The European Social Charter: A Commentary

The European Social Charter: A Commentary

By

The Academic Network on the European Social Charter and Social Rights

Volume 3

Part II (Articles 11 to 19)

Edited by

Stefano Angeleri, Koldo Casla and Sébastien Van Drooghenbroeck

BRILL | NIJHOFF

LEIDEN | BOSTON

The Library of Congress Cataloging-in-Publication Data is available online at https://catalog.loc.gov
LC record available at https://lccn.loc.gov/2022018237

Typeface for the Latin, Greek, and Cyrillic scripts: "Brill". See and download: brill.com/brill-typeface.

ISSN 2949-7876
ISBN 978-90-04-43407-3 (hardback)
ISBN 978-90-04-43414-1 (e-book)
DOI 10.1163/9789004434141

This book is printed on acid-free paper and produced in a sustainable manner.

Contents

Foreword

For 60 years now, the European Social Charter has been instrumental in fulfilling the mission stated in the Council of Europe's Statute: "to achieve a greater unity between its members for the purpose of safeguarding and realising the ideals and principles which are their common heritage and facilitating their economic and social progress". Together with the European Convention on Human Rights, it forms the basis of human rights protection in Europe.

Our Committee of Ministers has regularly affirmed the importance of the Charter in guaranteeing social rights across the continent, most recently at its Hamburg Session in May this year. The timing of this statement was particularly apt, given the way in which the COVID-19 pandemic has exposed the fragility of human rights protections in times of sudden adversity. Moreover, while the long-term economic effects of the pandemic are still to be felt, we know that in periods of downturn it is often the poorest who suffer most. There has therefore never been a better moment to ensure the effectiveness of our social rights system.

In April of this year, I presented a series of reform proposals to the Committee of Ministers. These aim to strengthen political commitment and support for the Charter, and to improve and simplify its procedures while promoting dialogue, communication and visibility. The proposals also mark the beginning of a period of reflection on the possibility of further substantive and procedural developments.

My proposals stress the importance of awareness-raising activities and of disseminating knowledge on the case law of the European Committee of Social Rights. I also point to the importance of including the Charter in university and other higher education curricula and of providing information and training for legal professionals, including judges.

ANESC is playing its own awareness-raising role, doing first-rate work to increase the Charter's visibility. This publication is the latest, important example. The first instalment of a multi-volume scholarly commentary on the Charter and its procedures, it is set to become a reference for academics and practitioners. As a landmark document, it is fitting that it coincides with the Charter's 60th anniversary, and a statement of the centrality of social rights to modern European life.

Marija Pejčinović Burić
Secretary General of the Council of Europe
Strasbourg, July 2021

Preliminary Remarks and Acknowledgments

Dear reader,

We are pleased to present the third volume of an eight-part Commentary on the European Social Charter, prepared by the Academic Network on the European Social Charter and Social Rights (ANESC or the Network).[1]

As Giovanni Guiglia, former ANESC/RACSE's General Coordinator wrote: "Our Network aims to promote the European Social Charter and the other legal instruments for the protection of social rights, in law, policy-making and academic studies, across different countries and their academics, in Europe. To this end, the ANESC develops activities in the fields of education, training, research, and pro-bono legal practice. The Network is composed of nearly 200 members from 14 European countries (Belgium, Cyprus, France, Greece, Hungary, Ireland, Italy, Poland, Portugal, Romania, Slovenia, Switzerland, Turkey and the United Kingdom). These are mainly academics who work in different legal fields, including social, constitutional, international and labour law, as well as few judges, lawyers and human rights consultants".[2]

A few years ago, the ANESC's governing bodies decided that the Network would start the drafting of the first-ever-published Commentary on the European Social Charter (ESC) System, following the numbering of the Revised Charter: Volume 1 (Cross-cutting themes – published in may 2022); Volume 2 (Preamble, Part I, Part II – Articles 1 to 10 – published in February 2023); Volume 3 (Part II – Articles 11 to 19); Volume 4 (Part II – Articles 20 to 31 – publishing ongoing); Volume 5 (Part III, Art A and B, Part IV, Art C); Volume 6 (Part IV, art D – Collective complaints); Volume 7 (Part V – Art E, F, G, H, I, J, Part VI – Art K, L, M, N, O and introduction of the Appendix); Volume 8 (Rules of the European Committee of Social Rights). The last four volumes will be published during the next two years.

This third volume, which examines critical ESC welfare rights for the general population and specific groups of people against the European Committee of Social Rights' jurisprudence and other international standards, is the result of the efforts of several members of the ANESC, under our editorial lead. We congratulate the authors of this volume, senior and junior academics and human rights experts, for their valuable research and all those ANESC members that

1 The network website at: https://www.racse-anesc.org/en/.

2 "Preliminary Remarks & Acknowledgments", in ANESC, Stefano Angeleri, and Carole Nivard (eds.), The European Social Charter: A Commentary. Volume 1, Cross-cutting Themes, Brill, 2022, p. x.

contributed, together with us, to reviewing this volume's chapters (Giovanni Cavaggion, Lorenza Mola, Murat Engin, Nikos Papadopoulos, Cristina Samboan, Fabrizio Proietti, Kübra Yenisey, Marco Rocca, Mouloud Boumghar, Carole Nivard, Padraic Kenna, Anna Panarella, Kostantina Chatzilaou, Manuel Fontaine, Guido Van Limberghen, Despina Kiltidou). Finally, we acknowledge the priceless of contribution of Professor R. J. Blaise MacLean, our proof-reader, and that of Raphaël Denayer for his support to formal editing.

We wish you a good reading and hope that this this Commentary, together with the other seven volumes, can become a particularly useful companion for academics and human rights practitioners to navigate European social standards and procedures vis-à-vis the many socioeconomic challenges of our times.

Belfast / Colchester / Brussels,
August 2023

Stefano Angeleri
Queen's University Belfast

Koldo Casla
University of Essex

Sébastien Van Drooghenbroeck
UCLouvain – St. Louis Bruxelles

Abbreviations

ACHPR	African Charter on Human and Peoples' Rights
ACHR	American Convention on Human Rights
CEDAW	Convention on the Elimination of all Forms of Discrimination against Women
CERD	International Convention on the Elimination of all Forms of Racial Discrimination
CJEU	Court of Justice of the European Union
CM	Committee of Ministers of the Council of Europe
CoE	Council of Europe
CRC	Convention on the Rights of the Child
CRPD	Convention on the Rights of Persons with Disabilities
CSE	Charte sociale européenne
CSE (rev)	Charte sociale européenne révisée
ECHR	European Convention on Human Rights
ECmHR	European Commission of Human Rights
ECSR	European Committee of Social Rights
ECtHR	European Court of Human Rights
ESC	European Social Charter
ESC (rev)	European Social Charter (Revised)
ETUC	European Trade Union Confederation
EU	European Union
HRC	Human Rights Committee
IACtHR	Inter-American Court of Human Rights
ICCPR	International Covenant on Civil and Political Rights
ICESCR	International Covenant on Economic, Social and Cultural Rights
ICJ	International Court of Justice
ICRMW	International Convention on the Protection of the Rights of all Migrant Workers and Members of their Families
ILO	International Labour Organization
NGO(s)	Non-Governmental Organization(s)
OAS	Organization of American States
OECD	Organisation for Economic Co-operation and Development
OJ	Official Journal
TEU	Treaty on European Union
TFEU	Treaty on the Functioning of the European Union
UDHR	Universal Declaration of Human Rights
UN	United Nations Organization
WHO	World Health Organization

Table of Cases

European Committee of Social Rights

ECSR, *International Commission of Jurists (ICJ) v. Portugal,* complaint No 1/1998, decision on the merits of 9 September 1999.

ECSR, *Syndicat national des Professions du tourisme v. France,* Complaint no. 6/1999, decision on the merits of 10 October 2000.

ECSR, *Autism-Europe v. France,* complaint No. 13/2002, decision on the merits of 4 November 2003.

ECSR, *International Federation of Human Rights Leagues (FIDH) v. France,* collective complaint No. 14/2003, decision on the merits of 8 September 2004.

ECSR, *World Organisation against Torture (OMCT) v. Greece* (complaint No. 17/2003), *Italy* (complaint No. 19/2003), *Ireland* (complaint No. 18/2003), *Portugal* (complaint No. 20/2003) and *Belgium* (complaint No. 21/2003), decisions on the merits of 7 December 2004.

ECSR, *European Roma Rights Centre (ERRC) v. Italy,* complaint No. 27/2004, decision on the merits of 7 December 2005.

ECSR, *European Roma Rights Centre (ERRC) v. Greece,* complaint No. 15/2003, decision on the merits of 8 December 2005.

ECSR, *European Roma Rights Centre v. Bulgaria,* complaint No. 31/2005, decision on the merits of 18 October 2006.

ECSR, *Marangopoulos Foundation for Human Rights (MFHR) v. Greece,* complaint No. 30/2005, decision on the merits of 6 December 2006.

ECSR, *World Organisation against Torture (OMCT) v. Portugal,* complaint No. 34/2006, decision on the merits of 6 December 2006.

ECSR, *Mental Disability Advocacy Center (MDAC) v. Bulgaria,* complaint No. 41/2007, decision on admissibility of 26 June 2007.

ECSR, *Swedish Trade Union Confederation (LO) and Swedish Confederation of Professional Employees (TCO) v. Sweden,* complaint No. 85/2012, decision on the merits of 3 July 2007.

ECSR, *International Movement ATD Fourth World v. France,* complaint No. 33/2006, decision on the merits of 5 December 2007.

ECSR, *European Federation of National Organisations Working with the Homeless (FEANTSA) v. France,* complaint No. 39/2006, decision on the merits of 5 December 2007.

ECSR, *Mental Disability Advocacy Centre (MDAC) v. Bulgaria,* complaint No. 41/2007, decision on the merits of 3 June 2008.

ECSR, *European Roma Rights Centre (ERRC) v. Bulgaria,* collective complaint No. 46/2007, decision on the Merit of 3 December 2008.

ESCR, *European Roma Rights Centre* (*ERRC*) *v. Bulgaria*, complaint No. 48/2008, decision on the merits of 18 February 2009.

ECSR, *International Centre for the Legal Protection of Human Rights* (*INTERIGHTS*) *v. Croatia*, complaint No. 45/2007, decision on the merits of 30 March 2009.

ECSR, *FEANTSA v. Slovenia*, complaint No. 53/2008, decision on the merits of 8 September 2009.

ECSR, *Confédération française démocratique du travail* (*CFDT*) *v. France*, complaint No. 50/2008, decision on the merits of 9 September 2009.

ECSR, *European Roma Rights Centre* (*ERRC*) *v. France*, complaint No. 51/2008, decision on the merits of 19 October 2009.

ECSR, *Defence for Children International* (*DCI*) *v. the Netherlands*, complaint No. 47/2008, decision on the merits of 20 October 2009.

ECSR, *Confédération Générale du Travail* (*CGT*) *v. France*, Complaint no. 55/2009, decision on the merits of 23 June 2010.

ECSR, *Centre on Housing Rights and Evictions* (*COHRE*) *v. Italy*, complaint No. 58/2009, decision on the merits of 25 June 2010.

ECSR, *Centre on Housing Rights and Evictions* (*COHRE*) *v. France*, collective complaint No. 63/2010, decision on the merits of 28 June 2011.

ECSR, *Federation of Employed Pensioners of Greece* (*IKA-ETAM*) *v. Greece*, complaint no. 76/2012, decision on the merits of 2 January 2012.

ECSR, *European Roma and Travellers Forum* (*ERTF*) *v. France*, complaint No. 64/2011, decision on the merits of 24 January 2012.

ECSR, *General Federation of employees of the national electric power corporation* (*GENOP-DEI*) / *Confederation of Greek Civil Servants Trade Unions* (*ADEDY*) *v. Greece*, complaint no. 66/2011, decision on 23 May 2012.

ECSR, *Médecins du Monde – International v. France*, collective complaint No. 67/2011, decision on the merits of 11 September 2012.

ECSR, *Defence for Children International* (*DCI*) *v. Belgium*, complaint No. 69/2011, decision on the merits of 23 October 2012.

ECSR, *Panhellenic Federation of pensioners of the public electricity corporation* (*POS-DEI*) *v. Greece*, complaint no. 79/2012, decision on the merits of 7 December 2012.

ECSR, *International Federation for Human Rights* (*FIDH*) *v. Greece*, collective complaint No. 72/2011, decision on the merits of 23 January 2013.

ECSR, *International Federation for Human Rights* (*FIDH*) *v. Belgium*, complaint No. 75/2011, decision on the merits of 18 March 2013.

ECSR, *European Committee for Home-Based Priority Action for the Child and the Family* (*EUROCEF*) *v. France*, complaint No. 82/2012, decision on admissibility and the merits of 19 March 2013.

ECSR, *Association for the protection of All Children* (*APPROACH*) *Ltd. v. Cyprus*, complaint No. 97/2013, decision on admissibility of 2 July 2013.

ECSR, *Swedish Trade Union Confederation* (*LO*) *and Swedish Confederation of Professional Employees* (*TCO*) *v. Sweden,* complaint No. 85/2012, decision on the merits of 3 July 2013.

ECSR, *International Planned Parenthood Federation – European Network* (*IPPF EN*) *v. Italy*, complaint No. 87/2012, Decision on the merits of 10 September 2013.

ECSR, *European Action of the Disabled,* (*AEH*) *v. France,* complaint No. 81/2012, decision on the merits of 11 September 2013.

ECSR, *Conference of European Churches* (*CEC*) *v. the Netherlands,* complaint No. 30/2013, decision on the merits of 1 July 2014.

ECSR, *European Federation of National Organisations working with the Homeless* (*FEANSA*) *v. the Netherlands*, complaint No. 86/2012, decision on the merits of 2 July 2014.

ECSR, *Finnish Society of Social Rights v. Finland,* complaint no. 88/2012, decision on the merits of 9 September 2014.

ECSR, *Association for the Protection of All Children* (*APPROACH*) *Ltd. v. France,* complaint No. 92/2013, decision on the merits of 12 September 2014.

ECSR, *Association for the Protection of All Children* (*APPROACH*) *Ltd v. Ireland,* complaint No. 93/2013, decision on the merits of 2 December 2014.

ECSR, *Association for the Protection of All Children* (*APPROACH*) *Ltd. v. Italy,* complaint No. 94/2013, decision on the merits of 5 December 2014.

ECSR, *Association for the Protection of All Children* (*APPROACH*) *Ltd. v. Slovenia,* complaint No. 95/2013, decision on the merits of 5 December 2014.

ECSR, *Association for the Protection of All Children* (*APPROACH*) *Ltd.* v. *Czech Republic,* complaint No. 96/2013, decision on the merits of 20 January 2015.

ECSR, *Association for the Protection of All Children* (*APPROACH*) *Ltd.* v. *Belgium,* complaint No. 98/2013, decision on the merits of 20 January 2015.

ECSR, *Centre on Housing Rights and Evictions* (*COHRE*) *v. Italy,* complaint No. 58/2009, decision on the merits of 25 June 2010.

ECSR, *Confederazione Generale Italiana del Lavoro* (*CGIL*) *v. Italy,* complaint No. 91/2013, decision on admissibility and merits of 12 October 2015.

ECSR, *Associazione sindacale « La Voce dei Giusti »* v. Italy, complaint No. 105/2014, decision on the merits of 18 October 2016.

ECSR, *European Federation of Public Service Employees* (*EUROFEDOP*) *v. Greece,* complaint No. 115/2015, decision on the merits of 13 September 2017.

ECSR, *Mental Disability Advocacy Center* (*MDAC*) *v. Belgium,* complaint No. 109/2014, decision on admissibility and the merits, 16 October 2017.

ECSR, *European Roma and Travellers Forum (ERTF) v. France*, complaint No. 119/2015, decision on the merits of 5 December 2017.

ECSR, *European Committee on Priority Home Action for Children and Families (EUROCEF) v. France*, complaint No. 114/2015, decision on the merits of 24 January 2018.

ECSR, *Transgender Europe and ILGA Europe v. Czech Republic*, complaint No. 117/2014, decision on the merits of 15 May 2018.

ECSR, *Equal Rights Trust v. Bulgaria*, complaint No. 121/2016, decision on the merits of 16 October 2018.

ECSR, *European Roma Rights Centre (ERRC) v. Bulgaria*, Complaint No. 151/2017, Decision on the Merits of 5 December 2018.

ECSR, *European Roma Rights Centre (ERRC) v. Belgium*, complaint No. 185/2019, decision on admissibility and immediate measures of 14 May 2020.

ESCR, *European Roma Rights Centre (ERRC) and Mental Disability Advocacy Centre (MDAC) v. Czech Republic*, complaint No. 157/2017, decision on the merits of 17 June 2020.

ECSR, *International Commission of Jurists (ICJ) v. Czech Republic*, Complaint No. 148/2017, decision on the merits of 20 October 2020.

ECSR, *International Commission of Jurists (ICJ) and European Council for Refugees and Exiles (ECRE) v. Greece*, complaint No. 173/2018, decision on the merits of 26 January 2021.

ECSR, *Defence for Children International (DCI), European Federation of National Organisations working with the Homeless (FEANTSA), Magistrats Européens pour la Démocratie et les Libertés (MEDEL), Confederación Sindical de Comisiones Obreras and International Movement ATD Fourth World v. Spain*, complaint No. 206/2022, decision on admissibility and immediate measures of 19 October 2022.

European Commission of Human Rights

ECmHR, 7 July 1986, *Khan v. the United Kingdom*, No. 11579/85.

ECmHR, 19 October 1994, *Akdıvar and others v. Turkey*, no. 21893/93.

European Court of Human Rights

ECtHR, 23 July 1968, *"Relating to certain aspects of the laws on the use of languages in education in Belgium" v. Belgium*, Nos. 1474/62, 1677/62, 1691/62, 1769/63, 1994/63 and 2126/64.

ECtHR, 25 April 1978, *Tyrer v. the United Kingdom*, No. 5856/72.
ECtHR, 13 June 1979, *Marckx v. Belgium*, No. 6833/74.
ECtHR, 9 October 1979, *Airey v. Ireland,* No. 6289/73.
ECtHR, 25 February 1982, *Campbell and Cosans v. the United Kingdom*, Nos. 7511/76 and 7743/76.
ECtHR, 7 July 1989, *Gaskin v. the United Kingdom*, No. 10454/83.
ECtHR, 26 May 1994, *Keegan v. Ireland*, No. 16969/90.
ECtHR, 9 December 1994, *Stran Greek Refinieries and Stratis Andeadis v. Greece*, No. 13427/87.
ECtHR, 4 July 1995, *Klerks v. the Netherlands*, No. 25212/94.
ECtHR, 16 September 1996, *Gaygusuz v Austria*, No. 17371/90.
ECtHR, 23 September 1998, *A v. the United Kingdom*, No. 25599/94.
ECtHR, 21 October 1998, *McIntyre v. United Kingdom*, No. 29046/95.
ECtHR, dec., 4 May 1999, *Marzari v. Italy*, No. 36448/97.
ECtHR, dec., 28 October 1999, *Pancenko v. Latvia*, No. 40772/98.
ECtHR, dec., 13 January 2000, *Maggiolini v. Italy*, no. 35800/97.
ECtHR [GC], 6 April 2000, *Thlimmenos c. Grece*, no 34369/97.
ECtHR, 13 July 2000, *Scozzari and Giunta v. Italy*, No. 39221/98 and No. 41963/98.
ECtHR, 3 October 2000, *Camp and Bourimi v. the Netherlands*, No. 28369/95.
ECtHR, [GC], 26 October 2000, *Kudła v. Poland*, No. 30210/96.
ECtHR, 28 November 2000, *Fiorenza v. Italy*, No. 44393/98.
ECtHR, [GC], 18 January 2001, *Chapman v. the United Kingdom*, No. 27238/95.
ECtHR, 10 May 2001, *Z. and Others v. the United Kingdom*, No. 29392/95.
ECtHR, dec., 26 June 2001, *O' Rourke v. the United Kingdom*, No. 39022/97.
ECtHR, [GC], 12 July 2001, *Prince Hans-Adam II of Liechtenstein v. Germany*, No. 42527/98.
ECtHR, 17 January 2002, *Calvelli and Ciglio v. Italy*, No. 32967/96.
ECtHR, dec., 21 March 2002, *Nitecki v. Poland*, No. 65653/01.
ECtHR, dec., 14 May 2002, *Zehnalová and Zehnal v. Czech Republic*, no. 38621/97.
ECtHR, 4 June 2002, *Wessels-Bergervoet v. the Netherlands,* No. 34462/97.
ECtHR, dec., 8 July 2003, *Sentges v. the Netherlands,* no. 27677/02.
ECtHR, 13 July 2004, *Pla and Puncernau v. Andorra*, No. 69498/01.
ECtHR, 12 October 2004, *Kjartan Ásmundsson v. Iceland*, No. 60669/00.
ECtHR, dec., 4 January 2005, *Pentiacova and Others v. Moldova*, no. 14462/03.
ECtHR, 9 June 2005, *Fadeyeva v. Russia,* No. 55723/00.
ECtHR, 12 July 2005, *Moldovan and others v. Romania* (No. 2), No. 41138/98, 64320/01.
ECtHR, 12 July 2005, *Solodyuk v. Russia*, No. 67099/01.
ECtHR, dec., 11 April 2006, *Molka v. Poland*, no. 56550/00.

ECtHR, [GC], 12 April 2006, *Stec and Others v. the United Kingdom,* No. 65731/01, 65900/01.
ECtHR, 11 July 2006, *Pastorino Et Autres C. Italie,* No. 17640/02.
ECtHR, 13 July 2006, *Jäggi v. Switzerland,* No. 58757/00.
ECtHR, 29 June 2007, *Folgerø and Others v. Norway,* No. 15472/02.
ECtHR,13 November 2007, *D.H. and Others v. the Czech Republic,* No. 57325/00.
ECtHR, 27 November 2008, *Salduz v. Turkey,* No. 36391/02.
ECTHR, 30 April 2009, *Glor v. Switzerland,* no. 13444/04.
ECtHR, 28 May 2009, *Brauer v. Germany,* No. 3545/04.
ECtHR, dec., 18 June 2009, *Budina v. Russia,* No. 45603/05.
ECtHR, 15 September 2009, *E.S. and Others v. Slovakia,* No. 8227/04.
ECtHR, dec., 10 November 2009, *Bladh v. Sweden,* No. 46125/06.
ECtHR, 2 March 2010, *Adamkiewic v. Poland,* No. 54729/00.
ECtHR, 16 March 2010, *Oršuš and Others v. Croatia,* No. 15766/03.
ECtHR, [GC], 16 March 2010, *Carson and Others v the United Kingdom,* No. 42184/05.
ECtHR, 24 June 2010, *Schalk and Kopf v. Austria,* no. 30141/04.
ECtHR, [GC], 21 January 2011, *M.S.S. v. Belgium and Greece,* No. 30696/09.
ECtHR, 27 September 2011, *Bah v. the United Kingdom,* No. 56328/07.
ECtHR, 11 October 2011, *Genovese v. Malta,* No. 53124/09.
ECtHR [GC], 17 January 2012, *Stanev v. Bulgaria,* no.36760/06.
ECtHR, 19 January 2012, *Dukic v. Bosnia and Herzegovina,* No. 4543/09.
ECtHR, 14 February 2012, *A. M. M. v. Romania,* No. 2151/10.
ECtHR, 10 April 2012, *Panaitescu v. Romania,* No. 30909/06.
ECtHR, 24 April 2012, *Yordanova and others v. Bulgaria,* No. 25446/06.
ECtHR, 25 September 2012, *Godelli v. Italy,* No. 33783/09.
ECtHR, 7 February 2013, *Fabris v. France,* No. 16574/08.
ECtHR, 9 April 2013, *Mehmet Şenturk and Bekir Şenturk v. Turkey,* No. 13423/09.
ECtHR, 18 June 2013, *Nencheva and others v. Bulgaria,* No. 48609/06.
ECtHR, [GC], 17 October 2013, *Winterstein and others v. France,* No. 27013/07.
ECtHR [GC], 7 November 2013, *Vallianatos and others v. Greece,* nos. 29381/09 and 32684/09.
ECtHR, 28 January 2014, *O'Keeffe v. Ireland,* No. 35810/09.
ECtHR, [GC], 17 July 2014, *Centre for Legal Resources on behalf of Valentin Câmpeanu v. Romania,* No. 47848/08.
ECtHR, [GC], 4 November 2014, *Tarakhel v. Switzerland,* No. 29217/12.
ECtHR, dec., 2 December 2014, *Strzelecka v. Poland,* no. 14217/10.
ECtHR [GC], 16 June 2015, *Chiragov and others v. Armenia,* no. 13216/05.
ECtHR, 16 June 2015, *Sargsyan v. Azerbaijan,* no. 40167/06.
ECtHR, 3 September 2015, *M. and M. v. Croatia,* No. 10161/13.

ECtHR, 13 October 2015, *S.H. v. Italy*, No. 52557/14.
ECtHR, 8 December 2015, *Z.H. and R.H. v. Switzerland*, No. 60119/12.
ECtHR, 23 February 2016, *Çam v. Turkey*, no. 51500/08.
ECtHR, 23 February 2016, *Paijc v. Croatia*, No. 68453/13.
ECtHR, 17 March 2016, *Vasileva v. Bulgaria*, No. 23796/10.
ECtHR, 22 March 2016, *Guberina v. Croatia*, no. 23682/13.
ECtHR [GC], 26 April 2016, *Murray v. The Netherlands*, No.10511/10.
ECtHR, 24 May 2016, *I.C. v. Romania*, No. 36934/08.
ECtHR, 30 June 2016, *Taddeucci and McCall v. Italy*, No. 51362/09.
ECtHR, 6 September 2016, *C.P. v. United Kingdom*, No. 300/11.
ECtHR, [GC], 13 December 2016, *Paposhvili v. Belgium*, No. 41738/10.
ECtHR, [GC], 13 December 2016, *Béláné Nagy v. Hungary*, No. 53090/13.
ECtHR, 9 February 2017, *Mitzinger v. Germany*, No. 29762/10.
ECtHR, 7 March 2017, *Baczúr v. Hungary*, No. 8263/15.
ECtHR, 3 October 2017, *D.M.D. v. Romania*, No. 23022/13.
ECtHR [GC], 19 December 2017, *Lopes De Sousa Fernandes v. Portugal*, No. 56080/13.
ECtHR, 30 January 2018, *Enver Şahin v. Turkey*, no. 3065/12.
ECtHR, 26 April 2018, *Cakarevic v. Croatia*, No. 48921/13.
ECtHR, dec., 29 January 2019, *Neagu v. Romania*, no. 49561/16.
ECtHR, dec., 25 June 2019, *Glaisen v. Switzerland*, no. 40477/13.
ECtHR [GC], 25 June 2019, *Nicolae Virgiliu Tănase v. Romania*, No. 41720/13.
ECtHR, 18 July 2019, *R.V. and Others v. Italy*, No. 37748/13.
ECtHR, 24 October 2019, *J.D. and A. v. the United Kingdom*, nos. 32949/17 and 34614/17.
ECtHR, 23 January 2020, *I.R. v. North Macedonia*, no. 38067/15.
ECtHR, 4 June 2020, *Association Innocence en Danger v. France* and *Association Enfance et Partage v. France*, No. 15343/15 and No. 16806/15.
ECtHR, 10 December 2020, *G.L. v. Italy*, no. 59751/15.
ECtHR [GC], 8 April 2021 *Vavřička and Others v. The Czech Republic*, No. 47621/13, 3867/14, 73094/14.
ECtHR, 22 June 2021, *R.B. v. Estonia*, No. 22597/16.
ECtHR, 25 January 2022, *Negovanović and Others v. Serbia*, nos. 29907/16, 30022/16, 30322/16 and 31142/16.
ECtHR, 31 May 2022, *Arnar Helgi Lárusson v. Iceland*, no. 23077/19.
ECtHR, 7 June 2022, *I.G.D. v. Bulgaria*, No. 70139/14.
ECtHR, 21 July 2022, *Darboe and Camara v. Italy*, No. 5797/17.
ECtHR, 11 October 2022, *Beeler v. Switzerland*, No. 78630/12.
ECtHR, 3 November 2022, *Loste v. France*, No. 59227/12.
ECtHR, 6 December 2022, *Scalzo v. Italy*, No. 8790/21.

ECtHR, 13 December 2022, *Elmazova and Others v. North Macedonia*, Nos. 11811/20 and 13550/20.

ECtHR [GC], 17 January 2023, *Fedotova and others*, nos. 40792/10, 30538/14 and 43439/14.

ECtHR, 23 May 2023, *Buhuceanu and others v. Romania*, nos. 20081/19 and 20.

Court of Justice of the European Union

CJEU, 2 July 1996, *Commission of the European Communities v Hellenic Republic*, C-290/94.

CJEU, 20 September 2001, *Rudy Grzelczyk v. Centre public d'aide sociale d'Ottignies-Louvain-la-Neuve*, C-184/99.

CJEU, 23 March 2004, *Brian Francis Collins v. Secretary of State for Work and Pensions*, C-138/02.

CJEU, 4 June 2009, *Athanasios Vatsouras and Josif Koupatantze v. Arbeitsgemeinschaft (ARGE) Nürnberg*, C-22/08 and C-23/08.

CJEU, 23 May 2011, *André Rossius and Marc Collard v. État belge – Service public fédéral Finances*, C-267/10 and C-268/2010.

CJEU, 24 April 2012, *Servet Kamberaj v Social Housing Institute of the Autonomous Province of Bolzano (IPES) and others*, Case C-571/10.

CJEU, 11 April 2013, *HK Danmark*, C-335/11 and C-337/11.

CJEU, 19 September 2013, *Pensionsversicherungsanstalt v. Peter Brey*, C-140/12.

CJEU, 17 July 2014, *Milica Široká v. Úrad verejného zdravotníctva Slovenskej republiky*, C-459/13.

CJEU, 10 September 2014, *Iraklis Haralambidis v Calogero Casilli*, C-270/13.

CJEU, 11 November 2014, *Elisabeta Dano, Florin Dano v. Jobcenter Leipzig*, C-333/13.

CJEU, 18 December 2014, *Centre public d'action sociale d'Ottignies-Louvain-la-Neuve v. Moussa Abdida*, C-562/13.

CJEU, 5 February 2015, *European Commission v Kingdom of Belgium*, C-317/14.

CJEU, 6 March 2015, *Gérard Fenoll v. Centre d'aide par le travail 'La Jouvene', Association de parents et d'amis de personnes handicapées mentales (APEI) d'Avignon*, C-316/13.

CJEU, 5 June 2018, *Relu Adrian Coman and Others v Inspectoratul General pentru Imigrări and Ministerul Afacerilor Interne*, C-673/16.

CJEU, 11 September 2019, *DW v. Nobel Plastiques Ibérica SA*, C-397/18.

CJEU, 15 July 2021, *XX v. Tartu Vangla*, C-795/19.

CJEU, 21 October 2021, *TC and UB v. Komisia za zashtita ot diskriminatsia and VA*, C-824/19.

CJEU, 14 December 2021, *V.A. v. Stolichna obshtina, rayon 'Pancharevo'*, C-490/20.

CJEU, 10 February 2022, *XXXX v. HR Rail SA*, C-485/20.

African Commission on Human and Peoples' Rights

ACHPR, *Social and Economic Rights Action Center, Center for Economic and Social Rights v. Nigeria*, communications no. 155/96, October 2001.

Inter-American Court of Human Rights

IACtHR, 1 September 2015, Case *Gonzales Lluy et Al. v. Ecuador* (Preliminary Objections, Merits, Reparations and Costs), Series C No. 298.

IACtHR, 8 March 2018, Case *Poblete Vilches et al. v. Chile* (Merits, Reparations and Costs), Series C No. 349.

UN Committee on Economic, Social and Cultural Rights

CESCR, dec., 4 March 2016, *Miguel Ángel López Rodríguez v. Spain* no. 1/2013, E/C.12/57/D/1/2013.

CESCR, 21 July 2017, *Mohamed Ben Djazia and Naouel Bellili v. Spain*, Communication No. 5/2015, E/C.12/61/D/5/2015.

CESCR, dec., 26 March 2018, *Trujillo Calero v. Ecuador* No. 10/2015, E/C.12/63/D/10/2015.

UN Human Rights Committee

CCPR, 30 August 2017, *Petr Gatilov v. Russian Federation*, Communication No. 2171/2012, CCPR/C/120/D/2171/2012.

Notes on Contributors

Stefano Angeleri
is a Marie Skłodowska-Curie postdoctoral researcher at Queen's University Belfast and visiting scientist at FXB Center for Health & Human Rights at Harvard University. He holds a PhD in Law from the Irish Centre for Human Rights (University of Galway, 2019) and is the national coordinator of the IE/UK section of the Academic Network on the European Social Charter and Social Rights. His research focuses on human rights law, health and social rights, migration and international law. Recent publications include the monograph 'Irregular Migrants and the Right to Health' (Cambridge University Press, 2022) and "Parsing human rights, promoting health equity: reflections on Colombia's response to Venezuelan migration", *Medical Law Review*, Volume 31, Issue 2, Spring 2023, Pages 187–204, https://doi.org/10.1093/medlaw/fwac053 (with Thérèse Murphy). Email: s.angeleri@qub.ac.uk

Nilay Arat
is professor of administrative law at the Faculty of Law, Kadir Has University, İstanbul, Turkey. She is a member of Turkish section of the Academic Network on European Social Charter and of the European Public Law Organization. Recent publications include: Nilay Arat, "Legal Aid Under Turkish Administrative Judiciary", *Annales de la Faculté de Droit d'Istanbul*, No.72, 2023, 71–95; Nilay Arat, "Right to Personal Liberty v. Administrative Detention? The case of Immigrants under Turkish Administrative Law", *European Review of Public Law*, Vol. 29, No. 1, 2017, 273–289; Nilay Arat, "Alternative Dispute Resolution Methods on Relations Between Public Authorities and Private Parties", *L'influence du droit européen en Suisse et en Turquie*, Lausanne 2015, 285–299. Email: aratnilay@yahoo.com

Lyle Barker
is a Researcher at Newcastle Law School. His main research interests are poverty and social rights. Previously, Barker was a Research Officer at the University of Essex Law School and Human Rights Centre, providing human rights research under the project Human Rights Local (2021–2023), and Human Rights Officer at Just Fair, leading on the organisation's social rights movement building and community work (2022–2023). He is the co-author with Dr Koldo Casla of Poverty and Social Rights in Essex (University of Essex Law School and Human Rights Centre 2022) and "I have walked this journey alone; my soul is tired:" Poverty, Child Protection and the Right to the Protection and Assistance

to the Family (University of Essex Law School and Human Rights Centre 2023). Email: lylebarker@btinternet.com

Demirhan Burak Çelik

PhD, is associate professor at the Faculty of Law, Department of Constitutional Law, Galatasaray University, İstanbul, Turkey. He is a Member of Turkish section of the Academic Network on European Social Charter and of the Association of Research on Constitutional Law (ARCL). Recent publications include: Barış Bahçeci and Demirhan Burak Çelik, "The Question of Interaction Between the Tax and Criminal Proceedings in the ECtHR Case-Law", *Intertaxv* Vol. 50, Issue 8/9, 2022, pp. 649 – 662; Demirhan Burak Çelik, 'The First Big Constitutional Breakthrough in Ottoman-Turkish Constitutionalism: The 1921 Constitution' *IACL-AIDC Blog* (11 March 2021), available at: https://blog-iacl-aidc.org/centenary-of-the-turkish-constitution/2021/3/11/the-first-big-constitutional-breakthrough-in-ottoman-turkish-constitutionalism-the-1921-constitution; Ronay Aybay, Demirhan Burak Çelik and İnsan Hakları Hukuku, *Human Rights Law*, 5th. Ed., Der Publications, İstanbul, Turkey, 2021. Email: mailto:dburakcelik@gmail.com

Koldo Casla

PhD, is a Senior Lecturer in International Law at the University of Essex. He leads the Human Rights Local project of the Human Rights Centre of the same university, and he is the Director of Essex Human Rights Centre Clinic. Previously, Casla was Research Associate at the Institute of Health & Society of Newcastle University (2017–19), where he co-drafted the first Bill on Economic, Social and Cultural Rights in the UK. He was also Policy Director of the UK social rights NGO Just Fair (2016–19), independent researcher on social rights for Amnesty International Spain (2013–19), and Chief of Staff of the Human Rights Commissioner of the Parliament of the Basque Country, Ararteko (2011–13). Among other publications, Casla is the author of Politics of International Human Rights Law Promotion in Western Europe: Order versus Justice (Routledge 2019) and Spain and Its Achilles' Heels: The Strong Foundations of a Country's Weaknesses (Rowman & Littlefield 2021), as well as the co-editor of Social Rights and the Constitutional Moment: Learning from Chile and International Experiences (Hart 2022).

Elisabeth David

is a teaching assistant and researcher in Belgian constitutional law at the UCLouvain – Saint-Louis Bruxelles and legal officer at the Belgian ministry of Justice in the EU criminal law department (focus on Belgian presidency of the Council of the EU). Research interests are Belgian constitutional law, EU constitutional law and EU criminal law. Email address: elisabeth.david@usaintlouis.be

Emmanuel Guematcha
is a senior lecturer in international law at the University of French Guiana and a lecturer in transitional justice at the University of Paris-Nanterre, France. He has been working on human rights and transitional justice issues. He has recently published a book on *The trial of Hissein Habré*, a former Chadian head of state, and has co-edited the French journal *Annuaire de justice transitionnelle* (Transitional Justice Yearbook). Email address: emmanuel.guematcha@univ-guyane.fr; guematcha@hotmail.com

Sedef Koç
PhD, is assistant professor at the Faculty of Law, Department of Labour and Social Security Law, Galatasaray University, İstanbul, Turkey. Her publications include: Sedef Koç Tangün and Evde Çalışanların Sosyal Güvenliği, İş Hukukunda Yeni Yaklaşımlar IV (Working from home and social security), On İki Levha, İstanbul, 2021; Sedef Koç Tangün, "Stajyer Kavramı ve Stajyerlerin Sigortalılığı" (Intern concept and interns' social security), *SİCİL Dergisi*, S. 40, 2018; Sedef Koç Tangün, "La protection de la maternité en droit du travail turc: Une analyse de point de vue de la non-discrimination et de la protection de l'emploi" (Maternity protection in Turkish labor law), *IOSR Journal of Humanities and Social Science*, Vol. 22, No. 3. Email: skoc@gsu.edu.tr; kocsedef@gmail.com

Nikolaos A. Papadopoulos
is a research fellow at the Law Department of the University of Turin, Italy. He currently serves as an International Consultant to the Council of Europe Department of Social Rights and as the coordinator of the Greek section of ANESC/RACSE. Nikolaos holds a PhD in international and European human rights law from the Law Faculty of Maastricht University in the Netherlands. His doctoral dissertation examined the renewed dynamics of the European Social Charter for the judicial enforcement and the protection of economic and social rights at the national level in a Europe in crisis. Email: nikolaos_papadopoulos@hotmail.com

Cinzia Peraro
PhD, is Associate Professor of European Union Law at the Law Department of the University of Bergamo (Italy). Her main research areas cover EU law

matters, fundamental rights, and EU private international law. Among her publications, the monograph focuses on fundamental social rights and collective redress in the European Union; some essays analyse social rights and the protection of workers; others deal with EU family law and children's rights, but also EU fundamental principles, privacy and competition. She is a member of research teams in several European and national projects. E-mail: cinzia.peraro@unibg.it

Inês Pereira de Sousa
is an Invited Lecturer and PhD candidate at the Porto Law School, Universidade Católica Portuguesa. She is a researcher of Católica Research Centre for the Future of Law/CEID and a member of ANESC and EUCRIM. Her research focus is in the area of European Criminal Law. Some of her most recent publications are: "Revisiting the paradigm of private sphere on personal data protection in the European Union – a Portuguese approach", *Book of 23rd Annual Meeting of the Nanterre Network – Legal and Interdisciplinary Challenges in Contemporary Society*. Ed. Lorenzo Bujosa Vadell, Fábio da Silva Veiga, Otmar Seul, Stephanie Rohlfing-Dijoux, 191–201. Salamanca: Faculty of Law, University of Salamanca, 2019; "Is the ECJ revisiting the European 'fifth amendment'? The CJEU rules on the right to silence?", *Expert insight into EU law developments – EU Law Analysis,* 1 de Agosto de 2021, available at http://eulawanalysis.blogspot.com/2021/08/is-ecj-revisiting-european-fifth.html. Email: isousa@ucp.pt

Ana Teresa Ribeiro
PhD, is an Assistant Professor at the Porto Faculty of Law, Universidade Católica Portuguesa and a researcher at the Católica Research Centre for the Future of Law, Porto, Portugal. She is also a member of several national and international labour law associations, such as ANESC and CIELO laboral. Her research focuses on Labour Law (particularly, on the collective relations), a subject on which she has possesses several conference participations and publications, such as: «The impact of the EU economic governance in Portugal», *European Labour Law Journal*, 2022, Vol. 13, n.º 2, pp. 193–213 (with Catarina Carvalho); «Gender discrimination (particularly) in wage matters: An analysis of the decision on the merits from the European Committee of Social Rights, University Women of Europe [UWE] v. Portugal, Complaint no. 136/2016», *Lex Social: Revista De Derechos Sociales*, 2022, 12(1), pp. 548–579 (with Milena Rouxinol), Email: aribeiro@ucp.pt.

Felicia Roşioru

PhD, is Associate Professor of Labour Law and EU Employment Law, Faculty of Law, Babeş-Bolyai University, Romania. Her research interests revolve around platform workers (status and collective rights), equality and non-discrimination, economically dependent workers. Recent publications include: "The 'Smart' Trade Union: New Strategies for a Digitalised Labour Market", in J.M. Miranda Boto and E. Bameshuber (eds.), *Collective Bargaining and the Gig economy: A Traditional Tool for New Business Model*, Oxford, Hart Publishing, 2022; "The social protection of platform workers in Romania: Meeting the growing demands for affordable and adequate coverage?", *International Social Security Review*, 2021, vol. 74, nos. 3–4. E-mail: felicia.rosioru@law.ubbcluj.ro

Milena Rouxinol

is an Assistant Professor at the Faculty of Law of the Catholic Portuguese University, with a PhD in Business Legal Sciences, concluded in 2014 at Coimbra University – Faculty of Law. Her main area of research is Labour Law; she is member of editorial borad of *Questões Laborais*, a Portuguese peer reviewed scientific journal and is also a member of important scientific national and international associations such as Associação Portuguesa de Direito do Trabalho, ANESC, or CIELO – Comunidad para la Investigación y el Estudio Laboral y Ocupacional. Some recent publications include: "Il regime dei lavoratori distaccati in Portogallo (dopo la direttiva 2018/957/UE) [The Posted Workers' Regime in Portugal (after Directive 2018/957/EU)]", Variazioni su Temi di Diritto del Lavoro, 2022-II, pp. 383–408 (with António Frada de Sousa); "A Tutela Antidiscriminatória do Trabalhador Sobrevivente de Cancro – Subsídio para um Enquadramento Dogmático-Normativo [The Antidiscriminatory Protection of a Cancer Survivor Employee – Contribution for a Dogmatic and Legal Framework]" in AA.VV (coord. Nuno Cerejeira Namora, Lourdes Mella Méndez, Duarte Abrunhosa e Sousa, Gonçalo Cerejeira Namora e Eduardo Castro Marques), Health at Work, Ageing and Environmental Effects on Future Social Security and Labour Law Systems, Cambridge Scholar Publishing, New Castle, 2018, p. 136–165. E-mail: mrouxinol@ucp.pt

Aslı Topukcu

is assistant professor at the Faculty of Law, Department of Constitutional Law, Yaşar University, İzmir, Turkey. She completed her doctoral studies at Istanbul University, Department of Public Law, with a dissertation on the judicial dialogue between constitutional courts. Her research interests focus on comparative constitutional law and human rights. Recent publications include: Nilay Arat and Aslı Topukcu, "The 1921 Constitution and Beyond: Any

Inspiration After 100 Years?", *Annales de la Faculté de Droit d'Istanbul*, No. 71, 2022, pp. 27–39; Aslı Topukcu, "Interaction Between Judiciary and Politics in Turkey: The Role of the Turkish Constitutional Court", *European Review of Public Law*, Vol. 28, No. 3, 2016, pp. 1091–1121. Email: asli.topukcu@yasar.edu.tr

Sébastien Van Drooghenbroeck

is full professor at the UCLouvain – St. Louis-Bruxelles, guest professor at the Université Paris Panthéon Assas, and Assessor in the Belgian Council of State. He is also coordinator (with Guido Van Limberghen) of the Belgian Section of the Academic Network on the European Social Charter and Social Rights, and national expert for the *European network of legal experts in gender equality and non-discrimination*. His main research concerns Human Rights Law, Constitutional Law and anti-discrimination law. Email: sebastien.vandroogh-enbroeck@usaintlouis.be

ARTICLE 11

The Right to Protection of Health

Emmanuel Guematcha

With a view to ensuring the effective exercise of the right to protection of health, the Parties undertake, either directly or in cooperation with public or private organisations, to take appropriate measures designed inter alia:

1 to remove as far as possible the causes of ill-health;
2 to provide advisory and educational facilities for the promotion of health and the encouragement of individual responsibility in matters of health;
3 to prevent as far as possible epidemic, endemic and other diseases.

Introduction

The first reference to the right to protection of health is generally said to have been made in the Preamble to the Constitution of the World Health Organization (WHO) in 1946 after the Second World War.[1] Certainly, there were other legal references to the protection of health far before the end of the war. Adam Gaffney, who has conducted a deep historical analysis on that matter, traces the roots of the right to health back as far as antiquity.[2] Some States gave consideration to health protection in their constitutions. This was the case, for example, of the 1917 Mexican Constitution[3] and the 1919 Weimar Constitution.[4]

1 Constitution of the World Health Organization, opened for signature 22 July 1946, 14 UNTS 185, entered into force 7 April 1948.
2 Adam Gaffney, *To Heal Humankind: The Right to Health in History*, New York-London, Routledge, 2017, pp. 6–13.
3 Article 72 (XVI) of the Mexican Constitution, 31 January 1917, referred to the protection of health in case of epidemics and diseases. Article 123, B (XI-C) of the same constitution also referred to medical attention, for women for example. For an analysis of this constitution regarding health protection, see John Tobin, *The Right to Health in International Law*, Oxford University Press, 2012, p. 22.
4 Article 119 of the Weimar Constitution, 11 August 1919 referred to the role of the German State in the field of health.

 | DOI:10.1163/9789004434141_002

During the 19th century and early 20th century, international sanitary conferences were organized by various States.[5] Some international legal instruments insisted on sanitary measures to be taken in cases of diseases and on the need to protect individuals against diseases.[6] After the Second World War, the protection of the right to the protection of health progressively became a common feature of the European constitutional tradition, in the context of the advent of the Welfare State, with the State being notably "charged with guaranteeing to deliver health care to its citizens".[7] Some post-war European constitutions referred to the right to health protection or at least to health protection,- notably in France[8] and in Italy[9]- and this movement extended far beyond the immediate post-war era.[10]

However, the Preamble of the Constitution of the WHO was the first international instrument to proclaim that "[t]he enjoyment of the highest attainable standard of health is one of the fundamental rights of every human being without distinction of race, religion, political belief, economic or social condition". It also defined health as a "state of complete physical, mental and social well-being and not merely the absence of disease or infirmity". Despite this recognition in an international legal source, the right to health protection did not become a "right" with corresponding legal and binding international obligations during the late 1940s and the 1950s. During this period, within the newly created United Nations, negotiations took place for the adoption of an international instrument that would recognise human rights. The right

5 For example, International Sanitary Conference, Paris, 1851; The International Sanitary Conference, Paris, 1903. For a list of these conferences, see Norman Howard-Jones, *The Scientific Background of the International Sanitary Conferences 1851–1938*, World Health Organization, Geneva 1975.

6 See e. g., Convention sanitaire internationale, signée à Paris le 3 décembre 1903 ; Convention internationale sanitaire, signée à Paris le 17 janvier 1912, et ratifiée le 7 octobre 1920 en vue d'arrêter les mesures propres à sauvegarder la santé publique contre l'invasion et la propagation de la peste, du choléra et de la fièvre jaune ; The Pan American Sanitary Code, signed in Havana on 14 November 1924. For more on that topic, see Guillaume Le Floch, « Rapport introductif-Santé et droit international: l'ébullition permanente », in Guillaume Le Floch and Thibaut Fleury Graff (ed.), *Santé et droit international*, SFDI, colloque de Rennes, Paris, Pedone, 2019, pp. 8–9.

7 Richard Freeman, Heinz Rothgang, "Health", in Francis G. Castles, Stephan Leibfried, Jane Lewis, Herbert Obinger and Christopher Pierson (eds), *The Oxford Handbook of the Welfare State*, Oxford, OUP, 2010, p. 308.

8 Preamble of the French Constitution, 26 October 1946, para. 11.

9 Article 32 of the Italian Constitution, 22 December 1947.

10 Kinney Eleanor and Clark Brian, "Provisions for Health and Health Care in the Constitutions of the Countries Around the World", *Cornell International Law Journal*, vol. 37, 2005, pp. 285–355.

to health protection was one of the rights considered.[11] The very first international instruments that proclaimed human rights took into consideration the right to health protection. In April 1948, Article XI of the American Declaration of the Rights and Duties of Man referred to the "[r]ight to the preservation of health and to wellbeing", and a few months later, Article 25 of the Universal Declaration of Human Rights (UDHR) of 10 December 1948 recognised the right to protection of health through the "right to adequate standard of living", stating that "[e]vryone has the right to a standard of living adequate for the health and well-being of himself and of his family". However, these international instruments were declarations and therefore not treaties imposing binding obligations upon States.

In 1950, the European States of the Council of Europe negotiated and adopted the European Convention on Human Rights that did not include the right to health protection.[12] In an international context where human rights would progressively be considered as divided into two different categories,[13] European States only dealt with the first category, civil and political rights, and not with the second category, economic, social and cultural rights to which the right to protection of health would be integrated. However, the Council of Europe a few years later decided to launch another international instrument that would specifically recognise social rights, including the field of "health protection".[14] At the same time and after the adoption of the UDHR, discussions and negotiations also took place within the United Nations for the adoption of a binding covenant on economic, social and cultural rights, which included the right to health protection.[15] The European States of the Council of Europe moved more

---

11 See e.g., Draft Resolution for the General Assembly submitted by the representative of India, UN Doc. E/CN.4/11, 31 January 1947, § 1 (c). Annex 'C' Revision of the Draft International Declaration of Human Rights prepared by the Commission on Human Rights, Article 15, UN Doc. E/CN.4/82/Add.12, 3 June 1948.

12 European Convention for the Protection of Human Rights and Fundamental Freedoms, opened for signature 4 November 1950, 213 UNTS 222, entered into force 3 September 1953.

13 William Schabas (ed.), *The Universal Declaration of Human Rights, The Travaux Préparatoires*, Cambridge, Cambridge University Press, 2013, p. lxxxviii; Ben Saul, David Kinley, Jacqueline Mowbray, *The International Covenant on Economic, Social and Cultural Rights: Commentary, Cases, and Materials*, Oxford, OUP, 2014, p. 4.

14 Memorandum of the Secretariat General of the Council of Europe on the Role of the Council of Europe in the Social Field, Strasbourg, doc. SG (53) 1, 16 April 1953, I-European Social Charter, § 16. Document available in: Council of Europe, European Social Charter, Collected (Provisional) Edition of the "Travaux Préparatoires", vol. I, 1953–1954, pp. 4–7.

15 Draft International Covenants on Human Rights, Report of the Third Committee, UN Doc. A/3525, 9 February 1957, pp. 51–57, §§ 145–157; Ben Saul, David Kinley, Jacqueline Mowbray, *cit.*, p. 4.

quickly. In 1961, they adopted a European Social Charter (the Charter) in which health was taken into account in many provisions that dealt with healthy working conditions (Article 3), children's health (Article 7), social and medical assistance (Article 13), and the health of migrant workers and their families (Article 19).[16] Furthermore, some provisions of the Charter were solely devoted to the protection of health as a right. In Part I on the rights and principles which were the "aim" of the policy of the States Parties, the Charter proclaimed: "Everyone has the right to benefit from any measures enabling him to enjoy the highest possible standard of health attainable".[17] The Charter explicitly recognised this right in Article 11, entitled "The right to protection of health".

The Charter was indeed the first adopted human rights treaty to recognise the right to health protection, and it was later followed by other international human rights treaties.[18] In 1996, a revised version of the Charter was adopted.[19] Some new provisions related to health were added to protect the health of the elderly (Article 23) and the poor or socially excluded (Article 30). The provisions relating to the right to protection of health were mostly retained, although in the 1996 revised version, the word "Parties" was preferred to the 1961 version that used "Contracting Parties" to refer to States. However, accidents were included in the list of what States must prevent. In the new Article 11 paragraph 3 of the revised version, it was provided that States shall "prevent as far as possible epidemic, endemic and other diseases, as well as accidents".

Article 11, in both the 1961 and revised versions, is one of the most widely accepted provisions of the Charter.[20] Of the 43 European States that became Parties to either the 1961 Charter or to the revised 1996 version, 42 chose to be bound by all the paragraphs of Article 11.[21] Only Armenia did not do so.[22]

---

16 European Social Charter, opened for signature 18 October 1961, 529 UNTS 89, entered into force 26 February 1965.

17 Part I, § 11, European Social Charter.

18 The right to health is also recognised in the 1966 International Covenant on Economic, Social and Cultural Rights (Article 12), the 1981 African Charter on Human and Peoples' Rights (Article 16), the 1988 Additional Protocol to the American Convention on Human Rights in the Area of Economic, Social and Cultural Rights (Article 10), the 2000 European Charter of Fundamental Rights (Article 35) and the 2004 Arab Charter on Human Rights (Article 39).

19 European Social Charter (revised), opened for signature 3 May 1996, (ETS No. 163), entered into force, 01 July 1999.

20 The Charter (1961 and 1996) established an "à la carte" system that allowed States Parties to choose which social rights they wished to implement, see Part III of the Charter.

21 See: Table of accepted provisions, Acceptance of the provisions of the revised European Social Charter (1996) as of 1 January 2021 in European Committee of Social Rights, *Progress Report 2020*, Council of Europe, July 2021, pp. 118–119; Acceptance of the provisions of the European Social Charter (1961), *ibid.*, p.124.

22 *Ibid.*, Acceptance of the provisions of the Revised European Social Charter (1996) on 1 January 2021, p. 118.

This chapter examines Article 11 of the revised 1996 Charter, which deals with the right to protection of health. First, it presents the history of the drafting and adoption of the right to protection of health. Second, it compares Article 11 of the Charter with other international provisions on the right to health. Third, it outlines the content of Article 11 also with reference to the European Committee of Social Rights' practice. Fourth, it analyses the nature of the obligations of the States Parties that have agreed to implement this right, and five, it underlines the indivisibility of human rights as confirmed by the links between the right to health protection and other human rights.

1 The Drafting and Adoption of Article 11

When the Council of Europe began to consider the adoption of a European Social Charter, health protection was taken into account from the outset and, later, there was a transition from the protection of health as a collective interest to the protection of health as an individual right that symbolised the transition from the liberal to the social-democratic form of State. The 1953 Memorandum drafted by the Secretariat General of the Council of Europe, which examined the role of international organisations in the social field, listed "general health protection" as one of the main "principles whose inclusion might be considered" in such a Charter.[23] However, when the European States began to negotiate, there were concerns that the issue of public health would raise difficulties, either because the creation of a "supra-national Specialised Authority" in this area might hinder the prospect of ratification by the States, or because the desirability of considering the issue of public health was questioned, since it was at the heart of the work of a new international organisation, the WHO.[24] It was considered important, particularly in the Committee on Social Questions of the Council of Europe which played a central role in the process of drafting the Charter, to exchange views on this issue with the WHO, which had a

23 Memorandum of the General Secretariat of the Council of Europe on the role of the Council of Europe in the Social Field, Strasbourg, *cit.*, p. 6.

24 Document available in: Council of Europe, European Social Charter, Collected (Provisional) Edition of the "Travaux Préparatoires", vol. I, 1953–1954; see the views of Santero, representing Italy, and Heyman, representing Belgium, pp. 33–34.

regional office for Europe.[25] It is not surprising that the first steps towards the recognition of the right to health protection in Europe came close to the wording of the Preamble of the WHO Constitution. In April 1955, the preliminary draft of the Charter referred to a "high standard of health" in Article 3, which stated, "Every person should have access to facilities for ensuring a high standard of health".[26] The right to health was thus limited to "access to facilities". This April 1955 version of the right to health detailed the measures to be taken by the States to give effect to this right:

> The measures to be taken by the signatory Governments to secure the enjoyment of this right, in cases where the private resources and initiatives of individuals or communities are inadequate, will include:
> (a) the reduction of infant mortality and provision for the healthy physical and moral development of the child; assistance to mentally defective children and those deserted or in distress; re-education of maladjusted children;
> (b) the improvement of nutrition, housing, education, recreation and other health factors connected with his surroundings;
> (c) the prevention, treatment and control of epidemic, endemic and other diseases;
> (d) the organisation of services and facilities to ensure for all effective medical attention in the event of sickness
> (e) free basic medical care and treatment.[27]

Some of these elements, such as the protection of children and the prevention, treatment and control of epidemic, endemic and other diseases,

25 *Ibid.*, see Heyman's intervention, p. 34. See also on that topic, Claire Lougarre, "What does the Right to Health Mean. The Interpretation of Article 11 of the European Social Charter by the European Committee of Social Rights", *Netherlands Quarterly of Human Rights*, vol. 33, no. 3, 2015, p. 329.

26 Article 3, Preliminary draft Social Charter submitted by the Secretariat of the Committee, Strasbourg, 19 April 1955, doc. AS/Soc I (6)1, in Council of Europe, European Social Charter, Collected (Provisional) Edition of the "Travaux Préparatoires", vol. II, 1955, p. 15.

27 *Ibid.* Most of these elements are included in the June 1955 version: Article 12, Preliminary draft Social Charter prepared by the Working Party for the preparation of a draft European Social Charter, Strasbourg, 18 June 1955. RXS/Soc (6) 28, in Council of Europe, *ibid.*, p. 90. See also the October 1955 version (Article 12, Recommendation, Draft European Social Charter Seventh Ordinary Session, 26th October 1955, doc. 403, Appendix), in Council of Europe, *ibid.*, p. 147.

were also found in the WHO Constitution, which listed the functions of the organisation.[28]

From this draft text on the right to health protection, new proposals were made and many amendments were adopted throughout the drafting process. In June 1955, a different formulation was preferred, stating that "[e]very person should have the benefit of facilities for ensuring a high standard of health".[29] Thus, the word "access", which seemed restrictive, was replaced by the word "benefit". In February 1956, the first sentence of the draft article proclaiming the right to health ("Every person should have the benefit of facilities for ensuring a high standard of health") was deleted from the Charter's draft articles.[30] However, this did not mean that the reference to a "high standard of health" was dropped. In fact, the reference to a high standard of health was moved to the title of Article 9, which recognised the right to health. The title of this article reflected "the right to a high standard of health".[31] This Article directly underlined the obligations of the States, without reference to the individual's right to health and the measures to be taken "in cases where the private resources and initiatives of individuals or communities are inadequate", a phrase which seemed to partially exempt States from acting when other initiatives were taken by others. Article 9 also stipulated that States "will take all appropriate measures" that were listed.[32] While the list contained measures to be taken for children, including many health factors and the prevention and organisation of facilities, the reference to "free basic medical care and treatment" that appeared in the April 1955 version was deleted. The reason for this deletion was, according to the Travaux Préparatoires, based on the fact that "free basic medical care and treatment" was covered by another article which dealt with "social security benefits".[33]

In September 1956, when the list of measures to be taken by States in the field of health was revised, a new proposal was added. In ensuring the right to health, measures taken by States would be "directly or in co-operation with

---

28 Article 2 of the WHO Constitution.

29 Article 12, Preliminary draft Social Charter drawn up by the Working Party on the preparation of a draft European Social Charter, Strasbourg, 18 June 1955. RXS/Soc (6) 28, in Council of Europe, *cit.*, vol. II, 1955, p. 90.

30 Draft report by Mr. Kalbitzer, Revised draft Social Charter submitted as a consolidated amendment to the draft Social Charter contained in Document 403, Strasbourg, 28th February 1956, Doc. AC/EC (7) 24, in Council of Europe, European Social Charter, Collected (Provisional) Edition of the "Travaux Préparatoires", vol. III, 1956, p. 75.

31 *Ibid.*

32 *Ibid.*

33 *Ibid.* ("p. 109" of the PDF document. There is no pagination number on that page).

local authorities and competent private organisations".[34] The idea here, according to the General Affairs Committee, was to take into account the activities of private organisations in the field of health.[35] A questionnaire was submitted to the European States asking them to express their views on the Charter, including the right to protection of health.[36] Germany proposed to define the right to health protection in the form of a declaration of principle.[37] This proposal was supported by Denmark, Belgium, Turkey and the UK.[38] A proposal for a declaration was made in 1957, which would be separate from the binding text on the right to health protection.[39] In December 1957, the draft Charter contained proposals for a declaration of principle on the right to protection of health[40] and a binding text.[41] Finally, it was in this form that the right to protection of health was recognised in 1961 with, on the one hand, paragraph 11 of Part I of the 1961 Charter proclaiming the individual right to health and, on the other hand, Article 11 emphasising the measures that European States must take in the area of the right to health protection. Article 11 of the Charter insisted, "*inter alia*", on the elimination "as far as possible [of] the causes of ill-health", the provision of "advisory and educational facilities", and the prevention, "as

34 Draft recommendation for the establishment of a European Convention on Social and Economic Rights, presented on behalf of the Committee on General Affairs by Mr L. Toncic, Rapporteur, Appendix, Draft European Convention on Social and Economic Rights, 27 September 1956, Doc. 536, § 1, in Council of Europe, *cit.*, vol. III, 1956, p. 542.

35 *Ibid.*, Explanatory Memorandum, presented by Mr. Toncic, rapporteur, in Council of Europe, *cit.*, vol. III, 1956, p. 561.

36 Social Committee (Fifth Session), European Social Charter (Rights relating to health, to an adequate standard of living, etc.), Report prepared by the Social Division of the Research Directorate on the basis of the replies of governments to the questionnaire drawn up by the Social Committee, Strasbourg, 20 June 1957, doc. EC/Soc (57) 12, in Council of Europe, European Social Charter, Collected (Provisional) Edition of the "Travaux Préparatoires", vol. IV, 1957, p. 121.

37 *Ibid.*, p. 123.

38 *Ibid.*

39 *Ibid.*, pp. 124–125.

40 Report of the Social Committee submitting the draft European Social Charter, Strasbourg, 20 December 1957, doc. CM (57) 176, Draft Text of the European Social Charter, Part 1, § 10 ("Everyone has the right to benefit from all measures enabling him to enjoy the highest possible standard of health attainable"), in Council of Europe, *ibid.*, p. 387.

41 *Ibid.*, p. 393: "XI Right to protection of Health With a view to ensuring the effective exercise of this right, the High Contracting Parties undertake, either directly or in co-operation with public or private organisations, to take appropriate measures designed *inter alia*: "(36) to remove as far as possible the causes of ill-health; (37) to provide advisory and educational facilities for the promotion of health and the encouragement of individual responsibility in matters of health; (38) to prevent as far as possible epidemic, endemic and other diseases"".

far as possible", of "epidemic, endemic and other diseases". In 1996, as mentioned in the introduction to this chapter, accidents were added to Article 11 paragraph 3 of the revised Charter as one of the elements that States must prevent. The recognition of the right to health in 1961 by the Charter marked the beginning of a movement towards the adoption of provisions protecting the right to health in other international human rights treaties.

II Comparing Other International Provisions on the Right to Health with Article 11 of the ESC

The right to health is protected by many general human rights treaties. It is recognised by Article 12 of the 1966 International Covenant on Economic, Social and Cultural Rights (ICESCR),[42] Article 16 of the 1981 African Charter on Human and Peoples' Rights (ACHPR),[43] Article 10 of the 1988 Additional Protocol to the American Convention on Human Rights in the Area of Economic, Social and Cultural Rights (Protocol of San Salvador),[44] Article 35

42 "1. The States Parties to the present Covenant recognize the right of everyone to the enjoyment of the highest attainable standard of physical and mental health. 2. The steps to be taken by the States Parties to the present Covenant to achieve the full realization of this right shall include those necessary for: (a) The provision for the reduction of the stillbirth-rate and of infant mortality and for the healthy development of the child; (b) The improvement of all aspects of environmental and industrial hygiene; (c) The prevention, treatment and control of epidemic, endemic, occupational and other diseases;(d) The creation of conditions which would assure to all medical service and medical attention in the event of sickness."

43 "1. Every individual shall have the right to enjoy the best attainable state of physical and mental health. 2. States Parties to the present Charter shall take the necessary measures to protect the health of their people and to ensure that they receive medical attention when they are sick."

44 "1. Everyone shall have the right to health, understood to mean the enjoyment of the highest level of physical, mental and social well-being. 2. In order to ensure the exercise of the right to health, the States Parties agree to recognize health as a public good and, particularly, to adopt the following measures to ensure that right: a. Primary health care, that is, essential health care made available to all individuals and families in the community; b. Extension of the benefits of health services to all individuals subject to the State's jurisdiction; c. Universal immunization against the principal infectious diseases; d. Prevention and treatment of endemic, occupational and other diseases; e. Education of the population on the prevention and treatment of health problems, and f. Satisfaction of the health needs of the highest risk groups and of those whose poverty makes them the most vulnerable."

of the 2000 Charter of Fundamental Rights of the European Union (CFRUE),[45] and Article 39 of the 2004 Arab Charter on Human Rights (Arab Charter).[46] Some international human rights treaties devoted to the protection of specific categories of people or specific human rights violations also recognise the right to health. Examples include the International Convention on the Elimination of All Forms of Racial Discrimination of 1965,[47] the Convention on the Elimination of All Forms of Discrimination against Women of 1979,[48] the Convention on the Rights of the Child of 1989,[49] the Convention on the Rights of Persons with Disabilities of 2006,[50] the Inter-American Convention on Protecting the Human Rights of Older Persons of 2015,[51] and the Protocol to the African Charter on Human and Peoples' Rights on the Rights of Persons with Disabilities in Africa of 2018.[52]

However, the structure of most of these provisions is different from that of Article 11 of the Charter. In the Charter, the right of health is proclaimed in paragraph 11 of Part I and Article 11 lists some measures that States must take to implement that right. In most other human rights treaties, the recognition of the right to health contains two parts in the same article.

In the first part, the individual right to health is affirmed, and in the second part, the measures to be taken by States parties to the treaty are enumerated. Article 35 of the Charter of Fundamental Rights of the European Union

45 "Everyone has the right of access to preventive health care and the right to benefit from medical treatment under the conditions established by national laws and practices. A high level of human health protection shall be ensured in the definition and implementation of all the Union's policies and activities".

46 "1. The States parties recognize the right of every member of society to the enjoyment of the highest attainable standard of physical and mental health and the right of the citizen to free basic health-care services and to have access to medical facilities without discrimination of any kind. 2. The measures taken by States parties shall include the following: (a) Development of basic health-care services and the guaranteeing of free and easy access to the centres that provide these services, regardless of geographical location or economic status; (b) Efforts to control disease by means of prevention and cure in order to reduce the mortality rate; (c) Promotion of health awareness and health education; (d) Suppression of traditional practices which are harmful to the health of the individual; (e) Provision of basic nutrition and safe drinking water for all; (f) Combating environmental pollution and providing proper sanitation systems; (g) Combating drugs, psychotropic substances, smoking and substances that are damaging to health."

47 Article 5 (e) (iv).

48 Articles 11.1 (f) and 12.

49 Article 24.

50 Article 25.

51 Article 19.

52 Article 17.

is one of the exceptions because it does not contain a list of measures to be adopted by States.[53] Moreover, Article 35 of the European Charter is quite different from Article 11 of the Charter and other treaty provisions on the right to health, as it recognises an individual right to "health care" that is limited to "the right of access to preventive health care and the right to benefit from medical treatment under the conditions established by national laws and practices".[54] The other provisions of general international human rights treaties, as well as paragraph 11 of Part I of the Charter, use a formulation close to the WHO Constitution when recognizing the right to health. They all emphasise the idea that individuals shall enjoy the highest or best attainable standard of health. Indeed, Article 12 paragraph 1 of the International Covenant on Economic, Social and Cultural Rights refers to "the enjoyment of the highest attainable standard of physical and mental health", Article 16 paragraph 1 of the ACHPR to the enjoyment of "the best attainable state of physical and mental health", Article 10 paragraph 1 of the 1988 Protocol of San Salvador to "the enjoyment of the highest level of physical, mental and social well-being", and Article 39 paragraph 1 of the Arab Charter to "the enjoyment of the highest attainable standard of physical and mental health".

With regard to the lists of measures that States must take to implement the right to health, they all have in common that they are not exhaustive. States may take other measures that are not listed. The measures listed in these treaties also vary from text to text and are sometimes close to Article 11 of the Charter. While the ACHPR is quite brief and refers to the need to take measures in the field of health and to provide "medical attention" to those in need, many treaties contain a detailed list of measures to be taken that include, as in Article 11 of the Charter,[55] measures that can be likened to those

---

53 See also the International Convention on the Elimination of All Forms of Racial Discrimination of 1965 and the Convention on the Elimination of All Forms of Discrimination against Women of 1979, which do not have a list of States obligations regarding the right to health.

54 On that difference between the EU Charter and the ESC, see Tamara K. Hervey, "We Don't See a Connection: The 'Right to Health' in the EU Charter and European Social Charter", in Gráinne De Búrca, Bruno De Witte, and Larissa Ogertschnig (eds), *Social Rights in Europe*, Oxford, OUP, 2005, pp. 305–336.

55 For example, article 12 para. 2 (b) of the ICESCR that refers to "[t]he improvement of all aspects of environmental and industrial hygiene"; article 10 para. 2 (f) of the 1988 Protocol to the ACHR that refers to "Satisfaction of the health needs of the highest risk groups and of those whose poverty makes them the most vulnerable" and article 39 para. 2 (e) of the 2004 Arab Charter on Human Rights that refers to the "[p]rovision of basic nutrition and safe drinking water for all".

aimed at removing the causes of illnesses, taking advisory and educational initiatives,[56] and preventing diseases.[57]

Nevertheless, some human rights treaties go well beyond what is included in Article 11 of the Charter by referring directly, for example, to the need for measures in the areas of "[u]niversal immunization against the principal infectious diseases",[58] and "[p]rovision of basic nutrition and safe drinking water for all".[59] Some international human rights bodies have also interpreted the right to health broadly. For example, the Committee on Economic, Social and Cultural Rights has given a broad interpretation to the right to health and has included elements that are not mentioned in Article 12 of the ICESCR. Among other things, it considered that the right to health includes "essential elements" and, with regard to health facilities and the provision of health care, it emphasised availability, accessibility, acceptability, and quality.[60] In a broad interpretation of Article 16 of the ACHPR, the African Commission on Human and Peoples' Rights noted that the right to health included "freedoms such as control over one's own body and health, including sexual and reproductive freedom".[61] However, these international developments do not mean that Article 11 of the Charter is overly narrow as compared to the provisions of other human rights treaties. Its content and meaning have been gradually clarified and sometimes expanded by the European Committee of Social Rights.

56 For example, article 10 para. 2 (e) of the 1988 Protocol to the ACHR that refers to the "[e]ducation of the population on the prevention and treatment of health problems" and article 39 para. 2 (c) of the 2004 Arab Charter on Human Rights that refers to the "[p]romotion of health awareness and health education".

57 For example, article 12 para. 2 (c) of the ICESCR that refers to "[t]he prevention, treatment and control of epidemic, endemic, occupational and other diseases"; article 10 para. 2 (d) of the 1988 Protocol to the ACHR that refers to the "Prevention and treatment of endemic, occupational and other diseases;" and article 39 para. 2 (b) of the 2004 Arab Charter on Human Rights that refers to the "[e]fforts to control disease by means of prevention".

58 Article 10 para. 2 (c) of the 1988 Protocol to the ACHR.

59 Article 39 para. 2 (e) of the 2004 Arab Charter on Human Rights.

60 Committee on Economic, Social and Cultural Rights, General Comment No. 14 (2000), The right to the highest attainable standard of health (article 12 of the International Covenant on Economic, Social and Cultural Rights), para. 12, UN Doc. E/C.12/2000/4, 11 August 2000. See also on the right to health, Ben Saul, David Kinley, Jacqueline Mowbray, *The International Covenant on Economic, Social and Cultural Rights*, *op. cit.*, pp. 977–1083.

61 AcomHPR, Principles and Guidelines on the Implementation of Economic, Social and Cultural Rights in the African Charter on Human and Peoples' Rights, 2010, Para. 64.

III Content of Article 11: the Right to Protection of Health

Article 11 of the Charter consists of an introduction and three paragraphs that deal with different elements of the right to health protection. The introduction provides that States must take steps to render the right to health protection effective. Article 11 states: "With a view to ensuring the effective exercise of the right to protection of health, the Parties undertake, either directly or in cooperation with public or private organisations, to take appropriate measures designed *inter alia*". The reference to public and private organisations is a recognition of the role they play, alongside States, in the protection of health.[62] The insistence on the cooperation between States and these organisations can also be analysed as a means of maximising the enjoyment of the right to health protection, mobilising all the actors that intervene in this field, and avoiding any situation that could result in the denial of the right to health. This introduction also announces that States must "take appropriate measures designed *inter alia*". The use of the phrase "*inter alia*" indicates that the list of measures that follows is not exhaustive and that other measures should be taken where they are deemed necessary. However, the measures listed in Article 11 are the ones to be considered because they are explicit and the European Committee of Social Rights (ECSR) has detailed their content.

A *Removing "as Far as Possible the Causes of Ill-Health" (Article 11 Paragraph 1)*

Paragraph 1 of Article 11 of the Charter raises the question of which causes of ill health must, as far as possible, be removed. A review of the decisions and conclusions of the ECSR, which examined that provision in a number of cases, provides some answers. Access to health care is one of the elements taken into account. In the case of *European Committee for Home Priority Action for Children and Families* (EUROCEF) *v. France*, France was accused of not respecting the rights of unaccompanied foreign minors who lived in difficult sanitary conditions, suffered from infections and, in a number of cases, had no access to medical care due to administrative and legal obstacles.[63] The ECSR found

62 On private-public cooperation in the public health sector, see Michael R. Reich, "Public-Private Partnerships for Public Health", in Michael R. Reich (ed.), *Public-Private Partnerships for Public Health*, Cambridge, Harvard University Press, 2002, pp. 1–18; Mariateresa Torchia, Andrea Calabrò and Michèle Morner, "Public-Private Partnerships in the Health Care Sector: A Systematic Review of the Literature", *Public Management Review*, vol. 17, no. 2, 2015, pp. 236–261.

63 ECSR, *European Committee on Priority Home Action for Children and Families* (EUROCEF) *v. France*, complaint No. 114/2015, decision on the merits of 24 January 2018, §§ 141–144.

that access to health care for unaccompanied foreign minors was covered by Article 11 paragraph 1 and declared that France did not guarantee such access and was therefore in violation of this provision.[64] In *Confederazione Generale Italiana del Lavoro* (CGIL) *v. Italy*, the ECSR found that Italy had violated Article 11 paragraph 1 because, *inter alia*, women "seeking access to abortion services [...] face[d] substantial difficulties in obtaining access to such services".[65]

The prohibition of a medical procedure being performed on an individual without the consent of that person and without considering the long-term health effects on that person has also been considered under that provision. In *Transgender Europe and* ILGA *Europe v. Czech Republic*,[66] which concerned the mandatory sterilisation imposed by law on transgender persons seeking to change their personal documents,[67] the complainants argued that "sterilisation [was] a major medical procedure, with irreversible consequences for a person's health, especially reproductive health, self-conception and mental wellbeing".[68] The ECSR found that the Czech Republic's legislation imposing sterilisation on transgender persons seeking to harmonise their identity with their appearance was contrary to Article 11 paragraph 1 of the Charter. It strongly asserted "that the condition attached for the recognition of transgender person's gender identity vitiates free consent, and therefore such a requirement violates physical integrity, operates contrary to the notion of human dignity and consequently cannot be considered as compatible with the right to protection of health as guaranteed by Article 11 § 1 of the Charter".[69] In this case, the ECSR stated that Article 11 paragraph 1 "encompasses, *inter alia*, the right to the highest possible standard of health and the right of access to health care".[70] In recent years, these two elements have been consistently taken into account by the ECSR when presenting its conclusions on the national reports submitted by European States. For example, in 2018, in its conclusions on Iceland, it examined measures designed "to ensure the highest possible standard of health", noting that life expectancy in Iceland was one of the highest in Europe, and the infant mortality rate one of the lowest.[71] With regard to "access

64 *Ibid.*, §§ 154–155.

65 ECSR, *Confederazione Generale Italiana del Lavoro* (CGIL) *v. Italy*, complaint No. 91/2013, decision on admissibility and merits of 12 October 2015, §§ 190–193.

66 ECSR, *Transgender Europe and* ILGA *Europe v. Czech Republic*, complaint No. 117/2014, decision on the merits of 15 May 2018.

67 *Ibid.*, § 10.

68 *Ibid.*, § 51.

69 *Ibid.*, § 86.

70 *Ibid.*, § 71.

71 ECSR, Conclusions XXI-2 (2018), Iceland, Article 11 § 1.

to health care", the ECSR asked Iceland to provide information on dental care and on the availability of mental health care in its future report.[72] Mortality rates and life expectancy, and the reality of access to health care facilities and specific treatments, are measures that the ECSR has included in the conclusions of its reports on many European States, such as Germany,[73] Spain,[74] Belgium[75] and Azerbaijan.[76]

The risk that the environment may pose has also been analysed in the context of Article 11 paragraph 1. Here, what is generally argued is that an unhealthy environment may be a cause of ill health. This reasoning is found in many cases brought to the attention of the ESCR. In one of its decisions dealing with environmental issues, the ECSR recalled that "under Article 11 § 1 of the Charter, health systems must respond appropriately to avoidable health risks, i.e. ones that can be controlled by human action, and States must guarantee the best possible results in line with the available knowledge".[77] In another important case, *Marangopoulos Foundation for Human Rights (MFHR) v. Greece*, the plaintiffs accused Greece of failing to protect the public from air pollution because it had authorised the activity of a company "without taking sufficient account of the environmental impact and without taking all necessary steps to reduce this impact".[78] The ECSR found that "[m]easures required under Article 11 should be designed, in the light of current knowledge, to remove the causes of ill-health resulting from environmental threats such as pollution",[79] and concluded that there had been a violation of Article 11 paragraph 1.[80] This evolutive interpretation of article 11 by the ESCR has certainly been prompted by the surge of awareness on environmental issues at the international level and in European societies beginning in the 1970s.[81] By taking into consideration the

72 *Ibid.*

73 ECSR, Conclusions XXI-2 (2017), Germany, Article 11 § 1.

74 ECSR, Conclusions XXI-2 (2019), Spain, Article 11 § 1.

75 ECSR, Conclusions 2017, Belgium, Article 11 § 1.

76 ECSR, Conclusions 2017, Azerbaijan, Article 11 § 1.

77 ECSR, *International Federation for Human Rights (FIDH) v. Greece*, collective complaint No. 72/2011, decision on the merits of 23 January 2013, § 144.

78 ECSR, *Marangopoulos Foundation for Human Rights (MFHR) v. Greece*, complaint No. 30/2005, decision on the merits of 6 December 2006, § 11.

79 *Ibid.*, § 202.

80 *Ibid.*, § 221. For an analysis of this case, see Mirja Trilsch, "European Committee of Social Rights: The Right to a Healthy Environment", *International Journal of Constitutional Law*, vol. 7, no. 3, July 2009, pp. 529–538.

81 On that awareness, see David R. Boyd, "Catalyst for Change. Evaluating Forty Years of Experience in Implementing the Right to a Healthy Environment" in John H. Knox, Ramin Pejan, *The Human Right to a Healthy Environment*, Cambridge, Cambridge University Press, 2018, pp. 17–23.

consequences of environment degradation on health, the ECSR also fills a gap of the Charter, which does not recognize a right to a healthy environment.[82] Thus, according to the ECSR, the right to a healthy environment is part of the right to protection of health. Paragraph 1 of Article 11 allows for the protection of persons against the causes of ill-health. These causes are manifold and can be summarised under the term "avoidable risks"; being risks that must be mitigated by States Parties in order to ensure the enjoyment of the right to health protection.

B *Providing "Advisory and Educational Facilities for the Promotion of Health and the Encouragement of Individual Responsibility in Matters of Health" (Article 11 Paragraph 2)*

Health promotion and information on health issues are central in Article 11 paragraph 2. States are called upon to raise "awareness" or "public awareness" among individuals or the population in order to ensure the enjoyment of the right to health protection. The idea here is that States must inform or must give information to individuals about their health or the potential risks they may face.[83] Greece, for example, was found to be in breach of Article 11 paragraph 2 because it failed to adequately inform the population living in a certain region of the country about environmental problems that posed risks to their health.[84] Referring to these failures, the ECSR recalled that "[i]nforming the public, particularly through awareness-raising campaigns, must be a public health priority".[85] Bulgaria was also found responsible for failing to implement "systematic, long-term government measures to promote health awareness" among the Roma population whose health was not protected.[86] The scope of measures that States must take is very broad, encompassing education and communication with both individuals and the public. These measures are well summarised by the ECSR in *International Centre for the Legal Protection of*

---

82 On that topic, see Giuseppe Palmisano, "The Right to a Healthy or Decent Environment as a Social Right: Acquis and Future Prospects of the European Social Charter System", *Roma Tre Law Review*, vol. 2, 2020, pp. 7–24. This author defends the idea of "[a]dding to the European Social Charter one or more specific provisions recognising the right to a healthy or decent environment as a social right" (p. 17).

83 See for example: ECSR, *Marangopoulos Foundation for Human Rights (MFHR) v. Greece, cit.*, § 216.

84 ECSR, *International Federation for Human Rights (FIDH) v. Greece, cit.*, §§ 156–160.

85 *Ibid*, § 158.

86 ECSR, *European Roma Rights Centre (ERRC) v. Bulgaria*, collective complaint No. 46/2007, decision on the Merit of 3 December 2008, §§ 48 and 51.

Human Rights (*INTERIGHTS*) *v. Croatia.*[87] With regard to Article 11 paragraph 2, the ECSR stated:

> States must provide education and aim to raise public awareness in respect of health-related matters. States must adopt concrete measures with a view to implementing a public education policy which is directed towards the population at large as well as particular population groups which are affected by specific health problems. The measures taken should seek to prevent activities that are damaging to health, such as smoking, excessive alcohol consumption and the use of drugs, and encourage the development of a sense of individual responsibility in respect of matters such as healthy diet, sexual and reproductive health and the environment.[88]

Paragraph 2 of Article 11 also covers health education in schools, periodic and preventive medical check-ups, consultations, counselling and screening, especially for certain categories of people such as children, adolescents and pregnant women.[89] Overall, these measures are seen as helping to advise, educate and raise awareness of health issues.

C *Preventing "as Far as Possible Epidemic, Endemic and Other Diseases, as Well as Accidents"* (*Article 11 Paragraph 3*)

Paragraph 3 of Article 11 deals with the prevention of various elements: epidemics, endemics, other diseases and accidents. Preventing these means that States must analyse current situations that may pose risks and assess their potential negative effects. Then they must take precautionary measures to prevent negative outcomes. The meaning of this provision is well developed in *Marangopoulos Foundation for Human Rights* (*MFHR*) *v. Greece*. In this case, the applicants invoked Article 11 paragraph 3 and claimed under that provision that the Greek State had "failed to conduct regular, population-wide health assessments of the effects of air pollution on health".[90] The ECSR explicitly linked the right to health protection to the right to a healthy environment, noting that there was a growing consensus that the two were connected.[91] It

87 ECSR, *International Centre for the Legal Protection of Human Rights* (*INTERIGHTS*) *v. Croatia*, complaint No. 45/2007, decision on the merits of 30 March 2009.

88 *Ibid*, § 43.

89 For these elements in the ECSR's conclusions, see for example, ECSR, Conclusions XXI-2 (2018), Greece, Article 11 § 2; ECSR, Conclusions 2017, Moldova, Article 11 § 2.

90 ECSR, *Marangopoulos Foundation for Human Rights* (*MFHR*) *v. Greece*, *cit.*, § 86.

91 *Ibid.*, § 195.

concluded that Greece had violated Article 11 paragraph 3 as it did under the first two paragraphs of Article 11.[92] In some cases, such as the *International Commission of Jurists (ICJ) and European Council for Refugees and Exiles (ECRE) v. Greece*, the ECSR examined both Article 11 paragraph 3 and Article 11 paragraph 1, and found violations without distinguishing between them.[93] In this case, the applicants argued that Greece had violated these provisions. They accused Greece of not taking "steps to facilitate access to health care and services, to address the causes of ill-health and to prevent diseases and the worsening of illnesses among migrant children".[94] The ECSR found that Greece had violated both provisions by failing to provide shelter and accommodation for migrant children and to protect their health.[95] This shows that there is a close connection between paragraphs 1 and 3 of article 11 since they both deal with health risks related to potential ill-health. With regard to the prevention of diseases, the ECSR has also treated immunization and vaccination under paragraph 3 in its case law, underlying "that vaccinations on a large scale are recognised as the most efficient and most economical means of combating infectious and epidemic diseases".[96]

More generally, it is in the ECSR's conclusions after examination of the national reports that one finds clarification of the understanding and meaning of Article 11 paragraph 3. The conclusions are generally divided into the following categories: a healthy environment; use of tobacco, alcohol and drugs; vaccinations and epidemiological surveillance; and accidents. In the conclusions in its report on Iceland in 2015, the ECSR analysed Iceland's efforts to prevent disease, looking at these categories.[97] It did the same for Luxembourg,[98] the UK[99] and Denmark.[100] In some of its conclusions, it also assessed the measures taken in the field of preventing accidents.[101]

---

92 *Ibid.*, § 221.

93 ECSR, *International Commission of Jurists (ICJ) and European Council for Refugees and Exiles (ECRE) v. Greece*, complaint No. 173/2018, decision on the merits of 26 January 2021, §§ 218–230.

94 *Ibid.*, § 211.

95 *Ibid.*, § 230.

96 ECSR, *Médecins du Monde – International v. France*, collective complaint No. 67/2011, decision on the merits of 11 September 2012, § 160.

97 ECSR, Conclusions XXI-2 (2018), Iceland, Article 11 § 3.

98 ECSR, Conclusions XXI-2 (2018), Luxembourg, Article 11 § 3.

99 ECSR, Conclusions XXI-2 (2017), United Kingdom, Article 11 § 3, 08/12/2017.

100 ECSR, Conclusions XXI-2 (2017), Denmark, Article 11 § 3.

101 ECSR, Conclusions 2017, France, Article 11 § 3; ECSR, Conclusions 2017, Belgium, Article 11 § 3.

Recently, immunisation programmes have been analysed by the ECSR as an important element of Article 11 paragraph 3. In its statement of interpretation on the right to protection of health in times of a pandemic, published in the context of the COVID-19 pandemic, the ECSR stated that States Parties to the Charter "must operate widely accessible immunisation programmes. They must maintain high coverage rates not only to reduce the incidence of these diseases, but also to neutralise the reservoir of the virus and thus achieve the goals set by the WHO to eradicate a range of infectious diseases. Vaccine research should be promoted, adequately funded and efficiently coordinated across public and private actors".[102] As with several other elements within Article 11, this emphasis on vaccination places this provision firmly within the framework of the prevention of harm to health, while affirming the increased role of those States whose obligations are clearly defined.

IV Obligations of the States Parties

It is now common knowledge among legal experts that the evolution of human rights into two main categories (civil and political rights, on the one hand, and economic, social and cultural rights, on the other) has led to questions about the nature of States' international obligations to implement these rights. It has been claimed that the obligations imposed on States in relation to social rights are positive, with States required to take action and measures to implement these rights. With regard to civil and political rights, States' obligations have been considered negative, with States required to refrain from taking measures that impede the enjoyment of these rights. This separation of human rights into two categories has been criticised and there is now considerable evidence that States have both positive and negative obligations when implementing all human rights. The right to the protection of health under the Charter is further evidence of this. The ECSR has held that European States have both positive and negative obligations when it comes to implementing Article 11. In the case of *Transgender Europe and ILGA Europe v. Czech Republic*, the ECSR clearly indicated that "Article 11 imposes a range of positive and negative obligations".[103] It also clearly considered that in the field of the right to health protection, States not only have to take positive measures and actions to promote

102 ECSR, 2020, Statement of interpretation on the right to protection of health in times of pandemic, p. 5.

103 ECSR, *Transgender Europe and ILGA Europe v. Czech Republic*, *cit.*, § 79.

the enjoyment of this right,[104] they also have to take negative measures since they must avoid interfering with the enjoyment of this right.[105]

A Positive Obligations

With regard to positive obligations, the ECSR has found in numerous decisions that States have failed to take action and that this has resulted in a violation of Article 11. For example, the ECSR found that by failing to provide adequate shelter and accommodation, as well as "sufficient health" to unaccompanied children, Greece violated Article 11 of the Charter.[106] It continued in the same vein against France, stating that France had failed to provide many "unaccompanied foreign minors" with access to "universal healthcare coverage" and "the state medical assistance".[107] The ECSR found that Bulgaria had failed to ensure "adequate access to health care" for pregnant Roma women and that this constituted indirect discrimination and a violation of Article 11 paragraph 1.[108] In other words, the Bulgarian State should have been proactive in avoiding this, including taking measures to ensure that these women had adequate access to health care. In another case, the ECSR found that Italy did not take the "necessary measures to remove the cause of ill health" of women wishing to terminate their pregnancy.[109] Despite its national legislation, Italy failed to ensure that "abortions requested in accordance with the applicable rules were performed in all cases, even when the number of objecting medical practitioners and other health personnel [was] high", and violated Article 11 paragraph 1.[110]

These positive obligations were also found in the statement of interpretation issued by the ECSR in the context of COVID-19. In this statement, the ECSR held that "States must take all necessary emergency measures in a pandemic", including "testing and tracing, physical distancing and self-isolation, the provision of adequate masks and disinfectant, as well as the imposition of quarantine and 'lockdown' arrangements".[111] Other measures, *inter alia*, include the

---

104 *Ibid.*

105 *Ibid.*

106 ECSR, *International Commission of Jurists (ICJ) and European Council for Refugees and Exiles (ECRE) v. Greece, cit.*, § 230.

107 ECSR, *European Committee on Priority Home Action for Children and Families (EUROCEF) v. France, cit.*, §§ 154–155.

108 ECSR, *European Roma Rights Centre (ERRC) v. Bulgaria*, Complaint No. 151/2017, Decision on the Merits of 5 December 2018, § 86.

109 ECSR, *International Planned Parenthood Federation – European Network (IPPF EN) v. Italy*, complaint No. 87/2012, Decision on the merits of 10 September 2013, § 176.

110 *Ibid.*, §§ 176–177.

111 ECSR, 2020: Statement of interpretation on the right to protection of health in times of pandemic, p. 3.

deployment of healthcare workers, raising awareness among people of the risks posed by the pandemic and promoting ways to mitigate contagion, preventing risks and so on.[112]

B *Negative Obligations*

With regard to negative obligations and the fact that States must not interfere with the enjoyment of the right to health protection, the ECSR found that the Czech Republic had not refrained from interfering with the rights of transgender persons because it required them to undergo "surgical gender reassignment [...] for a change of gender identity".[113] Before concluding that the Czech Republic had violated Article 11, the ECSR considered, *inter alia*, that "[o]bliging an individual to undergo such serious surgery which could in fact be harmful to health cannot be considered as being consistent with the obligation that the state refrain from interfering with the enjoyment of the right to health and in such cases, States must eliminate the interference".[114] The decisions of the ECSR that deal with environmental issues can also be viewed as an illustration of negative obligations of States in protecting health. If it is true that States must take measures to protect their populations against environmental pollution, they must also refrain from authorising activities of companies that can pollute the environment and affect public health. For example, in the case *Marangopoulos Foundation for Human Rights (MFHR) v. Greece*, Greece was held accountable because it did not take measures to avoid pollution in the context of a risk to health posed by lignite mining.[115] It is also possible in this case to argue that Greece should have refrained from giving authorisation to the activities of companies that were polluting the environment in the first place. Thus, these cases highlight two separate obligations for States: first, to protect the individual's health from harm (air pollution), which could be read as both a positive and a negative obligation; and second to restrain from imposing mandatory health treatments that are contrary to human dignity (sterilisation), which is mainly a negative obligation. When analysing the obligations of States regarding the right to health, the African Commission on Human and Peoples' Rights case went in that direction and insisted on these negative obligations regarding activities when it came to environmental pollution.[116] This

112 *Ibid.*, pp. 3–4.

113 ECSR, *Transgender Europe and ILGA Europe v. Czech Republic*, *cit.*, § 80.

114 *Ibid.*, § 80 and § 86.

115 ECSR, *Marangopoulos Foundation for Human Rights (MFHR) v. Greece*, *cit.*, §§ 220–221.

116 See ComADHP, *Social and Economic Rights Action Center, Center for Economic and Social Rights v. Nigeria*, communications n° 155/96, October 2001, § 52. For a comment on negative obligations of State in the context of pollution and the right to health, Michael Bothe,

consideration of the right to the protection of health as implying both negative and positive obligations illustrates the indivisibility of human rights.

V Links between the Right to Health Protection and Other Human Rights: Indivisibility of Human Rights

Human rights are indivisible and the separation into two categories (civil and political rights, on the one hand, and economic, social and cultural rights, on the other) has proven unrealistic because there are strong links between them. The right to protection of health is of particular concern because, although it is considered a social right, it shares strong links with civil and political rights. Globally, the ECSR has used dignity, which is a central concept in the enjoyment of all human rights, to insist on the importance of the right to health protection. It has stated that "health care is a prerequisite for the preservation of human dignity".[117] In a number of decisions, the ECSR has established links between the right to health protection and other civil and political rights. In dealing with the right to the protection of health, the ECSR "attaches great importance to the indivisibility of all human rights which shape the European system of human rights".[118] The most important link is between, on the one hand, the right to the protection of health and, on the other hand, the right to life, the prohibition of torture or inhuman or degrading treatment or punishment, and sometimes the right to respect for private and family life, which are respectively enshrined in Articles 2, 3 and 8 of the European Convention on Human Rights (ECHR). The ECSR has repeatedly stated that Article 11 of the Charter complements Articles 2 and 3 of the ECHR,[119] and that there are links between the right to health protection and Article 8 of the ECHR.[120]

"Les concepts fondamentaux du droit à la santé: le point de vue juridique", in René-Jean Dupuy, *The Right to Health as a Human Right*, Brill-Nijhoff, Leiden Boston, Colloques/ Workshop Series, The Hague Academy of International Law, 1979, pp. 14–34, p. 14.

117 ECSR, *International Federation of Human Rights Leagues* (*FIDH*) *v. France*, complaint No. 14/2003, decision on the merits of 3 November 2004, § 31.

118 For example, ECSR, *Transgender Europe and ILGA Europe v. Czech Republic, cit.*, § 83.

119 *Ibid.*,; ECSR, Conclusions 2005, Statement of interpretation, Article 11, 2005; ECSR, Statement of interpretation on the right to protection of health in times of pandemic, *cit.* p. 5.

120 For example, ECSR, *Transgender Europe and ILGA Europe v. Czech Republic, cit.*, § 83; ECSR, *International Federation of Human Rights Leagues* (*FIDH*) *v. Greece*, collective complaint No. 72/2011, decision on the merits, 23 January 2013, §. 51.

For its part, the European Court of Human Rights has taken that complementarity into consideration. Even if the Court had stated that the right to protection of health was not guaranteed by the ECHR and ruled inadmissible complaints based on that right,[121] it has in a number of cases established parallels between health, the right to health and Articles 2,[122] 3[123] and 8 of the ECHR.[124] In some cases, the Court has even referred to Article 11 of the Charter.[125] The Interamerican Court of Human Rights also went in the same direction. It established a link between the provision of health care and "the right to personal integrity and of the obligation not to endanger life", which derived from Articles 4 and 5 of the American Convention on Human Rights.[126] However, it went farther when it analysed Article 26 of the American Convention on Human Rights, which provides that States "undertake to adopt measures [...] with a view to achieving progressively [...] the full realization of the rights implicit in the economic, social, educational, scientific, and cultural standards". Even if the right to health is not explicitly recognised by the American Convention on Human Rights, and even if the justiciability of that right is not recognised under the 1988 San Salvador Protocol,[127] the Interamerican Court ruled that "the right to health is an autonomous right protected by Article 26 of the American Convention".[128]

The right to health protection is an important right enshrined in the European Social Charter. It imposes legal obligations on State Parties. The links between this right and non-derogable rights, such as the right to life and the prohibition of torture, argue for its enjoyment to be considered essential in States Parties to the Charter and, beyond, in other States. The COVID-19 pandemic exposed to the public, among other things, the overcrowding of medical

121 See, ECtHR, 28 November 2000, *Fiorenza v. Italy*, No. 44393/98; ECtHR, 11 July 2006, *Pastorino Et Autres C. Italie*, No. 17640/02, § 3.

122 ECtHR, 17 March 2016, *Vasileva v. Bulgaria*, No. 23796/10, § 63; ECtHR [GC], 25 June 2019, *Nicolae Virgiliu Tănase v. Romania*, No. 41720/13, § 127.

123 ECtHR [GC], 26 April 2016, *Murray v. The Netherlands*, No.10511/10.

124 For example, ECtHR, *Vasileva v. Bulgaria, cit.*, § 63; ECtHR [GC], *Nicolae Virgiliu Tănase v. Romania, cit.*, § 127.

125 ECtHR [GC], 19 December 2017, *Lopes De Sousa Fernandes v. Portugal*, No. 56080/13, § 114; ECtHR [GC], 8 April 2021 *Vavřička and Others v. The Czech Republic*, No. 47621/13, 3867/14, 73094/14, §§ 138–140.

126 IACtHR, 1 September 2015, Case *Gonzales Lluy et Al. v. Ecuador* (Preliminary Objections, Merits, Reparations and Costs), Series C No. 298, § 191.

127 Only trade union rights and the right to education are justiciable under that Protocol, see article 19 para. 6 of 1988 San Salvador Protocol.

128 IACtHR, 8 March 2018, Case *Poblete Vilches et al. v. Chile* (Merits, Reparations and Costs), Series C No. 349, § 174.

facilities, the lack of infrastructure and equipment in medical facilities in some countries, the overloading of the medical profession, the inequitable distribution of vaccines between the Global North and the Global South, the negative economic consequences and the deaths. It has demonstrated – if there was still any doubt – that health is at the heart of all human activity. Health protection must be, at all times, an absolute priority.

ARTICLE 12

The Right to Social Security

Lyle Barker

With a view to ensuring the effective exercise of the right to social security, the Parties undertake:

1. to establish or maintain a system of social security;
2. to maintain the social security system at a satisfactory level at least equal to that necessary for the ratification of the European Code of Social Security;
3. to endeavour to raise progressively the system of social security to a higher level;
4. to take steps, by the conclusion of appropriate bilateral and multilateral agreements or by other means, and subject to the conditions laid down in such agreements, in order to ensure:
   a) equal treatment with their own nationals of the nationals of other Parties in respect of social security rights, including the retention of benefits arising out of social security legislation, whatever movements the persons protected may undertake between the territories of the Parties;
   b) the granting, maintenance and resumption of social security rights by such means as the accumulation of insurance or employment periods completed under the legislation of each of the Parties.

Introduction

The right to social security is a fundamental human right recognised in various international and regional human rights law (IHRL) instruments. Although at a national level, some countries began implementing policies around social security in the late 19th century and early 20th century, the history of the human right to social security can be traced back to the mid-20th century when concerns over the economic and social well-being of individuals

 | DOI:10.1163/9789004434141_003

gained prominence following the aftermath of World War II.[1] The recognition of social security as a human right emerged as a response to the widespread poverty and social inequalities resulting from industrialisation and economic crises.[2]

The International Labour Organization (ILO) played a significant role in shaping the right to social security. In 1944, the ILO adopted the Declaration of Philadelphia, which stated that "all human beings, irrespective of race, creed, or sex, have the right to pursue both their material well-being and their spiritual development in conditions of freedom and dignity, economic security, and equal opportunity."[3] The ILO going on to stating in the Declaration that Member States should ensure "the extension of social security measures to provide a basic income to all in need of such protection and comprehensive medical care."[4]

The Universal Declaration of Human Rights (UDHR), adopted by the United Nations General Assembly in 1948, further solidified the recognition of social security as a human right. Article 25 of the UDHR declares that "everyone, as a member of society, has the right to social security and is entitled to realisation, through national effort and international cooperation and in accordance with the organisation and resources of each State, of the economic, social, and cultural rights indispensable for his dignity and the free development of his personality."[5]

Following the UDHR, in 1966 the United Nations General Assembly adopted the International Covenant on Economic, Social and Cultural Rights (ICESCR, or Covenant) with the aim of providing a more comprehensive and enforceable framework for the protection and promotion of economic, social, and cultural rights (ESC) to Member States of the UN. This included the ICESCR recognising the right to social security, affirming the right of everyone to social security, including social insurance under Article 9 of the Covenant.[6]

1 Jack Donnelly and Daniel J. Whelan, *International Human Rights*, Routledge, 2018, 5th ed, pp. 3–7.
2 Ibid.
3 International Labour Conference (26th Session) Declaration of Philadelphia, Declaration concerning the aims and purposes of the International Labour Organisation (Philadelphia 10 May 1944) § II (a).
4 Ibid § III (f).
5 Universal Declaration of Human Rights (adopted 10 December 1948) UNGA Res 217 A(III) (UDHR), Article 25.
6 International Covenant on Economic, Social and Cultural Rights (adopted 16 December 1966, entered into force 3 January 1976) (ICESCR) UNGA Res 2200A (XXI), Article 9.

At the European level, the European Social Charter (ESC, or Charter)[7] was adopted by the Council of Europe in 1961 with the aim of providing a robust and regional specific framework for the protection and promotion of the ESCR to Member States of the Council of Europe. However, Article 12 of the ESC differs from Article 9 of the ICESCR due to the requirement for State Parties' social security systems to meet the standards set by the 1965 European Code of Social Security[8] (and its 1990 revised version)[9] under Article 12 § 2 and the obligation to have equal treatment and retention of accrued rights for nationals of other Contracted Parties in respect of social security rights under Article 12 § 4. Through recognising the importance of social security in ensuring human dignity, the Charter aims to protect individuals and their families against the risks and uncertainties of life, such as unemployment, poverty, disability, old age, and other contingencies, by providing an explicit obligation for State Parties to provide adequate and accessible social protection systems. In affirming this, the governing body for the ESC, the European Committee of Social Rights (ECSR, or Committee) has stated that "it is of paramount importance that social security systems are adequate to protect the population", with the Committee making specific reference to groups such as disabled people and those from a lower socio-economic background.[10]

The right to social security under Article 12 of the ESC is one of the Articles contained in the original version of the Charter.[11] However, Article 12 § 2 was amended to include reference to the European Code of Social Security in the revised version of the instrument in 1996 (Revised ESC),[12] this was the only section of the Article that was amended. Article 12 of the ESC is one of the most complex rights contained within the Charter.[13] This is due to certain provisions under the Article, namely 12 § 4, requiring an extensive assessment of Contracted Parties' different national systems. As such, the ECSR has provided

7 The European Social Charter of 1961 (adopted 18 October 1961, entered into force 26 February 1965) CETS No. 35.

8 The European Code of Social Security (adopted 16 April 1964, entered into force 17 March 1968) CETS No. 48.

9 The European Code of Social Security (Revised) (adopted 6 November 1990) CENTS No. 139.

10 Council of Europe, *Case-law on the European Social Charter, Supplement No.3*, Council of Europe 1993, p. 113.

11 The European Social Charter of 1961 (adopted 18 October 1961, entered into force 26 February 1965) CETS No. 35 art 12.

12 The Revised European Social Charter of 1996 (adopted 3 May 1996, entered into force on 1 July 1999) CETS No. 163 art 12 § 2; Karin Lucas, "ARTICLE 12: THE RIGHT TO SOCIAL SECUIRTY", in Karin Lucas, *The Revised European Social Charter: An Article by Article Commentary*, Edwards Elgar, 2021, pp. 175–176.

13 Ibid p. 184.

extensive "jurisprudence" on this Article through the Reporting and Collective Complaint Procedures,[14] referencing other IHRL instruments and systems and other legal frameworks such as the European Code of Social Security.

This chapter will begin by offering an overview of the material and objective of Article 12 of the ESC. The first section looks towards the development of theoretical models of social security and their rationale, the drafting history of the Article, other relevant IHRL standards and the Article's relationship with other provisions within the ESC. Next section goes on to examine interpretations the ECSR has made in relation to this Article. The final section will make some concluding remarks in relation to the historical and ever-increasing importance of the right to social security under Article 12 of the ESC.

1 General Presentation

Between 1883–84, Germany became the pioneer in implementing a social insurance scheme, crafted by Otto von Bismarck.[15] The German Chancellor's impetus for implementing social insurance was twofold: to enhance the welfare of workers, ensuring optimal efficiency in the German economy, and to counter demands for more extreme socialist options.[16] Over time, the programs were expanded to include an old-age insurance program, supported in part by tax revenue.[17] Implemented was a social security system that has since served as a blueprint for social insurance: contributions from workers and employers were required to fund sickness insurance and workers' compensation.[18]

In the early 20th century, Scandinavia also witnessed the development of comprehensive social insurance policies that aimed to provide security and support to their citizens. Countries like Sweden and Denmark implemented progressive reforms to address social inequalities and improve living conditions.[19] These reforms were driven by the influence of labour movements and a welfare-oriented political climate, which created an environment conducive

---

14 Additional Protocol to the European Social Charter for Providing for a System of Collective Complaints (adopted 9 November 1995, entered into force 1 July 1998) CETS No. 158.

15 Martin Scheinin, "12. The Right to Social Security" in Asbjørn Eide, Catarina Krause, and Allan Rosas (eds), *Economic, Social and Cultural Rights: A Textbook* Brill, Leiden, Martinus Nijhoff Publishers, 2001, 2nd rev. ed p. 211.

16 Ibid.

17 Ibid.

18 Ibid.

19 Peter Baldwin, "The Scandinavian Origins of the Social Interpretation of the Welfare State," *Comparative Studies in Society and History*, vol. 31, no. 1, 1989.

to the implementation of social policies.[20] The Scandinavian models emphasised universal social insurance programs, shared responsibility between the state, employers, and workers, and investments in education, healthcare, and infrastructure.[21] These initiatives were instrumental in creating sustainable and inclusive welfare states in Scandinavia.[22]

In 1942, the conceptualisation of social security took another leap forward with William Beveridge's 'Social Insurance and Allied Service' report for a welfare state in the UK. Between 1942 and 1951, the report led to the establishment of the first "unified" social security system that was unique for its time in providing: universal coverage for the entire UK population, national insurance (a collective pool of funds through contributions from both employers and employees, which would be used to provide benefits when needed), cradle-to-grave welfare (the provision of benefits and services at various stages of life, including maternity grants, family allowances, unemployment benefits, and pensions), preventive and redistributive economic policies (the need for a progressive taxation system to redistribute income and reduce inequalities) and State responsibility (the need for the State to have responsibility in ensuring social security).[23]

A differentiation is frequently drawn between social security and social welfare. This classification aims to distinguish between the "earned" benefits of social security that are provided to workers and their families, and the assistance provided to individuals or groups based on their financial needs, funded by tax revenues.[24] Often, the term social security is used in a broader sense, encompassing both social insurance and social assistance.[25]

The legal justification for the benefits can serve as a basis for classifying them within or outside the scope of social security.[26] This criterion is commonly employed to categorise need-based social assistance as separate from social security.[27] However, the evolution of international safeguards for social

20 Ibid.
21 Ibid.
22 Ibid.
23 William Beveridge, 'The Beveridge Report: Social Insurance and Allied Services' (Majesty's Stationery Office, 1942) accessed <http://news.bbc.co.uk/2/shared/bsp/hi/pdfs/19_07_05_beveridge.pdf> accessed 1 May 2023, as complemented by William Beveridge, 'Full Employment in a Free Society' (The New Statesman and Nation and Reynolds News, 1944) accessed http://lib-161.lse.ac.uk/archives/beveridge/9A_79_Full_employment_in_a_free_society.pdf> accessed 1 May 2023.
24 Martin Scheinin, *cit.*, pp. 212–213.
25 Ibid.
26 Ibid.
27 Ibid.

and economic rights, particularly through the adoption of the European Social Charter (ESC), has altered this scenario. Now, "social assistance for individuals lacking sufficient resources, which is funded from general tax revenues rather than through individual contributions to an insurance-type scheme, must also be granted as an entitlement rather than at the discretion of the authorities."[28]

Article 25 of the UDHR, the ILO's Declaration of Philadelphia and Article 9 of the ICESCR would take on board lessons from the implementation and design of these models and began to shift understanding of social security as a universal human right. However, it would be the ILO's Social Security (Minimum Standards) Convention of 1952 (No. 102)[29] that would be most influential in the drafting of the right to social security under Article 12 of the ESC.

A *Drafting History*

The text of Article 12 underwent significant revisions in the drafting of the 1961 Charter, however, paragraph 2 is the only section of the Article that was amended in the Revised Charter.[30] In the drafting of the 1961 Charter, the article focused on specifying the services and situations covered by social insurance, including sickness, disability, widowhood, unemployment, and old age. It also encompassed benefits related to medical treatment, maternity, family support, and retirement pensions. However, these provisions were restructured to prioritise the establishment and maintenance of a satisfactory level of social security system, with a commitment from the State to progressively improve it.[31]

The initial draft of Article 12 in the 1961 Charter also made a reference to the European Code of Social Security, which outlined measures to protect the right to social security and the corresponding services and benefits.[32] However,

---

28 Council of Europe, *Conclusions of the Committee of Independent Experts of the European Social Charter – Conclusions XIII-1*, Council of Europe, 1998, pp. 55–57.

29 International Labour Organization (ILO) Convention Concerning Social Security (Minimum Standards), 1952 (No. 102) (adopted 28 June 1952, entered into force 27 April 195 5) ILO Treaty No 102.

30 Council of Europe 'Parliamentary Assembly, European Social Charter and European Economic and Social Council, Motion for a recommendation by Social, Health and Family Affairs Committee (rejected, not referred to the Committee of Ministers)' (1955) Doc. 403, 26; Karin Lucas, *cit.*, pp. 175–176.

31 Council of Europe 'Parliamentary Assembly, Draft European Social Charter, Report by the Committee of Ministers (Committee of Ministers' draft, officially published in February 1958)' (1959) Doc. 927, 12; Karin Lucas, *cit.*, pp. 175–176.

32 Council of Europe 'Parliamentary Assembly, Programme of Work of the Council of Europe, Communication by the Committee of Ministers' (1954); Karin Lucas, *cit.*, pp. 175–176.

subsequent drafts from 1959 did not delve into the specifics of these services and benefits since the term "social security" was considered a broad concept encompassing various forms of assistance.[33] Ultimately, due to the European Code of Social Security not being finished in 1961 (the instrument only being finalised in 1965), a reference was instead made to the ILO Convention No. 102.[34] The Convention provides nine specific forms of benefits that should be provided under social security:[35]

(1) medical care (part II)
(2) sickness benefit (part III)
(3) unemployment benefit (part IV)
(4) old-age benefit (part V)
(5) employment injury benefit (part VI)
(6) family benefit (part VII)
(7) maternity benefit (part VIII)
(8) invalidity benefit (part IX)
(9) survivors' benefit (part X)

Although, once the European Code of Social Security was completed, Article 12 § 2 of the Revised Charter was subsequently amended to align with the standards set by the European Code of Social Security, which follows the same nine forms of benefit for social security provided under ILO Convention No. 102.[36]

Paragraph 4 of the Charter acknowledges the principle that social security and social and medical assistance should be accessible to nationals of each party within the territories of other parties. This principle is referred to in connection with the European Interim Agreements on Social Security and the European Convention on Social and Medical Assistance. While Article 12 § 4 was not amended in the Revised Charter, in 1993, there was a proposal to introduce a new paragraph that would have obligated States to ensure pension

33 Council of Europe 'Parliamentary Assembly, Draft European Social Charter, Opinion by Social, Health and Family Affairs Committee (Committee of Ministers' draft as revised by the Consultative Assembly)' (1959) Doc. 1035, 12; Karin Lucas, *cit*, pp. 175–176.

34 Karin Lucas, *cit.*, pp. 175–176.

35 International Labour Organization (ILO) Convention Concerning Social Security (Minimum Standards), 1952 (No. 102) (adopted 28 June 1952, entered into force 27 April 195 5) ILO Treaty No 102.

36 The European Code of Social Security (Revised) (adopted 6 November 1990) CENTS No. 139.

payments to their nationals and nationals of other contracting parties residing abroad, but this proposal was ultimately rejected.[37]

B *Relevant International Standards*

As discussed, the right to social security is firmly embedded in the UDHR, ILO Convention No. 102 and the ICESCR. Moreover, in the reporting process under Article 9 of the CESCR, the nine categories of benefits outlined in ILO Convention No. 102 are utilised.[38] This highlights the significance of ILO standard-setting in comprehending the obligations outlined in the CESCR. This close association also indicates that the CESCR primarily concentrates on social security in a narrower scope, specifically focusing on cash benefits based on income and circumstances for workers and their families. Further interpretation of the right to social security under Article 9 of the ICESCR is provided by the treaty's governing body, the Committee on Economic, Social and Cultural Rights (CESCR), in its General Comment No. 19.[39] This guidance elucidates the various dimensions of social security, outlines State obligations, addresses implementation processes, and discusses the limitations associated with the right to social security.

The establishment of equality and non-discrimination in social security, including for migrant workers, is addressed by ILO Convention No. 118 on Equality of Treatment in Social Security (1962)[40] and Recommendation No. 167 on the Maintenance of Social Security Rights (1982).[41] Further ILO Conventions also set out standards and State obligations pertaining to different types of benefits such as sickness, unemployment, old age, and more.

Article 5(e)(iv) of the UN Convention on the Elimination of All Forms of Racial Discrimination (ICERD) mandates that the right to social security and social assistance be guaranteed without any form of discrimination.[42]

---

37 Council of Europe, 'Committee on the European Social Charter (Charte-Rel), Final Activity Report' (Council of Europe, 1994)Appendix IV, p. 48; Karin Lucas, *cit.*, pp. 175–176.

38 The reporting guidelines indicate that this clause relates not only to benefits in cash but also to 'medical and other' benefits. CESCR, Fact Sheet No.16 (Rev.1), A/CONF. 157/24 (Part 1), chap. III p. 9.

39 CESCR, general comments No. 19, The right to social security (Art. 9 of the Covenant).

40 International Labour Organization (ILO) Equality of Treatment (Social Security) Convention, 1962 (No. 118) (adopted 28 June 1962, entered into force 25 April 1964) ILO Treaty No 118.

41 ILO Maintenance of Social Security Rights Recommendation R167: Maintenance of Social Security Rights Recommendation, 1983 (No. 167) (69th Conference Session Geneva 1 June 1983).

42 Convention on the Elimination of All Forms of Racial Discrimination (adopted 21 December 1965, entered into force 4 January 1969) UNTS 195 (ICERD) Art 5(e)(iv).

Under its Article 11 § 1(e), the Convention on the Elimination of All Forms of Discrimination against Women (CEDAW) delves into the right to social security in greater detail, specifically identifying multiple forms of social security that must be provided to women without discrimination.[43] Consequently, this necessitates the identification of gender-specific needs and obstacles. Under Article 27 § 3 of the Convention on the Rights of the Child (CRC), the primary responsibility for ensuring the material well-being of a child lies with their parents.[44] However, State Parties are obligated to provide material assistance and support to fulfil these responsibilities.[45] Under Article 27 of the Convention on the Protection of the Rights of All Migrant Workers and Members of Their Families (CRMW), all migrant workers to social security, based on equal treatment with the nationals of the country of residence.[46] Furthermore, migrant workers in regular situations should enjoy certain additional rights to social security benefits and services, as outlined in Articles 45 and 54.[47]

At the regional level, the Inter-American, African and European systems all include provisions for the right to social security. In 1988, the Inter-American system adopted an Additional Protocol to the American Convention on Human Rights (ACHR) which included the right to social security under Article 9 of the Protocol.[48] Article 9 § 1 of the Protocol provides that "[e]veryone shall have the right to social security protecting him from the consequences of old age and of disability which prevents him, physically or mentally, from securing the means for a dignified and decent existence. In the event of the death of a beneficiary, social security benefits shall be applied to his dependents."[49] In regard to those

43 Convention on the Elimination of All Forms of Discrimination against Women (adopted 18 December 1979, entered into force 3 September 1981) UNTS 1249 (CEDAW) art 11 § 1(e).

44 Convention on the Rights of the Child (adopted 20 November 1989, entered into force 2 September 1990) 1577 UNTS 3 (CRC) art 27 § 3.

45 Ibid art 27 § 4.

46 Convention on the Protection of the Rights of All Migrant Workers and Members of Their Families (adopted 19 December 1990, entered into force 1 July 2003) UNTS 2220 (CRMW) art 27.

47 Ibid arts 45, 54.

48 American Convention on Human Rights "Pact of San Jose, Costa Rica" (adopted 22 November 1969, entered into force 19 July 1978) OAS Treaty Series No 36 (ACHR); Additional Protocol to the American Convention on Human Rights in the Area of Economic, Social and Cultural Rights (Protocol of San Salvador) (adopted 17 November 1988, entered into force 16 November 1999) OAS Treaty Series No 69 (1988) reprinted in Basic Documents Pertaining to Human Rights in the InterAmerican System OEA/Ser L V/II.82 Doc 6 Rev 1 at 67 (1992).

49 Additional Protocol to the American Convention on Human Rights in the Area of Economic, Social and Cultural Rights (Protocol of San Salvador) (adopted 17 November 1988, entered into force 16 November 1999) OAS Treaty Series No 69 (1988) reprinted in

in employment, Article 9 § 2 states that "the right to social security shall cover at least medical care and an allowance or retirement benefit in the case of work accidents or occupational disease and, in the case of women, paid maternity leave before and after childbirth."[50]

In 2022, the African Union adopted a Protocol on Social Protection and Social Security to the African Charter on Human and People's Rights (ACHPR).[51] Articles 3 and 4 of the Protocol require State Parties to ensure a minimum coverage of social protection and insurance for all, whilst also requiring States to progressively increase the coverage and standard of their social security systems.[52] Moreover, the Protocol is also expansive due to Articles 5 to 22 providing a descriptive list of requirements for various forms of social security and protection.[53] However, the legislation has still not yet come into force and requires further ratifications from State Parties of the ACHPR.[54] This piece of international law is not only a huge step forwards for Member States of the African Union but is also promising for the advancement and protection of the universal human right to social security as a whole.

The right to social security and social assistance is also encompassed in Article 34 of the Charter of Fundamental Rights of the European Union (EUCFR).[55] Specifically, Article 34 § 1 and § 2 establish this right for all individuals who are legally residing in the EU, subject to compliance with Community law and national laws and practices.[56] In the case of Kamberaj v. Autonomous Province of Bolzano, the Court of Justice of the European Union (CJEU) ruled that third-country nationals holding long-term residence status within the EU

Basic Documents Pertaining to Human Rights in the InterAmerican System OEA/Ser L V/ II.82 Doc 6 Rev 1 at 67 (1992) art 9 § 1.

50 Ibid art 9 § 2.

51 African Charter on Human and Peoples' Rights (adopted 27 June 1981, entered into force 21 October 1986) (1982) 21 ILM 58 (ACHPR); Protocol to the African Charter on Human and Peoples' Rights on the Rights of Citizens to Social Protection and Social Security (adopted February 2022, as amended).

52 Protocol to the African Charter on Human and Peoples' Rights on the Rights of Citizens to Social Protection and Social Security (adopted February 2022, as amended) arts 3, 4.

53 Ibid arts 5–22.

54 Pamhidzai H. Bamu and Laura Alfres, 'Why an Enforceable Protocol on Social Protection Is Essential in Africa' (*wiego.org*, *2022*) <https://www.wiego.org/blog/why-enforceable-protocol-social-protection-essential-africa#:~:text=The%20protocol%20calls%20for%20states,and%20adaptation%20of%20general%20schemes> accessed 5 June 2023.

55 Charter of Fundamental Rights of the European Union (European Union Charter, as amended) (EUCFR) art 34.

56 Ibid Article 34 § 1 and § 2.

are entitled to receive social benefits.[57] However, the interpretation of the criteria for long-term residency may vary among different national legislations, leading to restrictive and diverse approaches.

While the European Convention on Human Rights (ECHR) does not explicitly include a right to social security, the European Court of Human Rights (ECtHR) has developed case law pertaining to the right to social security under the right to property as stated in Article 1 of Protocol 1 and under Articles 8 and 14 of the Convention.[58] In the case of Gaygusuz v. Austria, the Court held that contributory cash benefits are a pecuniary right for the purposes of Article 1 of Protocol 1 and third-country nationals should be treated equally to national citizens in receipt of this payment.[59] In of Beeler v. Switzerland, the Court clarified that in order to determine if a social welfare benefit falls within the boundaries of Article 8, certain factors need to be considered, which include: (1) the purpose of the benefit; (2) the standards used to determine eligibility, calculation, and discontinuation of the benefit as outlined in the applicable laws; (3) how the benefit impacts the organisation of family life; and (4) the real-life consequences of the benefit considering the individual's specific circumstances and family life while receiving the benefit.[60] Moreover, the ECtHR has emphasised that while Article 8 does not ensure the entitlement to a social welfare benefit, if a country chooses to establish such a right, it must not implement discriminatory actions as defined in Article 14.[61]

C *Relationship with Other Charter's Provisions*

Article 12 of the ESC intricately linked with various provisions within the Charter, collectively shaping the social policy framework of the ESC. This framework is designed to promote the equitable access of all individuals in society to a comprehensive system of social protection that aligns with their specific circumstances and societal norms.[62] Its overarching objectives include mitigating the risk of marginalisation and alleviating poverty within society.[63] Interrelated rights under this framework include the right to social security

57 CJEU, 24 April 2012, *Servet Kamberaj v Social Housing Institute of the Autonomous Province of Bolzano (IPES) and others*, Case C-571/10 § 97.

58 Protocol 1 to the European Convention for the Protection of Human Rights and Fundamental Freedoms (adopted 20 March 1952, entered into force 18 May 1954) CENTS 9 art 1.

59 ECtHR, 16 September 1996, *Gaygusuz v Austria*, No. 17371/90 § 41.

60 ECtHR, 11 October 2022, *Beeler v. Switzerland*, No. 78630/12 § 72.

61 Ibid § 61.

62 ECSR, 'General Introduction to Conclusions XIV-1' p. 53.

63 Ibid.

under Article 12, the right to social and medical assistance under Article 13 and the right to benefit from welfare services under Article 14. In regard to Article 13, the Charter includes provisions for both social security and social assistance in distinct articles (Articles 12 and 13) with distinct obligations.[64] The Charter does not provide specific guidelines regarding the extent of these two concepts,[65] therefore, to determine whether a specific benefit falls under social security or social assistance, the primary criteria are the intended purpose of the benefit and the associated conditions.[66] The Committee defines "social assistance" as benefits where the primary criterion for eligibility is based on individual need, without any mandatory affiliation to a specific social security scheme intended to address a particular risk, or any requirement related to professional activity or payment of contributions.[67] The responsibilities arising from Article 14 of the Charter should not be interpreted as pertaining to a specific set of social security or social assistance benefits, but rather as a subsystem of social protection.[68] This interpretation is supported by the structure of Article 14, which is framed more as an individual right rather than merely a social benefit or systematic principle of State Parties' welfare policy.[69]

Other Articles within the Charter are also related to the right to social security under Article 12. The ECSR has stated that the right of persons with disabilities to independence, social integration and participation of life in the community under Article 15, State's must ensure that job and income losses of persons with disabilities are compensated by adequate social security benefits.[70] Under Article 16, the right of the family to social legal and economic protection, State Parties have an obligation to safeguard the economic well-being of families through suitable measures. The primary approach to fulfil this obligation should involve the provision of family or child benefits within the framework of social security, either universally or through means testing.[71] Likewise, the ECSR has also stated that there is strong link between the fulfilment of the right to protection against poverty and social exclusion and the fulfilment of the right to social security under Article 12.[72]

64 ESCR, 'Conclusions XIII-4 (1996), Statement of Interpretation on Articles 12 and 13'.
65 Ibid.
66 Ibid.
67 Ibid.
68 ECSCR, 'Conclusions 2005, Bulgaria'.
69 ESCR, *International Federation for Human Rights (FIDH) v. Belgium*, complaint no. 75/2011, decision on the merits of 18 March 2013, §108.
70 ECSR, 'Statement on Covid-19 and social rights adopted on 24 March 2021'.
71 ECSR, 'Conclusions 2019, Bosnia and Herzegovina.'
72 ECSR, 'Conclusions 2013. Statement of interpretation Article 30.'

II Interpretation by the European Committee of Social Rights

A *Article 12 § 1*

Article 12 § 1 of the Charter safeguards the right to social security by establishing and maintaining an adequate social security system. The Committee responsible for interpreting the Charter affirms that this right applies to workers, their dependents, and even self-employed individuals.[73] It is the responsibility of States that have ratified the Charter to ensure the realisation of this right by implementing a social security system through legislative measures and ensuring its effective functioning.

The concept of social security encompasses a wide range of benefits, including both universal schemes and those tailored to specific professions. These benefits can be either contributory or non-contributory, and they may also be combined to address particular risks. It is important to note that these benefits are provided in response to the occurrence of risks but are not intended to fully compensate for potential needs that may arise as a result of those risks.[74]

As per the Committee's interpretation, a social security system under Article 12 § 1 should fulfil the following criteria:[75]

– The system should encompass various risks and benefits that are relevant to social security, including medical care, sickness benefits, unemployment benefits, old age benefits, employment injury benefits, family benefits, and maternity benefits.[76]
– Health coverage and family benefits must be provided to a significant percentage of the population, extending beyond employment relationships.[77] Income-replacement benefits, such as sickness, maternity, unemployment benefits, pensions, and work accidents or occupational diseases benefits, should cover a substantial portion of the active population.[78]
– The financing of the social security system should be collective, involving contributions from employers, employees, and/or the

73 ECSR, 'Conclusions XIV-1(1998), Ireland'.

74 Revised European Social Charter of 1996 (entered into force on 1 July 1999) CETS No. 163; Council of Europe, 'Digest of the case law of the European Committee of Social Rights' (CoE, 2022) p. 120 <https://rm.coe.int/digest-ecsr-prems-106522-web-en/1680a95dbd> accessed 17 May 2023.

75 Ibid.

76 ECSR, 'Conclusions 2006, Bulgaria'.

77 ECSR, 'Conclusions 2017, Georgia'.

78 ECSR, 'Conclusions 2017, Georgia'; ECSR 'Conclusions 2017, Turkey'.

> State. When taxation is the funding mechanism, the system should ensure non-discriminatory coverage for individuals, while taking into account eligibility conditions such as means tests.[79] The principle of collective funding refers to the practice of financing social programs through contributions from employers, employees, and/or the state budget and the Committee regards collective funding as a fundamental aspect of a social security system envisioned by Article 12.[80] It is the view of the ECSR that this principle promotes equitable sharing of risk among community members and helps prevent discrimination against vulnerable worker groups.[81]

A social security system should ensure the effective realisation of the right to social security, particularly concerning the benefits provided under each category.[82] In the case of income replacement benefits, the level of benefits should be reasonably proportionate to the individual's previous income and should not fall below the poverty threshold. The poverty threshold is defined as 50 percent of the median equivalised income, calculated based on the Eurostat at-risk-of-poverty threshold value.[83]

If an income replacement benefit is set between 40 and 50 percent of the median equivalised income, the Committee will also consider other relevant benefits.[84] However, if the minimum level of an income replacement benefit falls below 40 percent of the median equivalised income, the benefits are deemed insufficient, and the availability of other benefits cannot rectify the situation to comply with the standards.[85]

The Committee's interpretation of Article 12 § 1 outlines specific conditions that must be met for unemployment benefits to comply with the Charter. These conditions include:

- Unemployment benefits should be paid for a reasonable duration.[86]

---

79 ECSR, 'Conclusions XVI-1 (2003), Statement of Interpretation on Article 12'; ECSR, *Finnish Society of Social Rights v Finland*, complaint no. 88/2012, decision on the merits of 9 September 2014, § 58.

80 ECSR, 'Conclusions XVIII-1 (2006), the Netherlands'.

81 Ibid.

82 ECSR, 'Conclusions XVI-1 (2003), Statement of Interpretation on Article 12'.

83 ECSR, 'Conclusions XXI-2 (2017), United Kingdom'.

84 ECSR, 'Conclusions 2013, Hungary'.

85 ECSR, 'Conclusions 2013, Finland'; ECSR, *Finnish Society of Social Rights v. Finland*, complaint no. 88/2012, decision on the merits of 9 September 2014, §§59–63; ECSR, *Federation of Employed Pensioners of Greece (IKA-ETAM) v. Greece*, complaint no. 76/2012, decision on the merits of 7 December 2012, § 74.

86 ECSR, 'Conclusions XVIII-1 (2006), Malta'.

- There should be an initial period during which an unemployed person can refuse a job or training offer that does not match their previous skills without losing unemployment benefits.[87] In cases where severe conditionalities are imposed, the loss of unemployment benefits due to refusal of employment may indirectly restrict the freedom to work, and this situation would be evaluated under Article 1§ 2 of the Charter.[88]

The Committee considers it punitive and discriminatory, violating the Charter, to link entitlement to sickness benefits to the nature and origin of a specific illness. Such a practice would be deemed discriminatory based on health status, as outlined in Article E of the Charter.[89] Regarding maternity and family benefits, their existence is taken into account under Article 12 § 1. However, the adequacy of these benefits in terms of scope and level is not explicitly addressed.[90]

B *Article 12 § 2*

Article 12 § 2 of the European Social Charter mandates that States parties establish and maintain a social security system that meets or exceeds the conditions required for ratification of the European Code of Social Security. The European Code of Social Security sets higher standards than ILO Convention No. 102, as it requires acceptance of a greater number of parts. For ratification, at least six out of the nine parts must be accepted, with certain branches counting for more than one part. For example, medical care is counted as two parts, and old age is counted as three parts.[91] Each part establishes minimum levels of personal coverage and benefits.[92]

In cases where a State has ratified the European Code of Social Security, the assessment under Article 12 § 2 is based on the Committee of Ministers' Resolutions, which take into account the evaluations of the ILO Committee of Experts, the Governmental Committee of the European Social Charter, and the European Code of Social Security.[93] Failure to comply with at least the minimum number of parts required for ratification of the European Code of Social Security will result in a determination of non-conformity with Article 12 § 2.[94]

---

87 ECSR, 'Conclusions XVIII-1 (2006), Germany'.
88 ECSR, 'Conclusions 2012, Statement of Interpretation on Article 1 § 2'.
89 ECSR, 'Conclusions 2013, Slovak Republic'.
90 ECSR, 'Conclusions XX-4 (2015), Statement of Interpretation on Article 8 § 1'.
91 ECSR, 'Conclusions 2013, Serbia'.
92 Ibid.
93 ECSR, 'Conclusions 2006, Italy'.
94 Ibid.

When a State has not ratified the European Code of Social Security, the Committee assesses the overall social security system under Article 12 § 2.[95] In order to determine whether the social security system meets the minimum level necessary for ratification of the Code, the Committee requires detailed information on the covered branches, the scope of personal coverage, and the level of benefits provided by the state party.[96] Findings under Article 12 § 1 are also taken into consideration during this assessment.[97]

C *Article 12 § 3*

Article 12 § 3 imposes an obligation on State Parties to continually enhance their social security systems. The purpose of this provision is to encourage States parties to progressively improve the scope and level of protection provided by their social security systems. This improvement can involve expanding benefit schemes, safeguarding against new risks, or increasing the level of benefits.[98] Additionally, a State's progress in improving its social security system may be considered compliant with Article 12 § 3, even if the requirements of Article 12 § 1 and 12 § 2 have not been fulfilled or if the State has not accepted these provisions.[99]

A partially restrictive development in the social security system, which may be referred to as a 'restriction' or 'limitation' on 'rights related to social security,' does not inherently constitute a violation of Article 12 § 3.[100] Instead, it should be evaluated in accordance with Article G of the Revised Charter.[101] The Committee's assessment of whether a State Party has made meaningful progress in improving its social security system takes into account various criteria, including:

- The nature of the changes, such as the scope and conditions for granting allowances, and the amounts of allowances.[102]
- The reasons behind the changes and the social and economic policy framework in which they are implemented.[103]

---

95 ECSR, 'Conclusions XIV-1 (1998), Finland'.

96 ECSR, 'Conclusions 2013, Serbia'.

97 ECSR, 'Conclusions 2017, Andorra'.

98 ECSR, 'Conclusions 2013, Georgia'; *Finnish Society of Social Rights v Finland* complaint no. 88/2012, decision on the merits of 9 September 2014, §§ 84–86.

99 ECSR, 'Conclusions 2009, Statement of Interpretation on Article 12 § 3'.

100 ECSR, *Federation of Employed Pensioners of Greece (IKA-ETAM) v. Greece*, complaint no. 76/2012, decision on the merits of 2 January 2012, § 70.

101 Ibid § 72.

102 ECSR, 'Conclusions XVI-1 (2002), Statement of Interpretation on Article 12 § 1, 12 § 2, 12 § 3.'

103 Ibid.

- The extent of the changes, including the categories and numbers of individuals affected and the levels of allowances before and after the alterations.[104]
- The necessity of the reform in question.[105]
- The presence of social assistance for individuals who find themselves in a situation of need as a result of the changes.[106]
- The outcomes and results achieved through the implemented changes.[107]

While individual restrictive measures may comply with the provisions of the Charter, their cumulative impact could potentially result in a violation of Article 12 § 3.[108] Measures aimed at consolidating public finances can be regarded as necessary for ensuring the stability and long-term viability of the social security system.[109] Considering the interconnectedness of the economy and social rights, the pursuit of economic objectives is not inherently incompatible with the principles outlined in Article 12.[110] Furthermore, provisions based on European Union directives and Community law do not automatically pass such an assessment.[111]

Nevertheless, when implementing consolidation measures, it is crucial to ensure that they do not undermine the fundamental structure of a national social security system or deprive individuals of the opportunity to benefit from its protection against significant social and economic risks.[112] Consequently, any modifications to a social security system must maintain an adequately comprehensive framework of mandatory social security and avoid the exclusion of entire groups of workers from the social safeguards provided by this system.[113] Additionally, these measures should not result in the transformation

---

104 Ibid.

105 ECSR, *Panhellenic Federation of pensioners of the public electricity corporation (POS-DEI) v. Greece*, complaint no. 79/2012, decision on the merits of 7 December 2012, §67.

106 ECSR, 'Conclusions XVI-1 (2002), Statement of Interpretation on Article 12 § 1, 12 § 2, 12 § 3.'

107 Ibid.

108 ECSR, *Federation of Employed Pensioners of Greece (IKA-ETAM) v. Greece*, complaint no. 76/2012, decision on the merits of 7 December 2012, §§ 78–83.

109 Ibid § 71.

110 Ibid § 41.

111 ECSR, *Confédération Générale du Travail (CGT) v. France*, Complaint no. 55/2009, decision on the merits of 23 June 2010, §§ 30–32.

112 ECSR, *Federation of Employed Pensioners of Greece (IKA-ETAM) v. Greece*, complaint no. 76/2012, decision on the merits of 7 December 2012, § 47.

113 ECSR, *General Federation of employees of the national electric power corporation (GENOP-DEI) / Confederation of Greek Civil Servants Trade Unions (ADEDY) v. Greece*, complaint no. 66/2011, decision on 23 May 2012, § 47.

of the social security system into a mere basic social assistance program.[114] Consolidation measures that disregard these boundaries represent regressive actions and cannot be considered compliant with the principles set forth in Article 12 § 3.[115]

D *Article 12 § 4*

The provision under Article 12 § 4 obligates State Parties to ensure the right to social security benefits for persons moving between the territories of State Parties. Specifically, State Parties must "undertake to take steps, by the conclusion of appropriate bilateral and multilateral agreements or by other means, and subject to the conditions laid down in such agreements, in order to ensure equal treatment with their own nationals of the nationals of other Parties in respect of social security rights, including the retention of benefits arising out of social security legislation, whatever movements the persons protected may undertake between the territories of the Parties."[116]

When determining the scope of Article 12 § 4, it is necessary to refer to paragraph 1 of the Appendix to the Charter, which states "[w]ithout prejudice to Article 12 § 4, the individuals covered by Articles 1 to 17 include foreigners only to the extent that they are nationals of other State Parties and are lawfully residing or regularly working within the territory of the State Party in question."[117] The Appendix to the Charter clarifies that Article 12(4) applies to individuals who are nationals of other State Parties and previously resided or regularly worked within the concerned territory, even if they no longer reside there.[118] These individuals have acquired social security rights based on their past residency or regular employment. Article 12(4) encompasses refugees and stateless persons, as well as self-employed workers.[119] The principle of reciprocity is not applicable to Article 12 § 4.[120]

When evaluating Article 12 § 4 (a), the Committee examines the "equal treatment of nationals from other States Parties, and retention (exportability)

114 ECSR, *Finnish Society of Social Rights v. Finland*, complaint no. 88/2012, decision on the merits of 9 September 2014, §85.

115 ECSR, *General Federation of employees of the national electric power corporation (GENOP-DEI) / Confederation of Greek Civil Servants Trade Unions (ADEDY) v. Greece*, complaint no. 66/2011, decision on 23 May 2012, § 47.

116 Digest, *cit.*, p. 123.

117 Ibid.

118 Ibid.

119 ECSR, 'Conclusions XIV-1 (1998), Turkey'.

120 ECSR, 'Statement of Interpretation on Article 12 § 4'.

of accrued rights of this group of persons."[121] To ensure equal treatment based on nationality as stated in Article 12 § 4 (a), States parties must take measures to eliminate and prevent discrimination in their social security legislation against nationals of other States Parties.[122] Both direct and indirect discrimination are encompassed by Article 12 § 4 (a). National legislation is prohibited from reserving social security benefits exclusively for nationals or imposing additional or more stringent conditions on foreigners.[123] Eligibility criteria for social security benefits cannot disproportionately affect foreigners compared to nationals, even if they are applied without reference to nationality.[124] However, legislation may require a reasonable period of residence for non-contributory benefits,[125] but a five-year period is considered excessive.[126]

Concerning child benefits, a requirement that the child resides in the paying State's territory may be compatible with Article 12 § 4.[127] The issue of child residence is exclusively examined under Article 12 § 4, rather than Article 16.[128] However, States implementing a "child residence requirement" are obligated to establish bilateral or multilateral agreements within a reasonable timeframe with States applying a different entitlement principle, in order to ensure equal treatment.[129] Equality of treatment does not necessarily entail that family allowances should be paid at the same amount when the children are not residents of the same country as the recipient.[130] In such cases, the level of benefit may be reduced proportionally to the cost-of-living differences in the respective countries.[131]

In regard to the retention (exportability) of accrued rights, beneficiaries have the right to retain (export) their accrued rights, including invalidity benefits, old age benefits, survivor's benefits, and occupational accident or disease benefits acquired under the legislation of one State, regardless of whether they relocate to another State.[132] The eligibility criteria specified in national legislation apply to these benefits irrespective of movement between States.[133]

---

121 Karin Lucas, *cit.*, p. 182.
122 ECSR 'Conclusions 2013, Lithuania'.
123 ECSR, 'Conclusions XIII-4 (1996), Statement of Interpretation on Article 12 § 4.'
124 Ibid.
125 ECSR, 'Conclusions 2004, Lithuania.'
126 Ibid.
127 ECSR, 'Conclusions 2006, Italy.'
128 ECSR, 'Conclusions XVI-1 (2002), Statement of Interpretation on Articles 12 § 4 and 16.'
129 ECSR, 'Conclusions 2006, Italy.'
130 ESCR, 'Conclusions XIII-4 (1996), Statement of Interpretation on Article 12.'
131 Ibid.
132 ECSR, 'Conclusions XIV-1 (1998), Finland'; ECSR 'Conclusions XIV-1 (1998), Norway'.
133 Ibid.

However, unemployment benefits, being short-term benefits closely tied to the labour market, are not required to be exportable according to the Committee's interpretation.[134] These obligations must be fulfilled independently, regardless of any other multilateral social security agreements in place.[135] To ensure the exportability of benefits, Article 12 § 4 (a) allows States Parties to choose between bilateral agreements or other appropriate means, such as unilateral, legislative, or administrative measures.[136]

The Committee assesses the maintenance of accruing rights under Article 12 § 4 (b). The ECSR in providing guidance on this provision has noted that a person who changes their country of employment should not face any disadvantage in terms of accruing rights, even if they have not fulfilled the required period of employment or insurance under national legislation to qualify for certain benefits or determine their amount.[137] To ensure the implementation of the right to maintain accruing rights, it may be necessary to consider the accumulation of employment or insurance periods completed in another territory.[138] In the case of long-term benefits, a pro-rata approach should also be adopted, taking into account the relevant periods of employment or insurance.[139]

State Parties have a certain degree of discretion in implementing Article 12 § 4 (b). Similar to Article 12 § 4 (a), they have the option to choose among different methods, such as multilateral conventions, bilateral or unilateral agreements, as well as legislative and administrative measures.[140] States that have ratified the European Convention on Social Security are considered to have made sufficient efforts to ensure the preservation of accruing rights.[141]

Concluding Remarks

The right to social security under Article 12 of the ESC is one of the cornerstones of the Charter and pivotal for the realisation of other interrelated rights within this instrument. Moreover, while there are various provisions across

134 ECSR, 'Conclusions XIV-1 (1998), Norway'.
135 Digest, *cit.*, p. 142.
136 ECSR 'Conclusions 2009, Finland'.
137 Digest, *cit.*, p. 124.
138 Ibid.
139 ECSR, 'Conclusions 2009, Finland'.
140 Ibid.
141 ECSR, 'Conclusions 2006, Italy'.

IHRL that contribute to the realisation of this right, under Article 12 § 3 and § 4, the ECSR provides a unique set of robust guidelines that aid State Parties in realising this right.

On the other hand, whilst it is acknowledged that States require time for the progressive improvement of their social security systems to fulfil the obligation under Article 12 § 3, with States also being somewhat justifiably unable to meet the complex requirements of equal treatment and retention of accrued rights under Article 12 § 4.[142] State Parties should nonetheless be striving to improve their social security systems and uphold the principles of equal treatment and the retention of accrued rights in order to cope with challenges such as ageing populations, underfunded and overstretched public services and the cost-of-living crisis.

---

142 During the 2017 ECSR monitoring cycle, none of the states were found to be in compliance with the requirements, primarily due to violations of equal treatment and the preservation of accruing rights. ECSR 'Conclusions, 2017'.

ARTICLE 13

The Right to Social and Medical Assistance

Stefano Angeleri

With a view to ensuring the effective exercise of the right to social and medical assistance, the Contracting Parties undertake:

1. to ensure that any person who is without adequate resources and who is unable to secure such resources either by his own efforts or from other sources, in particular by benefits under a social security scheme, be granted adequate assistance, and, in case of sickness, the care necessitated by his condition;
2. to ensure that persons receiving such assistance shall not, for that reason, suffer from a diminution of their political or social rights;
3. to provide that everyone may receive by appropriate public or private services such advice and personal help as may be required to prevent, to remove, or to alleviate personal or family want;
4. to apply the provisions referred to in paragraphs 1, 2 and 3 of this article on an equal footing with their nationals to nationals of other Contracting Parties lawfully within their territories, in accordance with their obligations under the European Convention on Social and Medical Assistance, signed at Paris on 11th December 1953.

Introduction

The inclusion of a provision on social and medical assistance in the European Social Charter (ESC) is a legacy of the post-World War II cultural and political environment in which a strong belief in the idea and concrete realisation of the European welfare or social state prevailed.[1] During the three decades that followed World War II, welfare or social programmes were gradually extended as part of the social and economic reconstruction of Europe,[2] which was

1 Georgios Katrougalos, "The (Dim) Perspectives of the European Social Citizenship", *Jean Monnet Working Paper NYU School of Law*, No. 5(7), 2012, p. 3.

2 Francis G. Castles *et al.*, "Introduction", in Francis G. Castles *et al.* (eds.), *The Oxford Handbook of the Welfare State*, Oxford, OUP, 2010, pp. 7–9.

 | DOI:10.1163/9789004434141_004

aimed at achieving long-lasting peace and social progress.[3] Indeed, during *les trente glorieuses*,[4] before the spread of the neoliberal market ideology that has characterised political and economic reality since the late 1970s, economic and social progress were regarded as intertwined goals.

The early history of social rights in the 20th century has paralleled that of the Western welfare state, with both of these phenomena gaining international mainstream recognition since World War II.[5] Indeed, the codification of social rights in European constitutions and treaties represented the legal endorsement of a system within which national governments undertook to provide a range of social services (including income support mechanisms) to people who needed them, to address the deepest social inequalities and target human well-being and full employment.[6] Social and medical assistance for the needy was considered an essential component of national social protection systems and a core social right as it represented the "baseline of social [and medical] protection below which nobody should be permitted to fall".[7] While the Charter gave an autonomous definition to social assistance and social security, overall, the former could be considered a species of the latter "just as social insurance, health care benefits and family benefits".[8] The constitutions of the European countries codified different takes on social security or species of it, as being either an individual right, a guiding principle of social policy

---

3 Universal Declaration of Human Rights (adopted 10 December 1948) UNGA Res 217 A(III) (UDHR), Preamble; European Social Charter (adopted 18 October 1961 entry into force 26 February 1965), ETS No. 35, Preamble; European Social Charter (Revised) (adopted 3 May 1996 entry into force 1 July 1999), ETS No. 163, Preamble.

4 The French economist Jean Fourastié defined as such the thirsty years of economic growth between the late 1940s and the early 1970s.

5 Toomas Kotkas, "The Short and Insignificant History of Social Rights Discourse in the Nordic Welfare State", in Toomas Kotkas and Kenneth Veitch (eds.), *Social Rights in the Welfare State: Origins and Transformations*, London, Routledge, 2016, p. 15.

6 The philosophy underlying the mid-20th century's welfare state is well exemplified by the Beveridge Report: William Beveridge, *Social Insurance and Allied Services*, London, Majestiy's Stationery Office, 1942, available at <http://news.bbc.co.uk/2/shared/bsp/hi/pdfs/19_07_05_beveridge.pdf>, as complemented by William Beveridge, *Full Employment in a Free Society*, London, The New Statesman and Nation and Reynolds News, 1944, available at <http://lib-161.lse.ac.uk/archives/beveridge/9A_79_Full_employment_in_a_free_society.pdf>.

7 Thomas Bahle, Michaela Pfeifer and Claus Wendt, "Social Assistance", in Francis G. Castles *et al.*, *cit.*, p. 449.

8 Gijsbert Vonk and Marius Olivier, "The Fundamental Right of Social Assistance: A Global, a Regional (Europe and Africa) and a National Perspective (Germany, the Netherlands and South Africa)", *European Journal of Social Security*, no. 21(3), 2019, p. 222.

or reaffirming the social responsibility of the state or its subnational governments in this area.[9]

As unpacked in the following pages, social and medical assistance consists of those support mechanisms that help persons living in poverty or at-risk-of-poverty to enjoy a minimally acceptable standard of living and necessary medical care. As Karin Lukas, former president of the European Committee of Social Rights (ECSR), affirmed, "from a structural and human rights point of view, it is certainly unusual that medical and social assistance are incorporated into one single article [considering that] usually, medical assistance is included in the right to health".[10]

Under the Charter system, such assistance is generally regarded as a last-resort measure that applies when social security mechanisms that protect against specific risks cannot meet an individual's basic needs. The term *medical assistance*, in this context, means necessary health care that is provided free of charge,[11] and it is precisely this financial element which constitutes the main difference between this right and the contingency-based benefit of medical care as per article 12 ESC (and Part II of the International Labour Organization Convention on Social Security). As far as *social assistance* is concerned, according to authoritative scholarship, applicable social benefits can be grouped into four main categories: general poverty-tested cash benefits provided to everyone in need; other means-tested benefits (e.g. family allowances); categorical assistance for specific groups (e.g. minimum pensions); and assistance for specific purposes (e.g. housing allowances).[12]

The ESC is the only human rights treaty to explicitly include a right to social and medical assistance, which the jurisprudence of the ECSR has made a concrete standard. This right is included in both its 1961 and 1996 versions and qualified as a "hardcore" provision of the Charter.[13] The original inclusion of

9 Alexandre Egorov and Marcin Wujczyk, *The Right to Social Security in the Constitutions of the World: Broadening the Moral and Legal Space for Social Justice*, Geneva, ILO, 2016, available at <https://www.ilo.org/wcmsp5/groups/public/---ed_norm/---normes/documents/publication/wcms_518153.pdf>.

10 Karin Lukas, *The Revised European Social Charter. An Article by Article Commentary*, Cheltenham, Elgar 2021, p. 198.

11 Further details cf. Section I. A; International Labour Conference (International Labour Organization), C102 – Social Security (Minimum Standards) Convention (Adopted 28 June 1952 entry into force 27 April 1955).

12 Tony Eardley *et. al.*, "Social Assistance in OECD Countries: Synthesis Report", *Research Report – Department of Social Security*, no. 46, London, HMSO, pp. 26–28, available at <http://eprints.whiterose.ac.uk/73427/1/>.

13 As indicated in the commentary to the Part III, article 20 of the 1961 Charter and article A of the Revised Charter, under the heading 'Undertakings', states are not automatically

this human rights provision in the ESC signalled a paradigm shift in how assistance programmes were conceived; they were no longer regarded as charity but as legal entitlements.[14] The *travaux préparatoires* show that the drafters of the ESC initially discussed social assistance as a component of a broader right to adequate standards of living and social security[15] but ended up regarding this right as worthy of an autonomous – although interrelated – provision.[16] However, it is undeniable that in welfare projects across Europe, social security programmes to protect people against certain risks, work-tied or group-specific benefits have, over the years, gained centrality[17] at the expense of need-based programmes. Yet, against this trend, both the Revised Charter and the case law of the ECSR have maintained a functional distinction between the right to social security (Article 12 ESC) and the right to social assistance (Article 13 ESC).[18] Furthermore, other human rights are deemed as strongly interrelated with Article 13 ESC given that it may be violated when states

---

bound by the entire text of the treaty upon ratification. They commit to be bound by a minimum number of undertakings (articles and paragraphs), some of which are to be chosen from a list at § 1 letter b) of the above provisions. These lists include Article 13, which is defined as a 'hard core' article by the Council of Europe's Explanatory Report to the European Social Charter (Revised) Strasbourg, 3 May 1996.

14 ECSR, Conclusions I (1969), Statement of Interpretation of article 13, as referred to in ECSR, Digest of the case law of the European Committee of Social Rights (June 2022), p. 124.

15 Consultative Assembly of the Council of Europe (now PACE), Draft European Social Charter by the Committee on Social Questions, 19 April 1955, p. 24; PACE, Draft Recommendation to the Committee of Ministers, 26 October 1955, Collected edition of the "Travaux préparatoires", vol. II (1955).

16 PACE, Draft European Social Charter by the Committee on Social Questions, 10 January 1956 and Committee on Economic Questions, 24 January 1956, article 8 § 2; PACE, Draft Recommendation to the Committee of Ministers, 14 April 1956, Article 9; PACE, Final Recommendation to the Committee of Ministers no. 104, October 1956; Committee of Ministers of the Council of Europe, Social Committee (3rd Session), Draft European Social Charter, 8 November 1956, Collected edition of the "Travaux préparatoires", vol. III (1956), pp. 870–872; Committee of Minsters of the Council of Europe, Draft European Social Charter by the Social Committee, 4th Session, April 1957; *ibid.*, 5th Session, June-September 1957; *ibid.*, 6th Session October-December 1957, Collected edition of the "Travaux préparatoires", vol. IV (1957).

17 Thomas Bahle, Michaela Pfeifer and Claus Wendt, *cit.*, p. 451.

18 For example: ECSR, *Finnish Society of Social Rights v. Finland*, complaint No. 88/2012, decision on the merits of 9 September 2014, § 33, 112–125; ECSR, *International Federation of Human Rights* (*FIDH*) *v. Belgium*, complaint No. 75/2011, decision on the merits of 18 March 2013, § 159–163; ECSR, *European Committee for Home-Based Priority Action for the Child and the Family* (*EUROCEF*) *v. France*, complaint No. 114/2015, decision on the merits of 24 January 2018, § 163.

fail to provide shelter, food, medical care, and clothing, which are necessary for protecting human dignity and for the "basic subsistence of any human being".[19]

While the next section analyses the normative content of Article 13 ESC in the light of the jurisprudence developed by the ECSR in the form of conclusions, decisions and statements of interpretation, the following and last part of this chapter is dedicated to comparable, although not equivalent, provisions in other international and European legal instruments. From this analysis the right to social and medical assistance in the Charter will emerge as a rather unique provision in human rights law: it established an individual and clear legal entitlement, with correlative state obligations, to assistance linked to a poverty-based concept of needs, thereby establishing a baseline level of social well-being and health care.

1 The Normative Content of Article 13 ESC

This section explores, paragraph by paragraph, the scope of the application of the right to social and medical assistance, which the jurisprudence of the ECSR has contributed to unpacking,[20] and examines its organic interrelation with the other provisions of the Charter. States that have declared to accept the binding nature of Article 13 undertake to realise the right(s) therein in law, policy, and practice.[21] As is the case for all provisions of the ESC, the article begins by establishing the legal obligation to "ensur[e] the effective exercise of the right to social and medical assistance",[22] not merely theoretically and in legal instruments but also in fact and with operational

19 ECSR, *Conference of European Churches (CEC) v. the Netherlands*, complaint No. 30/2013, decision on the merits of 9 July 2014, § 105–126.

20 For a table that summarizes key Article 13 standards identified by the ECSR, see Maria Dalli, "The Content and Potential of the Right to Social Assistance in light of Article 13 of the European Social Charter", *European Journal of Social Security*, no. 22(1), 2020, pp. 10–13.

21 Article 20 of the Charter of 1961 and article E of the Revised Charter establish that neither of the versions of the Charter is entirely binding on state parties, but states can select a minimum number of articles and paragraphs and comply with the respective duties. For further details on this 'à-la-carte' approach cf. volume 5 of this Commentary. As far as article 13 ESC (which reads the same in both the Charter of 1961 and the Revised Charter) is concerned, 38 out of 43 state parties to either version of the Charter have accepted 2, 3 or all its paragraphs, cf. list of accepted provisions at <https://rm.coe.int/1680630742>.

22 Article 13 ESC, *cit.*.

implementation measures.[23] Accordingly, the scrutiny of the ECSR extends to these measures.[24]

The Charter requires that states fulfil their international obligations of both a progressive and immediate nature.[25] The textual interpretation of all paragraphs of Article 13 suggests that the establishment of means-based safety net mechanisms, aimed at preventing individuals without adequate resources from falling into destitution and illness, is an immediate duty of result. Reading Article 12 ESC is instructive in this regard: While Article 12 § 1 establishes an immediate obligation to ensure a minimum level of income-substituting social security benefits (to prevent people from falling into poverty), Article 12 § 3 obliges states to progressively enhance social security systems in terms of coverage and level of benefits.[26] No similar wording is employed in Article 13 on social and medical assistance, which may be due to the core function that this provision plays in the realisation of baseline assistance for the most vulnerable. According to the text of Article 13, as confirmed by the case law of the ECSR, everyone who is financially disadvantaged to the extent that they are[27] at risk of falling below the poverty line should "be granted adequate assistance and (...) care" anchored to means-tested indicators, which are outlined below.

A *Adequate Assistance for Persons in Need*

1 Eligibility Criteria

Article 13 § 1 conceptualises the right to social and medical assistance as a universal right:[28] special assistance for people with disabilities, families and the elderly are all Charter-compliant support mechanisms, but Article 13 envisages means-tested assistance that is not group- or contingency-based.[29] In this

---

23 ECSR, *International Commission of Jurists (ICJ) v. Portugal*, complaint No. 1/1998, decision on the merits of 9 September 1999, §32; ECSR, *European Federation of National Organisations working with the Homeless (FEANTSA) v. Slovenia*, complaint No. 53/2008, decision on the merits of 8 September 2009, §28; ECSR, *International Association Autism-Europe v. France*, complaint No.13/2002, decision on the merits of 4 November 2003, §53.

24 ECSR, *International Movement ATD Fourth World v. France*, complaint No.33/2006, decision on the merits of 5 December 2007, §61.

25 Secretariat of the ECSR, Digest 2022, *cit.*, p. 34.

26 ECSR, *Finnish Society of Social Rights v. Finland, cit.*, § 39.

27 The singular 'They' is employed throughout the chapter as a gender-neutral pronoun. Cf. <https://www.merriam-webster.com/words-at-play/singular-nonbinary-they>.

28 This statement of universality is qualified by the limits of the personal scope of the Charter, as per Appendix to the European Social Charter, 18 October 1961, § 1, and Appendix to the Revised Charter, 3 May 1996, § 1. Cf. section I. D. below.

29 ECSR, Conclusions 2017, Andorra, Article 13 § 1; ECSR, Conclusions 2017, Armenia, Article 13 § 1.

context, the adjective *universal* does not indicate that the Charter mandates the creation of a universal basic income but rather suggests that the only condition for having a right to such assistance is that one person must find themselves "without adequate resources" and "unable to secure such resources either by [their] own efforts or from other sources, in particular by benefits under a social security scheme". For the ECSR, to distinguish between social security benefits (Article 12 ESC) and social assistance benefits (Article 13) means to "pay attention to the purpose of and the conditions attached to the benefit in question". The right to social security provides for income-substituting benefits in the "event of risks which arise [such as sickness, unemployment, disability and old age,] but they are not intended to compensate for a potential state of need (which could result from the risk itself)".[30]

Individual need is thus the sole eligibility criterion for social and medical assistance; cash and in-kind benefits are offered to any person on the sole ground that they are in need.[31] The provision of specific benefits to people traditionally considered vulnerable (e.g., the elderly, children, people with disabilities) are not enough to meet the state obligations set out in Article 13, and persons who do not fall into these categories but are still without adequate resources should be offered appropriate assistance.[32] Being *in need* means not having the necessary resources to "live a decent life" and "meet basic needs in an adequate manner".[33] States must identify in law a precise income threshold below which a person is considered in need and eligible to assistance and the criteria and procedures underlying the granting of benefits.[34] In setting the eligibility threshold, however, they cannot go lower than the poverty threshold, which is set at 50% of the median equivalised income, as calculated below. The underlying purpose of this provision, which is considered "an essential ingredient of any strategy which is intended to combat social exclusion in a substantive and meaningful manner", is to allow individuals to "live in a manner compatible with human dignity".[35]

---

30 ECSR, Conclusions XIII-4 (1996), Statement of interpretation on Articles 12 and 13; ECSR, *Finnish Society of Social Rights, cit.*, § 33.

31 ECSR, Conclusions 2013, Bosnia and Herzegovina, Article 13 § 1.

32 ECSR, Conclusions 2013, Hungary, Article 13 § 1.

33 ECSR, Conclusions XIII-4 (1996), Statement of Interpretation of Article 13§1; ECSR, Conclusions XIV-1 (1998), Portugal, Article 13.

34 ESCR, Conclusions 2017, Andorra, Article 13 § 1.

35 ESCR, *European Roma Rights Centre (ERRC) v. Bulgaria*, complaint No. 48/2008, decision on the merits of 18 February 2009, § 37.

2 Levels and Types of Benefits

A personal situation of need triggers the entitlement to "adequate assistance and, in case of sickness, the care necessitated by [one's] condition". As outlined above, the ECSR used a series of indicators anchored to the concepts of income and poverty to determine the eligibility criteria and levels of benefits. Indeed, when monitoring the adequacy of the assistance-related benefits in a country, the ECSR verifies that the level of assistance (basic benefits and additional benefits)[36] to be offered to an individual person without autonomous resources do not fall (manifestly) below the poverty threshold of 50% of the median equivalised income, which is calculated on the basis of the Eurostat at-risk-of-poverty threshold value.[37] The "median equivalised disposable income" is a statistical measure used to calculate living standards in the European Union. It is calculated by Eurostat every year and for each country. It represents the "income of a household, after tax and other deductions, that is available for spending or saving, divided by the number of household members converted into equalised adults".[38] In the absence of such an indicator, the national poverty threshold is taken into account, and the assistance level is adequate where it covers "the monetary cost of the household basket containing the minimum quantity of food and non-food items which is necessary for the individual to maintain a decent living standard and be in good health".[39]

Article 13 § 1 does not specify "what form social assistance should take. It may therefore take the form of benefits in cash or in kind".[40] While "an income guarantee has been established in most Contracting Parties",[41] the right to social assistance requires states to raise the level of social benefits above the poverty threshold. The adequacy of social assistance is assessed by including universal income-replacement benefits offered to prevent poverty and, when applicable, additional allowances, such as compensatory benefits for payment of utility bills, rent allowance and one-off benefits. For example, the jurisprudence of the ECSR shows that Sweden's basic benefits alone did not reach the poverty threshold of 50% of the equalised income during the last reporting

---

36 ECSR, Conclusions 2017, Andorra, Article 13; ECSR, Conclusions 2017, France, Article 13 § 1.

37 ECSR, Conclusions XIX-2 (2009), Latvia, Article 13.

38 Eurostat Statistics Explained, "Glossary: Equivalised disposable income", 1 August 2018, available at <https://ec.europa.eu/eurostat/statistics-explained/index.php?title=Glossary:Equivalised_disposable_income>.

39 ECSR, Conclusions 2009, Armenia, Article 13 § 1.

40 Secretariat of the ECSR, Digest 2022, *cit.*, p. 126.

41 ECSR, Conclusions XIII-4 (1996), Statement of Interpretation of Article 13§1.

cycle but, in consideration of all additional benefits, the overall figure was considered to conform with Article 13 § 1.[42]

States may establish "a link between access to this right and a willingness to seek employment or to receive vocational training (…) provided that these conditions are reasonable [and pursue the aim of finding] a lasting solution to the person's problems in accessing the labour market".[43] In any case, assistance must be provided "as long as the situation of need persists and cannot therefore be subject to time-limits" and the withdrawal of social assistance "for unemployed persons in active age after 18, 12 or 6 months (…) cannot be considered to be a permissible" as it would subject a person in need to "the risk of the loss of basic means of subsistence".[44] Furthermore, it is worth recalling that Charter-compliant eligibility criteria for social and medical assistance must relate to a single person: family benefits are not relevant for assessment under Article 13 ESC as their inclusion would mean that eligibility criteria were not genuinely universal and based on individual needs and personal vulnerability.[45] For those countries that have not accepted Article 23 ESC (the right of elderly persons to social protection), the ECSR assesses the level of non-contributory pensions paid to a single elderly person without resources under Article 13 § 1.[46]

Although all "conclusions" on the implementation of Article 13 by the ECSR record a detailed analysis of the reporting states' *social* (assistance) benefits, the examination of information regarding *medical* assistance-related measures (outside the specific case of emergency medical care for irregular migrants[47]) is not explicit across all reporting cycles. Complementary information on the conformity of the health care system and medical care with the Charter stems, however, from the scrutiny of the right to protection of health (accessibility of health care) (Article 11 § 1) and the right to social security (Article 12 § 1). The latter is often the case when medical assistance for people in need is provided as part of a health insurance system.[48] According to the established jurisprudence of the ECSR, medical assistance as per Article 13 § 1 is intended to be

42 ECSR, Conclusions 2017, Sweden, Article 13 § 1.

43 ECSR, *European Roma Rights Centre* (*ERRC*) *v. Bulgaria*, complaint No. 48/2008, decision on the merits of 18 February 2009, § 39.

44 ECSR, *ERRC v. Bulgaria* (2009), *cit.*, § 39–40.

45 ECSR, Conclusions 2013, Italy, Article 13 § 1.

46 This is the case of Armenia, Andorra, Austria, Belgium, Lithuania, and Moldova (as of 30 April 2020).

47 Cf. section I. D. below.

48 For example, this is the case of Serbia, Macedonia, and Germany (ECSR, Conclusions 2017 and XXI-2).

"free or subsidised health care or payments to enable persons [without adequate resources] to pay for the care required by their condition".[49] The ECSR considers that the right to medical assistance is adequately protected where "primary and specialised outpatient medical care", as well as emergency care, are financially accessible "for poor or socially vulnerable persons who become sick" and specifies that "the seriousness of the illness cannot be a factor in refusing to grant medical assistance".[50] To confirm the existence of adequate and affordable medical assistance, state parties are required, inter alia, to share information with the ECSR on the number of co-payments that people in poverty or at risk of poverty are required to make to obtain necessary health care services and medicines.[51]

The condition of being a recipient of social assistance to be eligible to access medical assistance provided via a subsidised health system is not considered compatible with Article 13 § 1. Indeed, in the 2008 collective complaint case of *ERRC v. Bulgaria*, the ECSR had to assess whether the health insurance system and existing medical assistance options allowed the most vulnerable people to receive the care necessitated by their conditions and whether the Roma community's access to health care were in practice, compliant with Articles 11 and 13 § 1, which are strongly correlated. The outcome of the procedure indicated that the Bulgarian legal and administrative system allowed certain people, such as temporarily unemployed people, without resources to fall outside the social assistance system. As a result, an important number of financially vulnerable people – in particular, members of the Roma community, whose poverty rate is particularly high and health insurance and social assistance affiliation especially low vis-à-vis the settled community – were prevented from accessing free necessary health care.[52]

According to the 2017 findings of the reporting procedure before the ECSR, only 7 out of the 35 states that had agreed to comply with Article 13 § 1 have actually established an adequate level of social benefits and medical care for people in need.[53] Due to the two-fold scope of this provision, either inadequate levels of social benefits or unaffordable medical assistance can lead

---

49 ECSR, Conclusions XIII-4 (1996), Statement of Interpretation of Article 13.

50 ECSR, *European Roma Rights Centre (ERRC) v. Bulgaria*, complaint No 46/2007, decision on the merits of 3 December 2008, § 44; ECSR, Conclusions, Bosnia and Herzegovina, Article 13 § 1; ECSR, Conclusions XIII-4 (1996), Greece, Article 13.

51 ECSR, Conclusion 2017, Latvia, Article 13 § 1; ECSR, Conclusion 2017, Moldova, Article 13 § 1.

52 ECSR, *ERRC v. Bulgaria*, (2008), *cit.*, § 41–43.

53 ECSR, Conclusions 2017, Andorra, Belgium, Iceland, Luxemburg, The Netherlands, Sweden, The United Kingdom.

to a conclusion of non-conformity of a state law or practice with Article 13 § 1.[54] The picture that emerged from the 2021 Conclusions of the ECSR is even more concerning: compliance with article 13 § 1 was examined in 25 country reports. Only one state was found to be in conformity (the Netherlands) and non-conformity conclusions were mainly taken on the following grounds: the lack of universality of social or medical assistance systems, inadequate levels of social assistance, excessively lengthy residence requirements to access assistance for foreigners lawfully resident and withdrawal of social assistance to persons in needs as a penalty for having refused a job offer.[55]

The *adequate* level of medical and social assistance that Article 13 § 1 requires states to fulfil – indicated above – only applies to those people who are either nationals or legal residents in a given state party to the Charter.[56] People who are either legally present or irregularly staying in a country are entitled to *emergency* medical and social assistance, the meaning of which is outlined in section D below.

3 Procedural and Formal Requirements

As mentioned above, social assistance and medical assistance are conceptualised as *human* rights in the Charter system. As such, the law of state parties must recognise them and define the elements to be "taken into account in order to assess the state of need and make the criteria for assessment of that need clear, as well as [establish a] procedure for determining whether a person lacks adequate resources".[57] Every national or local decision that denies, reduces or rejects the renewal of social and medical assistance must be subject to appeal before a review body. This body can be either a court or an administrative body that can guarantee independence from the executive and the parties. The scope of the right to appeal must include first-instance appeals and a subsequent level of review, and the reviewing body must have the power to judge on the merits of the case rather than solely on procedural points of law. Finally, as prospective beneficiaries of social and medical assistance are people

54 For example, the 2017 findings of the ECSR with regards to article 13 § 1 in the case of Spain and Romania point to the conclusion that both states have failed to comply with the required level of benefits exactly for this reason: Spanish medical assistance was considered sufficiently inclusive and affordable but their level of social assistance inadequate; Romanian's levels of social benefits appeared overall in compliance with the indicators of the ECSR, but necessary health care was not accessible and affordable for people in need, who tend to fall outside the national health insurance system.

55 ECSR (Secretariat), Press Briefing Elements – Conclusions 2021, 14 March 2022, pp. 13–14.

56 Appendix to the Charter, *cit.*, § 1.

57 ECSR, Conclusions XIII-4 (1996), Statement of Interpretation of Article 13.

who claim financial and social vulnerability, to make the right to appeal an effective entitlement, "legal aid must be provided".[58] The analysis of the 2017 and 2021 *conclusions* of the ECSR and the national reports submitted by state parties show a significant lack of applicable information on this point.[59]

B *Prohibition of the Diminution of Political and Social Rights*

Article 13 § 2 is aimed at preventing a person's status as a recipient of social or medical assistance being used to justify restricting that person's enjoyment of social and political rights. To assess compliance with this provision, the ECSR requires states to share information on "whether legal provisions enshrining the principle of equality and prohibiting discrimination in the exercise of political or social rights exist". These provisions must prevent arbitrary differentiation – of a direct or an indirect nature[60] – in the enjoyment of rights on the basis of receiving social or medical assistance[61] or on the ground of social status or any other personal circumstances, including having a particular health condition.[62] The existence (and implementation) of this anti-discriminatory legislation is a good indicator of compliance with Article 13 § 2. In HUDOC-ESC, the database of the jurisprudence of the ECSR, only a handful of cases are coded as having a finding of *non-conformity.* Most of these are based on the fact that, regardless of reiterated requests of information, the country reports had not displayed enough details on the above anti-discriminatory measures.[63] Only the case of Ireland, soon redressed in the early 1970s, gave rise to a conclusion of substantive non-conformity with the Charter on the ground that "a person who ha[d] received assistance benefits m[ight] not become a member of an assistance authority until after the expiration of a period of twelve months". This represented a non-justified limitation of the right to access employment.[64]

58 ESCR, Conclusions 2017, Hungary and Latvia, Article 13 § 1; ECSR, Conclusions XIII-4 (1996), Statement of Interpretation of Article 13.

59 Cf. recent ECSR's conclusions on the realisation of Article 13, available at <https://www.coe.int/en/web/european-social-charter/-/several-states-parties-to-the-european-social-charter-marked-by-a-high-levels-of-poverty-in-2017> and at <https://www.coe.int/en/web/european-social-charter/-/several-problems-relating-to-health-and-social-protection-still-persist-in-europe>.

60 ECSR, Conclusions XVIII-1 (2006), Croatia, Article 13 § 2; ECSR, Conclusions 2017, Andorra, Article 13 § 2.

61 ECSR, Conclusions 2017, Andorra, *cit.*

62 ECSR, Conclusions 2002, Article 13 § 2.

63 ECSR, Conclusions XIX-2 (2010), Croatia Article 13 § 2; ECSR, Conclusions 2009 and 2021, Moldova, Article 13 § 2; ECSR, Conclusions XVI-1 (2003) Malta, Article 13 §2.

64 ECSR, Conclusions I (1969), II (1971), III (1973), Ireland, Article 13 § 2.

C Empowering Social Services

The scope of the right to social assistance encompasses access to non-monetary benefits, in the form of free social services that target the prevention, removal and alleviation of personal and family needs as per Article 13 § 3. These services constitute an essential element of an integrated strategy of poverty alleviation and empowerment of dependant adults to help them regain their place as fully active members of society through means appropriate to their personal situation.[65] The provision of advice and practical help regarding the exercise the entitlement to social and medical assistance and on employment opportunities, vocational training or re-training, and the offer of counselling are examples of the services covered by the scope of Article 13 § 3.[66]

The case of *FIDH v. Belgium*, which was decided by the ECSR in 2013 and concerned the alleged insufficient availability of welfare services and anti-poverty strategies for highly dependent persons with disabilities, offers useful insights into the slight differences in scope between Articles 13 § 3 and 14 ESC. The Committee restates that there is indeed an overlap between the two provisions, to the extent that "they refer to services of the same kind (social), despite their slightly different wording".[67] However, the "advice and personal help" in Article 13 § 3 is aimed at enabling people without adequate resources "to overcome difficulties arising from their state of want, avoid benefit dependency and re-establish their autonomy".[68] For this reason, Article 13 § 3 goes "hand in hand with a material commitment of the States Parties aimed at enabling those entitled to social assistance eventually to reintegrate into social life through their own efforts and means". As such its *function* does not seem to be the most relevant for "examining the conformity with the Charter of the defendant State's policy with regard to highly dependent persons with disabilities".[69]

Another main difference between Articles 13 § 3 and 14 ESC is that Article 14 states that social services "may be provided subject to fees, fixed or variable, (…) [although] they must not be so high as to prevent the effective access to

65 Secretariat of the ECSR, Digest 2022, *cit.*, p. 130.

66 ECSR, Conclusions XIII-4 (1996), Statement of Interpretation of Article 13; ECSR, Conclusions XIV-1 (1998), Statement of Interpretation of Article 13; ECSR, Conclusions, Romania 2013, Article 13 § 3; ECSR, Conclusions, Slovak Republic 2008, Article 13 § 3.

67 ECSR, *International Federation of Human Rights* (*FIDH*) *v. Belgium*, complaint No. 75/2011, decision on the merits of 18 March 2013, § 158.

68 ECSR, *FIDH v. Belgium, cit.*, § 159.

69 ECSR, *FIDH v. Belgium, cit.*, § 163.

these services. For persons lacking adequate financial resources in terms of Article 13 § 1 such services should be provided free of charge".[70]

To comply with their obligations under Article 13 § 3, states are required to allocate adequate financial resources and qualified staff to provide social services, including advice and personal help, for people without adequate resources.[71] Furthermore, like Article 14 ESC, Article 13 § 3 requires that social services and institutions have adequate geographical distribution so as to guarantee equal and effective access by their target users across all of a state's territory.[72] For further analysis of the scope and normative development of the services of Article 14 ESC, I refer to the commentary in this volume.

D *The Personal Scope of Article 13*

The interactions between various paragraphs of Article 13 and the Appendix to the Charter, as interpreted by the jurisprudence of the ECSR, create different normative regimes in terms of the levels of social and medical assistance for nationals and regularly resident foreigners on the one hand and legally present people and irregular migrants on the other. This section examines how the drafters of the Charter and the ECSR have responded to the ideological dilemma between ethnocentrism and ethno-heterogeneity in relation to welfare provisions.[73]

The personal scope of the ESC extends to "foreigners only in so far as they are nationals of other contracting parties lawfully *resident* or *working* regularly within the territory of the contracting party concerned".[74] Extra-European immigration was not particularly topical when the Charter was being drafted, and the *travaux préparatoires* of the Charter of 1961 show that states were principally concerned with eliminating barriers to the enjoyment of socio-economic rights for the nationals of European countries[75] under the assumption that the

70 ECSR, Conclusions 2005, Statement of Interpretation of Article 14 § 1, as recalled by ECSR, *The Central Association of Carers in Finland v. Finland*, complaint No. 71/2011, decision on the merits of 4 December 2012, § 49.

71 ECSR, Conclusions XIII-4 (1996), Statement of Interpretation of Article 13; ECSR, Conclusions XX-2 (2013), Spain, Article 13 § 3.

72 ECSR, Conclusions 2017, Austria and Belgium, Article 13 § 3.

73 Diane Sainsbury, *Welfare States and Immigrant Rights. The Politics of Inclusion and Exclusion*, Oxford, Oxford University Press, 2012, pp. 1–10.

74 Appendix to the Charter, *cit.*, § 1.

75 Secretary General of the Council of Europe, Memorandum on the Role of the Council of Europe in the Social Field, SG (53) 1, 16 April 1953, § 14, available at <https://rm.coe.int/CoERMPublicCommonSearchServices/DisplayDCTMContent?documentId=0900001680 6c1c47>.

full entitlement to social rights were matters concerning legal and settled communities as identifiable taxpayers.[76] However, globalisation and contemporary forms of human mobility that emerged in the last few decades are realities that the ECSR had to address: it did so by emphasising a contextual and teleological interpretation of the Charter as a human rights treaty.[77]

Article 13 § 1, read in conjunction with the Appendix, is the correct legal source that applies to nationals and foreigners who are nationals of one of the state parties to the Charter, are "lawfully resident or working regularly" in the territory of another state party and lack adequate resources within the meaning explained above. This category of foreigners must enjoy an individual right to appropriate social and medical assistance on an equal footing with nationals.[78] This provision also applies to refugees and, for State Parties to the Revised Charter, to stateless people.[79] The guarantee of equal treatment must be enshrined in legislation, or at least in administrative acts.[80] Lawfully resident non-nationals in the territory of a state party "cannot be repatriated on the sole ground that they need assistance".[81] Indeed, when a residence or work permit has expired, this right to equal treatment no longer applies.[82]

It is worth recalling that, like most pieces of international law, the ESC does not regulate procedures for admitting foreigners into the territory of its state parties or for determining residence status. These are deemed areas for domestic decision making and legislation.[83] Accordingly, the right to equal treatment concerning social and medical assistance must be enjoyed only when a person's work or residence status has been processed with a positive outcome by national authorities. Once the person is authorised to enter and stay in a given state, fulfilling a length of residence requirement as a condition for equal treatment in respect to social and medical assistance is not considered to conform to the obligations set out in the Charter.[84]

---

76 Francesca Biondi Dal Monte, "Lo Stato Sociale di Fronte alle Migrazioni. Diritti Sociali, Appartenenza e Dignità della Persona", *Rivista del Gruppo di Pisa*, no. 3(12), 2012, p. 2.

77 ESCR, *International Federation of Human Rights League* (*FIDH*) *v. France*, complaint No. 14/2003, decision of 3 November 2004, § 26–32.

78 ECSR, Conclusions XIII-4 (1996), Statement of Interpretation of Article 13.

79 Appendix to the Charter of 1961, *cit.*, § 2 and to the Revised Charter, *cit.*, § 2 and 3; ECSR, *FEANTSA v. the Netherlands, cit.*, § 140; ECSR, Conclusions 2013, Bosnia and Herzegovina, Article 13.

80 ECSR, Conclusions XIV-1 (1998), Greece.

81 ECSR, Conclusions 2017, Bosnia and Herzegovina, Article 13 § 1.

82 ECSR, Conclusions 2017, Bosnia and Herzegovina, Article 13 § 1.

83 ECSR, Conclusions 2017, Austria, Article 13 § 1.

84 ECSR, Conclusions 2017, Austria, Article 13 § 1; ECSR, Conclusions 2017, Finland, Article 13 § 1.

Article 13 § 4 extends the right to social and medical assistance to foreign nationals of other contracting parties who are legally *present* in a given state party, although not resident therein, with reference to the personal scope of the 1953 European Convention on Social and Medical Assistance.[85] While the Statement of Interpretation of Article 13 attached to the ECSR's Conclusions 2013 indicates that the level of social and medical assistance to be provided to people who are "lawfully within the territories" of the state concerned is *adequate assistance* equalised to that to which nationals and residents are entitled,[86] the reporting cycles of the ECSR have consistently required states to provide a right to *emergency* assistance for legally present people under Article 13 § 4.[87]

The reference to the European Convention on Social and Medical Assistance, a coordination treaty,[88] complements the material scope of Article 13 only to the extent that it establishes conditions under which all state parties to the Charter (and not only the parties to the Convention itself) can repatriate non-resident foreigners without resources on the ground that they need assistance: in particular, persons must be in a fit state of health to be transported, and no objection on humanitarian grounds must exist.[89]

Article 13 § 1 has, since 2013,[90] been employed as the appropriate legal source to ground the right to emergency medical and social assistance for *irregular* or undocumented migrants, which the ECSR terms "foreign nationals unlawfully present in the territory". Due to the centrality of the right to social and medical assistance as a baseline human right for people in need in the Charter system, Article 13 has been heavily relied upon to permit the jurisprudential extension of the personal scope of the Charter to people who are, in principle, excluded from its scope due to their not being entitled to stay or reside in a state territory and, as such, being deportable.[91]

85 European Convention on Social and Medical Assistance, ETS No. 014 (adopted 11 December 1953 entry into force 1 July 1954), Article 1.

86 ECSR, Conclusions 2013, Statement of Interpretation of Article 13.

87 Cf. headings and findings reading article 13 § 4 in the ECSR, Conclusions 2017, *cit.*.

88 Explanatory report to the European Convention on Social and Medical Assistance, § 3, available at <https://rm.coe.int/CoERMPublicCommonSearchServices/DisplayDCTMContent?documentId=090000168oocg2ba>.

89 European Convention on Social and Medical Assistance, *cit.*, Article 7. a. ii. and 7. b..

90 ECSR, Statement of Interpretation of Article 13.

91 Elspeth Guild, "Who is an Irregular Migrant?", in Barbara Bogusz *et al.* (eds.), *Irregular Migration and Human Rights: Theoretical, European and International Perspectives* (*Immigration and Asylum Law and Policy in Europe*), Leiden, Martinus Nijhoff Publishers, 2004, p. 3.

As early as 2004, the ECSR established that "legislation or practice which denies entitlement to medical assistance to foreign nationals, within the territory of a State Party, even if they are there illegally, is contrary to the Charter".[92] While the case from which this quote is taken concerned foreign minors with irregular status, further cases confirmed that state parties to the Charter must provide at least emergency social and medical assistance to everyone, including irregular migrant adults, to meet their urgent and immediate needs, such as shelter, food, emergency medical care and clothing.[93] The enjoyment of these rights is necessary for protecting human dignity and for the "basic subsistence of any human being".[94] A finding to the contrary would potentially deprive irregular migrants of the protection of the most fundamental rights, such as the right to life, the right to physical and mental integrity and the right to human dignity.[95] These rights must be guaranteed in law and practice.[96] Regarding the severity of a situation of socio-economic deprivation that would trigger the applicability of the Charter, the ECSR clarified that the criteria of "urgency and seriousness" concerning individual material needs must not be interpreted too narrowly.[97] Emergency social and medical assistance "should be supported by a right to appeal to an independent body".[98] As far as minors are concerned, in line with other international obligations under different treaties, the ECSR considers them entitled to receive health care beyond urgent medical assistance so as to include primary and secondary care, as well as psychological assistance.[99]

The ECSR established a strong synergy of action among state measures that target Article 13 and other provisions of the Charter. For example, the right to

---

92 ECSR, *International Federation of Human Rights Leagues* (*FIDH*) *v. France*, complaint No. 14/2003, decision on the merits of 8 September 2004, § 32.

93 ECSR, *FEANTSA v. the Netherlands, cit.*, §§ 171–173; ECSR, *Conference of European Churches* (*CEC*) *v. the Netherlands*, complaint No. 30/2013, decision on the merits of 1 July 2014, §§ 105–126.

94 ECSR, *FEANTSA v the Netherlands, cit.*, §§ 171–173; ESCR, *CEC v. the Netherlands, cit.*, § 122. For further analysis, see Carole Nivard, "Précisions sur les droits de la Charte sociale Européenne bénéficiant aux étrangers en situation irrégulière", *La Revue des Droits de L'Homme – Actualité Droits-Libertés*, 2014, pp. 1–12.

95 ECSR, *Defence for Children International* (*DCI*) *v. Belgium*, complaint No. 69/2011, decision on the merits of 23 October 2012, § 28; ECSR, *Defence for Children International* (*DCI*) *v. the Netherlands*, complaint No. 47/2008, decision on the merits of 20 October 2009, § 19; ECSR, *FIDH v. France, cit.*, § 30 and 31.

96 ECSR, Conclusions 2017, Belgium, Article 13 § 1.

97 ECSR, *FEANTSA, cit.*, § 171.

98 ECSR, Conclusions 2004, The Netherlands, Article 13.

99 ECSR, *DCI v. Belgium, cit.*, §§ 128 and 131.

shelter of irregular migrants is described as a form of emergency assistance in both *FEANTSA v. the Netherlands* and *CEC v. the Netherlands*.[100] With reference to *EUROCEF v. France*, a case concerning conditions of inadequate accommodation for unaccompanied foreign minors, the ECSR recalled "that the obligation to provide emergency social and medical assistance is not respected in cases when minors are left in a situation of wandering and living on the streets".[101] Furthermore, it is worth recalling that the principle of non-discrimination as per Article E Revised Charter was read in conjunction with Article 13 § 1 and § 4 ESC in the 2012 case of *Médecins du Monde International v. France*.[102] This collective complaint concerned whether the treatment of migrant Roma, mostly from Romania and Bulgaria, living in severe poverty in France and often subjected to evictions, was compliant with several articles of the ESC, including the right to the protection of health (Article 11), the right to social and medical assistance (Article 13) and the right to protection against poverty and social exclusion (Article 30). The several findings of violation were grounded in the fact that ECSR considered that for equal treatment to be achieved, "differences between individuals should be taken into account [… and that] special consideration should be given to the needs and different lifestyle of the Roma, which are a specific type of disadvantaged group and a vulnerable minority",[103] regardless of whether they are lawfully resident or irregular staying people. Regarding migrant Roma who had resided or worked legally for more than 3 months in France, the ECSR found that the concrete implementation of the French administrative procedures to obtain medical assistance violated Article E in conjunction with Article 13 because they failed to adequately consider the especially vulnerable situation of this ethnic minority with migrant status as also characterised by recurring residence changes due to regular evictions. Furthermore, as the French *universal* sickness coverage was found not to be accessible by those migrants who had resided lawfully or worked regularly in France for less than 3 months, the Committee found an "unjustified difference in treatment" on the ground of nationality and a violation of Article 13 § 4 ESC. In contrast to these two findings of violation, the ECSR considered the

100 ECSR, *CEC v. the Netherlands, cit.*, § 144; ECSR, *FEANTSA v. the Netherlands, cit.*, §§ 53, 182 and 185.

101 ECSR, *European Committee for Home-Based Priority Action for the Child and the Family (EUROCEF) v. France*, complaint No. 114/2015, decision on the merits of 15 June 2018, § 163.

102 ECSR, *Médecins du Monde International v. France*, complaint No. 67/2011, decision on the merits of 11 September 2012.

103 ECSR, *Médecins du Monde International, cit.*, §§ 39 and 40.

emergency treatment offered to irregular migrants (of Roma origin) to be compliant with the Charter's standards.[104]

II Comparable Protection in Other Instruments of European and International Law

A *The European Convention on Human Rights*

The European Convention on Human Rights (ECHR) and the case law of the European Court of Human Rights (ECtHR or the Court) are highly regarded in the interpretation of the ESC by the ECSR. Indeed, the Charter "was envisaged as a human rights instrument t[hat] complement[s]" the ECHR.[105] It is precisely the universal scope of the ECHR and the need to protect the right to life and human dignity that allowed the extension of Article 13 ESC, via the contextual interpretation of the Charter, to cover emergency social and medical assistance for irregular migrants,[106] whose rights were not textually included in the personal scope of the Charter.[107]

Considering the relative weakness of the ESC system vis-à-vis the legally enforceable judgements of the ECtHR,[108] the ECHR has, since the 1980s, also been employed to advance socio-economic interests. Though the ECHR is essentially directed at the protection of civil and political rights, many of these rights "have implications of a socio-economic nature".[109] Indeed, the right to life (Article 2 ECHR), the prohibition of inhuman or degrading treatment (Article 3 ECHR), the right to private and family life (Article 8 ECHR) and the right to peaceful enjoyment of property (Article 1 Protocol 1 ECHR) have grounded complaints before the ECtHR regarding social benefits, health protection and housing issues. However, the Court specified that the "Convention does not guarantee, as such, socio-economic rights, including the right to charge-free dwelling, the right to work, the right to free medical assistance, or the right to claim financial assistance from a State to maintain a certain level

104 ECSR, *Médecins du Monde International, cit.*, §§ 172–182.
105 ESCR, *FIDH v. France, cit.*, § 27.
106 ESCR, *FIDH v. France, cit.*, §§ 30 and 31; ECSR, *CEC v.* the Netherlands, *cit.*, § 74; ECSR, *DCI v. Belgium*, *cit.*, § 36.
107 Appendix to the Charter, *cit.*, § 1.
108 Holly Cullen, "The Collective Complaints System of the European Social Charter: Interpretative Methods of the European Committee of Social Rights", *Human Rights Law Review*, no. 9(1), 2009, p. 66.
109 ECtHR, 9 October 1979, *Airey v. Ireland*, No. 6289/73, § 26.

of living".[110] In other words, socio-economic interests are indirectly protected within this legal framework only when the concrete circumstances of a case before the Court are found to be particularly suitable to fit the scope of the civil rights provisions in the ECHR as developed by the interpretative techniques of the ECtHR.

Article 2 ECHR has been employed in the area of health care in situations whose scope overlaps that of both Article 11 and Article 13 ESC. In the case of *Şenturk,* as far as a right to free medical assistance is concerned, the ECtHR recognised that the denial of emergency medical treatment, which was made conditional upon the payment of fees and that eventually led to the death of a pregnant patient, constituted a violation of the obligation to protect a person's physical integrity under the substantive limb of Article 2 ECHR.[111] In the context of public health, Article 2 requires states to fulfil a due diligence obligation to "make regulations compelling hospitals (...) to adopt appropriate measures for the protection of their patients' life".[112] In two cases concerning access to life-saving drugs, *Nitecki* and *Panitescu,* the Court offered a right-compliant solution which partially realised the right to medical assistance. Indeed, instead of the required full refund, a state refund of 70% of the cost of an essential drug was deemed compatible with Article 2 ECHR.[113] Further, where a person is, in practice, refused access to free medicine, in spite of a court ordering the same on the ground of supportive medical assessment, there may be a violation of Article 2 because this course of action would constitute failure to "prevent the applicant's life from being avoidably put at risk by not providing him [or her with] the appropriate health-care".[114] Additional emergency-oriented approaches stem from cases concerning a lack of medical care and social assistance for children entrusted to the care of the state that eventually died. In the cases of *Nencheva* and *Câmpeanu*, severe socio-economic deprivation, intersectional vulnerabilities of the victims, and state awareness of abusive circumstances were the core arguments that led to a finding of violation of Article 2 ECHR. In these cases, the Court held that responding states failed to adequately protect these children from serious and immediate threats to their lives, including cold and shortages of food, medicines and basic necessities.[115]

---

110 ECtHR, dec., 28 October 1999, *Pancenko v. Latvia,* No. 40772/98, § 2 (the law).

111 ECtHR, 9 April 2013, *Mehmet Şenturk and Bekir Şenturk v. Turkey,* No. 13423/09, §§ 84–97.

112 ECtHR, 17 January 2002, *Calvelli and Ciglio v. Italy,* No. 32967/96, § 49.

113 ECtHR, dec., 21 March 2002, *Nitecki v. Poland,* No. 65653/01, § 1 (the law).

114 ECtHR, 10 April 2012, *Panaitescu v. Romania,* No. 30909/06, §§ 27–37.

115 ECtHR, [GC], 17 July 2014, *Centre for Legal Resources on behalf of Valentin Câmpeanu v. Romania,* No. 47848/08; ECtHR, 18 June 2013, *Nencheva and others v. Bulgaria,* No. 48609/06.

In the ECHR framework injuries to physical and mental integrity may be outlawed via Article 3 ECHR under which "No one shall be subjected to torture or to inhuman or degrading treatment or punishment".[116] However, the use of Article 3 ECHR as a legal standard to advance the socio-economic well-being of people and to grant them necessary social and medical assistance is constrained: the level of "deprivation and want incompatible with human dignity" and the "minimum level of severity" that is needed to reach the threshold of applicability of this provision is difficult to achieve.[117] In the case of *Moldovan*, Article 3 ECHR was triggered because the state-led destruction of the applicants' houses placed them in a situation where they "lived, and some of them still live, in crowded and improper conditions – cellars, hen-houses, stables, etc. – and frequently changed address, moving in with friends or family in extremely overcrowded conditions".[118] Furthermore, it is worth mentioning the case of *M.S.S.*, concerning, inter alia, the severe socio-economic deprivation to which asylum seekers – a vulnerable group who were fully dependant on state support for their survival – were exposed in Greece, which included a failure to meet their "most basic needs: food, hygiene and a place to live".[119] In this case, while no general obligation of financial assistance for the asylum seekers or any other person applied, the Court held the state accountable because it was the state's passivity regarding the circumstances of people who depend on the state for their survival that caused the unacceptably dire living conditions of the applicants. Furthermore, in exceptional circumstances, Article 3 ECHR has been employed to prevent the deportation of migrants to places where emergency social and medical assistance are not granted, and people are consequently deprived of the bare minimum level of health and healthy living conditions.[120]

Regarding the establishment of "general measures of economic and social strategy", state parties to the ECHR maintain a wide margin of discretion. As a general rule, only "manifestly unreasonable" socio-economic measures, not necessary in a democratic society, are ruled out by the Court.[121] These principles

116 Ingrid Leijten, *Core Socio-Economic Rights and the European Court of Human Rights*, Cambridge, Cambridge University Press, 2018, p. 50.

117 ECtHR, dec., 18 June 2009, *Budina v. Russia*, No. 45603/05; ECtHR, [GC], 26 October 2000, *Kudła v. Poland*, No. 30210/96, § 91. Emphasis added.

118 ECtHR, 12 July 2005, *Moldovan and others v. Romania* (No. 2), No. 41138/98, 64320/01, § 103.

119 ECtHR, [GC], 21 January 2011, *M.S.S. v. Belgium and Greece*, No. 30696/09, §§ 252–254.

120 ECtHR, [GC], 4 November 2014, *Tarakhel v. Switzerland*, No. 29217/12, § 120; ECtHR, [GC], 13 December 2016, *Paposhvili v. Belgium*, No. 41738/10, § 183.

121 For example, see: ECtHR, [GC], 12 April 2006, *Stec and Others v. the United Kingdom*, No. 65731/01, 65900/01, § 52; ECtHR, [GC], 16 March 2010, *Carson and Others v the United Kingdom*, No. 42184/05, § 61.

normally apply in cases concerning limitable rights as per Article 8 and Article 1 Protocol 1 ECHR regarding complaints related to housing and social security.

As far as Article 8 ECHR is concerned, the actual detriment to an applicant's health and well-being needs to reach a certain "level of severity" in order to fall within the scope of this provision.[122] The social dimension of the right to respect for private and family life includes respect for the "peaceful enjoyment of one's existing residence"[123] but excludes the right to "be provided with a home".[124] However, in the assessment of the proportionality and necessity of an eviction procedure under such a negative right, adequate weight should be given to the vulnerability of certain groups, such as the Roma people,[125] people with disabilities[126] and severely ill-people.[127] Although Article 8 ECHR does not require states to offer housing benefits, those benefits that do fall within the ambit of Article 8 should be administered without discrimination,[128] as is the case with other social benefits.[129]

Article 1 Protocol 1 ECHR (protection of property), though relevant to the topic at hand, is extremely difficult to activate in situations protected by Article 13 ESC. Older case law on the right to the protection of property in the area of social protection clearly distinguished between contributory and non-contributory benefits, with only the former falling within the ambit of Article 1 Protocol 1. As indicated in the case of *Gaygusuz* "entitlement to this social benefit is therefore linked to the payment of contributions to the unemployment insurance fund, which is a precondition for the payment of unemployment benefits (…). It follows that there is no entitlement to emergency assistance where such contributions have not been made".[130] The concept of *possessions* was linked to the payment of taxes and contributions.[131] A shift occurred with the Grand Chamber's judgement in *Stec*, where the Court held that "if (…) a contracting state has in force legislation providing for the payment as of right of a welfare benefit – whether conditional or not on the prior payment of contributions – that legislation must be regarded as generating a proprietary

122 ECtHR, 9 June 2005, *Fadeyeva v. Russia,* No. 55723/00, § 69.

123 ECtHR, 19 January 2012, *Dukic v. Bosnia and Herzegovina,* No. 4543/09, § 40.

124 ECtHR, [GC], 18 January 2001, *Chapman v. the United Kingdom,* No. 27238/95, § 99.

125 ECtHR, 24 April 2012, *Yordanova and others v. Bulgaria,* No. 25446/06; ECtHR, [GC], 17 October 2013, *Winterstein and others v. France,* No. 27013/07.

126 ECtHR, dec., 4 May 1999, *Marzari v. Italy,* No. 36448/97.

127 ECtHR, dec., 26 June 2001, *O'Rourke v. the United Kingdom,* No. 39022/97.

128 ECtHR, 27 September 2011, *Bah v. the United Kingdom,* No. 56328/07, § 40.

129 ECtHR, *Stec, cit.,* § 55.

130 ECtHR, 16 September 1996, *Gaygusuz v. Austria,* No. 17371/90, § 39.

131 ECtHR, 4 June 2002, *Wessels-Bergervoet v. the Netherlands,* No. 34462/97.

interest falling within the ambit of Article 1 of Protocol No. 1 for persons satisfying its requirements".[132] The case law of the Court has indicated that Article 1 Protocol 1 is triggered when someone is already in receipt of some sort of benefit or has the legitimate expectation of receiving such benefit when all domestic legal requirements for entitlement are fulfilled.[133] A violation may occur when the payment of this benefit, to which the applicant is entitled, is delayed, reduced or withdrawn to the extent of being considered an "excessive burden" on the applicant's proprietary interest, and also in consideration of the fact that the benefit may be her or his sole source of income.[134] When assessing the proportionality of such a reduction or denial of social benefits, the Court has recently begun to emphasise the impact of the state measure on a "subsistence minimum" for vulnerable people.[135] However, applicable jurisprudence has proven that is it extremely difficult to successfully employ Article 1 Protocol 1 in the field of social protection: all the above possession-related conditions of applicability still apply, and it cannot be held that a "self-standing right to a minimum subsistence" or to social assistance should be included in the interpretation of Article 1 Protocol 1 ECHR.[136]

The ECtHR considers certain groups to be "especially vulnerable", and applicants who belong to these categories may encounter a certain favour by the ECtHR when their socio-economic interests are assessed for violation of ECHR.[137] As indicated above, regarding Roma, asylum seekers, the elderly, children, people with disabilities and individuals who are HIV positive, the threshold of severity to trigger the violation of Articles 2 and 3 has been lowered and

132 ECtHR, *Stec and Others v. the United Kingdom, cit.*, §54. Therefore, a proprietary interest would fall within the interpretation of the concept of possessions.

133 ECtHR, 9 December 1994, *Stran Greek Refinieries and Stratis Andeadis v. Greece*, No. 13427/87, § 59, the Court noted that an existing right should be "sufficiently established to be enforceable". The mere hope of receiving a benefit is not enough, cf. ECtHR, [GC], 12 July 2001, *Prince Hans-Adam II of Liechtenstein v. Germany*, No. 42527/98; ECtHR, dec., 10 November 2009, *Bladh v. Sweden*, No. 46125/06, § 46.

134 ECtHR, 12 July 2005, *Solodyuk v. Russia*, No. 67099/01; ECtHR, 12 October 2004, *Kjartan Ásmundsson v. Iceland*, No. 60669/00.

135 ECtHR, 7 March 2017, *Baczúr v. Hungary*, No. 8263/15, § 29; ECtHR, [GC], 13 December 2016, *Béláné Nagy v. Hungary*, No. 53090/13, § 118; ECtHR, 26 April 2018, *Cakarevic v. Croatia*, No. 48921/13, § 64.

136 Ingrid Leijten, "The Right to Minimum Subsistence and Property Protection under the ECHR: Never the Twain shall Meet?", *European Journal of Social Security*, No. 21(4), 2019, p. 320.

137 Lourdes Peroni and Alexandra Timmer, "Vulnerable Groups: The Promise of an Emerging Concept in European Human Rights Convention Law", *International Journal of Constitutional Law*, No. 11(4), 2013, pp. 1074–1082.

the state margin of appreciation in implementing Articles 8, 14 and 1 Protocol 1 reduced. Considering the current stage of interpretation of the ECHR, the provision of *adequate* social and medical assistance for *everyone in need* as per Article 13 ESC is far from being made a state duty under the ECHR; instead, the Court of Strasbourg takes an emergency-oriented approach that targets the most vulnerable people and groups in our societies and offers social protection to people who can demonstrate that they have a proprietary interest, that is those who are already in receipt of allowances or benefits in compliance with national law. This conclusion makes the correct implementation of the ESC particularly important for the realisation of an adequate right to a social minimum.

B *European Union Law*

There are no autonomous and uniform definitions of social security, social assistance or social protection under EU law, and it is the responsibility of each EU member state to materialise their detailed content in legal and administrative standards and procedures. However, EU law only establishes that this regulatory framework should meet the limits of EU free movement law and give due consideration to the principles provided for under Article 34 of the EU Charter of Fundamental Rights (CFR).[138] Article 34 CFR appears to distinguish social assistance from social security on the basis of their purposes. Indeed, social security schemes provide protection "in cases such as maternity, illness, industrial accidents, dependency or old age, and in the case of loss of employment",[139] while "social and housing assistance (…) ensure(s) a decent existence for all those who lack sufficient resources"[140] by enabling them to "meet their basic needs such as food, accommodation and health".[141] The normative content of both the right to social security and the right to social assistance in the CFR are shaped "in accordance with the rules laid down by Union law and national laws and practices". This shows the reluctance of the EU, including the Court of Justice of the European Union (CJEU) to engage substantially with the articulations of standards that are intimately linked to subject matters (social

138 Charter of Fundamental Rights of the European Union (CFR), 7 December 2000, originally published in OJEC 2000/C 364/01, text currently in force in OJ C 326, 26 October 2012.

139 CFR, *cit.*, Article 34 § 1.

140 CFR, *cit.*, Article 34 § 3.

141 CJEU, 24 April 2012, *Servet Kamberaj v. Istituto per l'Edilizia sociale della Provincia autonoma di Bolzano* (IPES), *Giunta della Provincia autonoma di Bolzano, Provincia autonoma di Bolzano*, C-571/10, § 91 and 92.

policy) that the treaties leave to the member states of the Union to regulate.[142] No full-fledged free-standing right to social and medical assistance exists in this legal framework; rather, the provision of such assistance is qualified as a *principle*.[143] This imbalance vis-à-vis other fundamental (civil) rights "may discourage the Court [CJEU] from imposing on the EU institutions positive duties to promote the guarantees listed in the Charter (...) [and it may] provide the Court with a justification for refusing to assess the validity of EU secondary legislation against the requirements of the Charter".[144] Beyond the applicability of the CFR, pieces of secondary legislation of the EU have established equal treatment rules and coordination mechanisms regarding the existing social security systems of the member states. They are intended to avoid barriers to the free movement of workers across internal borders and to enable them to retain the right to certain social security benefits granted by their member state of origin.[145]

As far as the entitlement to social assistance – the standard of which is determined at member state level – is concerned, the Citizen Rights Directive (CRD)[146] establishes different regimes for EU citizens who exercise their right to move freely in the EU according to their residence and working status.

---

142 The Explanations Relating to the Charter of Fundamental Rights, OJ C 303, 14 December 2007, pp. 17–35, indicate that: "The principle set out in Article 34(1) is based on Articles 153 and 156 of the Treaty on the Functioning of the European Union, Article 12 of the European Social Charter and (...) The Union must respect it when exercising the powers conferred on it by Articles 153 and 156 of the Treaty on the Functioning of the European Union". Similarly, article 35 is qualified as establishing a principle.

143 Explanation to the CFR, *cit.*; Cf. also Siofra O'leary, "Solidarity and Citizenship Rights in the Charter of Fundamental Rights of the EU", in Gráinne De Búrca (ed.), *EU Law and the Welfare State: In Search of Solidarity*, Oxford, Oxford University Press, 2005, p. 50.

144 Olivier De Schutter, "The European Pillar of Social Rights and the Role of the European Social Charter in the EU Legal Order", Study for the Secretariat of the European Social Charter and of the CoE-FRA-ENNHRI-Equinet Platform on Economic and Social Rights, 14 November 2018, p. 2, available at <https://www.coe.int/en/web/european-social-charter/-/study-on-the-european-pillar-of-social-rights-and-the-role-of-the-european-social-charter-in-the-european-union-legal-order>.

145 Regulation (EC) No 883/2004 of the European Parliament and of the Council of 29 April 2004 on the coordination of social security systems, OJ L 166, 30 April 2004, pp. 1–123, as amended; Regulation (EC) No 987/2009 of the European Parliament and of the Council of 16 September 2009 laying down the procedure for implementing Regulation (EC) No 883/2004 on the coordination of social security systems, OJ L 284, 30 October 2009, pp. 1–42, as amended.

146 Directive 2004/38/EC of the European Parliament and of the Council of 29 April 2004 on the right of citizens of the Union and their family members to move and reside freely within the territory of the Member States (...), OJ L 158, 30.4.2004, pp. 77–123, as amended (CRD).

No duty to provide social assistance to free moving citizens during the first 3 months of their residence in a new EU country exists under EU law.[147] After 3 months of residence, the social assistance benefits of the EU state of residence are reserved for economically active citizens who have moved within the EU, in which case an *equality of treatment* (with state nationals) clause applies.[148] However, EU nationals who have worked for less than a year in the new country of residence may have their social assistance limited to 6 months duration.[149] The provisions of the 2004 CRD on the links between residence and social assistance rights in the EU left space for interpretation; it also took consideration of a series of precedents that emphasised the principle of non-discrimination on the ground of nationality in the EU to grant allowances to job-seekers who "have established real links with the labour market of that State"[150] and social assistance to students[151] as potential – but not currently – economic actors. The case of *Brey* introduced the idea of granting a certain minimum level of social assistance benefits to non-economically active EU moving citizens based on a proportionality test: "the overall assessment of the specific burden which granting that benefit would place on the social assistance system as a whole by reference to the personal circumstances characterising the individual situation of the person concerned" should not lead to the finding that the burden is "unreasonable".[152] However, since the judgement in the *Dano* case,[153] the CJEU has consistently considered equality provisions regarding social assistance in the CRD to apply only to people who first comply with *residence* requirements under EU law. Social assistance is thus limited to economically active EU citizens, those who can temporarily retain the status of *worker* and people who have sufficient financial resources to move to another EU state. These findings have been extensively debated in the scholarship, and many have argued that they demonstrate the EU's affinity to a "Market state model"[154] and the idea of "earned" EU

147 CRD, *cit.*, Article 24 § 2.

148 CRD, *cit.*, Article 24 § 1.

149 CRD, *cit.*, Article 7 § 3.c..

150 CJEU, 23 March 2004, *Brian Francis Collins v. Secretary of State for Work and Pensions*, C-138/02; CJEU, 4 June 2009, *Athanasios Vatsouras and Josif Koupatantze v. Arbeitsgemeinschaft (ARGE) Nürnberg*, C-22/08 and C-23/08.

151 CJEU, 20 September 2001, *Rudy Grzelczyk v. Centre public d'aide sociale d'Ottignies-Louvain-la-Neuve*, C-184/99.

152 CJEU, 19 September 2013, *Pensionsversicherungsanstalt v. Peter Brey*, C-140/12, § 77, 78.

153 CJEU, 11 November 2014, *Elisabeta Dano, Florin Dano v. Jobcenter Leipzig*, C-333/13.

154 Charles Edward O'sullivan, "Social Assistance for Economically-Inactive Citizens within the EU's 'Market State' Model", *Irish Journal of European Law*, No. 19(1), 2016, pp. 64–75.

citizenship[155] and that they lead to the paradoxical situation whereby "a Union citizen would only be entitled to social assistance if he [or she] has sufficient resources and therefore is not in need of any social assistance".[156]

Where the rights of non-EU citizens are concerned, the conditions established in the Reception Condition Directive entitle all applicants for international protection in the EU who are without adequate resources to "material reception conditions that provide an adequate standard of living for applicants, which guarantees their subsistence and protects their physical and mental health".[157] As far as non-EU long-term residents are concerned, equal treatment with country nationals is the rule, but national law can reduce social assistance to "core benefits" according to the Long-Term Residence Directive.[158] In the case of *Kamberaj*, the CJEU specified that it is the responsibility of national courts to determine whether housing benefits are to be considered core benefits and that, in determining this, consideration should be given to the objectives of the Directive in the light of the *purpose* of the principle set out in Article 34(3) of the CFR. It follows that "in so far as the benefit in question (…) fulfils the purpose set out in (…) article [34] of the Charter [that is 'to ensure a decent existence for all those who lack sufficient resources'], it cannot be considered, under EU law, as not being part of core benefits within the meaning of Article 11(4) of Directive 2003/109".[159] Finally, concerning irregular migrants, applicable EU legislation is limited to the harmonisation of return procedures and the rights of these people pending return or while in pre-deportation detention. Only in these limited circumstances – and only *pending* removal – are these migrants entitled to "emergency health care and essential treatment of illness".[160]

155 Dion Kramer, "Earning Social Citizenship in the European Union: Free Movement and Access to Social Assistance Benefits Reconstructed", *Cambridge Yearbook of European Legal Studies*, No. 18, 2016, pp. 270–301.

156 Sandra Mantu and Paul Minderhoud, "Social rights as a case of Europeanization through law – the role of CJEU jurisprudence", *Nijmegen Migration Law Working Papers Series*, No. 1, 2016, p. 11.

157 Directive 2013/33/EU of the European Parliament and of the Council of 26 June 2013 laying down standards for the reception of applicants for international protection (recast), OJ L 180, 29 June 2013, pp. 96–116, articles 17–20.

158 Council Directive 2003/109/EC of 25 November 2003 concerning the status of third-country nationals who are long-term residents, OJ L 16, 23 January 2004, pp. 44–53, Article 11 § 1.d. and 11 § 4.

159 C-571/10, *Kamberaj, cit.*, § 92.

160 Directive 2008/115/EC of the European Parliament and of the Council of 16 December 2008 on common standards and procedures in Member States for returning illegally staying third-country nationals, OJ L 348, 24 December 2008, pp. 98–107, Articles 14 and 16 (Return Directive).

This brings us to a few remarks on the absence of a right to free medical care for people in need within the EU framework. Indeed, the first sentence of Article 35 CFR indicates that "Everyone has the right of access to preventive health care and the right to benefit from medical treatment under the conditions established by national laws and practices".[161] As any CFR's standard, this norm compels EU institutions and member states when they implement EU law to a certain course of action and cannot extend EU legislative powers.[162] The organisation of health care is a subject matter for EU member states to regulate comprehensively, and Articles 6 and 168 of the Treaty on the Functioning of the EU (TFEU) establish that public health is a policy area in which the Union supports, complements or supplements the actions of member states.[163] As the EU lacks any hard competence on the realisation of the individual right to health, which is closely related to the right to free medical care for people who lack adequate resources, the CJEU has tended to declare its incompetence when Article 35 CFR has been employed to ground complaints regarding the individual right to health[164] by reaffirming an unbreakable link between the protection of rights and the power of implementing them.[165] Therefore, it is not surprising that in *Abdida*, when judging the legality of deporting an irregular third-country national with a serious illness from the EU to a third country, the CJEU grounded its judgement on Article 19(2) CFR (principle of non-refoulment) and secondary legislation[166] and failed to address the issue of the (in)compatibility of the domestic practice with Article 35 CFR on health care, even though the Advocate General had recommended doing so.[167]

---

161 CFR, *cit.*, Article 35.

162 CFR, *cit.,* Articles 51 and 52.

163 For further details, see: Janne Rothmar Herrmann and Brigit Toebes, "The European Union and Health and Human Rights", in Brigit Toebes *et al.*, *Health and Human Rights in Europe*, Cambridge, Intersentia, 2012, p. 51.

164 E.g.: CJEU, 17 July 2014, *Milica Široká v. Úrad verejného zdravotníctva Slovenskej republiky*, C-459/13; CJEU, 23 May 2011, *André Rossius and Marc Collard v. État belge – Service public fédéral Finances*, C-267/10 and C-268/2010; Cf. Francesco Bestagno, "La tutela della salute tra competenze dell'Unione europea e degli Stati membri", in Laura Pineschi (ed.), *La tutela della salute nel diritto internazionale ed europeo tra interessi globali e interessi particolari,* Napoli, Editoriale Scientifica, 2017, p. 141.

165 Olivier De Schutter, *cit.,* p. 9.

166 Including the Return Directive, *cit.*

167 CJEU, 18 December 2014, *Centre public d'action sociale d'Ottignies-Louvain-la-Neuve v. Moussa Abdida*, C-562/13, §§ 50, 63 and 64; cf. Opinion of Advocate General in *Abdida,*, 4 September 2014, §§ 12 and 155.

EU citizens, provided that they reside legally in another EU state,[168] have access to state-determined medical care without discrimination on the ground of nationality when they comply with conditions for regular residence.[169] People who are staying for a short period in another EU state but who have not moved their residence can avail themselves of the European Health Insurance Card to access health care, the cost of which will be reimbursed by their state of residence.[170] EU patients can also access cross-border medical care and have the costs reimbursed by their own health insurance scheme, provided that the conditions of Directive 2011/24/EU are met.[171]

This section demonstrates the constrained contribution of EU law to the conceptualisation and implementation of a universal right to social and medical assistance. In particular, unlike Article 13 ESC, the eligibility criteria for social assistance in EU law are not exclusively means-tested and need-based: the lack of sufficient resources (at a level equivalent to the social assistance threshold) and of a clearly defined comprehensive sickness insurance are conditions that prevent EU citizens from obtaining legal residence (and long-term residence status)[172] in states that are not their own and, consequently, limit their access to domestically-defined social assistance benefits. People have access to health benefits under the regulations in a given EU state, without discrimination on EU nationality, but there is no EU norm that guarantees the harmonisation of free medical care standards for people in need. The articles on social rights within the CFR have rarely been used by the CJEU, probably due to its reluctance to elaborate on normative principles in social matters that are outside the Union's competences.[173] The imbalance between civil and social rights in

168 According to Article 7 CRD, *cit.*, the right to stay for more than 3 months in another EU Country is conditioned upon having an economically active status or to possess sufficient resources and a comprehensive sickness insurance, so as not to become burdens on the social assistance system of the host state. Sandra Mantu and Paul Minderhoud, "Exploring the Links between Residence and Social Rights for Economically Inactive EU Citizens", *European Journal of Migration and Law*, no. 21, 2019, pp. 322–326, pointed out that the condition of having comprehensive medical insurance is overlooked and underdeveloped by both EU law and national practices.

169 CRD, *cit.*, Article 24.

170 European Commission, health cover for temporary stays, cf. <https://europa.eu/youreurope/citizens/health/unplanned-healthcare/temporary-stays/index_en.htm>.

171 Directive 2011/24/EU of the European Parliament and of the Council of 9 March 2011 on the application of patients' rights in cross-border healthcare, OJ L 88, 4 April 2011; Cf. Janne Rothmar Herrmann and Brigit Toebes, *cit.*

172 Sandra Mantu and Paul Minderhoud, *cit.*, pp. 326 and 334.

173 Consolidated version of the Treaty on the Functioning of the European Union, OJ C 326, 26 October 2012, Articles 4 § 2. b) and k), 153, 156 and 168; CFR, *cit.*, article 51 § 1 and 52 § 2.

the EU legal framework is also confirmed by the fact that the ECHR is recalled to define the scope and contribute to the interpretation of equivalent rights in the CFR; no similar reference is made to the ESC system (outside of being a source of inspiration for the CFR's social rights).[174] This can only lead to the conclusion that the protection of social rights within the EU legal framework, including the right to social and medical assistance, is not presumed to conform to the ESC.[175] Finally, it is worth mentioning that the EU Pillar on Social Rights – an initiative led by the EU Commission – has largely emphasised access to adequate health care and income support mechanisms for people in need.[176] These soft law guidelines recommend that states and EU institutions adopt measures, within their respective competences,[177] to grant everyone ("citizens and third country nationals with legal residence")[178] access to *affordable*, preventive and curative health care of good quality, long-term care, a minimum income, an income in old age, a pension, as well as housing and assistance for the homeless and "support for access to [essential] services (…) for those in need".[179] Considering the above reflections on the standards and trends in EU primary and secondary legislation as interpreted by the CJEU, it is still unclear what impact this soft law initiative might have on the right to social and medical assistance under the EU legal framework and whether it can push EU law towards a more synergic relationship with the ESC.[180]

C *International Instruments*

The universal system of human rights or international human rights law (IHRL) does not textually address any right to social and medical assistance; however, its normative content is derived from the right to social security, as interlinked with other social rights. The Universal Declaration of Human Rights (UDHR), which has an authoritative but aspirational nature, is built on the premise that

174 CFR, *cit.*, Article 52 § 3.
175 ECSR, *Confédération générale du travail* (CGT) *v. France*, Complaint No. 55/2009, decision on the merits of 23 June 2010, § 35. Emphasis added.
176 Cf. background, aims and documents of this EU initiative at <https://ec.europa.eu/commission/priorities/deeper-and-fairer-economic-and-monetary-union/european-pillar-social-rights_en>.
177 Commission Recommendation of 26 April 2017 on the European Pillar of Social Rights, C (2017) 2600 final, Preamble, § 12, 17–19.
178 Commission Recommendation EPSR, *cit.*, Preamble, § 15.
179 Commission Recommendation EPSR, *cit.*, Chapter III: Social protection and inclusion.
180 Ane Aranguiz and Miriam Quené, "Is There a Way Where There's a Will? The Tensions between the Court's Case Law and the Pillar in Delimiting Transnational Solidarity", *European Journal of Migration and Law*, No. 21, 2019, pp. 528–539; Olivier De Shutter, *cit.*, pp. 47–50.

"freedom from (...) want" should be eradicated and "social progress and better standards of life" be promoted and progressively achieved.[181] Article 22 UDHR establishes that "Everyone, as a member of society, has the right to social security and is entitled to realization (...) of the economic, social and cultural rights indispensable for his dignity and the free development of his [or her] personality". This instrumental conception of social security, including cash or in-kind benefits in response to certain listed contingencies or "other lack of livelihood"[182] for the realisation of people's basic socio-economic rights is also reflected in Article 25 UDHR on the "right to a standard of living adequate for one's health and well-being".

Article 9 of the International Covenant on Economic, Social and Cultural Rights (ICESCR), which is the shortest provision of this key United Nations treaty, simply establishes that states "recognize the right of everyone to social security, including social insurance". In terms of normative development, this provision of the ICESCR has long been underexplored. Indeed, it touches contentious political issues of resource allocation and redistribution which are difficult to harmonise on a global level.[183] Indeed, the general obligations of the Covenant, including obligations in the field of social security (broadly intended) are progressive in nature, requiring states to move as swiftly as possible, within the limits of available resources, towards the full realisation of the right to social security and all other rights contained in the ICESCR.[184] However, there is a strong presumption that "retrogressive measures taken in relation to the right to social security (...) are prohibited under the Covenant".[185] As far as social assistance is concerned, General Comment No. 19 of the Committee on Economic, Social and Cultural Rights (CESCR) – which is a soft law document prepared by the monitoring body of the Covenant which provides an authoritative interpretation of state obligations arising from Article 9 ICESCR – established that the scope of Article 9 goes beyond contingency-based, contributory or insurance-based (social security) schemes and that states "must establish non-contributory schemes or other social assistance measures to provide

181 UDHR, *cit.*, Preamble.
182 UDHR, *cit.*, Article 25.
183 Jennifer Tooze, "The Rights to Social Security and Social Assistance: Towards an Analytical Framework", in Mashood A. Baderin and Robert Mccorquodale (eds.), *Economic, Social and Cultural Rights in Action*, Oxford / New York, Oxford University Press, 2007, p. 331.
184 International Covenant on Economic, Social and Cultural Rights (adopted 16 December 1966 entry into force 3 January 1976) (ICESCR) UNGA Res 2200A (XXI), Article 2 § 1.
185 Committee on Economic Social and Cultural Rights (CESCR), general comment No. 19, The Right to Social Security (Article 9 ICESCR), E/C.12/GC/19, 4 February 2008, § 42.

support to those individuals and groups who are [in need of social protection and are] unable to make sufficient contributions for their own protection".[186]

While general state obligations arising out of the Covenant are progressive in nature, the CESCR identifies some *core obligations* that require the state to immediately "ensure the satisfaction of, at the very least, minimum essential levels of each of the rights enunciated in the Covenant".[187] Regarding social security and social assistance, state parties must ensure access to non-discriminatory schemes to "provide a minimum essential level of benefits to all individuals and families that will enable them to acquire at least essential health care, basic shelter and housing, water and sanitation, foodstuffs, and the most basic forms of education".[188] This demonstrates that the rights to social security and adequate standards of living and health are strongly integrated and interdependent.[189] General Comment No. 14 on the right to health also indicated that state core obligations include the duties to ensure "access to the minimum essential food (…) and access to basic shelter, housing and sanitation, and an adequate supply of safe and potable water".[190] These core obligations, read in conjunction with the principle of non-discrimination in the Covenant, led the CESCR to indicate that "States have a special obligation to provide those who do not have sufficient means with the necessary health insurance and health-care facilities".[191]

The "concluding observations" of the CESCR concerning the states belonging to the European region,[192] issued during the last 10 years, have raised serious concerns regarding the adequacy of the level of available social benefits, in particular social assistance programmes, to guarantee an adequate standard of living to poor people. The CESCR has recommended that a subsistence minimum should be guaranteed in all states and that methods of calculating the subsistence level and the level of social assistance be periodically reviewed

---

186 CESCR, gen. comm. 19, *cit.*, § 4 b); CESCR, dec., 4 March 2016, *Miguel Ángel López Rodríguez v. Spain* no. 1/2013, E/C.12/57/D/1/2013, § 10.4.

187 CESCR, General comment No. 3, the nature of States parties' obligations (art.2, para.1 of the Covenant), § 10, as recalled in CESCR, dec., 26 March 2018, *Trujillo Calero v. Ecuador* No. 10/2015, E/C.12/63/D/10/2015, § 11.2.

188 CESCR, gen. comm. 19, *cit.*, § 59 a) b); cf. similarly CESCR, Miguel Ángel López Rodríguez, *cit.*, § 10.3.

189 World Conference on Human Rights, Vienna Declaration and Programme of Action Vienna (12 July 1993) A/CONF.157/23, § 5.

190 CESCR, gen. comm. 14, *cit.*, § 43 b) c).

191 CESCR, gen. comm. 14, *cit.*, § 18, 19.

192 These findings constitute the outcome of a monitoring process on periodic state reports. Their function is overall equivalent to the 'conclusions' in the Charter's state reporting system.

and indexed to the real cost of living.[193] Several concerns have been raised on the limited coverage of certain programmes and on their unclear and hard-to-meet eligibility criteria, including strict resident requirements that disproportionally affect people who are most in need of assistance.[194] Furthermore, cases of discrimination on the basis of nationality and migration status regarding access to social benefits and health care in law and practice have been recommended for redress.[195]

To design the normative contours of the right to social security, the CESCR has often made reference to the legal and recommendatory standards developed by the International Labour Organization (ILO)[196] –the United Nations agency responsible for the advancement of international labour standards and for targeting social justice. While several ILO conventions have defined standards of social protection against traditional social risks and contingencies,[197] the ILO recommendation on the implementation of social protection floors applies to the area of social and medical assistance.[198] Indeed, the ILO must

193 CESCR, concl. obs.: Ukraine, 6 March 2020, E/C.12/63/D/10/2015, § 33; Denmark, 12 November 2019, E/C.12/DNK/CO/6, § 39 ;Bulgaria, 29 March 2019, E/C.12/BGR/CO/6, § 25; Germany, 27 November 2018, E/C.12/DEU/CO/6, §§ 46 and 47; Spain, 25 April 2018, E/C.12/ESP/CO/6, § 31; Cyprus, 28 October 2016, E/C.12/CYP/CO/6, §§ 29 and 30; the United Kingdom, 13 July 2016, E/C.12/GBR/CO/6, §§ 40 and 41; Italy, 28 October 2015, E/C.12/ITA/CO/5, §§ 35 and 46; Greece, 27 October 2015, E/C.12/GRC/CO/2, §§ 23 and 24; Finland, 17 December 2014, E/C.12/FIN/CO/6, § 20; Montenegro, 15 December 2014, E/C.12/MNE/CO/1, § 16; Slovenia, 14 December 2014, E/C.12/SVN/CO/2, §§ 18 and 23; Romania, 9 December 2014, E/C.12/ROU/CO/3–5, § 16; Portugal, Lithuania, 24 June 2014, E/C.12/LTU/CO/2, § 10; Czech Republic, 23 June 2014, E/C.12/CZE/CO/2, § 14.

194 CESCR, concl. obs.: Denmark, *cit.*, §§ 36 and 37; Bulgaria, *cit.*, §§ 27 and 28; Republic of Moldova, 19 October 2017, E/C.12/MDA/CO/3, § 40; Russian Federation, 16 October 2017, § 36; The Netherlands, 6 July 2017, E/C.12/NLD/CO/6, § 39; North Macedonia, 27 June 2016, E/C.12/MKD/CO/2–4; § 37; Ireland, 8 July 2015, E/C.12/IRL/CO/3, §§ 20 and 21; Slovenia, *cit.*, § 18; Romania, *cit.*, § 21.

195 CESCR, concl. obs.: Norway, 6 march 2020, E/C.12/NOR/CO/6, §§ 28 and 38; Switzerland, 18 November 2019, E/C.12/CHE/CO/4 § 39; Slovakia, E/C.12/SVK/CO/3, § 46; Denmark, *cit.*, § 62; Bulgaria, *cit.*, §§ 38 and 39; Germany, *cit.*, §§ 58 and 59; Cyprus, *cit.*, §§ 15 and 16; the United Kingdom, *cit.*, §§ 24 and 25; Italy, *cit.*, §§ 18 and 19; Greece, *cit.*, §§ 11 and 35; Finland, *cit.*, § 27; Romania, *cit.*, § 12; Serbia, 10 July 2014, E/C.12/SRB/CO/2, § 14; Czech Republic, *cit.*, § 15.

196 E.g., CESCR, gen. comm. 19, *cit.*

197 For example, see: ILC (ILO) C102, *cit.*; C118 Equality of Treatment (Social Security) Convention 1962; C130 Medical Care and Sickness Benefits Convention 1969; C157 Maintenance of Social Security Rights Convention 1982; C182 Maternity Protection Convention 2000.

198 International Labour Conference (International Labour Organization), Recommendation No. 202 concerning National Floors for Social Protection, 14 June 2012, 101st Session of the ILC, Record no. 14A.

contribute to "achiev[ing] (...) the extension of social security measures to provide a basic income to all in need of such protection and comprehensive medical care".[199] This recommendation marked the culmination of several years of international discussion[200] on the need to establish nationally defined "sets of basic social security guarantees which secure protection aimed at preventing or alleviating poverty, vulnerability and social exclusion", including basic income security and medical care for people in need.[201] Binding ILO conventions apply to social protection, while measures targeting social assistance are contained in the above-mentioned soft-law instrument. It is also worth mentioning that the United Nations' Agenda for Sustainable Development reaffirmed these basic social guarantees in its "no poverty" Goal No. 1, according to which states should "implement nationally appropriate social protection systems and measures for all, including floors, and by 2030 achieve substantial coverage of the poor and the vulnerable".[202] Regardless of the very authoritative nature of this agenda, social assistance is conceived as a goal for progressive realisation rather than an – at least partially – immediately enforceable human right. For the CESCR, the realisation of social protection floors is regarded as an essential element of the right to social security and a primary feature of a rights-based social protection mechanism, consistent with the aforementioned concept of core obligations regarding Article 9 ICESCR.[203]

Finally, the United Nations Special Rapporteurs on extreme poverty and human rights have greatly contributed to systematising state obligations concerning social protection (including, to use the Charter's terminology, social security and social and medical assistance) under a human rights-based approach (HRBA), as an essential part of a comprehensive approach to poverty reduction.[204] This includes distinguishing between progressive and core obligations and considering the centrality of the principles of non-discrimination

199 ILC (ILO), Declaration of Philadelphia concerning the aims and purposes of the International Labour Organisation, 10 May 1944, § III, letter f.

200 Philip Alston, "Report of the Special Rapporteur on extreme poverty and human rights. The implementation of the right to social protection through the adoption of social protection floors", A/69/297, 11 August 2014, p. 6.

201 ILC (ILO), Social Protection Floors Recommendation, *cit.*, Articles 2 and 5.

202 General Assembly of the United Nations, "Transforming Our World: The 2030 Agenda for Sustainable Development", UNGA Res 70/1, 25 September 2015, Goal 1.3.

203 CESCR, Statement, Social protection floors: an essential element of the right to social security and of the sustainable development goals, E/C.12/2015/1, 15 April 2015, §§ 1, 7 and 8.

204 This contribution is outlined in Magdalena Sepúlveda Carmona and Carly Nyst, *The Human Rights Approach to Social Protection*, Helsinki, Ministry of Foreign Affairs of Finland; Cf. also: Philip Alston, *cit.*

and equality in social protection systems and content-related and process-related obligations.[205] In brief, the United Nations' HRBA to the right to social protection entails developing and implementing adequately funded and legally based income support mechanisms that are accessible, adaptable, acceptable and adequate and that incorporate gender and vulnerability perspectives.[206] Further core requirements of a genuine HRBA to social security that can empower the "poor" include developing protection systems with the participation of key stakeholders and ensuring that eligibility criteria and related information are transparent and that states are fully accountable for their shortcomings in this field.[207]

Concluding Remarks

This commentary aimed at describing and assessing the unique features of Article 13 ESC within the broader context of human rights law. Indeed, this analysis has demonstrated that the legal frameworks of the ECHR and EU law, as interpreted by the ECtHR and the CJEU, respectively, do not currently compel states to realise and implement a free-standing right to social and medical assistance. A claim to receive financial assistance or necessary health care is unlikely to be successful before the ECtHR as this body has clarified that the Convention is applicable in the field of social protection only when people have a proprietary interest or when severe situations of socio-economic deprivation arise.[208] In the EU context, the provision of social benefits and health care are regulated at the domestic level, and EU law only intervenes to establish regimes for the acquisition of a right to equal treatment of individuals who settle, reside or work in an EU country of which they are not nationals, using the social provisions offered to that country's nationals as a reference standard. Entitlement to these benefits is normally linked to legal residence or an economically active status. As a result, economically inactive people do not hold a right to social assistance in the EU legal framework.[209]

---

205 CESCR, gen. com. 19, *cit.*, §§ 40–61; Magdalena Sepúlveda Carmona and Carly Nyst, *cit.*, pp. 11 and 32.

206 CESCR, gen. com. 19, *cit.*, §§ 11–32; Magdalena Sepúlveda Carmona and Carly Nyst, *cit.*, pp. 32–47.

207 CESCR, gen. com. 19, *cit.*, §§ 24, 26, 69, 70, 77–80; Magdalena Sepúlveda Carmona and Carly Nyst, *cit.*, pp. 54–62.

208 Cf. section II. A.

209 Cf. section II. B.

By ratifying the ESC and accepting Article 13 on the right to social and medical assistance, state parties assume the positive duty to provide *adequate* financial or in-kind assistance for people who are – or who may fall – below the poverty threshold. A right to free *necessary* medical care complements the provision of social benefits to meet people's basic needs. The practice of the ECSR consistently shows that the main eligibility condition is having insufficient resources to meet one's basic needs, which is calculated with reference to a periodically updated median equivalised income (per country) and, subsidiarily, using the relative poverty threshold (per country). Article 13 established a full-fledged human right that responds to the ethical concept of equity in service provision and realises human dignity by preventing people from falling below a certain standard of living that is linked to sufficiently clear and flexible indicators. Creating social protection and health care systems that are responsive to the needs of people who do not have adequate resources, without further qualifiers, such as having paid contributions or membership of a vulnerable group, is a state duty of an immediate nature under the Charter system.[210]

Under IHRL, which is applicable on a global scale, social protection (which encompasses social security and social and medical assistance) is a right to be realised progressively, but its core content –"a minimum essential level of benefits to all individuals and families that will enable them to acquire at least essential health care, basic shelter and housing, water and sanitation, foodstuffs, and the most basic forms of education"[211] – should be realised immediately, according to the authoritative but not binding CESCR's jurisprudence. Within this framework, core obligations generally correspond to the *emergency* assistance set out by the ECSR ("assistance to cope with an immediate state of need. For this purpose, accommodation, food, emergency medical care and clothing"),[212] except for the reference to "essential health care". International monitoring activities indicate that social benefits should be set at a level that guarantees at least a subsistence minimum and should be progressively increased to ensure an adequate standard of living.[213]

Considering the limited personal scope of the ESC (even when extended by the jurisprudence of the ECSR),[214] IHRL would appear to provide more generous standards regarding the health care of non-residents and non-nationals: members of these groups (including irregular migrants) should have

210 Cf. section I. A. 1.

211 Cf. for instance: CESCR, gen. comm. No. 19, *cit.*, § 59 a) b).

212 Cf. for instance, ECSR, *FEANTSA*, *cit.*, § 171.

213 Cf. section II. C.

214 ECSR, *FIDH v. France*, *cit.* § 32; ECSR, *CEC v. the Netherlands*, *cit.*, §§ 66 and 122.

affordable access to *essential* health care (including preventive, primary and emergency care) under IHRL,[215] while the Charter refers to *emergency* care, although it stipulates that urgent needs "must not be interpreted too narrowly".[216] Outside these circumstances, the detailed conceptualisation of the right to social and medical assistance and the empowering level of benefits of the Charter system (via statements of interpretation, conclusions, and decisions) is difficult to find in other international legal frameworks. Articles 13 ESC (which require the establishment of a baseline safety net for everyone who is without adequate resources and the provision of empowering services that prevent or alleviate personal want) and Article 30 ESC (the right to protection against poverty and social exclusion) combine immediate core duties with the progressive realisation of those conditions that target the underlying causes of poverty via intersectoral measures.[217] While the organic and interdependent relationship between the provisions of the Charter prevents normative floors from becoming ceilings of social rights protection,[218] the contextual interpretation of the ESC, in line with the most contemporary HRBA to social rights, has facilitated the development, in social and medical assistance litigation, of arguments centred on dignity, universality and vulnerability.[219]

---

215 CESCR, gen. com. 19, *cit.*, § 37. Cf. Stefano Angeleri, 'The Impact of the Economic Crisis on the Right to Health of Irregular Migrants, as Reflected in the Jurisprudence of the UN Committee on Economic, Social and Cultural Rights', *European Journal of Migration and Law*, 19(2), 2017, pp. 165–190.

216 Cf. for instance: ECSR, *FEANTSA*, *cit.*, § 171.

217 Philip Alston, *cit.*, p. 9; Cf. for instance: ECSR, EUROCEF, *cit.*, §§ 181–183.

218 On the 'floors / ceiling' discussion regarding core socio-econimc rights. Cf. Audrey R. Chapman and Sage Russel (eds), *Core Obligations: Building a Framework for Economic, Social and Cultural Rights*, Intersentia NV, Mortsel, 2002, p. 9.

219 ECSR, *DCI v. The Netherlands*, *cit.*, § 35; ECSR, *DCI v. Belgium*, *cit.*, §§ 29, 33 and 36; ECSR, *CEC v. the Netherlands*, *cit.*, §§ 68 and 74.

ARTICLE 14

The Right to Benefit from Social Welfare Services

Nikolaos A. Papadopoulos

With a view to ensuring the effective exercise of the right to benefit from social welfare services, the Parties undertake:

1 to promote or provide services which, by using methods of social work, would contribute to the welfare and development of both individuals and groups in the community, and to their adjustment to the social environment;

2 to encourage the participation of individuals and voluntary or other organisations in the establishment and maintenance of such services.

Introduction

Article 14 of the European Social Charter (ESC, or Charter) is one of the articles originally contained in the ESC of 1961[1] that was not amended during the revision of the Treaty in 1996 (Revised ESC).[2] It recognises a unique right that has its own specific content and purpose. Through the recognition of the right to benefit from social welfare services under Article 14, the ESC requires the Contracting Parties to not only promote but also to provide and guarantee the effectiveness of an organised set of social protection services for individuals and groups of people, by methods of social work. The objective is for these services to contribute to the welfare and development of individuals in a situation of vulnerability, thereby ensuring personal autonomy and minimising the threat of dependency and marginalisation.

Article 14 is closely linked with several Charter provisions which, together, form a guide not only for social policy in general or for national social policy but, in particular, for "a common European social policy".[3] However, although the European Committee of Social Rights (ECSR, or Committee), the Charter's

1 European Social Charter of 1961 (entered into force on 26 February 1965) (CETS No. 35).

2 Revised European Social Charter of 1996 (entered into force on 1 July 1999) (CETS No. 163).

3 Council of Europe, European Social Charter, Collected (provisional) edition of the *travaux préparatoires*, vol. I, 1953–1954, p. 46.

 | DOI:10.1163/9789004434141_005

monitoring body, has over the years elaborated in detail on the content of Article 14 through its "jurisprudence" under the Reporting Procedure, there still appears to exist some confusion and uncertainty as to its actual scope and significance. This conclusion is amplified by the fact that, with very few exceptions, Article 14 has not received particular attention from complainant organisations under the Collective Complaints Procedure.[4] As a result, it appears that the true potential of the right to benefit from social welfare services for the social protection systems of the States Parties remains somewhat underdeveloped.

Against this background, this chapter first provides a general presentation of the content and purpose of Article 14 of the Charter. It looks in particular into the drafting history of Article 14 and compares it with relevant international standards. In addition, it distinguishes its protective scope from other relevant ESC provisions. Thereafter, the chapter brings forward the interpretive work on Article 14 by the ECSR, which has concretised the commitments of States Parties and has provided substance and impetus to the right to benefit from social welfare services, as well as its enforceability. The study concludes by drawing pertinent conclusions as to the role and significance of Article 14 for the protection of economic and social rights across Europe.

1 General Presentation

It is important to point out, as a preliminary remark, that, unlike the European Convention on Human Rights (ECHR, or Convention)[5] or other human rights treaties, the ESC presents a unique characteristic, which it has borrowed from certain International Labour Organization (ILO) Conventions.[6] It allows any State that ratifies the Treaty the option to not accept and ratify all its provisions, but to exclude some of them.[7] This possibility of an "*à la carte*" or "pick and choose" acceptance of the ESC provisions was intended to be a temporary means to make it easier for some States to adapt their acceptance of the

4 Additional Protocol to the European Social Charter Providing for a System of Collective Complaints, 9 November 1995 (CETS No. 158).

5 European Convention for the Protection of Human Rights and Fundamental Freedoms of 1950 (CETS No. 5).

6 See Stein Evju, "The European Social Charter and the International Labour Organisation – Interlinks Past and Present", in Wolfgang Däubler and Reingard Zimmer (eds.), *Arbeitsvölkerrecht. Festschrift für Klaus Lörcher*, Baden-Baden, Nomos, 2013, pp. 146–153.

7 See Part III, Article A of the Revised ESC (and the corresponding Part III, Article 20 of the ESC of 1961).

Charter to their own capacities, considering the existing differences in economic and social structures among European countries. Evidently, this practice of selective acceptance leads to a non-uniform application of the ESC and has been criticised for being one of the ESC's structural weaknesses – being at odds with the principle of indivisibility of human rights. Nonetheless, it has greatly facilitated the accession of many Council of Europe countries to the Charter.[8]

The minimum number of articles or paragraphs of Part II of the Charter that a State acceding to the Revised ESC must necessarily select and accept in their entirety is 16 articles (and 10 in the case of the ESC of 1961) or 63 paragraphs (and 45 in the case of the ESC of 1961). At the same time, each State, by acceding to the Charter, must accept at least six of the nine articles which, in the opinion of the drafters of the Charter, belong to the hard core of the rights it establishes (Articles 1, 5, 6, 7, 12, 13, 16, 19 and 20). Nevertheless, an examination of the provisions accepted by each of the Contracting Parties shows that the vast majority of States accept far more commitments than are necessary to satisfy the Treaty's requirements.[9]

Article 14, in particular, may be considered a widely accepted ESC article by Contracting Parties, even though it does not belong to the hard core of the articles that States are required to accept. Forty-two out of the 46 Council of Europe Member States have ratified either the ESC of 1961 or the Revised ESC.[10] Among those 42 Member States, 36 have accepted being bound by both paragraphs of Article 14 of the Charter,[11] while two Member States have accepted

8 The ECSR has, through the object-and-purpose interpretation of the ESC under Article 31 § 1 of the Vienna Convention on the Law of Treaties of 1969 (1155 UNTS 331) and through a holistic approach of the ESC's – interconnected and sometimes overlapping – provisions, attempted to mitigate the negative impact of the procedure's '*à la carte*' nature. See on this: Peggy Ducoulombier, "La liberté des États parties à la Charte sociale européenne dans le choix de leur engagement: une liberté surveillée", *Revue trimestrielle des droits de l'homme*, no. 96, 2013, pp. 829–857.

9 Olivier De Schutter and Matthias Sant'ana, "The European Committee of Social Rights (the ECSR)", in Gauthier De Beco (ed.), *Human Rights Monitoring Mechanisms of the Council of Europe*, Oxfordshire, Routledge, 2012, pp. 71–99, p. 75.

10 Switzerland and Lichtenstein have only signed the ESC of 1961. San Marino and Monaco have only signed the Revised ESC.

11 Andorra, Austria, Azerbaijan, Belgium, Bosnia and Herzegovina, Bulgaria, Croatia (has ratified only the ESC of 1961), Czech Republic (has ratified only the ESC of 1961), Cyprus, Denmark (has ratified only the ESC of 1961), Estonia, Finland, France, Georgia, Germany, Greece, Hungary, Iceland (has ratified only the ESC of 1961), Ireland, Italy, Latvia, Lithuania, Luxembourg (has ratified only the ESC of 1961), Malta, Montenegro, Netherlands, Norway, Portugal, Serbia, Slovakia, Slovenia, Spain, Sweden, Türkiye, Ukraine, United Kingdom (has ratified only the ESC of 1961).

being bound by one of its paragraphs.[12] Four Member States have not accepted being bound by Article 14 of the Charter.[13]

As with most of the Articles of Part II of the Revised ESC, Article 14 begins with the words "[w]ith a view to ensuring the effective exercise" of the right enshrined therein, before expressing that States "undertake" to do something. Therefore, the use of the word "effectiveness" in the operative part of the Charter seems to refer to the exercise of a right – here the right to benefit from social welfare services – that exists in reality, and to the guarantee that the obligations arising therefrom are intended to ensure that a given right will have an impact on reality.[14]

However, the obligations that stem from Article 14 of the Charter should not be considered as pointing to a set of social security or social assistance benefits but rather to a social protection subsystem.[15] This is exemplified by the structure of Article 14, which is formulated as more of an individual right rather than as a social benefit or a merely programmatic principle of the Contracting Parties' welfare policy. On the other hand, we cannot speak of a fully enforceable individual right to benefit from social welfare services, as the wording of Article 14 provides a rather wide mandate and offers different options (§ 1: "promote or provide services" [...] § 2: "encourage the participation") to the public authorities of the Contracting Parties for its implementation. Rather,

12 Armenia has accepted only Article 14 § 2 and Poland has accepted only Article 14 § 1 of the Charter. In its latest report on the non-accepted provisions of the ESC in Armenia, the ECSR stated there were no obstacles to the acceptance of Article 14 § 1 by Armenia. There is no available report on the non-accepted provisions of the ESC in Poland on the European Social Charter country profiles web page, at: https://www.coe.int/en/web/european-social-charter/country-profiles.

13 Albania, North Macedonia, Moldova and Romania. In its latest reports on the non-accepted provisions of the ESC in these four countries, the ECSR has considered that Albania, Moldova and Romania could accept both paragraphs of Article 14. Albania must however aim at increasing the quality and quantity of social services, whereas Romania must take measures to improve the mechanisms for supervising the adequacy of services, as well as the data collection mechanisms in relation to Article 14. The ECSR has invited North Macedonia to continue its consideration of Article 14 with a view to its possible acceptance in the near future.

14 Julien Betaille, *Les conditions juridiques de l'effectivité de la norme en droit public interne, illustrations en droit de l'urbanisme et en droit de l'environnement*, PhD thesis, Université de Limoges, 2012, pp. 23–24.

15 Cristóbal Molina Navarette, "Derecho a los beneficios de los servicios sociales: Articulo 14 de la Carta Social Europea", in Cristina Monereo Atienza and José Luis Monereo Pérez (eds.), *La garantía multinivel de los derechos fundamentales en el Consejo de Europa: el Convenio Europeo de Derechos Humanos y la Carta Social Europea*, Granada, Editorial Comares, 2017, pp. 669–681, p. 673.

Article 14 requires and is conditioned upon the co-ordinated actions and policies of each Contracting Party to give effect to its content through legislative, regulatory or other appropriate means.[16] In addition, Article 14 does not foresee an exclusive State obligation to provide free access to welfare services but is based upon the need for public-private cooperation, in which individual and voluntary or other organisations participate in the establishment and maintenance of such services.

Furthermore, unlike other ESC provisions, Article 14 is of a "horizontal nature" insofar as it includes everyone (who is in an exclusionary or difficult situation) within its personal scope and not only specific groups of people who lack adequate resources or are in a vulnerable situation (e.g. children, women, persons with disabilities, migrant workers, or older persons).[17] This conclusion is confirmed by the declaratory Part I of the Charter, which lays down in an abstract way the rights enshrined in the Charter and precedes Part II which is binding. According to the *travaux préparatoires* of the Charter, Part I of the Treaty was also regarded during the negotiations as a preamble in itself or, more precisely, as a continuum to the preamble, because it is a declaration of social policy principles and objectives.[18] As a result, it may guide the interpretation of the rights listed in Part II of the Charter.[19] Therefore, Article 14 of the operative Part II of the Charter should be read together with § 14 of Part I, according to which "Everyone has the right to benefit from social welfare services". However, in light of the well-known limitations of the Charter's scope

16 See Article I, § 1 of Part V of the Revised ESC that is entitled "Implementation of the undertakings given". See on this Evelyne Schmid, "Part V, Art I – Implementation of the undertakings given", in Academic Network on the European Social Charter And Social Rights *et al.* (eds.), *The European Social Charter: A Commentary* (forthcoming), Leiden, Brill/Nijhoff Academic Publishers, 2024, available at <https://serval.unil.ch/resource/serval:BIB_A6B49C5487E2.P001/REF>.

17 Katarzyna Dunaj and Joanna Ryszka, "The Protection of Vulnerable People in the Charter System", in Stefano Angeleri and Carole Nivard (eds.), *The European Social Charter: A Commentary*, vol. 1, *Cross-cutting Themes*, Leiden, Brill/Nijhoff Academic Publishers, 2022, pp. 319–348, p. 341.

18 Nikolaos A. Papadopoulos, "Revisiting the Preamble of the European Social Charter: Paper Tiger or Blessing in Disguise?", *Human Rights Law Review*, vol. 22, issue 1, 2022, pp. 1–21, p. 5.

19 Olivier De Schutter, "The Two Lives of the European Social Charter", in Jean-Yves Carlier, Olivier De Schutter and Marc Verdussen (eds.), *The European Social Charter: A Social Constitution for Europe*, Cheltenham, Edward Elgar Publishing, 2010, pp. 11–37, p. 15–16; Albert Bleckmann, "Interprétation et application en droit interne de la Charte sociale européenne, notamment du droit de grève", *Cahiers de droit européen*, no. 4, 1967, pp. 388–412, p. 389.

ratione personae,[20] it should be concluded, under a textual interpretation, that only nationals of States that are Parties to the Treaty and foreigners lawfully resident (i.e. authorised to enter and reside) or working regularly (i.e. authorised to enter and work) within the territory of those States are entitled (under the same conditions as nationals) to the right to benefit from social welfare services; this interpretation excludes unlawfully residing migrants.[21]

A *Drafting History*

According to the preparatory work on the ESC of 1961, the "right to social and cultural aid and guidance", as the right to benefit from social welfare services was provisionally called at the time, was not recognised in a separate article. Rather, it comprised part of the old Article 13, which was entitled "social services" and related to the problem of the social and cultural adaptation of the individual and the family to conditions resulting from mechanisation and industrialisation.[22] The objective of the ESC in that regard was to protect the economically weak and establish social services in all fields where, due to modern economic and social conditions, individual and family resources were not adequate.[23] In addition, the underlying idea was the need to set up, on both a national and a local scale, general assistance and guidance services – rather than welfare benefits – which would be accessible to every individual and family and would help them to manage their way through the maze of administrative and other bodies acting within their own specific field of social life.[24]

20 The Charter's Appendix (§ 1) reads: "Without prejudice to Article 12, paragraph 4, and Article 13, paragraph 4, the persons covered by Articles 1 to 17 and 20 to 31 include foreigners only in so far as they are nationals of other Parties lawfully resident or working regularly within the territory of the Party concerned, subject to the understanding that these articles are to be interpreted in the light of the provisions of Articles 18 and 19". According to Claudio Panzera, during the drafting of the ESC of 1961, "social protection of foreigners was deemed to be a matter of real importance only in so far they had established a deep and durable linkage within that territory". Claudio Panzera, "The Personal Scope of the European Social Charter: Questioning Equality", *Revista Europea de Derechos Fundamentales*, vol. 24, 2014, pp. 51–73, p. 55.

21 Bige Açimuz and Olgun Akbulut, "The Values Underlying the European Social Charter", in Stefano Angeleri and Carole Nivard, *cit.*, pp. 264–292, p. 285.

22 Council of Europe, European Social Charter, Collected (provisional) edition of the travaux préparatoires, vol. III, 1956, p. 434.

23 Council of Europe, European Social Charter, Collected (provisional) edition of the travaux préparatoires, vol. I, 1953–1954, p. 46.

24 Council of Europe, European Social Charter, Collected (provisional) edition of the travaux préparatoires, vol. IV, 1957, p. 127.

The governments of the United Kingdom and the Federal Republic of Germany saw no purpose in the ESC containing a general provision on social services, since social services were already specifically covered within the context of other rights. The governments of the Netherlands and Denmark, on the other side, were in favour of a general provision, while the government of Belgium was of the view that social services should come under the section on social security. Eventually, in the draft text of 1959, Article 14 was included as an independent article, taking a universal approach, highlighting the need for efficiency and equal access by everyone to social welfare services through methods of social work.[25] This choice was based on the fact that a more economics-driven perspective was finally adopted with respect to Article 13, which enshrines the right to social and medical assistance but only addresses those without, or at risk of becoming persons without adequate resources.

B *Relevant International Standards*

Article 14 of the Charter contains a unique and autonomous set of provisions enshrining the right to benefit from social welfare services, that fall under the scope of the modern macro-concept "social protection", rather than the classic concept of "social security and social assistance".[26] Remarkably, there is no equivalent article to Article 14 of the Charter in other legally binding universal or regional treaties, which provide only for the latter concept.

Such examples are ILO Convention No. 102 of 1952, known as the Social Security (Minimum Standards) Convention,[27] and the Council of Europe's European Convention on Social and Medical Assistance of 1953[28] and European Code of Social Security of 1964.[29] Similarly, the International Covenant on Economic, Social and Cultural Rights (ICESCR)[30] of the United Nations only recognises, in Article 9, the right of everyone to social security, including social insurance,[31] while the Charter of Fundamental Rights of the European Union

25 Karin Lukas, *The Revised European Social Charter: An Article by Article Commentary*, Cheltenham, Edward Elgar Publishing, 2021, p. 187.

26 Cristóbal Molina Navarette, *cit.*, p. 673.

27 Sixty-three States have ratified the Social Security (Minimum Standards) Convention of the ILO, 32 of which are Member States of the Council of Europe.

28 Eighteen Members States of the Council of Europe have ratified the European Convention on Social and Medical Assistance (CETS No. 14), most in the 1950s and 1960s.

29 Twenty-one Members States of the Council of Europe have ratified the European Code of Social Security (CETS No. 48).

30 International Covenant on Economic, Social and Cultural Rights of 1966 (993 UNTS 3).

31 See also the relevant interpretation of the Committee on Economic, Social and Cultural Rights (General Comment No. 19: The right to social security (Art. 9), 4 February 2008, E/C.12/GC/19).

(CFREU)[32] only includes, in Article 34, the right to social security and social assistance.[33] Although the CFREU makes mention of social services in Article 34 § 1,, these concern typical complementary benefits to social security. This conclusion is confirmed by the fact that, unlike Articles 12, 13, 30 and 31 of the Revised ESC, Article 14 of the ESC is not mentioned in the Explanation on Article 34 of the CFREU.[34]

Furthermore, as noted by Karin Lukas, the relevant case law of the Court of Justice of the European Union only concerns specific aspects of the system of national welfare services that fall under the scope of Article 13 of the ESC (the right to social and medical assistance), rather than Article 14.[35] This is also the case with respect to the case law of the European Court of Human Rights (ECtHR), when it broadly interprets Articles 2 (right to life), 3 (prohibition of torture), 6 (right to a fair trial), 8 (right to respect for private and family life) and 14 (prohibition of discrimination) of the ECHR, as well as Article 1 of the 1st Addition Protocol to the Convention[36] (right to property), to extend their applicability to many cases within the social security and social assistance sphere.[37]

C *Relationship with Other ESC Provisions*

Article 14 is closely interconnected with several Charter provisions, forming together the social policy of the ESC, which aims to facilitate the equal access of every member of society to a coherent system of social protection that matches their personal situation and social traditions, to reduce the risk of marginalisation and to alleviate poverty.[38] These provisions are, primarily, the right to social and medical assistance under Article 13[39] and the right to social

---

32 European Union, Charter of Fundamental Rights of the European Union, 26 October 2012, OJ C 326/02.

33 As is likewise the case with Article 10 of the European Community Charter of the Fundamental Social Rights of Workers of 1989.

34 European Union, Explanations relating to the Charter of Fundamental Rights, OJ C 303, 14.12.2007, pp. 17–35.

35 Karin Lukas, *cit.*, p. 200.

36 Protocol to the Convention for the Protection of Human Rights and Fundamental Freedoms of 1952 (CETS No. 9).

37 See e.g.: Ingrid Leijten, *Core Socio-Economic Rights and the European Court of Human Rights*, Cambridge, Cambridge University Press, 2018, pp. 233 ff.

38 ECSR, General Introduction to Conclusions XIV-1, p. 53.

39 See María Dalli, "The Content and Potential of the Right to Social Assistance in Light of Article 13 of the European Social Charter", *European Journal of Social Security*, vol. 22, issue 1, 2020, pp. 3–23.

security under Article 12,[40] which relate to the social benefits system of non-contributory, contributory or mixed nature.

In particular, Article 14 plays the role of the more general article in the field of social services, while Articles 13 § 1 and § 3 are the more specific (and narrow) provisions, concerning, respectively, the entitlement of persons without adequate resources to adequate assistance, including care in case of sickness, and to advice and personal help in order to prevent, to remove, or to alleviate personal or family want. Article 13 § 3 and Article 14 § 1 also have close ties with the right to protection against poverty and social exclusion under Article 30 (of the Revised ESC), which shares the same purpose but differs in technique.[41]

In fact, the ECSR had to deal with the delicate problem of interpretation that arose from the possible overlap between Article 14 and Article 13 § 3, given the "*à la carte*" nature of the Charter's acceptance procedure.[42] In the view of the Committee, Article 13 § 3 is much more restricted, as it concerns only a specific form of social welfare service (advice, in particular about the existence of various forms of assistance, and personal help) for persons without, or liable to be without, adequate resources. Article 14, on the other hand, is much broader in its application, as it concerns social welfare services in general and addresses all persons. This differentiation could be explained by the fact that Article 14 is one of the ESC articles that seeks "to give scope to the individual" in highly developed societies, rather than to remedy a need, which is the general objective of Article 13.[43]

Therefore, the manner in which the Contracting Parties implement the two provisions needs to be assessed separately. On the basis of this assessment, a Contracting Party could be deemed to be complying with the requirements of Article 14, even if its social services do not meet all the requirements of Article 13 § 3. Conversely, complying with Article 13 § 3 does not necessarily mean that the requirements of Article 14 are fulfilled.[44] In countries where the services under Article 13 § 3 are part of the general social services, the ECSR makes its assessment of the situation under Article 14 § 1, as long as these services are provided free of charge.[45]

---

40 George Katrougalos, "Social Security in the 'Case Law' of the Social Rights Committee", in Frans Pennings and Gijsbert Vonk (eds.), *Research Handbook on European Social Security Law*, Cheltenham, Edward Elgar Publishing, 2015, pp. 84–102.

41 Cristóbal Molina Navarette, *cit.*, p. 673.

42 Council of Europe, Social Protection in the European Social Charter, Social Charter Monographs No. 7, Council of Europe Publishing, 1999, p. 105.

43 ECSR, Conclusions I, p. 75.

44 ECSR, Conclusions I (1969), Statement of Interpretation of Article 13.

45 ECSR, Conclusions 2009, Statement of Interpretation of Article 14 § 1.

Secondarily, the right to benefit from social welfare services under Article 14 relates to but is distinct from other "social protection rights" that are enshrined in the Charter, which directly address specific vulnerable groups of people. These are, in particular, persons with disabilities under Article 15, family members under Article 16, children and young persons under Article 17, migrant workers and their families under Article 19, elderly persons under Article 23 and homeless persons under Article 31. To protect vulnerable groups of people, States have the obligation to draw up strategic objectives on the basis of relevant indicators and criteria, as well as to make choices regarding public spending to make sure that sufficient resources are devoted to social welfare.[46] According to the ECSR, issues such as childcare, services for the elderly, social housing services, or measures to combat homelessness are dealt with under the above-mentioned articles and not under Article 14 of the Charter.[47] Under Article 14, the Committee reviews the overall availability of such services and refers to those other articles for the detailed analysis of the services afforded.[48] When a State Party has not accepted these articles, then the ECSR assesses the situation for the specific groups of people under Article 14.[49]

II Interpretation by the ECSR

The Conclusions of the ECSR under the Reporting Procedure and its Decisions under the Collective Complaints Procedure have played an indispensable role in the interpretation of the Charter provisions. There has been a theoretical debate on whether the ECSR is given the exclusive competence by the Treaty and its additional protocols to interpret the ESC provisions or whether, according to the starting point under international law, only those Parties that have the power to amend a treaty may give an authoritative interpretation of the treaty.[50] Admittedly, there is no provision in the Charter similar to Article 32 ECHR, which explicitly confers on the ECtHR the competence to interpret and apply the Convention.

46 Katarzyna Dunaj and Joanna Ryszka, *cit.*, p. 344.

47 ECSR, Conclusions XII-1, General Introduction, 5.11 social services; Conclusions 2005, Bulgaria, Article 14; *The Central Association of Carers in Finland v. Finland*, complaint No. 71/2011, decision on the merits of 4 December 2012, § 55.

48 ECSR, Conclusions 2005, Statement of Interpretation of Article 14 § 1.

49 ECSR, Conclusions 2009, Statement of Interpretation of Article 14 § 1.

50 Joanna Harrington, "The Human Rights Committee, Treaty Interpretation, and the Last Word", EJIL: Talk! 5 August 2015, available at <https://www.ejiltalk.org/the-human-rights-committee-treaty-interpretation-and-the-last-word/>.

However, the ECSR has been given an express and comparably clear mandate by the ESC's drafters to ascertain, from a legal standpoint, whether Contracting Parties are complying with the Treaty's provisions.[51] Furthermore, States Parties have explicitly accepted that competence of the Committee. Therefore, by accepting the ESC's monitoring system and cooperating with the ECSR, States have also accepted the power of the Treaty's monitoring body to interpret the Treaty in order to assess State compliance with the Charter provisions.[52] As a result, although there is no provision in the ESC explicitly establishing an interpretive monopoly for the ECSR, the Charter and its additional protocols require the Committee to engage in a legal interpretation of the various provisions in order to assess State compliance. They thus confer great authority on the Committee and its pronouncements.

In that context, as best depicted by Stein Evju, "just as the vague notions of the ECHR [e.g. 'private and family life' or 'freedom of thought, conscience and religion'] cannot be applied without awareness of ECtHR case law, the ESC provisions cannot be properly appreciated without knowledge of ECSR case law".[53] As a result, the Committee, with its authoritative interpretation, gives normative content and precise meaning to the Charter provisions, even when they may at first seem vague and imprecise,[54] and helps the understanding of individual rights to emerge from the wording of the Charter provisions.[55]

For example, as remarked by Martin Scheinin, the Committee in its first set of Conclusions in 1982 had already asserted, despite the seemingly abstract

51 See Article 24 § 2 of the Amending Protocol reforming the supervisory mechanism, 21 October 1991 (CETS No. 142) and Article 12 of the Additional Protocol providing for a system of collective complaints, 9 November 1995 (CETS No. 158).

52 See Petros Stangos, "Challenges and reasons for reforming the collective complaints procedure of the European Committee of Social Rights – Towards a 'third life' of the European Social Charter?", *Epitheoressis Ergatikou Dikeou*, vol. 79, issue 10, 2020, pp. 1193–1214; Antonis Bredimas, "The 'decisions' of quasi-judicial bodies on human rights and their place in the domestic legal order of states", *Nomiko Vima*, vol. 66, issue 3, 2019, pp. 417–426, p. 422 (both in Greek).

53 Stein Evju, "Application by Domestic Courts of the European Social Charter", *Nordic Journal of Human Rights*, vol. 28, no. 3–4, 2010, pp. 401–421, p. 413.

54 See on this: Jean-François Akandji-Kombé, "La justiciabilité des droits sociaux et de la Charte sociale européenne n'est pas une utopie", in Jean-François Akandji-Kombé (ed.), *L'homme dans la société internationale: Mélanges en hommage au professeur Paul Tavernier*, Brussels, Bruylant, 2013, pp. 475–503, p. 487; Patrick Wachsmann, *Les droits de l'homme*, 5th ed., Paris, Dalloz, 2008, p. 58; Carole Nivard, *La justiciabilité des droits sociaux: étude de droit conventionnel européen*, Brussels, Bruylant, 2012, pp. 187–188.

55 Gisella Gori, "Domestic Enforcement of the European Social Charter: The Way Forward", in Gráinne De Búrca and Bruno De Witte (eds.), *Social Rights in Europe*, Oxford, Oxford University Press, 2005, pp. 69–88, p. 82.

and programmatic wording of Article 13 § 1 of the ESC, enshrining the right to social and medical assistance, that it conferred an individual right that is enforceable in court.[56] The Committee has also interpreted several other ESC provisions as giving rise to individual rights,[57] among which is Article 14. In particular, according to the ECSR, "Article 14 provides for an individual right ['subject to an effective right of appeal'[58]], for all persons who find themselves in a dependent situation to benefit from services using methods of social work".

It should be noted, generally, that contrary to the ICESCR, which explicitly recognises and regards the principle of progressive realisation and resource availability as fundamental,[59] the text of the ESC (including its preamble and protocols) does not explicitly refer to this principle.[60] Nevertheless, the ECSR has deduced the principle of progressive realisation of economic and social rights from a conjunctive reading of the Charter's preambular paragraphs, thus bringing the Charter closer to the ICESCR in that respect.[61] In particular, the ECSR has shown its willingness to give full consideration to the principle of progressive realisation and resource availability only "when it is exceptionally complex and expensive to secure one of the rights protected by the Revised Charter".[62] In that case, in the view of the Committee,

> the measures taken by the State to achieve the Revised Charter's aims must fulfil the following three criteria: (i) a reasonable timeframe, (ii) a measurable progress, and (iii) a financing consistent with the maximum use of available resources.[63]

---

56 Martin Scheinin, "Economic, Social and Cultural Rights as Legal Rights", in Asbjørn Eide, Catarina Krause and Allan Rosas (eds.), *Economic, Social, and Cultural Rights: A Textbook*, 2nd rev. ed., Leiden, Martinus Nijhoff Publishers, 2001, pp. 29–54, p. 43–45; See also Stein Evju, "Application by Domestic Courts", *cit.*, p. 406.

57 See e.g. the following Revised ESC provisions: Article 1 § 2; Article 2; Article 4 § 2, § 3, § 4 and § 5; Article 5; Article 6 § 3 and § 4; Article 7; Article 17; Article 19 § 6 and § 8; Article 20; Article 24; Article 25; Article 28; and Article 31 § 1. See also: Gisella Gori, *cit.*, p. 83.

58 ECSR, *International Federation for Human Rights (FIDH) v. Belgium*, complaint No. 75/2011, decision on the merits of 18 March 2013, § 105.

59 See Article 2, § 1 of Part II of the ICESCR, as well as the fifth recital of the preamble of the Optional Protocol to the ICESCR.

60 Olivier De Schutter and Matthias Sant'ana, *cit.*, pp. 76–77.

61 ECSR, *Centre on Housing Rights and Evictions (COHRE) v. Italy*, complaint No. 58/2009, decision on the merits of 25 June 2010, § 27.

62 ECSR, *Mental Disability Advocacy Centre (MDAC) v. Bulgaria*, complaint No. 41/2007, decision on the merits of 3 June 2008, § 39.

63 ECSR, *European Roma Rights Centre v. Bulgaria*, complaint No. 31/2005, decision on the merits of 18 October 2006, § 37; *Autism-Europe v. France*, complaint No. 13/2000, decision on the merits of 4 November 2003, § 53.

Furthermore, according to the Committee, States "enjoy a margin of appreciation in determining the steps to be taken to ensure compliance with the Charter, in particular as regards the choices which must be made in terms of priorities and resources".[64] In order to comply with the Charter, a number of assessment criteria must be fulfilled:

> States Parties must: (a) adopt the necessary legal, financial and operational means of ensuring steady progress towards the goals laid down in the Charter, (b) maintain meaningful statistics on needs, resources and results, (c) undertake regular reviews of the impact of the strategies adopted, (d) establish a timetable and not defer indefinitely the deadline for achieving the objectives of each stage, and (e) pay close attention to the impact of the policies adopted on each of the categories of persons concerned, particularly the most vulnerable.[65]

A *Article 14 § 1*

The ECSR reviews the overall organisation and functioning of social welfare services under Article 14 § 1, which requires Contracting Parties to set up a network of social services to help people to reach or maintain well-being and to overcome any problems of social adjustment.[66] This provision relates to the encouragement of the creation of services responsible to give advice and personal aid, rather than to the promotion of granting material assistance.[67] According to the Committee, the following services are included within the meaning of "social welfare services": counselling, advice, rehabilitation and other forms of support from social workers, home help services (assistance in the running of the home, personal hygiene, social support, delivery of meals), residential care, and social emergency care (shelters).[68] The content of Article 14 § 1 could be considered to be "dynamic", in the sense that the social welfare services included within its scope have the vocation of progressively broadening and multiplying their field of action.[69]

The ECSR has confirmed in its "jurisprudence" that the right to benefit from social welfare services under Article 14 of the Charter must potentially apply to

---

64 ECSR, *European Roma Rights Centre v. Bulgaria*, § 35.

65 ECSR, *FEANTSA v. Slovenia,* complaint No. 53/2008, decision on the merits of 8 September 2009, § 28.

66 ECSR, Conclusions 2005, Bulgaria.

67 ECSR, Conclusions XV-2, Poland.

68 ECSR, Conclusions 2005, Statement of Interpretation of Article 14 § 1.

69 Council of Europe, Social Protection [...], *cit.*, p. 100; ECSR, Conclusions I, p. 69.

the whole population,[70] namely to anyone with a social problem likely to need such services, unlike other specialised ESC articles targeting specific groups.[71] The Committee has provided a non-exhaustive list of groups of people who may find themselves in a situation of dependency and social marginalisation or at risk: children, older persons, people with disabilities, young persons in difficulty and young offenders, minorities (migrants, refugees, Roma, Travellers and other ethnic groups), homeless people, alcoholics and drug addicts, women who have experienced violence and former detainees.[72]

In line with its settled interpretive approach on the effectiveness of the ESC, as a human rights instrument,[73] which alludes to the ECtHR's line of reasoning, rendering the Convention "practical and effective",[74] the ECSR has stressed that the right to benefit from social welfare services must be guaranteed in law and practice. This means that there must be effective and equal access to social welfare services, with certain guarantees of transparency, equity and quality, which necessitate that:[75]

a) The general eligibility criterion to have access to such services is the lack of personal capabilities and means to cope with the situation;
b) An individual right of access to counselling and advice from social services shall be guaranteed to everyone likely to need it, while access to other kinds of services can be organised according to eligibility criteria that are not excessively restricted and, at any event, ensure care in case of urgent need;
c) The rights of the beneficiaries shall be protected, and any decision should be made in consultation with them and not against their will. At the same time, remedies must be available for those wishing to complain about the provision of social welfare services – particularly where the persons' requests for a social service have been rejected[76] – and a right to appeal to an independent body must be available where allegations of discrimination and violation of human dignity are made;

70 ECSR, Conclusions 2009, Statement of Interpretation of Article 14 § 1.
71 See *supra*, Section I and Section I.C.
72 ECSR, Conclusions 2009, Statement of Interpretation of Article 14 § 1.
73 ECSR, *International Commission of Jurists (ICJ) v. Portugal*, complaint No 1/1998, decision on the merits of 9 September 1999, § 32; *FEANTSA v. Slovenia*, *cit.*, § 28.
74 David Harris *et al.* (eds.), *Law of the European Convention on Human Rights*, 4th ed., Oxford, Oxford University Press, 2018, p. 18.
75 ECSR, Conclusions 2005, Statement of Interpretation of Article 14 § 1; Conclusions 2005, Bulgaria; Conclusions 2009, Statement of Interpretation of Article 14 § 1.
76 ECSR, Conclusions 2009, Georgia.

d) The provision of social welfare services may be subject to fees (fixed or variable), but they must not be so high as to prevent effective access. Such services should be provided free of charge to persons without adequate financial resources (within the meaning of Article 13 § 1 of the Charter);
e) The geographical distribution of social welfare services shall be sufficiently wide. In that context, it is important that these services cover a wide region, including cities and rural areas;[77]
f) Recourse to such services must not interfere with people's right to privacy, including the protection of personal data, and the resources provided must match the responsibilities and changing needs of the users.[78] This implies that the staff shall be qualified and in sufficient numbers, decision-making shall be as close to users as possible, and there must be mechanisms for supervising the adequacy of services (public and private).

Furthermore, as emphasised by the ECSR in *International Federation for Human Rights (FIDH) v. Belgium*, access to social welfare services can be regarded as equal and effective if the Contracting Parties offer varied and multiple methods of care for people likely to need them. The Committee cannot impose on States Parties a particular method of community care for such persons and, therefore, it is for States to decide which means is the most appropriate and most closely matches their needs. This falls, according to the Committee, within the States' margin of appreciation in implementing Article 14 of the Charter. However, Article 14 may be undermined if the approach taken, which may reasonably be regarded as being within the margin of appreciation of the State concerned as that most suited to the needs of these persons, is particularly deficient.[79] Also, the number and quality of the social welfare services actually provided need to correspond as closely as possible to the specific, practical and individual needs of the persons concerned, so that a free choice can be made by the users and, above all, by their families, provided that they act on behalf of these persons and not instead of them.[80]

---

77 ECSR, General Introduction to Conclusions XII-1 and XII-2, p. 35 and p. 41; Conclusions XIII-4, Ireland, pp. 233–234.

78 ECSR, Conclusions 2009, Slovak Republic.

79 ECSR, *International Federation for Human Rights (FIDH) v. Belgium*, complaint No. 75/2011, *cit.*, § § 121–122.

80 *Ibid.*, § 110.

In the same collective complaints case – the only one so far concerning Article 14 of the Charter that has been considered by the ECSR on the merits[81] – the ECSR also elaborated on the normative content of Article 14 § 1, thus providing further impetus to its enforceability. Remarkably, the ECSR drew a link in that regard with its general approach to the principles of progressive realisation and resource availability in the field of economic and social rights, as discussed above. In particular, according to the Committee,

> Article 14 § 1 of the Charter forms part of the articles of the Charter which require States Parties to devise and implement appropriate measures in order to ensure, gradually and in due course, the effective exercise of the right in question. The fact that this provision does not require the States Parties to guarantee immediate results or to adopt conduct which may be capable in the absolute of guaranteeing the right immediately (immediate due diligence) does not mean that the conduct of a State Party, which fails to comply with the legal obligation to offer a particular social service to the extent that it denies access to this service to the persons concerned and excludes them from any solution of this type, can be deemed to comply with this provision of the Charter.[82]

In that light, the Committee considered that Belgium violated Article 14 § 1 of the Charter, given that, over a period of time that the Committee considered to have taken long enough, the Belgian authorities had failed to make any progress in organising the available financial resources in order to prevent the many genuine cases of highly dependent persons with disabilities being denied access to any care or accommodation solution.[83]

Consequently, even in the case of Charter rights – such as the right to benefit from social welfare services under Article 14 of the ESC – which are worded more vaguely than others, and therefore being addressed only to the legislature

---

81 In another collective complaints case in which Article 14 was invoked by the complainant organisation (ECSR, *The Central Association of Carers in Finland v. Finland*, complaint No. 71/2011, *cit.*, § 55), the ECSR held that the matter in question belonged under Article 23 of the Revised Charter and no separate issues arise under Article 14. So was the case with the ECSR decisions on the merits in *European Disability Forum (EDF) and Inclusion Europe v. France*, complaint No. 168/2018, and *Validity Foundation v. Finland*, complaint No. 197/2020, where the allegations were examined under Article 15 § 3 of the ESC.

82 ECSR, *International Federation for Human Rights (FIDH) v. Belgium*, complaint No. 75/2011, *cit.*, § 145.

83 ECSR, *International Federation for Human Rights (FIDH) v. Belgium*, complaint No. 75/2011, *cit.*, § 149 ff.

or the executive and requiring implementing measures in due time, the States Parties may nonetheless violate the Treaty under specific circumstances. This is so, especially, where no measures (legislative, regulatory or other) or inadequate measures have been taken by a State to fulfill an obligation stemming from the Charter.

Finally, in the context of the Covid-19 crisis, the ECSR noted that the rapid digitalisation of social and other services during the pandemic has tended to accentuate the social exclusion of people living in poverty due to lack of equipment, broadband connections and digital skills. As a result, the ECSR drew attention to Article 14 of the Charter, highlighting that delivery of social welfare services frequently involves and depends upon in-person contact and, where digital delivery becomes preferable or necessary in the current context, States Parties should ensure that users of social welfare services have effective access to the requisite technology.[84]

To that end, in the 2021 monitoring cycle, the States were asked to reply to a targeted question, namely how and to what extent the operation of social services was maintained during the Covid-19 crisis and whether specific measures were taken in view of possible similar crises arising in the future. A targeted question was put to the State Parties concerning the user involvement in social services and, in particular, how such involvement is ensured and promoted in legislation, budget allocations and decision-making at all levels, as well as in the design and delivery of services in practice.[85]

B *Article 14 § 2*

Article 14 § 2 provides for the State obligation to encourage and support individuals and voluntary or other organisations in participating in the establishment and maintenance of effective and equally accessible social welfare services, according to the criteria analysed with respect to Article 14 § 1.[86] Traditionally, the establishment of social welfare services was associated with the public sector. However, Article 14 § 2 reflects the effort of the Charter's drafters to reinforce solidarity among members of the society,[87] towards the direction of maintaining and improving social welfare services, not only through State but also through individual action. The phrase "voluntary or other organisations"

84 ECSR, Statement on COVID-19 and social rights adopted on 24 March 2021, 2021, available at <https://rm.coe.int/statement-of-the-ecsr-on-covid-19-and-social-rights/1680a230ca>.

85 ECSR, Press Briefing Elements: Conclusions 2021, 2022, pp. 14–15, available at <https://rm.coe.int/conclusions-2021-press-briefing-final-en/1680a5eed6>.

86 ECSR, Conclusions 2005, Statement of Interpretation of Article 14 § 2.

87 Council of Europe, Social Protection […], *cit.*, p. 102.

refers to nongovernmental organisations and private firms, either non-profit or for-profit, as well as organisations of workers or employers.[88]

Evidently, the manner in which this obligation has been formulated reveals that States Parties have a wide margin of discretion in implementing this provision. According to the ECSR, no uniform model is imposed on States Parties for the implementation of Article 14 § 2. This means that States may promote the establishment of social welfare services jointly run by public bodies, private concerns and voluntary associations, or may leave the provision of certain services entirely to the voluntary sector.[89] In any case, according to the Committee, the States Parties support the establishment and maintenance of social welfare services financially, and these services cannot be deprived of this commitment, even if the intervention of the organisations and the individuals is enormous.[90] The Committee generally demands information from States Parties about the financing and the financial organisation of social welfare services.

Contracting Parties have the obligation to ensure that public and private services are properly coordinated,[91] and that efficiency does not suffer because of the number of providers involved. The Committee examines all forms of support and care mentioned under Article 14 § 1, as well as financial assistance or tax incentives in this area. For purposes of controlling the quality of services provided and ensuring the rights of the users, as well as the respect of human dignity and basic freedoms, an effective preventive and reparative supervisory system is required.

Furthermore, Contracting Parties are required to encourage individuals and voluntary or other organisations to participate in maintaining social services, for example by taking action to strengthen the dialogue with the civil society in areas of welfare policy that affect social welfare services. According to the ECSR, this includes action to promote the representation of specific user-groups in bodies where the public authorities are also represented, and action to promote consultation of users on questions concerning the organisation of the various social services and the aid they provide.[92]

---

88 ECSR, Conclusions III, Austria, p. 78; Conclusions VI, Italy, p. 100; Conclusions XIII-3, Portugal, p. 387.

89 ECSR, Conclusions 2005, Statement of Interpretation of Article 14 § 2.

90 ECSR, Conclusions XII-1, United Kingdom, p. 214; General introduction to Conclusions XII-1, p. 41.

91 ECSR, Conclusions VI, Italy, p. 100; Conclusions VIII, Spain, p. 177.

92 ECSR, Conclusions 2005, Bulgaria; See also: Council of Europe-Department of the ESC, Digest of the Case Law of the European Committee of Social Rights, 2022, p. 134, available at <https://rm.coe.int/digest-ecsr-prems-106522-web-en/1680a95dbd>.

In the 2021 monitoring cycle, the States Parties were requested to provide information on user involvement in social services ("co-production"), in particular on how such involvement is ensured and promoted in legislation, budget allocations and decision-making at all levels, as well as in the design and delivery of services in practice. Co-production is understood here to mean that social services work together with users of the services on the basis of fundamental principles, such as equality, diversity, accessibility and reciprocity.[93] To be able to take a position on this matter, the Committee requested the following information in order to be able to fully assess the situation in the States Parties concerned: statistical data on subsidies paid by the central government and local authorities to voluntary organisations which provide social services, and description of types of support that may exist for voluntary organisations, such as, for example, tax incentives; what kind of supervisory machinery in charge of monitoring the quality of services exists both for public and private institutions and in different entities; and how the dialogue with civil society in respect of social welfare services is ensured.[94]

Concluding Remarks

Article 14 is a widely accepted ESC article by Contracting Parties, of a horizontal and universal nature, with no counterpart in any other universal or regional treaty. Remarkably, the positive obligations that stem from Article 14 of the Charter point to a subsystem of social protection rather than to a set of social security or social assistance benefits. Although Article 14 is structured as more of an individual right rather than a social benefit, a conclusion which has also been confirmed by the ECSR, its standards are broadly formulated and it should be considered a right-institutional guarantee, conditioned on the actions of the Contracting Parties, in cooperation with voluntary and other organisations. Article 14 is the more general article in the field of social services, having close links with and complementing several other Charter provisions.

The ECSR has performed with care the demanding task of distinguishing, through its interpretive work, the actual content of Article 14 from other relevant ESC provisions and specifying the State obligations which have arisen, while remaining within the spirit of the drafters' intentions and respecting

93 See e.g.: ECSR, Conclusions 2021, Azerbaijan, 14 § 2.

94 See e.g.: ECSR, Conclusions 2021, Bosnia and Herzegovina, 14 § 2.

States' margin of appreciation. Consequently, the ECSR has provided a significant impetus to the right to benefit from social welfare services, solidifying its potential to serve as an effective tool for the social protection systems of the Contracting Parties and as a bulwark for individuals and vulnerable groups of persons in their struggle against dependency and marginalisation, especially in times of crisis.

As a result of its *lex generalis* nature, Article 14 of the Charter has posed few difficulties to States in its implementation. This nature of Article 14 implies that the ECSR may only perform an overall and not an in-depth assessment of the conformity of States Parties with their obligations to provide social welfare services under Article 14, unlike other more specialised ESC provisions.[95] This perhaps explains the little attention paid so far to Article 14 by complainant organisations under the Collective Complaints Procedure.

---

95 Karin Lukas, *cit.*, p. 203.

ARTICLE 15

The Right of Persons with Disabilities to Independence, Social Integration and Participation in the Life of the Community

Felicia Roșioru

With a view to ensuring to persons with disabilities, irrespective of age and the nature and origin of their disabilities, the effective exercise of the right to independence, social integration and participation in the life of the community, the Parties undertake, in particular:

1. to take the necessary measures to provide persons with disabilities with guidance, education and vocational training in the framework of general schemes wherever possible or, where this is not possible, through specialised bodies, public or private;
2. to promote their access to employment through all measures tending to encourage employers to hire and keep in employment persons with disabilities in the ordinary working environment and to adjust the working conditions to the needs of the disabled or, where this is not possible by reason of the disability, by arranging for or creating sheltered employment according to the level of disability. In certain cases, such measures may require recourse to specialised placement and support services;
3. to promote their full social integration and participation in the life of the community in particular through measures, including technical aids, aiming to overcome barriers to communication and mobility and enabling access to transport, housing, cultural activities and leisure.

Introduction

After almost 10 years of preparatory work by the Council of Europe and its Member States, the European Social Charter was opened for signature by the Member States on 18 October 1961. It was meant to create a social bedrock of fundamental rights, the Social Constitution of Europe, that "would inspire

 | DOI:10.1163/9789004434141_006

confidence in the Council of Europe and further progressive social development",[1] by continuing the Council's work in the field of human rights.[2] Among the principles of European social policy which the Member States were willing to undertake, special protection was granted to vulnerable groups, including "physically and mentally handicapped".[3] Looking back, we notice that, besides of the obviously outdated terminology, the protection initially granted was rather limited, as Article 15 of the Charter of 1961 focused on "vocational training, rehabilitation and social resettlement" of persons with disabilities. A certain segregation was envisaged, as protection included specialised institutions and placement services, as well as sheltered employment. The Charter of 1961 did not contain any obligations for the employers to adapt the working conditions of the "ordinary" workplaces for workers with disabilities, nor a preference for employment in such workplaces.[4] However, when highlighting this relatively limited initial scope of protection of Article 15, it should be noted the specific context in which the Charter of 1961 was adopted and the reluctance of certain European States to move towards a binding instrument setting precise obligations in the social field. This reluctance is illustrated by the fact that the rights guaranteed by Article 15 are not listed among the particularly significant rights guaranteed by the Charter[5] and, in many Member States, the protection of people with disabilities has adhered to a charitable, segregation and welfare policy approach. This perspective has gradually changed and the Revised European Social Charter, adopted in April 1996, has the merit of being the first international instrument to mention disabled persons as true human rights holders and not as "subjects of rehabilitation".

The analysis of Article 15 is also particularly relevant in order to highlight the role of the European Social Charter, as one of the pillars of the "continent's human rights architecture".[6] The Revised Charter guarantees fundamental

---

1 Secretariat-General of the Council of Europe, *Memorandum on the Role of the Council of Europe in the Social Field*, Strasbourg, 16th April 1953, SG (53) 1, § 1, p. 4.

2 Committee of Ministers, Report of the ad hoc Committee of Social Experts on the European Social Charter, 13 September 1953, CM (53) 99, p. 11.

3 SG (53) 1, *Memorandum*, *cit.*, § 16, p. 7.

4 Mark Bell, "Article 15 RESC", in Edoardo Ales, Marrk Bell, Olaf Deinert *et al.* (eds.), *International and European Labour Law*, Baden-Baden, Beck/Hart/Nomos, 2018, p. 308.

5 European Social Charter of 1961, adopted 18 October 1961, entered into force 26 February 1965 (ETS No. 035) (herein after: Charter of 1961), Article 20 § 1b; European Social Charter (revised), adopted 3 May 1996, entered into force 1 July 1999 (ETS No. 163) (hereinafter: Revised Charter), Part III, Article A § 1b.

6 Secretary General of the Council of Europe, *State of democracy, human rights and the rule of law in Europe A shared responsibility for democratic security in Europe*, SG (2015), April 2015, p. 76.

social and economic human rights covering employment, but also everyday aspects, such as housing, health, education, social protection and welfare. Some people are more vulnerable than others in these everyday aspects; therefore, the revised Charter specifically protects elderly people, children, people with disabilities and migrants.[7] The Charter provides an extensive and complete protection of social rights, serving as point of reference in the EU, as most of the social rights in the Charter of Fundamental Rights in the EU are founded upon the articles of the European Social Charter. Article 26 CFREU on integration of persons with disabilities[8] is based on Article 15 of the European Social Charter and on point 26 of the Community Charter of the Fundamental Social Rights of Workers.[9]

The scope of protection of persons with disabilities was extended by the revised Charter and, more importantly, social policy in this field was set on different coordinates, focusing on respect, independence and inclusion. Article 15 was amended, granting persons with disabilities the right to an independent life, irrespective of age and the nature and origin of their disabilities.[10] Therefore, vocational rehabilitation was replaced by personal autonomy, independent social integration and participation in the life of the community. The *revised* perspective on the protection of people with disabilities is in line the fundamental value of human dignity, set down by the Council of Europe as bedrock of European Society.[11]

There was also an evolution with regard to the rights holders protected by Article 15, from "physically or mentally disabled" (in the Charter of 1961) to "persons with disabilities, irrespective of age and the nature and origin of their disabilities" (in the 1996 Revised Charter). The terms used by the revised Charter mark a clear separation from the traditional medical model, focusing on the

7 Katarzyna Dunaj and Joanna Ryszka, "Chapter 12 The Protection of Vulnerable People in the Charter System", in Stefano Angeleri and Carole Nivard (eds.) *The European Social Charter: A Commentary. Volume 1, Cross-cutting Themes,* Brill, Leiden, 2022, pp. 319–348.

8 Persons with disabilities have the right (according to Article 26 CFREU) to benefit from measures designed to ensure their independence, social and occupational integration and participation in the life of the community, as well as (according to Principle 17 of the European Pillar of Social Rights) to income support, that ensures living in dignity, services enabling labour market and social participation and a work environment adapted to their needs.

9 Preamble – Explanations relating to the Charter of Fundamental Rights in the EU (hereinafter: CFREU), Official Journal of the European Union C 326, European Union, 2012.

10 Explanatory Report to the European Social Charter (Revised), Strasbourg, 3.V.1996, § 63, p. 7.

11 SG (53) 1, *Memorandum, cit.*, § 5, p. 5.

social conception[12] of disability. The paternalistic welfare policy, adopted by many European states towards persons with disabilities[13] was replaced with the focus on full social integration and participation in the life of the community, on education within the framework of general schemes and of work in the ordinary working environment. Article 15 does not specify who should be covered by its provisions as a person with disabilities but depends upon the social policies of the States Parties; but its scope is wide enough to include persons with psycho-social disorders.[14] The new wording of Article 15 of the revised Charter promotes a new approach to disability, seen as a question of citizenship and not in terms of the target group or individual problems; therefore, the whole community should focus on inclusion and remove the existing barriers.

Ten years after the European Social Charter was revised, focusing on social participation and access of persons with disabilities, the United Nations (UN) adopted the Convention on the Rights of Persons with Disabilities (CRPD),[15] in 2006, incorporating the new approach promoted by the revised Charter within a legally binding framework. Starting from the evolving concept of disability, as well as from the reality that persons with disabilities still face barriers to their participation as equal members of society as well as violations of their human rights, which is a breach of their dignity, the CRPD reaffirms the universal, indivisible interdependent and interrelated character of all human rights and fundamental freedoms, as well as the need for persons with disabilities to be guaranteed their full and equal enjoyment. The CRPD is built on the principles of individual autonomy and independence of persons with disabilities; respect for inherent dignity; non-discrimination, equality of opportunity; full and effective participation and inclusion in society; accessibility; respect for difference and acceptance of persons with disabilities as part of human diversity and humanity; and respect for the evolving capacities of children with disabilities and for their right to preserve their identities. States Parties to the CRPD must take positive action in order to render these rights effective.[16]

---

12 Olivier De Schutter, "The European Social Charter as a tool for the protection of the rights of persons with disabilities, with an emphasis on inclusive education", Work Forum on the Implementation of the UN Convention on the Rights of Persons with Disabilities.

13 Jarlath Clifford, "The UN Disability Convention and its Impact on European Equality Law", *The Equal Rights Review*, vol. 6, 2011, p. 22.

14 Conference of the INGOs of the Council of Europe, *Rights of persons with disabilities. Article 15 of the European Social Charter in the light of the United Nations Convention on the Rights of Persons with Disabilities*, 2015, p. 6.

15 Convention on the Rights of Persons with Disabilities (CRPD), adopted on 13 December 2006, entered into force on 3 May 2008.

16 Rosemary Kayess and Ben Fogarty, "The Rights and Dignity of Persons with Disabilities", *Alternative Law Journal*, vol. 32, no. 1, 2007, p. 23.

All Council of Europe member states have signed the CRPD and only one has not yet ratified it.[17] The CRPD sets its scope not by defining disability, but by describing the persons to whom it will apply, starting from the perspective of disability as the result of the person's impairments' interaction with the discriminating barriers that may be faced in everyday life.

This human rights-based approach has been envisaged since 1981, after the UN General Assembly has proclaimed 1981 as the International Year for Disabled Persons. The Parliamentary Assembly of the Council of Europe, noting that some member states have carried out "outstanding activities for physically, mentally and sensorially disabled persons", has seen this moment as the starting point to reflect on a renewed and updated policy "giving more weight to the seriousness of the disability than to its origin",[18] since poorly informed societies and inadequate housing policies have encouraged segregation rather than integration. The 1981 vision was revolutionary, as it has looked at disability as a restriction "caused by physical, psychological, sensory, social, cultural, legal or other obstacles",[19] preventing disabled people from fully integrating, as equal members, in family life and in the community. The burden was placed on society, which has the duty of adapting its standards to enable disabled people to lead independent lives. Rehabilitation was charted on new coordinates, overcoming the initial concept of medical care and recovery of functions,[20] and moving from viewing the disabled person as a patient to a citizen, entitled to equal rights. Subsequently, the Committee of Ministers' Recommendation on a coherent policy for people with disabilities included the World Health Organisation's (WHO) definition of disability as "any restriction or lack (resulting from an impairment)[21] of ability to perform an activity in the manner of or within the range considered normal for a human being".[22] In this Recommendation, it is the handicap that defines the person's relation with his or her environment. In 2001, the WHO[23] replaced impairment,

17 Liechtenstein has signed the CRPD in September 2020.

18 PACE, Rec.925(1981), Council of Europe's contribution to the International Year for Disabled Persons.

19 *Ibid.*

20 PACE, Report, Doc. 6581, (*Former*) *Social, Health and Family Affairs Committee*, Independent living: rehabilitation policies for the disabled, 26 February 1992, §§ 3 and 6.

21 According to the same Recommendation, impairment is "any loss or abnormality of psychological, physiological or anatomical structure or functions".

22 CM, Rec.(92)6 on a coherent policy for people with disabilities, p. 4.

23 World Health Organisation (WHO), *International Classification of Functioning and Disability*, 2001 (ICF), which is expressly mentioned in the Council of Europe's Action Plan to promote the rights and full participation of people with disabilities in society: improving the quality of life of people with disabilities in Europe 2006–2015 [Rec.(2006) 5].

disability and handicap with "body functions and structures" and "activities and participation", conceived not just from the bodily perspective, but also from an individual and social perspective, including the impact of personal factors and attitudes.[24]

In its Disability Action Plan 2006–2015, adopted in April 2006, there was no definition of disability included, as the Committee of Ministers of the Council of Europe has considered that this is an issue that should be settled by each member state, in its national policy. However, the Action Plan has clearly marked the shift to the human rights-based approach, as it has aimed to implement, at the European level, a coherent policy, based on the "principles of full citizenship and independent living".[25] The Council of Europe Strategy on the rights of persons with disabilities for 2017–2023 enhances the human rights-based policy, aiming to grant them effective access and enjoyment on an equal basis with others of all civil, political, economic, social and cultural rights, and safeguarded by the European Social Charter, the European Convention on Human Rights, the CRPD "as well as all other international human rights instruments".[26] The strategic priorities set by the Council of Europe are to be implemented in line with the CRPD principles, with the involvement of persons with disabilities, aiming to ensure respect for human rights, diversity, equality, dignity and equal opportunities.[27] Since the Council of Europe and the UN have convergent standards in protecting and promoting the human rights of persons with disabilities, the Council of Europe has set five rights-based priority areas[28] that correspond to Articles of the CRPD, aiming at its implementation in practice.[29] In line with this policy, the European Committee on Social Rights (ECSR) often relies, in its decisions on Article 15 of the Revised

---

24 Sujoy Kanti Ghoshal, "Concept of Disability – The Dynamic Trend", *International Research Journal of Commerce Arts and Science*, Volume 9, Issue 4, 2018, pp. 235–236.

25 CM, Rec.(2006) 5 on the Council of Europe Action Plan to promote the rights and full participation of people with disabilities in society: improving the quality of life of people with disabilities in Europe 2006–2015.

26 Council of Europe Disability Strategy 2017–2023: Human Rights: A Reality for All, March 2017, p. 7.

27 *Ibid*, pp. 8 and 10.

28 The priority areas are: equality and non-discrimination; awareness raising; accessibility; equal recognition before the law; freedom from exploitation, violence and abuse.

29 Council of Europe Disability Strategy 2017–2023, p. 11: "The interpretation and implementation of these priority areas will be done in line with the UNCRPD, the European Convention on Human Rights, the European Social Charter and the developing case law of the European Court of Human Rights. The evolving body of decisions, guidelines and General Comments of the UNCRPD Committee, as well as the conclusions and decisions of the European Committee of Social Rights are duly taken into account".

Charter, on the provisions of the CRPD and the comments of the Committee on the Rights of Persons with Disabilities.[30] Policies, activities and measures adopted by the Council of Europe and its member states bring added value to policies and measures adopted "in other regional and international contexts", such as the EU and the UN.[31] The CRPD, in its turn, does not affect "any provisions which are more conducive to the realisation of the rights of persons with disabilities",[32] contained in the law or in international law in force for a State Party to the convention.

The modern perspective of disability is that of an "umbrella term",[33] referring to a limitation relying on a social and individual perception rather than on reduced body functions, and the new wording of Article 15 marks the commitment of the Council of Europe to granting effective rights to all persons with disabilities, regardless of their impairments.

1 The Primary Rights Guaranteed by Article 15 of the Revised European Social Charter

Article 15 of the revised Charter guarantees the primary rights to independence, social integration and participation in the life of the community, aiming to grant an equal citizenship to persons with disabilities.[34] The rights initially guaranteed by the Charter of 1961– to vocational training and rehabilitation – gave expression to the will to the reintegration within society of people with disabilities, who had to be enabled to work and be independent.[35] The revised Article 15 marks an essential change of paradigm, "from treating disabled persons as objects of pity and towards respecting them as equal citizens"[36] who want to lead independent lives; from "rehabilitation and resettlement" to

30 ECSR, *Mental Disability Advocacy Center* (*MDAC*) *v. Belgium*, complaint No. 109/2014, decision on admissibility and the merits, 16 October 2017, §§ 22–24; ECSR, *European Action of the Disabled* (*AEH*) *v. France*, complaint No. 81/2012, decision on the merits of 11 September 2013, § 17.

31 Council of Europe Disability Strategy 2017–2023, p. 11.

32 CRPD, Article 4 § 4.

33 Edit Kajtar, "Changing Perspective on Social Inclusion of People with disabilities: A European-Hungarian Outlook", *Studia iuridica auctoritate Universitatis Pécs Publicata*, no. 141, 2008, p. 169.

34 ECSR, *International Association Autisme-Europe* (*AIAE*) *v. France*, Complaint No. 13/2002, Decision on the merits of 4 November 2003, § 48.

35 ECSR, Conclusions I, Interpretative statement of Article 15.

36 ECSR, Conclusions XVIII (2007), Statement of Interpretation of Article 15 § 1; ECSR *International Association Autisme-Europe* (*AIAE*) *v. France*, *cit.*, § 48.

inclusion and choice;[37] from welfare recipients to rights holders.[38] The disability policy has changed accordingly, now focusing on inclusion: rehabilitation and social resettlement were replaced by independence, social integration and participation in the life of the community. This advancement in the disability policy was promoted by the Council of Europe, with the adoption of several recommendations and resolutions by the Committee of Ministers,[39] aiming at establishing a coherent policy for people with disabilities;[40] to remove barriers and to adopt the universal design;[41] to ensure an effective right to education,[42] deinstitutionalisation and community living for children with disabilities;[43] to safeguard adults and children with disabilities against abuse[44] and to promote the human rights of older persons.[45]

The rights to independence, social integration and participation in the life of the community are granted both to children and to adults, irrespective of the nature and origin of their disabilities.[46] The paragraphs of Article 15 come together to achieve these rights.[47]

Under Article 15 of the Charter, the State Parties must adopt a coherent policy that reflects this modern approach to independence, social integration and participation in the life of the community, focusing on effective measures to provide: (A) guidance, education and vocational training, (B) access to

---

37 ECSR, *International Association Autisme-Europe (AIAE) v. France, cit.*, § 48.

38 ECSR, *European Action of the Disabled (AEH) v. France, cit.*., § 75; Committee on the Rights of Persons with Disabilities (CtRPD), *General comment No. 4 (2016) on the right to inclusive education*, CRPD/C/GC/4, 25 November 2016, § 1; Aneja N., "Human Rights of Persons with Disabilities: Contemporary Developments", *International Journal of Law Management & Humanities*, no. 5, 2022, pp. 1004–1007.

39 Available at: https://www.coe.int/en/web/disability/adopted-texts.

40 CM, Rec.(92)6 on a coherent policy for people with disabilities.

41 Res.AP(2001)1 on the introduction of the principles of universal design into the curricula of all occupations working on the built environment; Res.AP(2001)3 Towards full citizenship of persons with disabilities through inclusive new technologies; Res.AP(2007)3 and CM.Rec(2009)8 on achieving full participation through Universal Design.

42 Res.AP(95)3 on a Charter on the vocational assessment of people with disabilities; Res.AP(2007)4 and CM.Rec.(2009)9 on the education and social inclusion of children and young people with autism spectrum disorders.

43 CM. Rec.(2010)2 on deinstitutionalisation and community living of children with disabilities.

44 Res.AP(2005)1 on safeguarding adults and children with disabilities against abuse.

45 CM. Rec.(2009)6 on ageing and disability in the 21st century: sustainable frameworks to enable greater quality of life in an inclusive society; CM. Rec(2014)2 on the promotion of human rights of older persons.

46 Explanatory Report to the European Social Charter (Revised), *cit.*, § 63, p. 7.

47 ECSR, *European Action of the Disabled (AEH) v. France, cit.*, § 28.

employment and (C) full social integration and participation in the life of the community. As the Charter is a human rights protection instrument, protection has to be granted not just theoretically, but also in fact;[48] therefore, the legislation adopted by the States Parties has to be accompanied by practical action and an effective and rigorous control.[49]

Persons with disabilities are a vulnerable group, more likely to depend upon community care supported by public funds in order to live independently and in dignity, as compared with other persons in receipt of community care;[50] therefore, the policies adopted by the states may have a major impact on this group. State Parties have to adopt positive measures[51] and not just provide the possibility of the disabled persons to fully integrate in society and live an independent life. Among these measures, those related to an effective exercise of the right to education play a major role.

A *The Right to Guidance, Education and Training of Persons with Disabilities*

Initially, Article 15 of the Charter of 1961 was aiming to ensure the effective exercise of the rights to vocational training, rehabilitation and resettlement. Therefore, State Parties undertook, in line with the first paragraph of the text, to take adequate measures in order to provide training facilities to "the physically or mentally disabled".[52] Training facilities could have been provided, where necessary, by public or private specialised institutions. As traditional assistance policies became outdated, the importance of education and training was reconsidered as necessary steps towards economic independence and social integration. Education and training play an essential role in the person obtaining a position in the open labour market and employment is essential to leading a self-determined life. Education below the upper secondary level exposes young persons with disabilities to disadvantages in the employment

48 ECSR, *International Commission of Jurists* (*ICJ*) *v. Portugal*, complaint No. 1/1998, decision on the merits of 9 September 1999, § 32; ECSR, *European Federation of National Organisations working with the Homeless* (*FEANTSA*) *v. Slovenia*, complaint No. 53/2008, decision on the merits of 8 September 2009, § 28.

49 ECSR, *International Association Autisme-Europe* (*AIAE*) *v. France*, *cit.*, § 53.

50 ECSR, *MDAC*, *cit.*, § 77.

51 Explanatory Report to the European Social Charter (Revised), *cit.*, § 63, p. 7; ECSR, *International Association Autisme-Europe* (*AIAE*) *v. France*, *cit.*, § 53; ECSR, *ICJ*, *cit.*, § 32.

52 Charter of 1961, Article 15.

market,[53] thus "occupational integration is an essential element of social integration".[54]

1 Education, Vocational Training and Guidance

Article 15 § 1 of the revised Charter guarantees the right to guidance, education and vocational training within the framework of general schemes wherever possible or through specialised public or private bodies otherwise. The right to education and training encompasses primary education, general and vocational secondary education, as well as other forms of vocational training and all types of higher education, including university education.[55] After referring to disabled persons in Articles 9 (on vocational guidance) and 10 (on vocational training), the Charter raises the right of persons with disabilities to education and training to the level of a separate social right, requiring adequate means for bringing it into effect:[56] not just in the form of legal action, but also by making available the necessary resources and the operational procedures in order to give effectiveness to the rights specified and to the goals laid down by the Charter.[57] Therefore, Contracting States that have accepted this paragraph are bound to declare the steps taken in order to render the right effective, taking into consideration the type and number of main specialised institutions providing appropriate training, the number of persons receiving such training and of the staff engaged in such work.[58]

The right to education for children and adults with disabilities plays an essential role in advancing the citizenship rights[59] of independence, social integration and participation in the life of the community. This approach is in line with the vision promoted by the UN Committee on the Rights of Persons with Disabilities, that the right to inclusive education is a fundamental human right of all learners.[60] Education is essential to inclusion and any future choice of a professional activity, which plays an essential role in guaranteeing the person's fundamental rights.[61] Therefore, the revised Article 15 expressly mentions

53 Digest of the Case Law of the European Committee of Social Rights, December 2018, p. 158.

54 ECSR, Conclusions XIV-2 (1998), Statement of interpretation of Article 15.

55 ECSR, Conclusions 2012, Ireland.

56 ECSR, Conclusions I, Interpretative statement of Article 15.

57 ECSR, *International Movement ATD Fourth World v. France*, complaint No.33/2006, decision on the merits of 5 December 2007, § 61.

58 ECSR, Conclusions I, Interpretative statement of Article 15 § 1.

59 ECSR, *International Association Autisme-Europe (AIAE) v. France, cit.*, § 48.

60 CtRPD, *General Comment no. 4 cit.*, § 11, p. 3.

61 ECSR, Conclusions XIV-2, *cit.*

education and priority is given to "the framework of general schemes, wherever possible", that is to mainstream schools.[62] The aim of Article 15 § 1 of the revised Charter is "not just to set standards, but also to empower persons with disabilities to have effective access to mainstream education"[63] and to adequate teaching, as a condition of participation in community life, because schools play a fundamental role in enhancing the pupils' potential and in achieving self-fulfilment.[64]

Vocational training – in a restrictive way – focuses on the initial instruction of individuals, helping them to acquire the necessary knowledge and skills to enter the labour market and to achieve personal fulfilment and social integration.[65] Vocational training is linked to general education, comprising a "full range of education and training activities for individuals".[66] Vocational guidance has to be granted to all children and adults with disabilities in all aspects related to their occupational choice and progress. "Vocational rehabilitation" includes all the means and methods designed to enable persons with disabilities to find or to keep a job.[67]

The material scope of Articles 10 and 15 of the Charter overlap, as they both grant the right to vocational training. "As the Charter was conceived as a whole, its provisions complement each other and overlap in part".[68] However, the purpose of the two articles is complementary, but different.[69] Article 10 guarantees the right to effective and appropriate vocational training for the entire population, including persons with disabilities, balancing both the individual needs of persons, including adult workers, and the general needs of the labour market.[70] Vocational training should be provided or promoted in consultation with employers' and workers' organisations. Article 15 confers a wider protection for persons with disabilities, treating vocational training as a means of achieving independence, social integration, personal autonomy and participation in the life of the community.[71] The modern approach focuses on inclusion;

---

62 ECSR, *European Action of the Disabled (AEH) v. France, cit.*, § 78.
63 ECSR, *MDAC, cit.*, § 77.
64 ECSR, *European Action of the Disabled (AEH) v. France, cit.*, § 91.
65 *Ibid.*, § 101.
66 *Ibid.*, § 105.
67 ECSR, Conclusions XIV-2, *cit.*
68 ECSR, *Mental Disability Advocacy Center (MDAC) v. Bulgaria*, complaint No. 41/2007, decision on admissibility of 26 June 2007, § 9.
69 ECSR, *European Action of the Disabled (AEH) v. France, cit.*, § 24.
70 *Ibid.*, § 25.
71 Explanatory report to the European Social Charter (Revised), *cit.*, § 63; ECSR, *European Action of the Disabled (AEH) v. France, cit.*, § 29.

thus guidance, education and vocational training should be provided, whenever possible, within the framework of general schemes and not in specialised institutions.[72]

Article 15 § 1 should be read in conjunction with Article 17 § 1 of the revised Charter. As a part of the right of children and young persons to social, legal and economic protection, Article 17 focuses on the "full development of their personality", requiring an encouraging environment for the development of their physical and mental capacities. Such an environment is crucial for children with disabilities, especially "where the effects of ineffective or untimely intervention are ever likely to be undone".[73] As Article 17 embodies the modern approach to mainstreaming, it requires the establishment and maintenance of sufficient and adequate institutions and services for the education that children and young persons need.[74]

2 From Integration to Inclusion

There is a conceptual difference between integration and inclusion. The ECSR highlighted that a policy of integration basically requires that children with disabilities fit the mainstream system. On the other hand, inclusion focuses on the child's right to participate in mainstream schooling and involves the obligation of schools to accept the child and to provide reasonable accommodation, while taking into account his/her abilities and educational needs.[75] The right to inclusive education is "a fundamental human right to all learners",[76] and involves systemic reforms.[77] Thus, in order to overcome barriers, changes should be adopted, as regards the content, the teaching methods and approaches, and the structures and strategies in education. All students should benefit from "an equitable and participatory learning experience and environment that best corresponds to their requirements and preferences".[78] Integration programmes may be accepted upon condition that they lead to inclusive education for disabled children.[79]

72 *Ibid.*, § 64.

73 ECSR, *International Association Autisme-Europe* (*AIAE*) *v. France, cit.*, § 49.

74 *Ibid.*

75 ECSR, *MDAC v. Belgium, cit.*, § 66.

76 CtRPD, *General Comment no. 4*, § 11.

77 Will Momm and Andreas Konig, "Community Integration for Disabled People – A New Approach to Their Vocational Training and Employment", *International Labour Review*, vol.128, no. 4, 1989, pp. 497–510.

78 ECSR, *MDAC v. Belgium, cit.*, § 67.

79 *Ibid.*, § 68.

The ECSR relies in its decisions on Article 24 § 2 CRPD, stating that inclusive education system at all levels should be put in place by the State Parties by adopting specific measures within their social policies. A "set of measures" refers to access to the general education system: in particular, children with disabilities should not be excluded from free and compulsory primary education, or from secondary education, on the basis of their disability. Since disabled persons still face poor accessibility to schools,[80] they should be granted effective and equal access to "an inclusive, quality and free" primary and secondary education, in the communities in which they live.[81] Inclusive education requires effective individualized support measures within the general education system and reasonable accommodation, according to the needs of the person with a disability, and provided in environments that maximize academic and social development.[82] A coherent inclusive education strategy requires adequate resources: human, financial and material.[83] The elementary measures adopted by the State Parties include the support of teachers and the accessibility of premises in order to enable integration and must demonstrate that tangible progress is being made in setting up education systems which exclude no one.[84]

In line with the concept of inclusion, there is a breach of the obligations contained in Article 15 § 1 when the right to enrolment in mainstream schools is granted only to pupils who are able to follow the common-core curriculum, even if suitable and proportionate measures (of a "corrective, customised, compensatory and dispensatory nature")[85] apply and where enrolment may be annulled if the school considers that the accommodation needed for integrating the pupil into mainstream education would impose a disproportionate burden.[86] Such a right is based rather on integration than on inclusion, as the pupil is required to fit the mainstream system, rather than requiring the school to accept the child. Inclusive education implies support and reasonable accommodation measures, that are necessary for persons with disabilities to access schools effectively. Inclusive education is built on four pillars: availability, accessibility, acceptability and adaptability.[87] Under Article 15 § 1, the

---

80 *Ibid.*, § 23.

81 Article 24 § 2 CRPD; ECSR, *European Action of the Disabled* (AEH) *v. France*, *cit.*, § 17.

82 Article 24 § 2 (a)-(e) CRPD.

83 CtRPD, *Concluding observations on the initial report of Belgium*, adopted by the Committee at its 12th session (15 September-3 October 2014), § 36.

84 ECSR, Conclusions 2005, Cyprus.

85 ECSR, *MDAC v. Belgium*, *cit.*, § 65.

86 *Ibid.*, §§ 65–66.

87 *Ibid.*, § 105; ECSR, *MDAC v. Bulgaria*, *cit.*, § 37; CtRPD, *General Comment no. 4*, *cit.*, §§ 21–38.

measures taken by the State Parties must guarantee adequate teaching, in both mainstream and special schools. In addition, States have to make tangible progress in "setting up inclusive and adapted education systems",[88] involving an "in-depth transformation of education systems in legislation, policy and the mechanisms for financing, administering, designing, delivering and monitoring education".[89] In particular, for children and adolescents with autism, assistance at school is an important means for their inclusion in mainstream schools.[90] As there is still a lack of reasonable accommodation in mainstream education, children with disabilities are often compelled to attend special schools.[91] Adequate teaching must be provided both in mainstream schools, and in special schools if needed,[92] in order to guarantee an equal and non-discriminatory treatment of persons with disabilities.

3 Obligations of the State Parties under Article 15 § 1

States have to provide education for persons with disabilities, as well as vocational guidance and training "in one or other of the pillars of the education system, in other words [in] mainstream or special schools".[93] There is, however, a priority to education in mainstream establishments and State Parties do not enjoy a wide margin of appreciation when it comes to choosing the type of school for the education and training of persons with disabilities. Given the purpose of Article 15 § 1 – to promote the independence, integration and participation of persons with impairments – education should clearly be provided in mainstream schools. The debate is centred on inclusive education and segregated education should only be the exception.

Priority to education in mainstream schools is subject to a conditionality clause and public authorities have to take into account, on a case-by-case basis, the individual circumstances, including the type and severity of the disability.[94] For example, when the CRPD was adopted, Deaf and Blind organisations advocated that achieving skills, such as Braille or sign language, orientation and mobility is more effective in environments other than inclusive or mainstream education. However, these skills may be acquired at any stage of life, not just through a formal education system[95] and they should not limit access

88 ECSR, Conclusions XX-1 (2012), Austria.

89 CtRPD, *General Comment no. 4, cit.*, § 9.

90 ECSR, *European Action of the Disabled (AEH) v. France, cit.*, § 85.

91 ECSR, *MDAC v. Belgium, cit.*, § 23.

92 ECSR, *International Association Autisme-Europe (AIAE) v. France, cit.*, § 48.

93 *Ibid.*, § 78.

94 *Ibid., loc. cit.*; ECSR, *MDAC v. Belgium, cit.*, § 61.

95 Rosemary Kayess *et al., cit.*, p. 27.

to education in mainstream establishments. For the acquisition of these skills and for an education that maximizes academic and social development, State Parties must, under Article 24 § 4 CRPD, employ the necessary staff qualified in sign language and/or Braille (teachers, including teachers with disabilities). Professionals and staff who work at all levels of education should be trained to use appropriate augmentative and alternative modes, means and formats of communication, but also educational techniques and materials to support persons with disabilities; training should also include disability awareness. The ECSR has highlighted the need for teachers and staff trained for the specific needs of the disabled persons.[96]

States enjoy a margin of appreciation only related to the means they consider most appropriate for implementing the right to education in mainstream schools, "bearing in mind the cultural, political or financial circumstances in which their education system operates".[97] Among their duties lies the obligation to provide the human assistance that is needed for the school career of persons with disabilities.[98] There is a limit to the margin of appreciation of the States, as the choices made or the means adopted should not be of a nature or should not be applied "in a way that deprives the established right of its effectiveness and turns it into a purely theoretical right".[99] Thus, in practice, many school buildings are not accessible and teachers in mainstream schools are not usually trained to answer the specific needs of children with disabilities; therefore, such children rarely find a suitable school near their home.[100] Children with intellectual disabilities (mild, moderate or severe mental disabilities) face important barriers to accessing mainstream schooling and children with serious intellectual disabilities are exempted from compulsory schooling.

The ECSR highlighted that all persons with disabilities have the right to guidance, education and vocational training, even if it is provided in day-centres and institutions and not in formal schooling.[101] For children, adolescents or

---

96 ECSR, *MDAC v. Belgium cit.*, § 70; ECSR, *European Action of the Disabled (AEH) v. France, cit.*, § 90.

97 ECSR, *European Action of the Disabled (AEH) v. France, cit.*, §§ 80–81; ECSR, *MDAC, cit.*, § 61.

98 ECSR, *European Action of the Disabled (AEH) v. France, cit.*, § 80.

99 ECSR. *European Federation of National Organisations working with the Homeless (FEANTSA) v. France*, complaint No. 39/2006, decision on the merits of 5 December 2007, § 55; *MDAC v. Belgium, cit.*, § 61; ECSR, *European Action of the Disabled (AEH) v. France, cit.*, § 81.

100 ECSR, *MDAC v. Belgium, cit.*, § 70. Barriers exist also when children with disabilities have access to mainstream schooling (*European Action of the Disabled (AEH) v. France, cit.*, §§ 90–91).

101 ECSR, *MDAC v. Belgium, cit.*, § 68.

adults with disabilities, priority has to be given to education and training "within the framework of ordinary schemes and only where this is not possible, through special schools".[102] State Parties must prove that there is a genuine access to mainstream education or, at least, that substantial efforts are being made in order to achieve such a result.[103] Key figures are taken into consideration for this purpose, such as: the total number of persons with disabilities (including children) and the number of students with disabilities following mainstream or special education and vocational facilities; the percentage of such students entering the labour market,[104] as an indicator of adequate teaching and social inclusion; and the number of persons with disabilities (children and adults) living in institutions.[105] Conversely to inclusion, there is exclusion when persons with impairments are directly or indirectly prevented from, or denied access to, education; segregation occurs when students with disabilities are educated in separate environments, especially designed to respond to various impairments, but in isolation from students without disabilities. Integration occurs when persons with disabilities are placed in existing mainstream educational institutions, but they have to adapt to the standardized requirements of these institutions.[106] The ECSR held that there is a violation of Article 15 § 1 when the proportion of children with autism educated, in general or specialist schools, is much lower than in the case of other children, whether or not disabled, as well as when there is a chronic shortage of care and support facilities for autistic adults.[107]

The work done in specialised institutions, where care is provided for children and adolescents with autism should also be predominantly educational in nature.[108] The Charter requires State Parties, at the bare minimum, to provide care in medico-educational institutes or day-hospital units (in the health sector).[109] Article 15 § 1 refers to specialised institutions, but in the context of Article 15 as a whole; guidance, education and vocational training of persons with disabilities represent the most important means to secure their right to independence, social integration and participation. Access to employment and measures facilitating the communication and mobility of the persons with

102 ECSR, *International Association Autisme-Europe* (AIAE) *v. France, cit.*, § 48.
103 ECSR, Conclusions 2008, Andorra.
104 ECSR, Conclusions 2012, Russian Federation.
105 ECSR, Conclusions 2008, Lithuania.
106 CtRPD, *General Comment no. 4*, § 11.
107 ECSR, *International Association Autisme-Europe* (AIAE) *v. France, cit.*, § 54.
108 ECSR, *European Action of the Disabled* (AEH) *v. France, cit.*, § 121.
109 ECSR, *European Action of the Disabled* (AEH) *v. France, cit.*, § 113.

disabilities are ranked by Article 15 only in second and third place as means of securing fully-fledged citizenship of the persons concerned. Therefore, specialised institutions referred to in Article 15 § 1 have to ensure that guidance, education and vocational training are given with priority over other functions and duties of these institutions; their internal organisation and/or their working methods should be adapted for this purpose.[110]

In order to grant access to inclusive education, in addition to reasonable accommodation measures, State Parties must adopt non-discrimination legislation requiring at least a compelling justification for special or segregated educational systems and an effective remedy for those who are unlawfully excluded, segregated or denied an effective right to education.[111] Non-discrimination legislation may be of a general nature, specific legislation concerning education, or a combination of these.[112] Effective equal access to education and vocational training is also assessed based upon the relevant case law and the number of complaints concerning discrimination, on the ground of disability in relation to education and training, brought to the appropriate bodies.[113]

As Article 15 § 1 is "exceptionally complex and particularly expensive to resolve". The measures taken by States to achieve the Charter's objectives must meet three criteria: a reasonable timeframe, measurable progress and financing making the maximum use of available resources, by taking into consideration the impact of the choices made on the vulnerable groups and their families.[114] State Parties enjoy a large margin of appreciation in allocating the financial resources for the schooling of persons with disabilities. However, it cannot be considered that maximum use of resources is being made when a state finances travel to another state, where children with intellectual disabilities are accommodated and educated in specialised institutions, according to appropriate educational standards, rather than financing the implementation of such standards within specialised institutions on its own territory.[115]

4 Reasonable Accommodation

Reasonable accommodation is not expressly stated by Article 15 § 1, which mentions only the duty of the State Parties to take the measures necessary

110 *Ibid.*, §§ 110–111.

111 ECSR, Conclusions XVIII (2007), *cit.*; ECSR, *MDAC v. Belgium*, *cit.*, § 84.

112 ECSR, Conclusions XVIII (2007), *cit.*

113 ECSR, Conclusions 2008, Lithuania.

114 ECSR, *International Association Autisme-Europe (AIAE) v. France*, *cit.*, § 53.

115 ECSR, *European Action of the Disabled (AEH) v. France*, *cit.*, § 99.

to provide guidance, education and professional training for persons with disabilities. The ECSR has developed its case law relying on the provisions of the CRPD, according to which "reasonable accommodation" means the duty of the State Parties to adopt the necessary and appropriate modifications and adjustments, where needed in a particular case, in order to ensure that persons with disabilities enjoy or exercise all their human rights and fundamental freedoms, on an equal basis with others. Reasonable accommodation is a right and it should not be perceived merely as an advantage.[116] However, reasonable accommodation should not impose a disproportionate or undue burden. Proportionality and disproportionality depending on the context and the availability of accommodation measures should not be limited to a certain school, but to the educational resources that are available in the educational system. Provision of reasonable accommodation should be based on the evaluation of social barriers to education, rather than on a medical diagnosis of impairment[117] and it should relate to an individual and his/her needs, as it helps to correct factual inequalities.[118] Such measures may include: "changing the location of a class, providing different forms of in-class communication, enlarging print, materials and/or subjects in sign, or providing all handouts in an alternative format, providing students with a note-taker, or a language interpreter or allowing students to use assistive technology in learning and assessment situations. Provision of non-material accommodations, such as allowing a student more time, reducing levels of background noise, sensitivity to sensory overload, alternative evaluation methods or replacing an element of curriculum by an alternative element, must also be considered".[119] The State's failure to make provision for reasonable accommodations constitutes discrimination in the enjoyment of the rights granted by Article 15 § 1 of the revised Charter, that is, discrimination on grounds of intellectual disability.[120]

Individual support and reasonable accommodation should be free of charge at all compulsory levels of education as assistance is essential to effective access to education for children with disabilities.[121] In addition to "compulsory, quality, free and accessible primary education", State Parties should adopt measures to grant children with disabilities access to "complete, free, equitable and quality secondary education", as well as providing equal access for women

116 ECSR, *MDAC v. Belgium*, *cit.*, § 17.
117 CtRPD, *General Comment no. 4*, *cit.*, § 30.
118 ECSR, *MDAC v. Belgium*, *cit.*, § 72.
119 CtRPD, *General Comment*, *cit.*, §§ 29–30; ECSR, *MDAC v. Belgium*, *cit.*, § 24.
120 ECSR, *MDAC v. Belgium*, *cit.*, § 73.
121 *Ibid.*, § 17.

and men with disabilities to "affordable and quality technical, vocational and tertiary education, including university, and lifelong learning", in public and private academic institutions.[122]

B *The Right to Independent Life, Full and Equal Social Participation through Employment*

Article 15 § 2 of the revised Charter guarantees the effective exercise of the right of disabled persons to independence, social integration and participation through employment. The aim is to achieve "equal employment opportunities for persons with disabilities" by rethinking both the disability itself and the means of obtaining full, and equal participation of disabled persons in the life of the community.[123] Therefore, State Parties must take the measures required in order to promote the access of persons with disabilities to employment, by having recourse if necessary to specialised placement and support services. In particular, such measures should be directed towards encouraging employers to hire (offering tax incentives and recruitment premiums)[124] and, on the other hand, to retain in employment persons with disabilities, in "the ordinary working environment".[125] If necessary, the employers might need to adjust the working conditions to the needs of the persons with disabilities. If work in the ordinary working environment is not possible by reasons of disability, State Parties have to arrange for, or create, sheltered employment, according to the worker's level of disability. The Charter of 1961 has also envisaged, in Article 15 § 2, the obligation of the State Parties to take adequate measures in order to place disabled persons in employment. These measures were "special", including: specialised placing services, facilities for sheltered employment and measures to encourage employers to admit disabled persons to employment.[126]

An important aspect, that promotes access of persons with impairments to employment, is the shift from the assessment of working capacity based on a medical model of "incapacity"[127] to an assessment of the barriers which, in interaction with any long-term physical, mental or psychological impairment of the person, might hinder his/her full and effective participation in professional life on an equal basis with other workers.

---

122 *Ibid.*, § 24.
123 ECSR, Conclusions XIV-2, *cit.*
124 *Ibid.*
125 According to Article 15 § 2 of the revised Charter.
126 Article 15 § 2 of the Charter of 1961.
127 ECSR, Conclusions 2020, Serbia.

1 Work in the "Ordinary Working Environment" vs Sheltered Employment

Access to employment for persons with physical and/or intellectual disabilities[128] should be rendered effective, on an equal footing, in the first place, on the open labour market,[129] as a result of a "coherent policy" and positive measures adopted by the States Parties[130] and the involvement of employers and trade unions.[131] Measures to support persons with disabilities, including with respect to their employment, are a common national practice.[132] Article 15 § 2 of the revised Charter highlights the fact that social integration should be achieved through employment "in the ordinary working environment", through the use of "specialised placement and support services", if necessary. Such services include: "counselling, wage subsidies, and tax incentives, training, assistance to begin an independent activity or to start-up a business, special competitions for the civil service, support for sheltered workshops",[133] advice and training for employers, providing knowledge and guidance to support people with disabilities (employees or future employees); reimbursement of costs for professional coaching for remaining in employment after the expiry of the supported employment measure;[134] and "information campaigns to encourage employers to focus on people skills and abilities rather than barriers and disabilities".[135] Priority is given to individualized support for persons with impairments, including ongoing support after recruitment for a certain job.[136] State Parties are required to create opportunities for employment in the open labour market, rather than focusing on sheltered workplaces for persons with intellectual or psychosocial disabilities in particular.[137] Despite the traditional preference for sheltered employment, which leads to segregation of the employment market, State Parties should adapt their policy to offering jobs within ordinary working environments to persons with disabilities, corresponding to their skills and employment potential.[138] Changing the way of assessing working ability[139] and regular assessment of the vocational capacities, with

128 ECSR, Conclusions I (1969), Statement of Interpretation of article 15 § 2.
129 ECSR, Conclusions XX-1 (2012), Czech Republic.
130 Explanatory Report to the European Social Charter (Revised), § 64.
131 ECSR, Conclusions XIV-2, *cit.*
132 Mark Bell, *cit.,* p. 308.
133 ECSR, Conclusions 2020, Turkey.
134 ECSR, Conclusions XXII-1 (2020), Germany.
135 ECSR, Conclusions 2020, Sweden.
136 Mark Bell, *cit.,* p. 309.
137 ECSR, Conclusions 2020, Turkey.
138 ECSR, Conclusions XIV-2, *cit.*
139 ECSR, Conclusions 2020, Estonia.

the participation of persons with disabilities[140] are very important measures to promote and support their employment.

Sheltered employment is a "residual option"[141] and such facilities must be reserved only for those who cannot work in the open labour market, due to their disability. Sheltered employment also covers working co-operatives[142] and it is seen as a measure of transition, as it should aim at assisting persons with disabilities to enter the open labour market. State Parties must provide equal treatment to disabled persons working in sheltered employment facilities where production is the main activity, who are entitled to "the usual benefits of labour law", especially the right to fair remuneration and trade union rights.[143] The fact that Article 15 § 2 recognizes sheltered employment as a form of work[144] is important, as the ECSR is asking State Parties to provide information on the level of wages within sheltered employment and to the extent that trade unions operate in these workplaces.[145] Since sheltered employment is a form of work according to the Revised Charter, the national court will most likely decide, in such a case, that the disabled person is entitled to annual leave.[146]

2 The Employer's Obligation of Reasonable Accommodation

Although Article 15 § 2 imposes duties on the State Parties, an obligation of reasonable accommodation has been developed by the ECSR:[147] the employer is obliged to take the necessary measures to adjust the working conditions in order to ensure effective access to employment, on the one hand, and to keep in employment persons with disabilities, on the other. This obligation is called reasonable accommodation and an emphasis is placed on this duty when persons have become disabled as a result of an industrial accident or occupational illness.[148] The employer may benefit from public funds to adjust the workplace and work equipment[149] and render it accessible for workers with disabilities,

140 ECSR, Conclusions XIV-2, *cit.*
141 Mark Bell, *cit.*, p. 309.
142 Explanatory Report to the European Social Charter (Revised), *cit.*, § 63, p. 7.
143 ECSR, Conclusions XVII-2 (2005), Czech Republic.
144 Mark Bell, *cit.*, p. 309.
145 ECSR, Conclusions, XVI-2 (2004), Germany.
146 The decision of the national court in such case would also be in line with CJEU, 6 March 2015, *Gérard Fenoll v Centre d'aide par le travail 'La Jouvene', Association de parents et d'amis de personnes handicapées mentales (APEI) d'Avignon*, C-316/13, § 40.
147 ECSR, Conclusions 2007, Statement of Interpretation of Article 15 § 2.
148 *Ibid.*
149 ECSR, Conclusions 2020, Estonia.

including: purchasing a computer software, communication and orientation aids, adapting and purchasing ancillary technological equipment or adapting hygienic, thermal, light or noise conditions.[150] The mere legal provision that the employer has the duty of reasonable accommodation is not sufficient; it should be accompanied by guarantees of effectiveness. State Parties should provide information as to how reasonable accommodation is effectively guaranteed in practice and the number of employers having received funding for workplace adaptations and technical equipment.[151] In addition, the denial of such accommodation should be considered a form of discrimination, explicitly included in anti-discrimination laws.[152] There is a breach of Article 15 § 2 when there is a low general awareness of the notion and the precise content of the concept of reasonable accommodation and where employers do not face considerable liability if they fail to meet this requirement.[153]

While effective workplace accommodation is a duty of the employer, the means to achieve it, as well as the limits and the sanctions that might be encountered by non-compliant employers are established at the national level by the State Parties, who enjoy a margin of discretion – within certain limits – of the measures they deem to be necessary in order to ensure effective access to employment of persons with disabilities. Unlike the EU legal framework, the European Social Charter doesn't set specific limits to the employers' duty of reasonable accommodation, nor does it establish exemptions in case of a disproportionate burden. The ECSR assesses the effectiveness of the measures taken by the States and not directly the conduct of the employers.[154]

3 Obligations of the State Parties under Article 15 § 2

As in the case of the first paragraph of Article 15, State Parties enjoy a margin of discretion and may adopt the measures they deem to be necessary in order to promote access to employment of persons with disabilities. Article 15 § 2 does not require the introduction of quotas, even if such a system is widespread among the State Parties. If such a system is applied, the ECSR assesses its effectiveness[155] by requiring information on the total number of persons with disabilities, including those of working age; those employed, in the public and private sectors,[156] in ordinary and in sheltered employment; those benefiting

150 ECSR, Conclusions XXII-1 (2020), Czech Republic.
151 ECSR, Conclusions 2020, Serbia.
152 *Ibid.*
153 ECSR, Conclusions 2020, Hungary.
154 *Ibid.*
155 ECSR, Conclusions XIV-2 (1998), Belgium.
156 ECSR, Conclusions 2020, Estonia.

from employment promotion measures; those seeking employment; those who are unemployed, as well as "the general transfer rate of people with disabilities from sheltered to open market employment";[157] furthermore, disaggregated data (gender, age and disability) should be provided.[158] State Parties also have to provide information on the practical implementation of the obligation to ensure reasonable accommodation, examples and any relevant data on compliance, information on the mechanisms that monitor effective implementation[159] and to indicate whether reasonable accommodation has led to more persons with disabilities to be employed in the open labour market.[160] There is a specific duty on the State Parties to adopt legislation that prohibits discrimination and dismissal on the basis of disability,[161] and that creates a genuine equality of opportunities on the open labour market.[162] Those who were unlawfully discriminated against should have an effective remedy to tackle discrimination.[163]

As in the case of the first paragraph, Article 15 § 2 involves rights whose achievement "is exceptionally complex and particularly expensive to resolve". Therefore, the measures adopted by the State Parties must respect three conditions: "to be taken within a reasonable time, with measurable progress and to an extent consistent with the maximum use of available resources".[164] The measures adopted also have to be assessed from the perspective of their impact on groups with heightened vulnerabilities and their families, on whom falls the heaviest burden in the event of institutional shortcomings.[165]

C *The Right to Full Social Integration and Participation in the Life of the Community through Accessibility*

Article 15 § 3 of the revised Charter grants the right of persons with disabilities to full social integration and participation in the life of the community, focusing on the social model of disability. This model focuses on the barriers that persons with impairments face in society, such as inaccessible transport

157 ECSR, Conclusions 2012, Cyprus; Conclusions XVI-2 (2004), Belgium.
158 ECSR, Conclusions 2020, Cyprus.
159 *Ibid.*
160 ECSR, Conclusions 2016 and 2020, Turkey.
161 ECSR, Conclusions 2003, Slovenia.
162 ECSR, Conclusions 2012, Russian Federation.
163 ECSR, Conclusions XIX-1 (2008), Czech Republic.
164 ECSR, *International Association Autisme-Europe* (AIAE) *v. France*, *cit.*, § 53.
165 ECSR, *International Association Autisme-Europe* (AIAE) *v. France*, *cit.*, § 53.

or public buildings, thereby shifting from the individual medical problem[166] to the issue of disabling social barriers, that have to be eradicated.[167] The essence of the social model of disability relies on the fact that impairment is "individual and private", whereas disability "is structural and public".[168] The right to full integration is achieved through measures aiming at the removal of barriers to communication and mobility, including such measures as technical aids and other means necessary in order to enable the disabled persons' access to transport (by land, rail, sea and air), housing (public, social and private), cultural activities and leisure (social and sporting activities).[169]

To this end, State Parties to the ESC must adopt a coherent policy in the disability context, containing positive actions for the achievement of the goals of social integration and full participation of persons with impairments.[170] The policy has to take into consideration the needs of persons with disabilities who "should have a voice in the design, implementation and review of such a policy".[171] The positive action measures, legally established and coordinated,[172] should be reinforced by non-discrimination legislation, applicable both to the public and the private sphere and providing effective remedies for those who have been unlawfully treated. Such legislation should cover housing, transport, telecommunications and cultural and leisure activities and it may consist of specific legislation, general anti-discrimination legislation or a combination of the two.[173]

Fostering the integration and participation of disabled persons in community life requires,[174] first of all, that State Parties establish mechanisms to assess

166 Colin Barnes, "Understanding the social model of disability. Past, present and future", in Nick Watson, Alan Roulstone and Carol Thomas (eds.), *Routledge Handbook of Disability Studies,* 2nd ed., London, Routledge, 2019, pp. 12–22.

167 Mike Oliver, "The social model of disability: thirty years on", *Disability & Society*, vol. 28, no.7, 2013, pp. 1024–1026.

168 Tom Shakespeare, "The Social Model of Disability", in Lennard J. Davis, *The Disability Studies Reader*, 4th ed, London, Routledge, 2013, p. 216.

169 ECSR, Conclusions 2005, Norway; ECSR, *Defence for Children International (DCI), European Federation of National Organisations working with the Homeless (FEANTSA), Magistrats Européens pour la Démocratie et les Libertés (MEDEL), Confederación Sindical de Comisiones Obreras and International Movement ATD Fourth World v. Spain*, complaint No. 206/2022, decision on admissibility and immediate measures of, 19 October 2022, § 10 (lack of access to electricity).

170 ECSR, Conclusions 2007, Slovenia.

171 ECSR, Conclusions 2003, Italy.

172 ECSR, *International Federation for Human Rights (FIDH) v. Belgium*, complaint No. 75/2011, decision on the merits of 18 March 2013, § 172.

173 ECSR, Conclusions 2012, Estonia.

174 ECSR, Conclusions 2008, Statement of interpretation of Article 15 § 3.

the barriers to communication and mobility, in order to identify the support measures that are needed in order to assist them in overcoming these barriers. To this purpose, technical aids (such as prostheses, walkers, wheelchairs, guide dogs and appropriate housing support arrangements) and support services (personal assistance and auxiliary aids) must be available for persons with disabilities, at no cost or subject to an appropriate contribution, taking into account the beneficiary's means.[175] Persons with impairments may overcome barriers to communication and mobility through telecommunications and new information technology, which must be accessible;[176] in addition, sign language should have an official status.[177] Many means of transport and public buildings tend not to be accessible to persons with disabilities, due as well to constraints related to the cultural heritage of the buildings.[178] Under Article 15 § 3, public transportation (by land, rail, sea and air), as well as "all newly constructed or renovated public buildings, facilities and buildings open to the public, and cultural and leisure activities should be physically accessible".[179]

Accessibility is a precondition to an independent life and full and equal participation in society[180] and is a means to achieve *de facto* equality for all of persons with disabilities. There is an important difference between accessibility and reasonable accommodations: accessibility is related to groups and must be implemented gradually and unconditionally; reasonable accommodation is related to an individual, applies immediately to all of his/her rights and may be limited by disproportionality.[181] As the realization of accessibility takes time, "reasonable accommodation may be used as a means to provide access to an individual in the meantime, as it is an immediate duty".[182]

Article 15 § 3 is also applicable to highly dependent adults with disabilities, who have a critical state of health and particular lifestyle.[183] If they remain at home, being excluded from day or night care facilities, State Parties must make sure that home adaptations that are "necessary to permit these persons' integration and dignified existence within the family and social environment" are being

175 *Ibid.*
176 ECSR, Conclusions 2005, Estonia.
177 ECSR, Conclusions 2003, Slovenia.
178 ECtHR, 31 May 2022, *Arnar Helgi Lárusson v. Iceland*, no. 23077/19.
179 ECSR, Conclusions 2003, Italy.
180 CtRPD, *General Comment No. 2 (2014) on Article 9: Accessibility*, 22 May 2014, CRPD/C/GC/2, § 1.
181 CtRPD, *General Comment No. 6 (2018) on equality and nondiscrimination*, 26 April 2018, CRPD/C/GC/6, § 41.
182 *Ibid.*, § 42.
183 ECSR, *FIDH v. Belgium*, *cit.*, § 175.

taken by the social services.[184] More generally, housing policies must take into account the needs of persons with disabilities, including the adequate supply of suitable housing, either public, social or private in nature. Furthermore, financial assistance should be provided for the adaptation of existing housing".[185]

II Non-discrimination in the Exercise of Article 15 of the Revised European Social Charter

"The non-discrimination norm has a very important role in the disability context".[186] The scope of Article 15 includes discrimination based on disability and prohibits all form of discrimination.[187] Equality of treatment should exist, not only by law but also in practice, between persons with disabilities who are Nationals of a State Party and legally residing or regularly working on the territory of another State Party.[188]

The drafters of the Revised Charter paid a heightened importance to the principle of non-discrimination with respect to the effective enjoyment of the substantive rights contained by the Charter, an importance that is highlighted by the insertion of Article E into a separate Article.[189] Article E is not an autonomous right which could in itself provide independent grounds for a complaint; it can be analysed only in combination with a substantive right granted by the Revised Charter, securing the equal effective exercise of that right.[190] The wording of Article E is similar to that of Article 14 of the ECHR, and the ECSR makes reference[191] to the judgments of the European Court of Human Rights (ECtHR) for the definition of the principle of equality, which means "treating equals equally and unequals unequally".[192] Persons who are in significantly different situations should be treated differently by the State; consequently, there is discrimination when persons whose situations are different are treated in a uniform manner,[193] without objective and reasonable

184 *Ibid., loc.cit.*
185 ECSR, Conclusions 2003, Italy.
186 ESCR, Conclusions 2003, *cit.*
187 ECSR, *MDAC v. Belgium, cit.*, § 62.
188 Conclusions XIV-2, *cit.*
189 ECSR, *International Association Autisme-Europe (AIAE) v. France, cit.*, § 51.
190 *Ibid,* § 51.
191 *Ibid.*, § 52; ECSR, *European Action of the Disabled (AEH) v. France, cit.*, § 133.
192 ECtHR [GC], 6 April 2000, *Thlimmenos c. Grece*, no 34369/97, § 44.
193 ECSR, *Syndicat national des Professions du tourisme v. France,* Complaint no. 6/1999, Decision on the merits of 10 October 2000, § 56 (a difference in treatment between lecturer guides approved by national bodies and interpreter guides and national lecturers

justification.[194]

Disability is not explicitly listed as a prohibited ground of discrimination under Article E, yet the ECSR has considered that it is contained in the reference to "other status".[195] The Charter expresses solidarity and promotes social inclusion and State Parties must respect differences and avoid social exclusion.[196] Highly dependent adults with disabilities are particularly vulnerable if their individuality and human dignity are not respected.[197] Their situation has to be taken into consideration by the State Parties when adopting measures in the social services field, in order to guarantee effective access to the benefits of public policy, even if it means that persons with severe disabilities will be treated more favourably[198] than persons without or with minor/ moderate disabilities.[199] The Charter envisages a complete protection against discrimination, encompassing the right to education and vocational training, the right to work and accessibility and full participation in society, in cultural activities and in leisure.

Article E prohibits both direct discrimination and all forms of indirect discrimination, which "may arise by failing to take due and positive account of all relevant differences or by failing to take adequate steps to ensure that the rights and collective advantages that are open to all are genuinely accessible by and to all".[200] A difference in treatment indirectly based on disability may arise as a result of budget restrictions in social policy matters,[201] as an apparently neutral provision, criterion or practice would put persons with impairments at a particular disadvantage compared with other persons, unless it can be justified.[202] For an independent life and in dignity, a person with a disability is more likely to be dependent on community care, funded through the State

---

with a state diploma, as regards working conditions and the freedom to conduct guided tours constitutes discrimination); ECSR, *Associazione sindacale « La Voce dei Giusti »* v. Italy, Complaint No. 105/2014, Decision on the merits of 18 October 2016, § 80 (the terms of admission to a teaching qualification, the operating methods and the non- recognition of previous work experience constitutes discrimination as it affects disproportionately supply teachers).

194 ECtHR [GC], 6 April 2000, *Thlimmenos,* § 44.

195 ECSR, *International Association Autisme-Europe* (*AIAE*) *v. France, cit.*, § 51.

196 ECSR, *European Roma Rights Centre* (*ERRC*) *v. Italy,* complaint No. 27/2004, decision on the merits of 7 December 2004, § 19.

197 ECSR, *FIDH v. Belgium, cit.,* § 208.

198 *Ibid.,* § 209.

199 *Ibid.,* § 207.

200 ECSR, *International Association Autisme-Europe* (*AIAE*) *v. France, cit.*, § 52; *FIDH, cit.*, § 206.

201 ECSR, *European Action of the Disabled* (*AEH*) *v. France, cit.,* § 144.

202 *Ibid.,* § 143.

budget, than other persons receiving community care.[203] Therefore, not providing sufficient day and night care facilities constitutes discrimination, as many highly dependent persons with disabilities are excluded from this form of social welfare service, which would be appropriate to their specific needs.[204]

However, different budgets, for financing establishments specialising in the education and care of disabled children and for "ordinary schools", "does not in itself amount to discrimination, since it is primarily for States themselves to decide on the modalities of funding".[205] On the other hand, providing only limited funds for the education of children and adolescents with autism is a form of indirect discrimination.[206] The fact that the proportion of children with autism who are educated in general or specialist schools is much lower compared to other children constitutes discrimination.[207]

III Disability Protection in Other Instruments of European and International Law: Convergence or Divergence with the Charter?

The social model of disability has become predominant in recent decades, reflected in a series of European and international protection instruments focusing on ensuring the effectiveness of the rights of persons with disabilities and on adapting the environment to their needs. The rights guaranteed by Article 15 of the Charter can be found in other European and international protection instruments, but the scope of these rights or the means necessary to ensure their effectiveness may vary from one instrument to another.

The revised ESC and the EU framework find a point of convergence in the CRPD which permits a certain harmonization of their respective standards. The Council of Europe and its member states aim to bring added value to policies and measures adopted by the EU and the UN;[208] the EU has ratified the CRDP.[209] The CRPD, in turn, does not lower standards established in the

203 *Ibid.*, § 144.
204 ECSR, *FIDH v. Belgium*, *cit.*, § 210.
205 ECSR, *International Association Autisme-Europe* (*AIAE*) *v. France*, *cit.*, § 54.
206 ECSR, *European Action of the Disabled* (*AEH*) *v. France*, *cit.*, § 145.
207 ECSR, *International Association Autisme-Europe* (*AIAE*) *v. France*, *cit.*, § 54.
208 Council of Europe Disability Strategy 2017–2023, p. 11.
209 The EU signed the UN Convention on the Rights of People with Disabilities on 30 March 2007 and ratified it on 23 December 2010 (Council Decision of 26 November 2009 concerning the conclusion, by the European Community, of the United Nations Convention on the Rights of Persons with Disabilities, *OJ L 23, 27.1.2010, p. 35–36*).

national or international law in force for a State Party to the convention.[210] There is a certain conceptual convergence between the revised ESC, the CRPD and the EU legal framework, a convergence that is not always reflected in the jurisprudence of the bodies monitoring compliance with the European and international standards. With respect to the three paragraphs contained in Article 15 of the revised Charter, it is now worth examining the main equivalent or divergent protection standards across international and European law.

The duty of the State Parties to provide accessible education and the person's right not to be segregated and to be provided with reasonable accommodation, as established by Article 15 § 1 of the Charter and developed in the case-law of the ECSR,[211] is in line with the UNESCO Convention against Discrimination in Education, Article 24 § 1 CRPD[212] and with Article 23 § 3 of the Convention on the Rights of the Child. Article 24 § 1 CRPD focuses on inclusive education systems and lifelong learning, directed to fully developing the human potential, sense of dignity and self-worth of persons with disabilities.[213]

However, even if the Charter of Fundamental Rights in the EU is inspired by the European Social Charter, Article 26 CFREU on integration of persons with disabilities merely states the negative obligation of the EU to respect the rights of persons with disabilities to benefit from measures designed to ensure their independence, social and occupational integration and participation in the life of the community; it does not set duties for the EU Member States to take the necessary measures to that purpose. Due to the limited competencies of the EU in the field of disability and to the principle of subsidiarity, the EU mainly supports and complements the actions of the Member States in this field.[214] Similarly to the ESC, the EU also provides for the right of persons with disabilities, including "invisible disabilities such as autism, dyslexia, or hyperactivity" to education at all levels and forms, from early childhood to university degree, since education plays an essential role in combating poverty and in creating fully inclusive societies.[215] Both legislation and educational institutions must

---

210 CRPD, Article 4 § 4.

211 Supra, the analysis of Article 15 § 1 of the revised Charter.

212 CtRPD, *General Comment No. 4 (2016), cit.*, § 13.

213 *Ibid*, § 15.

214 Isabelle Hachez, "Article 26. Intégration des personnes handicapées", in Fabrice Picod and Sébastien Van Drooghenbroeck, "Charte de droits fondamentaux de l'Union européenne. Commentaire article par article", Bruxelles, Bruylant, 2018, p. 584.

215 Communication from the Commission to the European Parliament, the Council, the European Economic and Social Committee and the Committee of the Regions, *Union of Equality: Strategy for the Rights of Persons with Disabilities 2021–2030,* Brussels, 3.3.2021 – COM(2021) 101 final, p. 17.

provide conditions for an inclusive approach, as many students with disabilities still attend special schools, which do not always grant an effective access to the labour market. Among the EU initiatives which can be highlighted are: the support of education policies by the European Agency for Special Needs and Inclusive Education and the Strategy for the Rights of Persons with Disabilities 2021–2030[216] (promoting inclusive and accessible vocational programmes). The EU has acceded to the CRPD and it has undertaken to contribute "to the development of quality of education" and to implementing a vocational training policy supporting and supplementing the action of the Member States.[217]

Persons with disabilities face numerous employment-related barriers, high unemployment rates, a lack of accessibility of the work environment and lower standards in hiring conditions. They usually earn lower wages than persons without disabilities, are not appointed to managerial positions, are in vulnerable employment and face instability. Digital work, new technologies and artificial intelligence offer new pathways into the labour market, but may also create new barriers for persons with disabilities.[218] Article 27 CRPD recognizes the right to work of persons with disabilities, including "the right to the opportunity to gain a living by work freely chosen or accepted" in an open, inclusive and accessible labour market and work environment and provides a non-exhaustive list of the measures to be taken for that purpose, including just, favourable and safe working conditions; non-discrimination (including harassment) and the collective dimension of the right to work.[219]

The wording of Article 15 § 2 of the revised Charter refers to the social policy State Parties should adopt in the field of employment of persons with disabilities. Workplace accommodation, as a duty of the employer, has been developed by the ECSR,[220] but national social policy should determine the means to achieve it, the limits and the sanctions applicable to non-compliant employers.[221] Unlike the European Social Charter, the EU legal framework sets specific limits to the employers' duty of reasonable accommodation and it establishes exemptions in case of a disproportionate burden.

---

216 *Ibid.*, p. 12.

217 Council Decision of 26 November 2009 concerning the conclusion, by the European Community, of the United Nations Convention on the Rights of Persons with Disabilities, Annex II.

218 CtRPD, *General Comment No. 8 (2022) on the right of persons with disabilities to work and employment*, 9 September 2022, CRPD/C/GC/8, § 5.

219 *Ibid.*, § 6.

220 ECSR, Conclusions 2007, Statement of Interpretation on Article 15 § 2.

221 ECSR, Conclusions, 2020, Hungary.

Under Article 5 of Council Directive 2000/78/EC of 27 November 2000 establishing a general framework for equal treatment in employment and occupation, employers have a duty of reasonable accommodation, entailing appropriate measures to enable a person with disabilities to have access to, participate in, or advance in employment, or to undergo training, unless such measures would impose a disproportionate burden. The assessment of the disproportionate nature of the burden focuses on the financial and other costs entailed, compared to the scale and financial resources of the employer and the possibility of obtaining public funding or other assistance. Direct and indirect discrimination in employment and occupation on the ground of disability is prohibited and denial of reasonable accommodation in the case of a disabled person is a form of discrimination.[222] The CJEU has held that dismissal for 'objective reasons' of a disabled worker who has a productivity below a given rate, a low level of multi-skilling in the undertaking's posts and a high rate of absenteeism, constitutes indirect discrimination on grounds of disability, unless the employer has beforehand provided that worker with reasonable accommodation.[223] If this obligation is respected, there is no duty to recruit, promote, or maintain in employment or training a person who is not competent, capable and available to perform the essential functions of a job or to undergo the relevant training.[224]

Reasonable accommodation entails measures of a physical (material), organizational or educational nature:[225] adapting premises and equipment; the provision of training or integration resources; measures of work organisation (related to the rhythm or speed of work or a reduction in working hours)[226] and/or the distribution of tasks. The concept of 'reasonable accommodation' should be understood broadly, giving priority to the adaptation of the workplace, to keep the person in employment,[227] including (provided that there is at least one such vacancy) the reassignment to another position for which the person has the necessary competence, capability and availability, unless that measure imposes a disproportionate burden on the employer.[228]

---

222 CJEU, 11 September 2019, *DW v. Nobel Plastiques Ibérica SA*, C-397/18, § 72.

223 *Ibid*, § 75.

224 CJEU, 21 October 2021, *TC and UB v. Komisia za zashtita ot diskriminatsia and VA*, C-824/19, § 62.

225 CJEU, 15 July 2021, *XX v. Tartu Vangla*, C-795/19, § 48.

226 CJEU, 11 April 2013, *HK Danmark*, C-335/11 and C-337/11, §§ 55–56.

227 CJEU, 10 February 2022, *XXXX v. HR Rail SA*, C-485/20, § 41.

228 CJEU, 10 February 2022, *XXXX v. HR Rail SA*, *cit.*, § 49.

The EU Strategy for the Rights of Persons with Disabilities 2021–2030 aims to improve participation in employment of persons with impairments,[229] by providing: guidance and support in strengthening employment capacities and integration services, promoting hiring perspectives through affirmative action and combating stereotypes, ensuring reasonable accommodation at work, securing health and safety at work and vocational rehabilitation schemes in case of chronic diseases, sickness or accidents, and exploring quality jobs in sheltered employment and pathways to the open labour market.[230]

Transforming societies and ensuring accessibility of persons with disabilities to the life of the community, including cultural activities and leisure is the pre-condition to an effective social inclusion, as granted by Article 15 § 3 of the revised Charter. The right to participate in the cultural life of the community, enjoy the arts and share in scientific advancement and its benefits is contained in Article 27 of the Universal Declaration of Human Rights. Article 9 CRPD focuses on accessibility, as a pre-condition to full participation in all aspects of life. Equal access of persons with disabilities, in urban and in rural areas, to the physical environment, transportation, information and communications, as well as to other facilities and services open or provided to the public, must be granted. Effective measures to ensure personal mobility, under Article 20 CRPD, include, *inter alia*, facilitating access to quality mobility aids, devices, assistive technologies and forms of live assistance and intermediaries, as well as training in mobility skills to persons with disabilities and to specialist staff working with them. Article 30 CRPD recognizes the right of persons with disabilities to take part without discrimination in cultural life, recreation, leisure and sport. Therefore, accessible formats of different cultural materials and activities, access to places for cultural performances or services, to sporting, recreational and tourism venues, participation in mainstream sporting activities at all levels and in disability-specific sporting and recreational activities are required. Persons with disabilities should have the opportunity to develop and utilize their creative, artistic and intellectual potential and State Parties to the CRPD must recognise and support their specific cultural and linguistic identity, including sign languages and deaf culture. The importance of full participation of people with disabilities in society through accessibility is also stressed by different directives and regulations adopted at EU level.[231]

229 COM(2021) 101 final, *cit.*, p.13.

230 *Ibid.*, p. 14.

231 At EU level it worth mentioning: the European Accessibility Act – Directive (EU) 2019/882 of the European Parliament and of the Council of 17 April 2019 on the accessibility requirements for products and services; Directive (EU) 2016/2102 of the European Parliament and of the Council of 26 October 2016 on the accessibility of the websites and mobile

In this context, the ECtHR has found a violation of Article 3 (prohibition of degrading treatment) in the case of a man placed against his will in a psychiatric institution in a remote mountain location, in degrading conditions,[232] as well as in the case of an eight-year-old child, placed in an institute which could not accommodate his needs.[233] Among the grounds of discrimination entailing the application of Article 14 ECHR[234] and Article 1 of Protocol No. 12, the ECtHR recognises[235] disability, medical conditions or genetic features, as well as a reduced margin of appreciation for the States in establishing different legal treatment for people with disabilities.[236] There is a consensus on the need to protect people with disabilities from discriminatory treatment,[237] including reasonable accommodation to allow "the opportunity to fully realise their rights".[238] The denial of financial awards, in the case of a blind chess player winning similar international accolades (the Blind Chess Olympiads) as sighted players, who were granted the financial award as a form of national sporting recognition, is discriminatory on the basis of disability.[239]

The ECtHR has also analysed the lack of access to public buildings by disabled persons as a form of discrimination, balancing the interest of the person with impairments with the "disproportionate or undue burden" on the State,

---

applications of public sector bodies; Regulation (EC) No 1107/2006 of the European Parliament and of the Council of 5 July 2006 concerning the rights of disabled persons and persons with reduced mobility when travelling by air; Regulation (EU) No 181/2011 of the European Parliament and of the Council of 16 February 2011 concerning the rights of passengers in bus and coach transport (especially Article 9, 10 and 16); Regulation (EU) No 1177/2010 of the European Parliament and of the Council of 24 November 2010 concerning the rights of passengers when travelling by sea and inland waterway (especially Article 7 and 14) and Regulation (EC) No 1371/2007 of the European Parliament and of the Council of 23 October 2007 on rail passengers' rights and obligations. Other EU initiatives are related to accessibility standardization, EU Disability Card, EU Parking Card.

232 ECtHR [GC], 17 January 2012, *Stanev v. Bulgaria*, no.36760/06.

233 ECtHR, 23 January 2020, *I.R. v. North Macedonia*, no. 38067/15.

234 Convention for the Protection of Human Rights and Fundamental Freedoms, entered into force on 3 September 1953.

235 For an overview of the jurisprudence, ECtHR, *Guide on Article 14 of the European Convention on Human Rights and on Article 1 of Protocol No. 12 to the Convention, Prohibition of discrimination*, 2022.

236 ECtHR, 30 April 2009, *Glor v. Switzerland*, no. 13444/04, § 84.

237 ECtHR, *Glor v. Switzerland, cit.*, § 54.

238 ECtHR, 30 January 2018, *Enver Şahin v. Turkey*, no. 3065/12, §§ 67–69; ECtHR, 23 February 2016, *Çam v. Turkey*, no. 51500/08, §§ 65–67; ECtHR, 10 December 2020, *G.L. v. Italy*, no. 59751/15, §§ 60–66.

239 ECtHR, 25 January 2022, *Negovanović and Others v. Serbia*, nos. 29907/16, 30022/16, 30322/16 and 31142/16, § 92.

"within the confines of the available budget and having regard to the cultural heritage protection of the buildings".[240] In many cases, the Court declared the applications inadmissible, as the applicants had not demonstrated the existence of a special link between the lack of access to the buildings in question and the particular needs of their private life.[241] On the other hand, Article 8 was found to be relevant to complaints related to public funding that was necessary to facilitate the mobility and quality of life of disabled applicants.[242] Other judgments regard housing[243] and disability-based discrimination against the applicant on account of the disability of his child.[244]

An important part of the ECtHR case-law related to the protection of persons with disabilities focuses on the right to education, as guaranteed by Article 2 of Protocol No. 1 to the ECHR. The failure to conduct an individual assessment of a disabled student's concrete needs regarding access to university premises is discriminatory,[245] as is the refusal to enrol into a National Music Academy a student suffering from severe eyesight imparity (blindness).[246] In addition, the lack of specialised assistance, to which a child suffering from non-verbal autism was legally entitled, preventing her from continuing to attend primary school, is a "serious discrimination".[247]

Concluding Remarks

Protection of the human rights and dignity of persons with disabilities has followed a long path, but there remains a lengthy road ahead. As "unwanted members of the society, treated like second class citizens",[248] persons with

240 ECtHR, *Arnar Helgi Lárusson, cit.*, § 59.

241 ECtHR, dec., 14 May 2002, *Zehnalová and Zehnal v. Czech Republic*, no. 38621/97; ECtHR, dec., 11 April 2006, *Molka v. Poland*, no. 56550/00; ECtHR, dec., 25 June 2019, *Glaisen v. Switzerland*, no. 40477/13; ECtHR, dec., 29 January 2019, *Neagu v. Romania*, no. 49561/16.

242 ECtHR, dec., *Molka v. Poland,, cit.*, p. 16; ECtHR, dec., 4 May 1999, *Marzari v. Italy*, no. 36448/9; ECtHR, dec., 13 January 2000, *Maggiolini v. Italy*, no. 35800/97; ECtHR, dec., 8 July 2003, *Sentges v. the Netherlands*, no. 27677/02 (related to a demand of a robotic arm of a young man who was provided with an electric wheelchair with an adapted joystick); ECtHR, dec., 4 January 2005, *Pentiacova and Others v. Moldova*, no. 14462/03.

243 ECtHR, 22 March 2016, *Guberina v. Croatia*, no. 23682/13.

244 ECtHR, 24 October 2019, *J.D. and A. v. the United Kingdom*, nos. 32949/17 and 34614/17.

245 ECtHR, *Enver Şahin v. Turkey, cit.*, § 69.

246 ECtHR, *Çam v. Turkey, cit.*, §§ 65–69.

247 ECtHR, *G.L. v. Italy, cit.*, § 71.

248 Kiran Kori, "Safeguarding the Human Rights of Persons with Disabilities: An Analytical Approach", *International Journal of Law Management & Humanities*, No. 4, 2021, p. 1248.

impairments have long been treated as objects of pity,[249] and not as equal citizens. Consequently, social policy has followed mainly a charitable approach. In this context, the Charter has brought an essential change of perspective, focusing on the dignity of all human beings, irrespective of their physical or mental condition, as the very essence of human rights and bedrock of the European Society:[250] "The idea of human rights implies that the dignity of all individuals must be recognised and respected".[251] Persons with disabilities should enjoy an equal citizenship and be allowed to make their own choices, as rights holders.

Article 15 of the Charter is particularly important for the protection of human rights, ensuring that all citizens, including those with impairments, are granted effective rights and highlighting the vital link between safeguarding social rights and protecting human dignity.[252] The first paragraph of Article 15, granting the right to education, vocational training and guidance, is essential in the architecture of Article 15, as it improves the "employability" of disabled persons and their ability to remain in employment: occupational integration is an essential element of social integration.[253] Obtaining a position in the open labour market, guaranteed by the second paragraph of Article 15, is essential to living a self-determined life, that is, to effective and equal participation in the life of the community. Rendering societies more accessible, guaranteed by the third paragraph, as well as assessing disability as an interaction of health conditions, environmental factors and personal factors,[254] defines the difference between inclusion and integration.

Multiple sources aim at safeguarding the human rights and dignity of disabled persons: the revised ESC, the CRPD, the ECHR and various directives and initiatives adopted by the EU. The difficulty related to this diversity is that different standards of protection of persons with impairments may apply in practice. The common denominator of the revised ESC and the EU framework may be identified in the relevance of the CRPD. It would be inaccurate, however, to simply assimilate the revised ESC to the CRPD, as the ESC and, more generally, the Council of Europe, seek to add value to the existing work,

249 ECSR, *International Association Autisme-Europe (AIAE) v. France*, *cit.*, § 48; Conclusions XVIII (2007), *cit.*

250 SG (53), Memorandum, *cit.*, § 5, p. 5.

251 ECSR, Conclusions XIV-2 (1998), Statement of interpretation of Article 15.

252 ECSR, Conclusions XIV-2 (1998), Statement of interpretation of Article 15.

253 *Ibid.*

254 ECSR, Conclusions 2020, p. 3.

devised under different European and international instruments, in order to grant persons with disabilities effective rights on an equal footing with others. Even if the Charter is expressly mentioned by Article 151 TFEU, as a bedrock of fundamental social rights that the EU is aiming to achieve, the ESC – though it is sometimes used by the CJEU when interpreting EU law and as a source for the CFREU – it is still undervalued in the EU legal order.[255] Persons with disabilities still face barriers in their participation as equal members of society and violations of their human rights and dignity: a father may still not attend birthday parties with his children because the building is not accessible;[256] a student may still be refused enrolment to university or might lack specialised assistance.[257] Positively, the plurality of sources leads to a dialogue between the bodies monitoring compliance with the European and international standards and to a better protection of the rights of persons with disabilities: the ECSR usually relies on the CRPD in its decisions assessing compliance with the provisions of Article 15 of the Charter;[258] the CJUE[259] relies on the CRPD and the ECtHR[260] relies on the standards set by the ESC and the CRPD. Even if Article 15 is "exceptionally complex and particularly expensive to resolve", the ECSR rigorously monitors compliance with the standards set by the Charter, assessing if the national measures are taken within a reasonable timeframe, with measurable progress and financing making the maximum use of available resources.[261]

The Charter is a living instrument[262] and the interpretation of its rights and freedoms by the ECSR takes into consideration the current conditions,[263] new emerging issues and relevant international instruments,[264] leading to a more inclusive society, granting effective rights, equally, to all its citizens, regardless

255 Olivier De Schutter, "The European Social Charter in the context of implementation of the EU Charter of Fundamental Rights", European Union, 2016, pp. 19–21.

256 ECtHR, *Arnar Helgi Lárusson, cit.*, § 59.

257 EctHR, *Çam v. Turkey, cit.*, §§ 65–69; ECtHR, *G.L. v. Italy, cit.*, § 71.

258 ECSR, *MDAC, cit.*, §§ 22–24; ECSR, *European Action of the Disabled, cit.*, § 17.

259 CJEU, *Tartu Vangla,, cit.*, § 49; CJEU, *Komisia, cit.*, § 59.

260 ECtHR, *Arnar Helgi Lárusson, cit.*, § 23; ECtHR, [GC], 13 December 2016, *Béláné Nagy v. Hungary*, no. 53080/13, § 35.

261 ECSR, *International Association Autisme-Europe (AIAE) v. France, cit.*, § 53.

262 ECSR, *ILGA v. Czech Republic*, complaint No.117/2015, decision on the merits of 15 May 2018, § 75.

263 ECSR, *Marangopoulos Foundation for Human Rights v. Greece*, complaint No. 30/2005, decision on the merits of 6 December 2006, § 194.

264 ECSR, *FEANTSA v France, cit.*, § 64.

of their impairments. Article 15 of the revised Charter has had, and still plays, an important role in setting the standards of protection on different coordinates and in achieving full participation of persons with disabilities in the life of the community.

ARTICLE 16

The Right of the Family to Social, Legal and Economic Protection

Nilay Arat, Demirhan Burak Çelik, Sedef Koç and Aslı Topukcu

With a view to ensuring the necessary conditions for the full development of the family, which is a fundamental unit of society, the Contracting Parties undertake to promote the economic, legal and social protection of family life by such means as social and family benefits, fiscal arrangements, provision of family housing, benefits for the newly married, and other appropriate means.

Introduction

Article 16 is one of the "hard core provisions" of the European Social Charter (ESC)[1] and i is also one of the most accepted articles of the Charter, in both the 1961 and 1996 versions, which highlights the overall commitment of state parties to the socio-economic protection of the family.[2] By describing the family as "a fundamental unit of the society" and by imposing upon the States an obligation to take appropriate measures to protect it, this article reflects an approach similar to that of some basic UN documents such as the Universal Declaration of Human Rights (UDHR, Article 16), the International Covenant on Civil and Political Rights (ICCPR, Article 23), the International Covenant on Economic Social and Cultural Rights (ICESCR, Articles 10 and 11 § 1) and the Charter of Fundamental Rights of the European Union (CFREU, Article

1 European Social Charter (ESC), 1961, Article 20: "1. Each of the Contracting Parties undertakes … b. to consider itself bound by at least five of the following articles of Part II of this Charter: Article 1, 5, 6, 12, 13, 16 and 19"; ESC (rev), Part III, Article A: "1. Subject to the provisions of Article B below, each of the Parties undertakes … b. to consider itself bound by at least six of the following nine articles of Part II of this Charter: Article 1, 5, 6, 7, 12, 13, 16, 19 and 20."

2 The only five States who have not accepted Article 16 of the ESC (rev) are Albania, Andorra, Armenia, Cyprus and Georgia. For the chart of the acceptance of provisions by the States, see: <https://rm.coe.int/country-by-country-table-of-accepted-provisions/1680630742>.

 | DOI:10.1163/9789004434141_007

33).[3] At the same time, in terms of how it provides human rights protection to the family, Article 16 ESC differs from some other international and regional provisions such as Article 12 of the UDHR, Article 17 of the ICCPR, Articles 8 and 12 of the European Convention on Human Rights (ECHR) and Articles 7 and 9 of the CFREU, to the extent that it extends beyond the right to respect for private and family life or the right to marry and start a family.[4] Article 16 has a

3 UDHR, Article 16: "Men and women of full age, without any limitation due to race, nationality or religion, have the right to marry and to found a family. They are entitled to equal rights as to marriage, during marriage and at its dissolution. Marriage shall be entered into only with the free and full consent of the intending spouses. The family is the natural and fundamental group unit of society and is entitled to protection by society and the state."; ICCPR, Article 23: "1. The family is the natural and fundamental group unit of society and is entitled to protection by society and the state. 2. The right of men and women of marriageable age to marry and to found a family shall be recognized. 3. No marriage shall be entered into without the free and full consent of the intending spouses. 4. States parties to the present covenant shall take appropriate steps to ensure equality of rights and responsibilities of spouses as to marriage, during marriage and at its dissolution. In the case of dissolution, provision shall be made for the necessary protection of any children."; ICESCR, Article 10: "The States Parties to the present Covenant recognize that: 1. The widest possible protection and assistance should be accorded to the family, which is the natural and fundamental group unit of society, particularly for its establishment and while it is responsible for the care and education of dependent children. Marriage must be entered into with the free consent of the intending spouses. 2. Special protection should be accorded to mothers during a reasonable period before and after childbirth. During such period working mothers should be accorded paid leave or leave with adequate social security benefits. 3. Special measures of protection and assistance should be taken on behalf of all children and young persons without any discrimination for reasons of parentage or other conditions. Children and young persons should be protected from economic and social exploitation. Their employment in work harmful to their morals or health or dangerous to life or likely to hamper their normal development should be punishable by law. States should also set age limits below which the paid employment of child labour should be prohibited and punishable by law."; ICESCR, Article 11 § 1: "The States Parties to the present Covenant recognize the right of everyone to an adequate standard of living for himself and his family, including adequate food, clothing and housing, and to the continuous improvement of living conditions. The States Parties will take appropriate steps to ensure the realization of this right, recognizing to this effect the essential importance of international co-operation based on free consent."; CFREU, Article 33: "1. The family shall enjoy legal, economic and social protection. 2. To reconcile family and professional life, everyone shall have the right to protection from dismissal for a reason connected with maternity and the right to paid maternity leave and to parental leave following the birth or adoption of a child".

4 UDHR, Article 12: "No one shall be subjected to arbitrary interference with his privacy, family, home or correspondence, nor to attacks upon his honour and reputation. Everyone has the right to the protection of the law against such interference or attacks."; ICCPR, Article 17: "1. No one shall be subjected to arbitrary or unlawful interference with his privacy, family, home or correspondence, nor to unlawful attacks on his honour and reputation. 2. Everyone has the right to the protection of the law against such interference or attacks."; ECHR, Article 8: "1. Everyone has the right to respect for his private and family life, his home and his

wide scope in order to provide full protection for the family. It envisages that the family will not only be protected by laws but also by economic and social measures such as "social and family benefits, social arrangements, provision of family housing, benefits for the newly married." It must also be underlined that this is not an exhaustive list as the Article refers to "such means as ... and other appropriate means."

The first draft of the Article was longer and reflected certain social values widely accepted in the 1950s in Europe. The then Article 1 of the Section B which was entitled "Rights pertaining to the family and to children" read as follows:

> Every man shall have a right to found a family.
> The family is the foundation of society and as such entitled to the widest measure of protection.
> It is based on a marriage freely entered into by the prospective husband and wife.
> The unity of the family may not be impaired, save on the basis of respect for the natural, rights of the individuals concerned.
> The steps to be taken by the signatory Governments for the protection of the family shall include:
> (a) Payment of a supplementary allowance to the father of the family so that the mother may stay at home;
> (b) Assistance to large families, more particularly by the grant of allowances in proportion to the number of children;

correspondence. 2. There shall be no interference by a public authority with the exercise of this right except such as is in accordance with the law and is necessary in a democratic society in the interests of national security, public safety or the economic well-being of the country, for the prevention of disorder or crime, for the protection of health or morals, or for the protection of the rights and freedoms of others". It is also important to note that in the view of the European Committee of Social Rights, Article 16 also protects a right to personal development and the right to establish and develop relationships with other human beings and the outside world, in parallel with Article 8 of the European Convention on Human Rights. See: ESCR, *Centre on Housing Rights and Evictions* (COHRE) *v. Italy*, complaint No. 58/2009, decision on the merits of 25 June 2010, § 129; ECHR, Article 12: "Men and women of marriageable age have the right to marry and to found a family, according to the national laws governing the exercise of this right."; CFREU, Art 7: "Everyone has the right to respect for his or her private and family life, home and communications."; CFREU, Art 9: "The right to marry and the right to found a family shall be guaranteed in accordance with the national laws governing the exercise of these rights."

(c) Special protection accorded to mothers during reasonable periods before and after childbirth; the mother shall have the right to leave with pay for not less than six weeks before and six weeks after childbirth, the right to keep her job and to receive both medical attention for herself and her child and financial assistance during the nursing period.[5]

This approach, however, received negative feedback. For instance, the International Federation of Christian Trade Unions emphasized the importance of family wages but underlined that the head of the family could be either a man or a woman.[6] In a similar vein, it was proposed by a member of the Consultative Assembly (UK MP Burton) that sub-paragraph (b) of paragraph 5 be deleted as it encouraged women to stay at home.[7] It should also be noted that the Governments proposed a much more detailed list of measures such as tax relief, rent reduction, establishment of maternity aid institutions for social counselling, legal and medical assistance, general and special child welfare measures.[8] However, the Working Party, appointed by the Consultative Assembly to draft the Charter, decided to adopt only the first paragraph of the text prepared by the Secretariat, since the majority of the delegations considered that to be the best option to avoid provisions which were overly detailed or which did not come directly within the scope of the Social Charter.[9] In the end, Article 16 ESC was "formulated in a very generic way which led to a considerable body of case law by the Committee".[10] It is also worth noting that the States did not consider any revision of this Article in the Revised Charter, though the Appendix to the 1996 Revised Charter clarifies that: "It is understood that the protection afforded in this provision covers single-parent families" as, unlike the 1961 Charter,[11] the protection of mothers is covered by the scope of this provision.

In Europe, the mid-20th century's "traditional" notion of family consisting of "a white, heterosexual, married couple, with children, all living under the

5 Council of Europe, *European Social Charter Collected (Provisional) Edition of the "Travaux Préparatoires"*, vol. II, Strasbourg, 1955, p. 15 and 16.

6 *Ibid.*, p. 31.

7 *Ibid.*, p. 129.

8 Council of Europe, *European Social Charter Collected (Provisional) Edition of the "Travaux Préparatoires"*, vol. VI, Strasbourg, 1957, p. 34.

9 *Ibid.*, p. 60.

10 Karin Lukas, *The Revised European Social Charter, An Article By Article Commentary*, Cheltenham, Edward Elgar Publishing, 2021, p. 214.

11 ESC, 1961, art 17.

same roof, where the husband is the main breadwinner and the wife primary carer of children and other dependants"[12] has changed over years and been replaced by a more "expanded and pluralistic" approach, embracing new concepts such as single parent families, unmarried or same-sex couples, children born out of wedlock and gender equality.[13] The European Committee of Social Rights (ECSR), the European Court oif Human Rights (ECtHR) and the Court of Justice of the European Union (CJEU) have taken into account the social changes affecting the notion of "family" in their case law.[14]

As the idea of the "family" is flexible, the ECSR notes that the Charter applies to every family according to the definition of this term under domestic law. It therefore accepts the terminology used in domestic law to determine the concept of the family.[15] When it is not clear, the Committee requests that the

12 Care Mcglynn, *Families and the European Union: Law, Politics and Pluralism*, Cambridge, Cambridge University Press, 2006, p. 23.

13 On the evolution of the notion of family in Europe, see: *ibid.*, p. 23–41.

14 For instance, below is a summary of the case law on same-sex couples. After examining the rights of the same-sex couples under the notion of 'private life' for a long time, the ECtHR, with *Schalk and Kopf v. Austria* case, has accepted that a same-sex couple living in a stable relationship falls within the notion of family life, as well as private life, in the same way as a heterosexual couple, see: ECtHR, 24 June 2010, *Schalk and Kopf v. Austria,* no. 30141/04, §§ 92–95. In *Vallianatos and others v. Greece* case, the Court stated the currently emerging trend with regard to the introduction of forms of legal recognition of same-sex relationships (ECtHR [GC], 7 November 2013, *Vallianatos and others v. Greece,* nos. 29381/09 and 32684/09, § 91). Recently in in *Fedotova and others v. Russia* and *Buhuceanu and others v. Romania* cases, the ECtHR has pointed out that the States have a positive obligation to provide a legal framework allowing same-sex couples to be granted adequate recognition and protection of their relationship. Cf. ECtHR [GC], 17 January 2023, *Fedotova and others*, nos. 40792/10, 30538/14 and 43439/14, §§ 152–190; ECtHR, 23 May 2023, *Buhuceanu and others v. Romania,* nos. 20081/19 and 20 others. The CJEU has also developped a similar case law. In the landmark judgement of *Coman and others* case, the Luxembourg Court ruled that the member States are to recognize same-sex marriages performed in other EU members (CJEU, 5 June 2018, *Coman and others*, C-673/16). In *V.A. v. Stolichna obshtina, rayon 'Pancharevo'* case, the Court of Justice has determined that same-sex parentage should be legally recognized across all EU member States and that the child should be permitted to exercise, with each of the parents, the right to move and reside freely within the territory of the EU member States (CJEU, 14 December 2021, *V.A. v. Stolichna obshtina, rayon 'Pancharevo'*, C-490/20). The ECSR also notes and welcomes in its Conclusions the developments regarding the rights of same-sex couples (ECSR, Conclusions XVI-1 (2003), Belgium). It follows the draft acts concerning the issue. The Committee states whether there is a different treatment in law or in practice as well (ESCR, Conclusions XIII-4 (1996), the Netherlands). The Committee states whether there is a different treatment in law or in practice as well (ECSR, Conclusions XVIII-1 (2006), Belgium).

15 ECSR, Conclusions XX-4 (2015), Iceland: "According to the report the Icelandic term fjölskylda which corresponds to the term family may have slightly different connotations

States Parties explain how this concept is defined and to describe the legal situation of family types other than those based on marriage.[16] However, it should also be underlined that there are limits for the States Parties to define the notion of the family: "domestic law must not provide for an unduly restrictive definition ... the scope of Article 16 is, in any case, not restricted to family based on marriage ... In addition, single parent families enjoy the rights provided in Article 16[17]".

Furthermore, to provide the widest protection for the family, the ECSR case law indicates that there are interrelated obligations on the States Parties to implement family-protective policies. In the view of the Committee:

> This article, which states the family's right to economic, legal and social protection, must be seen in conjunction with a number of other provisions in the Charter, such as Articles 14 and 17, that aim rather to give scope to the individual in our highly developed society, than to remedy a need, as Article 13 does. All these provisions are clearly founded on the idea that, since the industrial revolution and the social upheavals it produced, the modern state has had to take on certain new tasks and, in particular, as provided in Article 16, to create the living conditions necessary to give the family its full scope. The traditional affirmation of the family as the fundamental unit of society is maintained in Article 16, which, however, adds the idea that family welfare cannot henceforth be left to individual effort, as in the liberal epoch. Acceptance of these principles led the authors of Article 16 to lay down in it an obligation to implement a true family policy which was intended to operate in those fields where the needs of families become particularly pressing because of the restricted

---

depending on the items of legislation in which they appear, but generally speaking the term refers to the closest family members, usually the person's spouse or cohabiting partner and their children, including step-children, adopted children and foster children, or parents, including step-parents, adoptive parents and foster parents, siblings, including step-siblings, adopted siblings and foster siblings and the most immediate relatives".

16 ECSR, Conclusions 2011, Italy: "According to Article 29 of the Constitution, 'the Republic recognises the rights of the family as a natural society founded on marriage'. Moreover, Article 30 stipulates that 'the law ensures such legal and social protection measures as are compatible with the rights of the members of the legitimate family to any children born out of wedlock'. The Committee asks that the next report explain how domestic law defines the 'family' concept and describe the legal situation of family types other than those based on marriage, notably in the light of Article 16 of the Charter, such as families with unmarried parents, and single-parent, reconstituted and homoparental families".

17 Digest of the Case Law of the European Committee of Social Rights, December 2012, p. 141, based on conclusions of the ECSR.

means they have available to meet them. In the Committee's opinion, a family policy of this sort must take the form of diversified action planned in harmony with and as a supplement to existing arrangements for assistance and social security.[18]

I Legal Protection of the Family

Within the scope of legal protection of the family, the European Committee of Social Rights (ECSR) evaluates such "equality of family treatment" issues as (A), equality between families, spouses and parents, (B) family mediation, (C) domestic violence and (D) childrens issues. While assessing the legal situation within the States Parties, the ECSR not only takes into account the States' reports but may also refer to other sources such as reports or resolutions prepared by experts,[19] different state institutions,[20] Council of Europe bodies such as the Committee of Ministers,[21] the Office of Commissioner for Human Rights,[22] European Commission against Racism and Intolerance (ECRI)[23] or EU institutions.[24]

A *Equality among Families, Spouses and Parents*

One of the obligations that the Social Charter imposes on States Parties is equal treatment among families. In this regard the Committee emphasizes that in accordance with the equal treatment principle, Article 16 ESC requires States parties to ensure the protection of vulnerable families, including Roma, Sinti and Traveller families.[25] The States should take meaures appropriate to these families' particular circumstances in order to safeguard their rights to housing and preventing them, as vulnerable groups, from becoming homeless.[26] Another obligation that Article 16 implies on States is data collection.

---

18 ECSR, Conclusions I, Statement of Interpretation on Article 16.

19 ECSR, Conclusions XVII-1(2005), Finland.

20 ECSR, Conclusions 2004, Norway or ECSR, Conclusions XVII-1 (2005), Spain.

21 ECSR, Conclusions 2004, Romania.

22 ECSR, Conclusions XVII-1 (2005), Greece.

23 ECSR, Conclusions XVIII-1 (2006), Poland.

24 ECSR, Conclusions 2004, Romania.

25 ECSR, *Centre on Housing Rights and Evictions* (*COHRE*) *v. Italy,* complaint No. 58/2009, decision on the merits of 25 june 2010, § 113; ECSR, *European Roma and Travellers Forum* (*ERTF*) *v. France,* complaint No. 64/2011, decision on the merits of 24 january 2012, § 143.

26 ECSR, *European Roma Rights Centre* (*ERRC*) *v. Italy,* complaint No. 27/2004, decision on the merits of 7 december 2005, § 21.

The Committee recalls that State authorities have a responsibility for collecting data on particular groups which are, or could be, discriminated against.[27] It is also important to underline that this collection of detailed information must respect minimum international standards.

It is also important to highlight that the principle of equal treatment implies that nationals of other Parties to the Revised European Social Charter and nationals of the other Contracting Parties to the 1961 European Social Charter, lawfully residing or regularly working in another State Party, are treated equally.[28] The Committee emphasises that family members who are in the territory of a Contracting Party in accordance with the right to family reunification guaranteed by Article 19 § 6 must be afforded equal treatment with nationals in all aspects related to the protection of the family.[29]

Guaranteeing equality between spouses and between parents is another requirement placed upon the States Parties. The Committee recalls that spouses must be equal, particularly in respect of rights and duties within the couple (eg., reciprocal responsibility, ownership, administration and use of property) and children (parental authority, management of children's property). It also states that in cases of family breakdown, Article 16 requires the provision of legal arrangements to settle marital conflicts and, in particular, conflicts relating to children: care and maintenance, custody and access to children.[30] The Committee concludes that, if the States do not adopt appropriate measures to guarantee equality between spouses, the situation is not in conformity with Article 16.[31]

B *Family Mediation*

Within the ambit of legal protection, the States are required to establish family mediation services to help settle disputes and ensure that future relations between parents and between they and their children are not unduly damaged.[32] The Committee states that to be in conformity with Article 16 ESC, these services must be easily accessible to all families. In particular families must not be deterred from availing of such services for financial reasons. If these services are free of charge, this constitutes an adequate measure to this

27 ECSR, *European Roma Rights Centre (ERRC) v. Greece*, complaint No. 15/2003, decision on the merits of 08/12/2005, § 27.

28 ECSR, Conclusions XVII-2 (2005), Latvia.

29 ECSR, Conclusions XVI-I (2002), Statement of interpretation of Articles 12–4 and 16.

30 ECSR, Conclusions 2015, Russian Federation.

31 ECSR, Conclusions XV-1 (2000), Turkey.

32 ECSR, Conclusions 2011, Hungary.

end. Otherwise, the possibility of access for families when needed should be provided.[33] The ECSR asks States Parties whether measures governing mediation are envisaged in practice. In this regard it examines whether they cover the entire country, are free of charge and how effective they are.[34]

C Domestic Violence

The Committee of Social Rights interprets Article 16 as covering the issue of domestic violence.[35] According to the ECSR, Article 16 requires that protection for women exists both in law (through appropriate measures and punishment for perpetrators, including restraining orders, fair compensation for the pecuniary and non-pecuniary damage sustained by victims, the possibility for victims – and associations acting on their behalf – to take their cases to court and special arrangements for the examination of victims in court) and in practice (through the collection and analysis of reliable data, training, particularly for police officers, and services to reduce the risk of violence and provide support and rehabilitation to victims). If the States' reports do not contain sufficient information on the situation in practice, the Committee may demand such information, particularly statistics.[36] If it determines that the measures taken to solve the problem of domestic violence in practice are inadequate it may conclude that the situation is not in conformity with Article 16.[37]

The Committee also refers to other Council of Europe norms on this issue such as the Recommendation Rec (2002)5 of the Committee of Ministers of the Council of Europe to member States on the Protection of Women Against Violence, Parliamentary Assembly Recommendation 1681 (2004) on a campaign to combat domestic violence against women in Europe and the Convention on Preventing and Combating Violence against Women and Domestic Violence (İstanbul Convention). It underlines the importance of İstanbul Convention by mentioning that the instruments of the CoM and the Parliamentary Assembly have been superseded by this text as a legally binding document for those states which have ratified it. The ECSR determines in its Conclusions whether a State Party has signed or ratified the İstanbul Convention.[38] When assesing the situation in the States which ratified the Convention, the ECSR also refers to the reports of the Council of Europe's Group

33 ECSR, Conclusions XX-4 (2016), Luxembourg.
34 ECSR, Conclusions 2011, Lithuania.
35 ECSR, Conclusions XVII-1 (2005), Belgium.
36 ECSR, Conclusions XIX-4 (2011), Czech Republic.
37 ECSR, Conclusions 2011, Turkey.
38 ECSR, Conclusions 2019, Azerbaijan; ECSR, Conclusions 2019, Estonia.

of Experts on Action against Violence against Women and Domestic Violence (GREVIO), the body responsible for monitoring the implementation.[39]

39 ECSR, Conclusions 2019, France: "Insofar as France has signed and ratified the Istanbul Convention on Preventing and Combating Violence against Women and Domestic Violence (which came into force in France on 1 November 2014), the Committee refers to the procedure to assess the conformity of the situation in France which took place in the context of this mechanism. It notes that in November 2019, the Council of Europe's Group of Experts on Action against Violence against Women and Domestic Violence (GREVIO) published its first baseline evaluation report on France. GREVIO noted the measures taken, notably in terms of legislation, in order to strengthen the legal framework for preventing and addressing violence, as well as the considerable increase in terms of resources allocated to combating such violence. Despite these measures, GREVIO has identified a number of areas where improvement is needed (see details in GREVIO report). The Committee asks the next report to provide updated information on domestic violence against women and related convictions, the implementation of the various measures described in the report and their impact on reducing domestic violence against women, also in the light of the abovementioned GREVIO recommendations"; ECSR, Conclusions 2019, Turkey: "Insofar as Turkey has signed and ratified the Istanbul Convention on Preventing and Combating Violence against Women and Domestic Violence (which came into force in Turkey on 1 August 2014), the Committee refers to the assessment procedure which took place in the context of this mechanism. It notes that in October 2018, the Council of Europe's Group of Experts on Action against Violence against Women and Domestic Violence (GREVIO) published its first baseline evaluation report on Turkey. GREVIO experts recognised progress with regard to measures to protect women from violence but pointed out the lack of evidence showing that cases of violence are effectively investigated, prosecuted and sanctioned. The report urged authorities among others to step up measures to identify and remedy gaps in the institutional response to violence against women, in accordance with the duty of due diligence, recognise forced marriage and stalking as separate offences and develop training programmes for law enforcement authorities. The Committee asks the next report to provide comprehensive and updated information on all aspects of domestic violence against women and related convictions, as well as on the use of protection orders, the implementation of the various measures described in the report and their impact on reducing domestic violence against women (including economic violence), also in the light of the abovementioned GREVIO recommendations. In the meantime, in the light of the information available, the Committee considers that it has not been established that women are ensured adequate protection, in law and in practice, against domestic violence.". It should be noted that Turkey has declared its withdrawal from the Istanbul Convention by a Presidential Decision in 2021. For the unconstitutionality of this Decision, see: "Statement from the Association of Research on Constitutional Law (ARCL) on the Presidential Decision on the Istanbul Convention", available online at <https://anayasader.org/statement-from-the-association-of-constitutional-research-on-the-presidential-decision-on-the-istanbul-convention>, accessed 15 May 2023. For an analysis of this withdrawal from the view of international and human rights law, see: Başak Çali and Laurence Helfer, "The Gender of Treaty Withdrawal: Lessons from the Istanbul Convention", available online at <https://www.ejiltalk.org/the-gender-of-treaty-withdrawal-lessons-from-the-istanbul-convention>, accessed 15 May 2023.

D Child Issues

The Committee of Social Rights points out that the ECSR treats children as individual rights' holders, since the human dignity inherent in each child fully entitles them to all fundamental rights granted to adults. Moreover, the specific situation of children, which combines vulnerability, limited autonomy and development needs, requires States to grant them specific rights enshrined in different substantive provisions of the Charter such as Article 31 § 2 (on the right to shelter); Articles 8, 11, 7, 19 § 2 (concerning right to health); Articles 9, 10, 15, 17, 19 §§ 11–12 (related to right to education); Articles 16, 27, 19§6 (protection of the family and right to family reunification); Articles 7 § 1, 17 (protection against danger and abuse); Articles 7 § 1 and § 3 (prohibition of child labour under the age of 15); and Article 17 (specific working conditions for children aged between 15 and 18 years old). In the view of the Committee, the European Social Charter is the most significant treaty at the European level for the human rights of children; it complements the European Convention on Human Rights in this area and reflects the United Nations Convention on the Rights of the Child. The ECSR also underscores that, when interpreting the ESC, it considers itself bound by the internationally recognised requirement to apply the principle of "best interests of the child[40]".

The Committee therefore states that any restrictions or limitations of custodial rights of parents should be based on adequate and reasonable criteria laid down in legislation and should not go beyond what is necessary for the protection and best interests of child and the rehabilitation of the family. In this regard it emphasizes that placement must be an exceptional measure, and is only justified when it is based on the needs of the child, namely if remaining in the family environment represents a danger for the child. Placement should not only be grounded on the financial conditions or material circumstances of the family and should be considered as a temporary solution, during which continuity of the relationship with the family should be maintained.[41]

Based upon this comprehensive approach, the Committee also stresses that the States should take relevant measures in law and in practice to guarantee that each child be able to express their views in proceedings concerning them.[42]

---

40 ECSR, *Defense for Children International* (DCI) *v. The Netherlands*, complaint No. 47/2008, decision on the merits of 20/05/2009, §§ 25, 26 and 29.

41 ECSR, Conclusions 2011, Statement of interpretation of Articles 16 and 17–1.

42 ECSR, Conclusions 2004, Slovenia.

II Social and Economic Protection of Family

A *Social Policies and Social Security Issues*

Article 16 ESC requires States to implement a genuine family policy through various means. It is their responsibility to ensure an adequate standard of living for families by establishing a system of family allowances or child benefits. These benefits – which may be subject to income conditions – must constitute an adequate income supplement for a significant number of families.[43] Other forms of economic protection, such as birth grants and additional benefits for large families may also contribute to the implementation of this obligation. It is only to the extent that these benefits comprise social security benefits within the meaning of Article 12 (the right to social security) that the Committee deals with them in relation to both Articles 12 and 16.

Article 16 also contains the obligation to provide childcare services, in particular for young children, that are sufficient in number to meet the needs of families, affordable and accessible to all. The services offered must be of good quality (the ratio of children in relation to the number of staff, staff training, appropriate premises). Article 27 of the Revised Charter (the right of workers with family responsabilities to equal opportunities and treatment) is closely linked to Article 16.

1 Childcare Facilities

Where a State Party has accepted Article 27 of the Charter, childcare facilities and arrangements are examined under this provision.[44] State Parties are required to ensure that childcare facilities are available, affordable and of good quality (eg. coverage with respect to the number of children aged 0–6, ratio of staff to children, staff training, suitable premises and cost of childcare to parents).[45]

---

43 ECSR, Conclusions 2006, Estonia: "The Committee considers that, to comply with Article 16 of the Revised Charter, child allowance must represent an adequate income supplement representing a significant percentage of the median equivalised income. According to MISSOC, the monthly child allowance is 150 Estonian kroons (EEK; 9.59 €). The report states that in 2004, the amount was increased to 300 EEK (20 €). According to Eurostat statistics for 2003, child allowances in Estonia amount to some 4.6 % of that income. Taking account of other family benefits and tax exemptions, the Committee considers that this amount is sufficient."

44 ECSR, Conclusions 2011, Azerbaijan.

45 ECSR, Conclusions XVII-1 (2004), Turkey: "The report indicates that the General Directorate of Social Services and Child Protection (SHÇEK) is responsible for the establishment and the running of childcare, including inspection. Childcare is provided by Crèches and Daily Care Centres (for 0 to 6 years old) and Children's Club (from 7 to

Families must be granteed access to appropriate social services, in particular in times of adversity. State Parties should provide *inter alia* family counselling and psychological guidance advice on childrearing.

In order to ensure that the views of families are taken into account in the formulation of family policy, all civil organisations representing families should be consulted by the relevant authorities.[46]

2 Economic Protection

a *Family Benefits*

State Parties are required to ensure the economic protection of the family by appropriate means. The primary means should be family or child benefits provided as part of social security, available either universally or subject to a means-test.[47]

The Committee emphasised that the drafters of the Charter appeared to intend family allowances to fall within the scope of Article 16 because that article specifically includes "family benefits" as a means of promoting the welfare of the family. Furthermore, it is possible to satisfy the provisions of Article 12 of the Charter by complying with the conditions for the ratification of ILO Convention N° 102, i.e. acceptance of at least three social security branches out of nine. While family benefits constitute one of the nine branches, there is no reason why a State could not comply with Article 12 without providing family benefits. Thus, if a State has accepted Article 16, it has accepted a more specific obligation than that of Article 12, i.e., an obligation to protect the family through various measures, including the provision of family benefits. Therefore, while the existence of a family benefits scheme is (with other benefits) a sufficient but not necessary condition for compliance with Article 12, it is a necessary condition for fulfilling Article 16.

---

12 years of age). Childcare structures can be public or private. According to the report, there are 12 public crèches and daily care centres run by SHÇEK gathering for about 540 children. 500 additional children attend temporary structures established after the 1999 earthquake. Private registered institutions (1,179) offer their service to some 17,430 children. Childcare is free both in public and private structures for low income families benefiting about 542 children. The Committee observes from other sources that, in 1998, about 4.5% of the children aged 3 to 6 were attending pre-school education, or that in 1999/2000, the enrolment rates were 10% in pre-school education. Taking into consideration that, according to official sources there are about 3.2 million children aged 0–4 years, the Committee finds the situation not to be in conformity with the Charter because of the manifestly inadequate provision of childcare places."

46 ECSR, Conclusions 2006, Statement of Interpretation on Article 16.

47 ECSR, Conclusions 2006, Statement of Interpretation on Article 16.

Thus, it is clear that the authors of the Charter envisaged that family allowances should form part of the family policy provided for under Article 16. Nevertheless, family allowances are a "social security" benefit and as such can be viewed within the context of Council of Europe instruments (specifically the 1953 Interim Agreements and the 1964 European Code of Social Security) which allow for a qualifying residence period of up to six months to be imposed in respect of non-contributory (family) allowances in order to prevent abuse.[48]

b *Family Benefits of a Sufficient Amount*

The Committee considers that, in order to comply with Article 16, family benefits must constitute an adequate income supplement, which is the case when it represents a significant percentage of the median equivalised income.[49] The level of benefit should be adjusted as necessary to keep pace with inflation. Other forms of economic protection, such as birth grants, additional payments to large families or tax relief in respect of children, are also applicable to the implementation of this provision.

According to the Committee, social vulnerability, which is linked to not being in a position to fulfill parental responsibilities, often goes hand in hand with increased economic hardship.[50] The measure of suspending for a period of one year and possibly terminating family allowances in cases of truancy (interruption due to the lack of school attendance for 3 successive months or for 6 months in one school year), would increase the economic and social vulnerability of the children concerned. Consequently, such measures are not in principle proportionate to the aim pursued and constitute an undue restriction on the right of families to social, legal and economic protection.[51]

---

48 ECSR, Conclusions XI-1 (1989), Denmark.

49 ECSR, Conclusions XX-4, Poland."Median equivalised income (Eurostat): the income of a household is established by summing all monetary income received from any source by each member of the household. In order to reflect differences in household size and composition, this total is divided by the number of 'equivalent adults' using a standard scale (the so-called modified OECD equivalence scale). The resulting figure is attributed to each member of the household." (ECSR, Conclusions 2006, Statement of Interpretation on Article 16; ECSR, Conclusions 2006, Estonia).

50 ECSR, *European Committee for Home-Based Priority Action for the Child and the Family (EUROCEF) v. France*, complaint No. 82/2012, decision on admissibility and the merits of 19 March 2013, § 41.

51 ECSR, *Equal Rights Trust v. Bulgaria*, complaint No. 121/2016, decision on the merits.

3 Vulnerable Families

State Parties are required to ensure the protection of vulnerable families, single-parent families and Roma families, in accordance with the principle of equality of treatment.

The Committee examines the means used by States to ensure the social, legal and economic protection of the various types of families in the population, especially single parent families, with a particular emphasis on vulnerable families, including Roma. States can choose such means freely, with the provison that they must not jeopardise the effective protection of Roma families.[52] For the situation to be compatible with the treaty, State Parties must (...) pay close attention to the impact of the policies adopted on each category of persons concerned, particularly the most vulnerable.[53]

4 Equal Treatment

State Parties must ensure equal treatment of foreign nationals of other State Parties who are lawfully resident or regularly working in their territory with respect to family benefits. However, by analogy with Article 12 § 4 and based on the Appendix, Article 16 precludes the application of length of residence requirements as far as contributory benefits are concerned, but States may apply a length of residence requirement as regards noncontributory benefits on condition that the length is not excessive.[54]

The proportionality of such length of residence requirements is examined on a case-by-case basis having regard to the nature and purpose of the benefit: a period of 6 months is reasonable and therefore in conformity with Article 16.[55] On the other hand, periods of 1 year, and *a fortiori*, 3–5 years are manifestly excessive and therefore in violation of Article 16.[56] The question as to whether the residency of a child in the territory is required before child benefits will be paid is examined exclusively under Article 12 § 4.[57]

The Committee recalls that Article E also prohibits all forms of indirect discrimination. Such indirect discrimination may arise by failing to take due and positive account of all relevant differences or by failing to take adequate steps

52 ECSR, Conclusions 2006, Statement of Interpretation on Article 16.

53 ECSR, *European Federation of National Organisations Working with the Homeless (FEANTSA) v. France*, complaint No. 39/2006, decision on the merits of 5 December 2007, § 54.

54 ECSR, Conclusions XIV-1 (1998), Sweden.

55 ECSR, Conclusions XIV-1 (1998), Sweden.

56 ECSR, Conclusions XVIII-1 (2006), Danemark.

57 ECSR, Conclusion XVI-1 (2002), Statement of Interpretation on Article 16.

to ensure that the rights and collective advantages that are open to all are genuinely accessible by and to all.[58] Applying different measures must not lead to give rise to a disproportionate impact on specific group.[59]

B *Housing*

1 General Remarks

The right to housing is regulated in Article 31 of the Revised European Social Charter of 1996 which determines the measures required to promote access to housing of an adequate standard, preventing and reducing homelessness with a view to its gradual elimination and making the price of housing accessible to those without adequate resources. Additionally, the scope and measures concerning the right to housing had been elaborated under the decisions and conclusions of the ECSR also with regards to Article 16 of the Social Charter prior to the revised charter coming into existence. Thus, Article 16 remains the sole legal protection on housing rights for the States that have not ratified the Revised Charter or have not accepted Article 31 in the Revised Charter.

In these cases, the ECSR referred to other international instruments and decisions in order to extend its jurisprudence to housing cases and clarify its scope.[60]

2 Housing in Respect of Family Protection

While monitoring and creating standards for the right to housing in respect of family protection, the ECSR focused its attention on particularly vulnerable people. The next section of this chapter discusses the personal scope of this jurisprudence, while the following will shed the light on the scope of this right.

a *Personal Scope*

According to the Article 31 § 1 of the Social Charter everyone has the right to suitable housing as a means of ensuring an adequate standard of living. In examining the ECSR decisions and conclusions on the subjects of the right to housing, we find that there is a distinctive group of individuals which is

58 ECSR, *Autism-Europe v. France*, complaint No. 13/2002, decision on the merits of 4 November 2003, § 52.

59 ECSR, Decision on the merits, *Equal Rights Trust v. Bulgaria*, complaint No. 121/2016.

60 ECSR, Conclusions XIII-3(1995), Turkey: "In this regard, the Committee also took note of the observations of the Turkish Government in relation to the questions posed in the previous conclusion as regards the evacuation and destruction of villages in south east Turkey. The Committee also took note of the report of the European Commission of Human Rights in a case brought before the European Court of Human Rights in December 1995 (Application No. 21893/93, Akdıvar and Others v. Turkey)".

addressed, such as elderly and disabled people, vulnerable families, newly married couples, young couples, families with children, single parent families, Roma Families, homeless people and persons rendered homeless.

Elderly and Disabled People: The ECSR evaluated elderly and disabled people as a particular group of individuals in terms of economic help and public sector housing. In one of its conclusions –in the report on United Kingdom– the ECSR found that the state continues to undertake its obligations under Article 16 through its sustained efforts as regards public sector housing for elderly and disabled people.[61] In this respect no further decisions or conclusions of the ECSR could be found, however, it is significant to note the jurisprudence and documents of other international human rights instruments. On this point, the ICESCR in its General Comment No. 4 mentions accessibility as a component of the right to adequate housing and further defines disadvantaged groups as the elderly, children, physically disabled, terminally ill, HIV-positive individuals, persons with persistent medical problems, mentally ill people, victims of natural disasters, people living in disaster-prone areas among those who must be accorded full and sustainable access to adequate housing.[62] In this sense, in the *Marzari v. Italy* case, which concerned a disabled individual, the ECtHR primarily stated that Article 8 does not guarantee that the state authorities must resolve housing problems of an individual, however, the refusal of the state to provide assistance to an individual suffering disease might cause in some circumstances – depending upon the impact on the private life – an issue under the Article 8 respect for private life of the ECHR.[63] Considering that the ECHR does not provide economic and social rights, the ECtHR placed special emphasis on the link between a protected right (right to private life) and a social right (right to housing).

61 ECSR, Conclusions VIII (1984), United Kingdom.

62 CESCR, General Comment No. 4 (1991), The right to adequate housing (Article 11(1) of the Covenant), 13 December 2001, E/1992/23, § 8(e).

63 ECtHR, dec., 2 December 2014, *Strzelecka v. Poland*, no. 14217/10, § 49: "The Court must first examine whether the applicant's rights under Article 8 were violated on account of the decision of the authorities to evict him despite his medical condition. It further has to examine whether the applicant's rights were violated on account of the authorities' alleged failure to provide him with adequate accommodation. The Court considers that, although Article 8 does not guarantee the right to have one's housing problem solved by the authorities, a refusal of the authorities to provide assistance in this respect to an individual suffering from a severe disease might in certain circumstances raise an issue under Article 8 of the Convention because of the impact of such refusal on the private life of the individual (ECtHR, *Marzari v. Italy*, App. No. 36448/97, Admissibility Decision, 04.05.1999)."

Vulnerable Families: The ECSR reiterates that the essential protection concerning the right to housing for vulnerable families is housing and rental allowances and their supplements.[64] The ECSR examined whether concrete steps have been taken in order to improve the living conditions of vulnerable families.[65] In addition to the concrete steps and statistics showing the position of the state, the ECSR also considered and relied upon non-state-oriented evidence/information in order to examine the issue. By doing so, the ECSR has sought to follow-up for possible negative effects measures taken by States.[66]

In this regard, the ICESCR in its General Comment No. 4 cites affordability as a component of the right to adequate housing particularly in respect to housing related costs depending on income levels, protection against unreasonable rent levels or rent increases and ensuring the ability to obtain housing supplies.[67]

Family Composition: Under the conclusions of the ECSR the composition of the family in terms of young couples (with/without children),[68] newly married couples[69] (as especially stated in Article 16 of the Social Charter), families with children[70] and single parent families[71] have been evaluated. The ECSR in its Conclusion on a Croatian Report on 2003–2004 collectively examines

---

64 ECSR, Conclusions VIII (1984), United Kingdom; Conclusions XX-4 (2015), Iceland.; Conclusions XX-4 (2015), Czech Republic.

65 ECSR, Conclusions 2017, Hungary: "The Committee takes note of the efforts made by Hungary; However nothing in the report allows it to assess the impact of those strategies on the situation of the persons concerned, in particular, the number of social housing units built, rehabilitated or renovated, the number of vulnerable families moved into an adequate housing and, measures undertaken to accompany families in finding adequate housing".

66 ECSR, Conclusions XX-4 (2015), Denmark: "Pursuant to the Danish Act on Social Housing, social housing is open to the entire population with a special focus on vulnerable groups with low income. (…) The report indicates that there are approximately 600,000 social housing units representing 22% of the total number of dwellings. In 2013, 83,000 households with children with low income had 42% of the rent covered by housing benefit. (…) The Committee notes from the comments submitted by Danish Institute for Human Rights' (DIHR) that the policies for improving living conditions in the challenged social housing neighbourhoods have the inverse effect of preventing vulnerable tenants from moving into these neighbourhoods. The Committee therefore asks the next report to indicate what steps are being taken to remedy this situation".

67 CESCR, General Comment No. 4 (1991), *cit.*, § 8(c).

68 ECSR, Conclusions 2006, Lithuania; ECSR, Conclusions XVIII-1 (2006), Croatia.

69 ECSR, Conclusions IX-2 (1986), Spain.

70 ECSR, Conclusions 2006, Lithuania; ECSR, Conclusions XVIII-1 (2006), Croatia; ECSR, Conclusions XX-4 (2015), Denmark.

71 ECSR, Conclusions 2006, Lithuania.

the issue of housing in terms of family and states that "Article 16 is concerned with maintaining family ties" and includes "household (s) composed of parents, including lone parents, with children, and young couples likely to have children".[72] In understanding the concept of family with regard to the right to adequate housing, it is significant to take into account General Comment No. 4 of the ICESCR. Therefore, the emphasis on the concept of family must be taken in a broad sense and any form of discrimination must be eliminated for purposes of the enjoyment of right to adequate housing.[73]

Persons Rendered Homeless: The ICESCR seeks multiple procedural and material remedies for persons rendered homeless by state action. In that sense, in its Conclusion on Turkish Reports of 1990–1991 and 1992–1993 the ECSR evaluated the situation of the state vacating or merging villages in the south-eastern part of Turkey to secure law and order, or to protect its inhabitants, and asks whether the authorities had taken measures to re-house or provide any compensation to persons who had been rendered homeless.[74] In examining the situation in Turkey, the ECSR – by referring to the ECHR case of *Akdıvar and others v. Turkey*[75] – concluded that the state had failed to re-house or to provide adequate financial support and compensation for the villagers deprived of their right to adequate housing.[76]

Roma Families: The concept of housing in respect of family life could be considered under the issue of "cultural identity"; this issue has been dealt with in respect to Roma Families.[77] The ECSR places special emphasis on Roma Families in regard to two main issues, one being economic and other being about discrimination. In its conclusions the ECSR addresses the issue of removing barriers faced by Roma families in their attempts to access adequate housing by advancing efforts dealing with the disadvantages faced these families.[78] In addition, the ECSR underlines the equality principle and further states that Roma Families should enjoy rights equal to those of nationals in

72 ECSR, Conclusions XVIII-1 (2006), Croatia.

73 CESCR, General Comment No. 4 (1991), *cit.*, § 6.

74 ECSR, Conclusions XIII-1 (1993), Turkey.

75 ECmHR, 19 October 1994, *Akdıvar and others v. Turkey*, no. 21893/93. See also: ECtHR [GC], 16 June 2015, *Chiragov and others v. Armenia*, no. 13216/05, Judgment; ECtHR, *Sargsyan v. Azerbaijan*, 16 June 2015, no. 40167/06.

76 ECSR, Conclusions XIII-3 (1993), Turkey.

77 Roma families issue under the right to housing has been elaborated by the ECtHR under the scope of the article 8 of the Convention. See: Bernadette Rainey, Elizabeth Wicks and Clare Ovey, *Jacobs, White & Ovey: The European Convention on Human Rights*, Sixth Ed., Oxford, Oxford University Press, 2014, p.383–386.

78 ECSR, Conclusions XX-4 (2015), United Kingdom.

terms of accessing social housing.[79] In addition, on the issue of discrimination against Roma Families, the ECSR refers to conclusions of the European Commission against Racism and Intolerance and points out the increase in socially excluded localities in the case of Roma Families.[80]

b *Material Scope*

The ECSR addresses the scope of the right to housing as it relates to adequate housing standards as an element of family protection. In its conclusions the ECSR states that the State Parties must ensure adequate standards of housing depending on the size, the composition and the needs of the family as well as essential services, such as heating and electricity.[81] Moreover, the ECSR stresses that the scope of the right to housing in terms of family protection extends to including both enjoyment of security of tenure in order to guarantee "the meaningful enjoyment of family life in a stable environment" and protection from unlawful eviction.[82]

Additionally, other international instruments also interpret the concept of the right to housing in a broad sense. One example would be General Comment No.4 of the ICESCR which under Article 7 states that right to housing guarantees the right to live somewhere in security, peace and dignity. Under the same General Comment ICESCR defines the concept of adequacy under Article 8 where it determines the meaning of adequacy through such factors as social, economic, cultural, climatic, ecological and other factors including legal security of tenure, availability of services, materials, facilities and infrastructure, affordability, habitability, accessibility, location and cultural adequacy.

As to the legal security of tenure, the ICESCR underlines the function of this concept as a guarantee of legal protection against forced eviction, harassment and other threats. At the same time in the conclusions and decisions of the ECSR, the issue of eviction[83] receives the weightiest attention in terms of discussing the availability of alternative housing/accommodation as a substantial safeguard. The ECSR notes that alternative housing/accommodation

79 ECSR, Conclusions XX-4 (2015), Denmark.

80 ECSR, Conclusions XX-4 (2015), Czech Republic.

81 ECSR, Conclusions 2017, Hungary.

82 ECSR, *European Roma Rights Centre v. Greece*, Collective complaint No: 15/2003, decision on the merits of 8 December 2004, § 24.

83 ECSR, *European Federation of National Organisations working with the Homeless (FEANTSA) v. France, cit.*, § 86: "*Eviction may be defined as the deprivation of housing which a person occupied on account of insolvency or wrongful occupation.*"

has to be provided in the case of eviction.[84] The ICESCR accords broad attention to the concept of eviction, regarding it as the last resort while all feasible alternatives are to be considered through prior consultation with all affected persons.[85] Regarding the standards for eviction, the ICESCR establishes the criteria in relation to other human rights and states that individuals facing forced eviction should not be rendered homeless or vulnerable to the violation of other human rights. Accordingly, States must take all appropriate measures to the maximum of their available resources to ensure adequate alternative housing.[86] The ICESCR stresses the significance of the protection of the family unit when dealing with eviction, especially when the persons being evicted are responsible for the care and education of the dependent children.[87]

c *Procedural Safeguards*

The ECSR places special emphasis on the procedural issues in order to guarantee lawful implementation of any eviction. The ECSR points out that the effective protection of the right to adequate housing must be implemented through adequate procedural safeguards.[88] ECSR sets the standards for eviction to be in compliance with the Social Charter as: "an obligation to consult the parties affected in order to find alternative solutions to eviction", "an obligation to fix a reasonable notice period before eviction", "accessibility to legal remedies", "accessibility to legal aid" and "compensation in case of illegal eviction[89]".

---

84 ECSR, *European Roma Rights Centre v. Greece*, Collective complaint No. 15/2003, decision on the merits of 8 december 2004, § 50.

85 CESCR, General Comment No. 7 (1997), The right to adequate housing (Article 11(1) of the Covenant), Forced evictions, 20 May 1997, E/1998/22, § 13.

86 *Ibid.*, § 16. See also: CCPR, 3 January 2017, *"I Elpida" – The Cultural Association of Greek Gypsies from Halandri and Suburbs, and Stylianos Kalamiotis v. Greece*, Communication No. 2242–2013, §12.2.

87 CESCR, 21 July 2017, *Mohamed Ben Djazia and Naouel Bellili v. Spain*, Communication No.5/2015, § 15.4: "Human rights are indivisible and interdependent. Accordingly, State obligations with regard to the right to housing should be interpreted together with all other human rights obligations and, in particular, in the context of eviction, with the obligation to provide the family with the widest possible protection (Article 10 (1) of the Covenant). The obligation of States parties to provide, to the maximum of their available resources, alternative accommodation for evicted persons who need it includes the protection of the family unit, especially when the persons are responsible for the care and education of dependent children".

88 ECSR, Conclusions XX-4 (2015), Netherlands Curaçao.

89 ECSR, Conclusions XX-4 (2015), Denmark; ECSR, Conclusions XX-4 (2015), Netherlands Aruba; ECSR, Conclusions XX-4 (2015), Netherlands Curaçao; ECSR, Conclusions 2017, Romania.

Reasonable notice period before eviction: Parties are required to give notice prior to eviction taking place. Such notice must be an official one ordered by a court.[90] The ECSR finds that a reasonable notice period should be no shorter than two months and has to rely on a court bailiff.[91] Further, as to the timing of the eviction, it is stated that the winter period and nighttime are not acceptable times for the eviction of those who have legal status in respect to the property.[92]

Accessibility to legal remedy and legal aid: An important component of a procedural safeguard against unlawful eviction is access to affordable and impartial judicial or other remedies,[93] including access to legal aid.[94] As to the legal aid, the affected persons may be granted a legal representative before the courts under legal proceedings, including pro bono assignment of an attorney.[95]

Compensation in the case of illegal eviction: Compensation for illegal evictions shall be provided.[96]

d *Interim Measures*

In order to "avoid irreparable injury or harm to the persons concerned" as provided in Rule 36 § 1 of the Rules of Procedure of the ECSR, the Committee may adopt interim measures. For instance in *European Roma Rights Centre (ERRC) v. Belgium*, the ECSR, indicated to the Government to adopt all possible measures "to guarantee that persons whose caravans have been seized are not rendered homeless or forced to live in unacceptable living conditions" and "to ensure that all affected persons have due access to water, sanitation, electricity,

90 CCPR, 30 August 2017, *Petr Gatilov v. Russian Federation*, Communication No.2171/2012, § 9.2.

91 ECSR, *European Federation of National Organisations working with the Homeless (FEANTSA) v. France, cit.*, § 87. The ESCR states that 30 days notice period for tenants and 5 days for occupiers before eviction are too short and does not the standards of the Charter. See: ECSR, Conclusions 2017, Romania.

92 ECSR, Conclusions 2017, Romania; ECSR, *European Federation of National Organisations working with the Homeless (FEANTSA) v. France, cit.*, § 87.

93 ECSR, Conclusions XX-4 (2015), Netherlands Curaçao.

94 ECSR, Conclusions XX-4 (2015) Czech Republic. See also CESCR, General Comment No. 7 (1997): The right to adequate housing (Article 11(1) of the Covenant): Forced evictions, *cit.*, § 13.

95 ECSR, Conclusions XX-4 (2015), Czech Republic.

96 ECSR, *European Federation of National Organisations working with the Homeless (FEANTSA) v. France, cit.*, § 86. See also: General Comment No. 7 (1997): The right to adequate housing (Article 11(1) of the Covenant): Forced evictions, *cit.*, § 13.

necessary medical and social assistance as well as to legal aid, in particular taking into account the needs of the vulnerable groups concerned (including children, persons with disabilities and elderly persons)[97]". Likewise, in *Defence for Children International* (*DCI*), *European Federation of National Organisations working with the Homeless* (*FEANTSA*), *Magistrats Européens pour la Démocratie et les Libertés* (*MEDEL*), *Confederación Sindical de Comisiones Obreras and International Movement ATD Fourth World v. Spain* the Committee invited the Government to adopt immediate measures "to ensure that all affected persons have access to electricity and heating, in particular taking into account the needs of the vulnerable groups concerned (including children, persons with disabilities, persons with medical conditions, persons with foreign origin, older persons and Roma)" and "to offer appropriate alternative accommodation to the affected persons where it is not possible, to safely ensure access to electricity and heating.[98]"

Concluding Remarks

Article 16 ESC, offering a wide legal and socioeconomic protection of the family, allowed the ECSR to extend the Charter's protection of family members to situations covered by other specific articles of the Charter which may not have been ratified by states. The importance of Article 16 on this point is more visible for instance, as to the right to housing, considering that only fifteen States (out of thirty-five) have agreed to be bound by Article 31, whereas the total number of States that have accepted Article 16 is thirty-seven (seven parties to the ESC and thirty parties to the revised ESC). For those who have not ratified the revised Charter or have not accepted Article 31, Article 16 remains as the sole legal protection of housing rights.

It is also worth highlighting that the ECSR has taken into consideration the social changes within the European states over the years and has not accepted or limited the scope of its caselaw to the 'classical notion of the family'. This has

97 ECSR, *European Roma Rights Centre* (*ERRC*) *v. Belgium*, complaint No. 185/2019, decision on admissibility and immediate measures of 14 May 2020.

98 ECSR, *Defence for Children International* (*DCI*), *European Federation of National Organisations working with the Homeless* (*FEANTSA*), *Magistrats Européens pour la Démocratie et les Libertés* (*MEDEL*), *Confederación Sindical de Comisiones Obreras and International Movement ATD Fourth World v. Spain*, complaint No. 206/2022, decision on admissibility and immediate measures of 19 October 2022.

granted the ECSR the opportunity to construe Article 16 as a pivotal provision safeguarding the rights of diverse family structures, including single-parent families, same-sex families, and offering protection to unmarried couples or to children born out of wedlock, thus making of the Social Charter 'a living instrument' around family issues and rights.

ARTICLE 17

The Right of Children and Young Persons to Social, Legal and Economic Protection

Cinzia Peraro

With a view to ensuring the effective exercise of the right of children and young persons to grow up in an environment which encourages the full development of their personality and of their physical and mental capacities, the Parties undertake, either directly or in co-operation with public and private organisations, to take all appropriate and necessary measures designed:

1. (a) to ensure that children and young persons, taking account of the rights and duties of their parents, have the care, the assistance, the education and the training they need, in particular by providing for the establishment or maintenance of institutions and services sufficient and adequate for this purpose;
   (b) to protect children and young persons against negligence, violence or exploitation;
   (c) to provide protection and special aid from the state for children and young persons temporarily or definitively deprived of their family's support;
2. to provide to children and young persons a free primary and secondary education as well as to encourage regular attendance at schools.

Introduction

Article 17 of Part I of the European Social Charter (ESC or the "Charter"), in its 1996 Revised version (RESC or Revised Charter), provides for the fundamental right of children and young persons to be appropriately protected at social, legal and economic levels. The content is further specified in Article 17 of Part II, which sets out the measures that the Parties shall undertake with a view to effectively guaranteeing their right to grow up in an environment where their full development and their personality as well as their physical and mental capacities are encouraged.

 | DOI:10.1163/9789004434141_008

Article 17 RESC covers issues similar to those protected by Article 7,[1] in particular under its § 10,[2] and by Article 16 RESC, which deals with the right of families to social, legal and economic protection. This latter provision also grants protection for mothers, which were previously contemplated jointly with children under former Article 17 of the 1961 Charter. Thus, Article 16 RESC covers children, but indirectly, insofar as they are considered as part of the family. Article 17 RESC, on the other hand, concerns the rights of the child as an individual.[3] Therefore, Article 17 does not apply to the matters covered by the other abovementioned Articles and specifically addresses the needs arising from the vulnerability of children, thus providing a protection "outside the context of work".[4]

1 Drafting History

The original version was drafted as an independent article in 1959,[5] although some paragraphs were included in other, different, articles. The version[6] accepted in the 1961 Charter did not contain specific details regarding the right to protection. In the previous drafts, references to the protection from

1 On children's protection in the Charter, see Katarzyna Dunaj and Joanna Ryszka, "The Protection of Vulnerable People in the Charter System", in Stefano Angeleri and Carole Nivard (eds.), *The European Social Charter: A Commentary*, vol. I: *Cross-cutting Themes*, Leiden, Brill, 2022, pp. 319–348, spec. part III.A. See also: Giuseppe Palmisano, *L'Europa dei diritti sociali. Significato, valore e prospettive della Carta sociale europea*, Bologna, Il Mulino, 2022, p. 93 ff.; CoE, *Digest of the Case Law of the European Committee of Social Rights*, June 2022, available online at <https://rm.coe.int/digest-ecsr-prems-106522-web-en/1680a95dbd>; Information Document prepared by the Secretariat of the ESC, *Children's rights under the European Social Charter*, 2008, available online at <https://rm.coe.int/1680474a4b>.

2 On their coordination and overlapping issues, see: ECSR, Conclusions XV-2 (2001), Statement of Interpretation on Article 17, 7 § 10, where the Committee affirmed that, with respect to the Contracting Parties having accepted both provisions, to deal with the following issues under Article 7 § 10: protection of children against moral dangers at work and outside work and involvement of children in the sex industry and in begging. Under Article 17, the following matters are covered: establishment of parentage and adoption; children and the law; children in public care; protection of children from ill-treatment and abuse. See also *supra* the comment under Article 7.

3 Holly Cullen, "Is the European Social Charter a Charter for children?", *Irish Jurist*, 2005, vol. 40, pp. 60–85, spec. p. 67.

4 Explanatory Report to the European Social Charter (Revised), Strasbourg, 3 May 1996, ETS No. 163, § 69.

5 Consultative Assembly of the Council of Europe, 12th January 1959, Doc. 927.

6 Consultative Assembly of the Council of Europe, 12th September 1959, Doc. 1035.

exploitation and negligence, or to providing children and young persons with a free primary and secondary education and welfare services had been proposed.[7] Additionally, the 1956 proposal[8] to include homeless children, juvenile delinquents and children with disabilities as coming under the personal scope of the rights to be protected, within categories to be supported by special services, was not retained.[9] The revised provision does not include any specification on the target groups, which were identified through the interpretation of the European Committee of Social Rights (ECSR or the Committee).[10]

Some amendments have been introduced into the RESC in comparison to the former Article 17 included in the 1961 Charter. The latter stated, in Part I, that "[m]others and children, irrespective of marital status and family relations, have the right to appropriate social and economic protection"; and, in Part II, that "[w]ith a view to ensuring the effective exercise of the right of mothers and children to social and economic protection, the Contracting Parties will take all appropriate and necessary measures to that end, including the establishment or maintenance of appropriate institutions or services". In addition to the inclusion of specific clarifications on actions required to fulfil the objective of granting protection to children and young persons in different contexts, two fundamental changes can be underlined with a view to understanding the core provisions included under Article 17 RESC.

One amendment concerns the beneficiaries of the three-fold protection under the RESC, which now covers children and young persons, but without any reference to the mothers. As mentioned above, mothers do indeed fall within the scope of application of Article 16 on the right of the family to social, legal and economic protection.[11] This demonstrates the intention to specifically address the rights of children, who are thus directly protected as individuals alone. Accordingly, this amendment facilitated the applicability of this provision to children in irregular situations, such as unaccompanied foreign minors.[12]

Second, Article 17 of the RESC also provides for the legal protection of children and young persons. The 1961 Charter only refers to social and economic

7 Lukas Karin, *The Revised European Social Charter: An Article by Article Commentary*, Cheltenham, UK, Edward Elgar Publishing Limited, 2021, p. 225.

8 Consultative Assembly of the Council of Europe, 14th April 1956, Doc. 488.

9 Holly Cullen, *cit.*, p. 65 ff.

10 See *infra*.

11 Explanatory Report, *cit.*, § 66; Holly Cullen, *cit.*, p. 65.

12 See *infra*; for a comment, Stefano Angeleri and Róisín Dunbar, "The Reform of the European Social Charter", in Stefano Angeleri and Carole Nivard (eds.), *The European Social Charter: A Commentary*, vol. I: *Cross-cutting Themes*, *cit.*, pp. 38–61, spec. p. 51.

protection. The new reference to legal protection clearly fits into the evolving approach of considering children as individuals in need of protection in different contexts. As clarified in the Explanatory Report, "[t]his provision protects children, irrespective of such factors as their birth status and the marital status of their parents. In confirmation of the case law of the Committee of Independent Experts, according to which certain rights such as the right of children to inheritance are covered by Article 17 of the Charter, the word 'legal' has been added to its title".[13] Therefore, this addition supports the broad interpretation of the provision, which is intended to grant protection in all situations.

II Other Instruments Establishing Similar Standards

Article 17 of the RESC encompasses many rights which are provided for at an international level in the principles of the UN Convention on the Rights of the Child (CRC) signed in New York on 20 November 1989 and which, in fact, inspired its drafting,[14] as well as of the 1950 European Convention on Human Rights (ECHR).

The amendments to Article 17 were in fact intended to align it with the UN CRC, as reflected in the preamble, where it recognises with regard to children "the full development of their personality and of their (...) capacities" as the target of the protection. This reference recalls Article 27 of the CRC regarding the right of every child to a standard of living adequate for the child's physical, mental, spiritual, moral and social development.[15] The principle of the best interests of the child, under Article 3 CRC, has been employed by the ECSR to develop its interpretation of the requirements of Article 17 RESC.[16] In its decisions, where relevant, the ECSR also made explicit reference to the CRC

13 Explanatory Report, *cit.*, § 70; see *infra*.

14 On the influence of the UN Convention, see: Francesca Ippolito, "The Convention on the Rights of the Child in Litigation Before the European Social Charter Committee and the European Court of Human Rights: «Why Then, Can One Desire Too Much of a Good Thing?»", *Diritti umani e diritto internazionale*, no. 1, 2020, pp. 93–119.

15 Stefano Angeleri and Róisín Dunbar, *cit.*, p. 51. For an assessment of the corresponding provisions among the two instruments, see: Holly Cullen, *cit.*, p. 63 ff.

16 See *infra* and Lukas Karin, *cit.*, p. 224. In *International Federation of Human Rights Leagues (FIDH) v. France*, complaint No. 14/2003, decision on the merits of 8 September 2004, the ECSR affirmed that "Article 17 of the Revised Charter is further directly inspired by the United Nations Convention on the Rights of the Child" (§ 36).

and the accompanying general comments of the UN Committee on the Rights of the Child.

The social rights enshrined in the European Social Charter stand alongside the European Convention of Human Rights, which encompasses civil and political rights, and thus have different structures and effects.[17] In some decisions, the ECSR makes references to the case law of the European Court of Human Rights (ECtHR) to support its interpretation and assessment of domestic legislation or practice.[18] In general, whenever comparable situations have been brought to their attention, their approach has been similar because it is aimed at granting the broadest protection possible.[19]

Other conventions have been adopted by the Council of Europe concerning issues related to specific children's rights.[20] Moreover, at the policy level, the 2006 programme "Building a Europe for and with children" represents a cross-disciplinary plan of action involving national governments, civil society, the EU, and other international organisations and stakeholders. Then, in 2020, the Steering Committee for the Rights of the Child was established as the successor to the Ad Hoc Committee for the Rights of the Child.[21] Various instruments offering practical guidance have been adopted by the Committee of Ministers

17 On the adoption of both instruments, see: Giuseppe Palmisano, *L'Europa dei diritti sociali*, *cit.*, p. 19 ff. See also: Lorenza Mola, *La Carta sociale europea e il controllo internazionale sulla sua applicazione*, Torino, Giappichelli, 2022, p. 1 ff.; Ann Skelton, "International Children's Rights Law: Complaints and Remedies", in Ursula Kilkelly and Ton Liefaard (eds.), *International Human Rights of Children*, Singapore, Springer Nature, 2019, pp. 65–91, spec. p. 86.

18 See, for instance, *infra* regarding the issue of corporal punishment. For comments on the relationship between the Charter and the ECHR, see: Christina Deliyanni-Dimitrakou, "The European Social Charter and the European Convention on Human Rights", in Stefano Angeleri and Carole Nivard (eds.), *The European Social Charter: A Commentary*, vol. I: *Cross-cutting Themes*, *cit.*, pp. 351–374; Giorgio Malinverni, "The Court of European Human Rights, the protection of social rights, its relationship with the European Committee of Social Rights", in Marilisa D'amico and Giovanni Guiglia (eds.), *European Social Charter and the challenges of the XXI century*, Napoli, Edizioni Scientifiche Italiane, 2014, pp. 97–112.

19 Findings of ECtHR jurisprudence are referenced in the footnotes of part III below.

20 See: Convention on the Protection of Children against Sexual Exploitation and Sexual Abuse (CETS No. 201), Lanzarote 25 October 2007; European Convention on the Exercise of Children's Rights, CETS No. 160, Strasbourg 25 January 1996; European Convention on the Legal Status of Children Born out of Wedlock, CETS No. 85, 15 October 1975; Convention on the Adoption of Children (revised), CETS No. 202, 27 November 2008; Convention on Contact concerning Children, CETS No. 192, 15 May 2003; Convention on Preventing and Combating Violence against Women and Domestic Violence, CETS No. 210, 11 May 2011.

21 See applicable information at <https://www.coe.int/en/web/children/cdenf>.

that implement the strategies for the rights of the child.[22] On 23 February 2022, the Committee of Ministers adopted the new Strategy for the Rights of the Child (2022–2027) entitled "Children's Rights in Action: from continuous implementation to joint innovation", which aims at advancing the protection and promotion of the rights of the child across Europe.[23]

At the European Union level, the scope of some articles of the Charter of Fundamental Rights (CFR) echoes the content of Article 17 RESC.[24] Article 24 CFR on the rights of the child is more extensive than Article 17 RESC.[25] It states:

1. Children shall have the right to such protection and care as is necessary for their well-being.
   They may express their views freely. Such views shall be taken into consideration on matters which concern them in accordance with their age and maturity.
2. In all actions relating to children, whether taken by public authorities or private institutions, the child's best interests must be a primary consideration.
3. Every child shall have the right to maintain on a regular basis a personal relationship and direct contact with both his or her parents, unless that is contrary to his or her interests.

---

22 See, for instance: Rec. CM/Rec(2009)10 on integrated national strategies for the protection of children from violence, 18 November 2009; Guidelines on child-friendly justice, 17 November 2010; Guidelines on child-friendly health care, 21 September 2011; Rec. CM/Rec(2011)12 on children's rights and social services friendly to children and families, 16 November 2011; Rec. CM/Rec(2012)2 on the participation of children and young people under the age of 18, 28 March 2012; Recommendation CM/Rec(2018)5 concerning children with imprisoned parents, 4 April 2018; Rec. CM/Rec(2018)7 on guidelines to respect, protect and fulfil the rights of the child in the digital environment, 4 July 2018; Rec. CM/Rec(2019)11 on effective guardianship for unaccompanied and separated children in the context of migration, 11 December 2019; Action Plan on Protecting Vulnerable Persons in the Context of Migration and Asylum in Europe (2021–2025), August 2021.

23 The 2022 Strategy identifies six strategic objectives: freedom from violence for all children, equal opportunities and social inclusion for all children, access to safe use of technologies for all children, child-friendly justice for all children, giving a voice to every child, children's rights in crisis and emergency situations. The Strategy is available online at <https://www.coe.int/en/web/children/strategy-for-the-rights-of-the-child>.

24 For an overview on the rights of the child in Europe, see: European Union Agency for Fundamental Rights, CoE and ECtHR, *Handbook on European law relating to the rights of the child*, 2022, available at <https://fra.europa.eu/en/publication/2022/handbook-european-law-child-rights>.

25 *Charter of Fundamental Rights of the European Union*, OJ C 202, 7.6.2016, p. 389 ff.

The Explanation to the EU CFR states that "Article 24 is based on the UN CRC, particularly Articles 3, 9, 12 and 13 thereof. Paragraph 3 takes account of the fact that, as part of the establishment of an area of freedom, security and justice, the legislation of the Union on civil matters having cross-border implications, for which Article 81 of the Treaty on the Functioning of the European Union confers power, may include notably visiting rights ensuring that children can maintain on a regular basis a personal and direct contact with both of their parents".[26]

Other EU Charter Articles may cover children's rights to protection in various fields. These include Article 7 on the respect for private and family life, Article 14 on the right to education, Article 21 on non-discrimination, Article 33§1 on the right to legal, social and economic protection of the family, Article 34 § 3 on the right to social and housing assistance and Article 47 on fair trial guarantees. Though those instruments have different scopes of application and legal weight, similarities can be outlined in the interpretation of the corresponding provisions, as well as in the light of other relevant conventions.[27]

---

26 *Explanations relating to the Charter of Fundamental Rights* (OJ C 303, 14.12.2007, p. 17 ff.), available online at <https://eur-lex.europa.eu/legal-content/EN/TXT/?uri=CELEX:32007X1214(01)>. However, according to the preamble to the Explanations, "[a]lthough they do not as such have the status of law, they [the Explanations] are a valuable tool of interpretation intended to clarify the provisions of the Charter" (see also Article 52 § 7 CFR). Among the relevant EU legislation on the rights of the child in civil judicial cooperation, see Council Regulation (EU) 2019/1111 of 25 June 2019 on jurisdiction, the recognition and enforcement of decisions in matrimonial matters and the matters of parental responsibility, and on international child abduction (recast) (OJ L 178, 2.7.2019, p. 1 ff.), that replaced Council Regulation (EC) No 2201/2003 of 27 November 2003; and the Proposal for a Council Regulation on jurisdiction, applicable law, recognition of decisions and acceptance of authentic instruments in matters of parenthood and on the creation of a European Certificate of Parenthood (COM(2022)695 final of 7 December 2022).

27 On the relationship between the EU Charter and the European Social Charter, see: Marco Rocca, "The European Social Charter and the European Union", in Stefano Angeleri and Carole Nivard (eds.), *The European Social Charter: A Commentary.* vol. I: *Cross-cutting Themes, cit.*, pp. 375–401; Olivier De Schutter, *The European Social Charter in the context of implementation of the EU Charter of Fundamental Rights*, Study for the European Parliament (PE 536.488), 2016, available online at <https://www.europarl.europa.eu/RegData/etudes/STUD/2016/536488/IPOL_STU(2016)536488_EN.pdf>. For a comment, see also: Federica Cristani, "The European Court of Justice and the protection of social rights: Which role for the European Committee of Social Rights?", in Marilisa D'amico and Giovanni Guiglia (eds.), *European Social Charter and the challenges of the XXI century, cit.*, pp. 113–142.

At a policy level, the European Union is committed to the protection of children's rights and promotes initiatives[28] such as the European Forum on the rights of the child, the EU Network for Children's Rights and EU Child Participation Platform, as well as adopting such soft-law as the latest Strategy on the rights of the child (2021–2024),[29] and the European Child Guarantee.[30]

III Analysis of the Provision

Part I of the RESC asserts the right of children and young persons to social, legal and economic protection, which is further implemented, under Part II, with recommended measures to be undertaken by States Parties to effectively grant such protection. The examination of the content of this provision addresses both the personal and material scopes, including references to the Committee's relevant decisions, which have contributed to the interpretation of the protection being guaranteed to the target groups.[31]

A *Personal Scope*

Article 17 of the RESC, as amended in relation to the original 1961 Charter, provides for the right to social, legal and economic protection in favour of children and young persons. The beneficiaries of the protections granted are children and young persons on an equal basis; the reference to these two groups is not intended to create any distinction. In fact, as explained in the Appendix to the RESC, the provision covers all persons under the age of 18 years[32] unless age of majority is attained earlier, under the national law applicable to the child. This indication is, however, without prejudice to the other specific provisions of

28 See applicable information at <https://ec.europa.eu/info/policies/justice-and-fundamental-rights/rights-child_en>.

29 COM(2021)142 final of 24 March 2021.

30 Council Recommendation (EU) 2021/1004 of 14 June 2021 establishing a European Child Guarantee (OJ L 223, 22.6.2021, p. 14 ff.), see its Recital 5 where it recalls the commitment included under Article 17 of the RESC.

31 For an overview on the practical application of the Charter, see: CoE, *Digest of the Case Law of the European Committee of Social Rights*, *cit.*; European Union Agency for Fundamental Rights, CoE and ECtHR, *Handbook on European law relating to the rights of the child*, *cit.*; Monika Smusz-Kulesza, Anahit Manasyan and Alla Fedorova, *Training programme for judges. European Social Charter and case law of the European Committee of Social Rights*, February 2021, available online at <https://rm.coe.int/15-judges-training-eng-soft/1680a39c11>, spec. p. 141 ff. on Article 17.

32 Lukas Karin, *cit.*, p. 351.

the Charter and in particular under to Article 7 which also, as specified in the Explanatory Report, covers the protection of children.[33]

Pursuant to Article 17 § 1(a) related to the adoption of measures addressed to care, assistance and education, States shall take into account the rights and duties of the parents of the children or young persons involved. Parents, according to the Explanatory Report, must be considered all those persons who are in charge of the legal care or assistance of children or young persons, such as legal guardians or other individuals legally responsible.[34] It thus requires States to consider and respect the responsibilities of those persons in charge of the child's care.

A relevant issue concerning the categorization of beneficiaries relates to the inclusion of foreign minors.[35] Pursuant to paragraph 1 of the Appendix, the persons covered in Article 17 RESC are – *inter alia* – to "include foreigners only in so far as they are nationals of other Parties lawfully resident or working regularly within the territory of the Party concerned, subject to the understanding that these articles are to be interpreted in the light of the provisions of Articles 18 and 19". Moreover, it specifies that "[t]his interpretation would not prejudice the extension of similar facilities to other persons by any of the Parties"[36] and that treatment as favourable as possible shall also be accorded to refugees[37] and stateless persons.[38]

The Committee's 2021 decision in *International Commission of Jurists* (ICJ) *and European Council for Refugees and Exiles* (ECRE) *v. Greece*[39] confirmed the applicability of both paragraphs of Article 17 RESC to foreign children who are in an irregular migration situation on the territory of a State Party, as affirmed in earlier cases, which are analysed below under their respective subject matters.

---

33 Explanatory Report, *cit.*, § 71.

34 *Ibid.*, § 72.

35 On this issue, see also: Bige Açimuz and Olgun Akbulut, "The Values Underlying the European Social Charter", in Stefano Angeleri and Carole Nivard (eds.), *The European Social Charter: A Commentary*, vol. I: *Cross-cutting Themes*, *cit.*, pp. 264–292, spec. part III.B; and, in general, Giuseppe Palmisano, "Overcoming the limits of the European Social Charter in terms of persons protected: the case of third State nationals and irregular migrants", in Marilisa D'amico and Giovanni Guiglia (eds.), *European Social Charter and the challenges of the XXI century*, *cit.*, pp. 171–192.

36 Appendix, *cit.*, § 1.

37 See also *infra* regarding ECSR, *International Commission of Jurists* (ICJ) *and European Council for Refugees and Exiles* (ECRE) *v. Greece*, complaint No. 173/2018, decision on the merits of 26 January 2021.

38 Appendix, *cit.*, § 1, second part, and § 2.

39 ECSR, *International Commission of Jurists* (ICJ) *and European Council for Refugees and Exiles* (ECRE) *v. Greece*, *cit.*, § 77.

The ECSR interpretation on the personal scope of this provision followed a teleological approach in order to ensure its conformity with other relevant international human rights instruments.[40] The Committee itself stated that "it is necessary to seek the interpretation of the treaty that is most appropriate in order to realise the aim and achieve the object of this treaty, not that which would restrict the Parties' obligations to the greatest possible degree".[41] Thus, paragraph 1 of the Appendix must not be interpreted "in such a way as to deny foreign minors unlawfully present in a country (whether accompanied or unaccompanied) the guarantee of their fundamental rights, including the right to preservation of their human dignity".[42]

In this regard, following the guidance of the UN Committee on the Rights of the Child, the ECSR considered that the personal scope of the Charter must be determined according to the principle of the child's best interests. It recalled that, pursuant to CRC General Comment No. 5,[43] "[e]very legislative, administrative and judicial body or institution is required to apply the best interests principle by systematically considering how children's rights and interests are or will be affected by their decisions and actions – by, for example, a proposed or existing law or policy or administrative action or court decision, including those which are not directly concerned with children, but indirectly affect children".[44]

On the interpretation of the personal scope, in *International Federation of Human Rights Leagues (FIDH) v. France* of 2004, the Committee stressed that

40 See: CoE, *Digest of the Case Law of the European Committee of Social Rights*, *cit.*, p. 213; Lukas Karin, *cit.*, p. 364.

41 ECSR, *European Committee for Home-Based Priority Action for the Child and the Family (EUROCEF) v. France*, complaint No. 114/2015, decision on the merits of 24 January 2018, § 53.

42 ECSR, *Defence for Children International (DCI) v. Belgium*, complaint No. 69/2011, decision on the merits of 23 October 2012, § 30. "A strict interpretation of paragraph 1 of the Appendix, which would result in the non-recognition of the States Parties' obligation to guarantee foreign minors unlawfully present in their territory the enjoyment of these fundamental rights, would be incompatible with international *jus cogens*" (*ibid.*, § 33). Moreover, according to the Committee, "a strict interpretation of the Appendix (…) would not be in harmony with the United Nations Convention on the Rights of the Child, which all member states of the Council of Europe have ratified. It is therefore justified for the Committee to have regard to this convention, adopting the interpretation given to it by the United Nations Committee on the Rights of the Child, when it rules on an alleged violation of any right conferred on children by the Charter" (ECSR, *European Committee for Home-Based Priority Action for the Child and the Family (EUROCEF) v. France*, *cit.*, § 53).

43 UN, Doc. CRC/GC/2003/5, §§ 45–47.

44 ECSR, *Defence for Children International (DCI) v. Belgium*, *cit.*, § 32. See: Lukas Karin, *cit.*, p. 364.

the Charter was "envisaged as a human rights instrument to complement the European Convention on Human Rights" and that, pursuant to the Vienna Declaration of 1993, "the Charter must be interpreted so as to give life and meaning to fundamental social rights.[45] It follows *inter alia* that limitations on rights are to be read restrictively, i.e., understood in such a manner as to preserve intact the essence of the right and to achieve the overall purpose of the Charter".[46] In that case, the Committee recognised that Article 17 RESC "protects in a general manner the right of children and young persons, including unaccompanied minors, to care and assistance". Thus, it found a violation of Article 17 because unaccompanied minors and children of illegal immigrants were only entitled to medical assistance in life-threatening situations and not in a promt way.[47]

As regards children unlawfully present in the territory of one State, in *Defence for Children International (DCI) v. the Netherlands* of 2009,[48] the Committee clarified that children fall within the personal scope of application of Article 17 RESC regardless of their residence status, whether following a failed asylum procedure, a failed regular immigration procedure and/or pending the results of a regular immigration procedure. This finding was then included in the Statement of Interpretation on Article 17 § 2.[49]

The ECSR noted in the *Defence for Children International (DCI) v. Belgium* case of 2012 that the implication of paragraph 1 of the Appendix is that foreign minors (accompanied and unaccompanied) unlawfully present in a country – in the specific case, non asylum-seeking unaccompanied foreign minors and children in families illegally resident – "would not come within the personal

45 ECSR, *International Federation of Human Rights Leagues (FIDH) v. France*, complaint No. 14/2003, decision on the merits of 8 September 2004, §§ 27–29.

46 ECSR, *International Federation of Human Rights Leagues (FIDH) v. France, cit.*

47 *Ibid*; see on this issue, Lukas Karin, *cit.*, p. 363. Unaccompanied foreign minors do fall within the personal scope of the ECHR, that applies, within the jurisdiction of the Contracting Parties, to everyone whatever their country of origin. Their protection is granted, for instance, with regard to the prohibition of ill-treatment under Article 3 ECHR (ECtHR, 28 February 2019, *Khan v. France*, No. 12267/16, on the failure of the authorities to provide foreign minors with care before and after the dismantling of the makeshift camps set up in the "lande de Calais"; in the same sense, 28 February 2019, ECtHR, *H.A. and Others v. Greece*, No. 19951/16) as well as under Article 8 ECHR on the right to respect for private and family life (for instance, in case of shortcomings in procedural guarantees afforded to a minor migrant preventing him to file an asylum request: ECtHR, 21 July 2022, *Darboe and Camara v. Italy*, No. 5797/17).

48 ECSR, *Defence for Children International (DCI) v. the Netherlands*, complaint No. 47/2008, decision on the merits of 20 October 2009, §§ 34–38 and 66.

49 ECSR, Conclusions 2011, Statement of Interpretation on Article 17 § 2.

scope of Article 17, as they are not nationals of other Parties 'lawfully resident or working regularly' within the territory of the Party concerned".[50] However, in the light of other relevant and applicable rules of international law,[51] the personal scope defined in "paragraph 1 of the Appendix should not be interpreted in such a way as to expose foreign minors unlawfully present in a country to serious impairments of their fundamental rights on account of a failure to give guarantee to the social rights enshrined in the revised Charter",[52] such as the rights to life, to physical integrity or to human dignity.[53]

The Committee pointed out that the application of the Charter's provisions to foreign migrants in an irregular situation is "entirely exceptional and is not applicable to all the provisions of the Charter". This is due to the fact that it is "justified solely in the event that excluding foreigners in an irregular migration situation from the protection afforded by the Charter would have seriously detrimental consequences for their fundamental rights" and would consequently place them "in an unacceptable situation, regarding the enjoyment of these rights, as compared with the situation of nationals and of lawfully resident foreigners".[54]

In the ECSR's opinion, "the risk of impairing fundamental rights is all the more likely where children – *a fortiori* migrant children unlawfully present in a country – are at stake. This is due to their condition as 'children' and to their specific situation as 'unlawful'[55] migrants, combining vulnerability and limited autonomy".[56] Indeed, children cannot be held genuinely responsible for their place of residence, because they are not able to decide for themselves whether to stay or to leave. So, in cases where they are unaccompanied, "their situation becomes even more vulnerable and the state should be managed entirely by the State, which has a duty to care for children living within its territory and not to deprive them of the most basic protection on account of their 'unlawful' migration status".[57]

---

50 ECSR, *Defence for Children International (DCI) v. Belgium, cit.*, § 28 ff.

51 *Ibid.*, § 29.

52 *Ibid.*, § 34. In this sense, see also: ECSR, *European Committee for Home-Based Priority Action for the Child and Family (EUROCEF) v. France, cit.*, § 55; *International Commission of Jurists (ICJ) and European Council for Refugees and Exiles (ECRE) v. Greece, cit.*, § 75.

53 ECSR, *Defence for Children International (DCI) v. Belgium, cit.*, § 29.

54 *Ibid.*, § 35; and lately *International Commission of Jurists (ICJ) and European Council for Refugees and Exiles (ECRE) v. Greece, cit.*, § 76.

55 On the interpretation of the issue of unlawful stay, see Claudio Panzera, "The personal scope of the European Social Charter: questioning equality", *Revista Europea de Derechos Fundamentales*, n. 24, 2014, pp. 51–73, spec. p. 60 ff.

56 ECSR, *Defence for Children International (DCI) v. Belgium, cit.*, § 37.

57 *Ibid.*

In addition, since according to Article 17 § 1 RESC States Parties are required to fulfil positive obligations relating to the accommodation, basic care and protection of children and young persons, "[n]ot considering that States Parties are bound to comply with these obligations in the case of foreign minors who are in a country unlawfully would therefore mean not guaranteeing their fundamental rights and exposing the children and young persons in question to serious threats to their rights to life, health and psychological and physical integrity and to the preservation of their human dignity".[58] It means that State authorities cannot shirk their responsibility to protect the rights of unaccompanied children by alleging their unregulated legal situation.[59]

In *International Commission of Jurists* (ICJ) *and European Council for Refugees and Exiles* (ECRE) *v. Greece*, in 2021,[60] the Committee reiterated its interpretation regarding the personal scope of Article 17 RESC, which therefore includes migrant children, whether accompanied or unaccompanied foreign children. This case concerned mostly children (accompanied and unaccompanied) who arrived in Greece and applied for asylum or international protection. As the ECSR noted, in the light of paragraph 2 of the Appendix, they therefore fall within the definition of refugees under the 1951 Geneva Convention on the Status of Refugees.[61] The Committee recalled that "the protection of a refugee under the Charter does not depend on the administrative recognition of refugee status by a State, which is done by the granting of asylum".[62] In this respect, it explicitly referred to its Statement of Interpretation on the rights of refugees under the Charter adopted in 2015.[63] The Committee then considered that refugees must be guaranteed social rights that are directly related to the right to life and human dignity and form part of an "non-derogable core" of rights,[64] among which Article 17 RESC is included.[65] Consequently, the personal scope

58 *Ibid.*, § 38.

59 See Bige Açimuz and Olgun Akbulut, *cit.*

60 ECSR, *International Commission of Jurists* (ICJ) *and European Council for Refugees and Exiles* (ECRE) *v. Greece*, *cit.*, § 75 ff.

61 *Ibid.*, § 80.

62 *Ibid.*, § 81.

63 ECSR, Statement of Interpretation on the rights of refugees under the European Social Charter, elaborated during the 280th session, 7–11 September 2015, § 6. See also: ECSR, Conclusions 2015, § 21, p. 8, on the rights of refugees under the Charter.

64 ECSR, Statement of Interpretation on the rights of refugees under the European Social Charter, *cit.*, § 11.

65 ECSR, *International Commission of Jurists* (ICJ) *and European Council for Refugees and Exiles* (ECRE) *v. Greece*, *cit.*, § 82.

of the Charter also covers refugee and asylum-seeking children, as long as their asylum claim has not been rejected by a body of final instance.[66]

B *Material Scope*

According to Article 17 RESC, children and young persons have the right to social, legal and economic protection, which must be granted by the Parties by implementing all appropriate and necessary measures, such as those listed in Part II, under paragraphs 1 and 2, taking into consideration any different contexts. Such measures must be aimed at ensuring the effective exercise of the rights of children and young persons to grow up in an environment which encourages the full development of their personality and of their physical and mental capacities.

A preliminary observation concerns the specification in Article 17 of Part I of the right to "appropriate" protection. It indeed stipulates that the States have a positive obligation to effectively undertake all necessary actions in favour of the vulnerable beneficiaries. In addition, the reference to the three levels of protection expresses the intention to comprehensively promote the rights of children and young persons in different situations which may, nonetheless, be mutually interconnected.

In general, under Article 17 RESC, States Parties are required to: ensure that children and young persons have the care, the assistance, the education and the training they need (§§ 1.a and 2); protect them against negligence, violence and exploitation (§ 1.b.) and; provide protection and aid for children and young persons deprived of their family's support (§ 1.c.). According to the Committee's decisions, the material scope of the provision in question covers the following issues: (1) the legal status of the child; (2) the rights of children in public care; (3) the protection of children from violence, ill-treatment and abuse; (4) young offenders; (5) the right to assistance and the situation of children in poverty; and (6) the right to education.

1 Legal Status of the Child

As to the legal protection, its introduction in the Revised Charter codifies the approach of the ECSR to legal issues concerning the status of children, as well as the need to protect their identity as such, which in fact covers various aspects of their personality and can also be relevant in order that they be able to benefit from the protection at social and economic levels.

66 *Ibid.*, § 83.

As clarified in the Explanatory Report, the protection to children must be granted irrespective of legal factors, such as their birth status and the marital status of their parents.[67] In particular, the Committee noted that Article 17 RESC permits no discrimination as between children born outside of marriage and children born within marriage, e.g., in respect of maintenance obligations and succession.[68] In addition, concerning the legal status of children, a new issue that may be brought to the attention of the Committee involves the protection of the rights of children having same-sex parents, due to the increasing amount of case law before national courts and uncertainties in domestic – as well as in international and EU – legislation, especially concerning surrogacy and stepchild adoption.[69]

67 Explanatory Report, *cit.*, § 70.

68 ECSR, Conclusions XVII-2, Malta; ECSR, Conclusions 2003, France; see also: CoE, *Digest of the Case Law of the European Committee of Social Rights*, *cit.*, p. 149. The ECSR interpretation is in line with the ECtHR, which grants protection to both natural and legal families especially concerning the status of the children by virtue of the principle of non-discrimination based on birth under Article 14 ECHR (see ECtHR, 13 June 1979, *Marckx v. Belgium*, No. 6833/74; ECtHR, 7 February 2013, *Fabris v. France*, No. 16574/08; ECtHR, 11 October 2011, *Genovese v. Malta*, No. 53124/09, where it reiterated that very weighty reasons would have had to be advanced to justify an arbitrary difference in treatment on the ground of birth), to *de facto* relations regardless of the gender of the parties (see ECtHR, 26 May 1994, *Keegan v. Ireland*, No. 16969/90; regarding same-sex partners, see: ECtHR, 24 June 2010, *Schalk and Kopf v. Austria*, No. 30141/04; ECtHR, 23 February 2016, *Paijc v. Croatia*, No. 68453/13; ECtHR, 30 June 2016, *Taddeucci and McCall v. Italy*, No. 51362/09); as well as in relation to inheritance rights, also in conjunction with Article 14 ECHR (see ECtHR, 3 October 2000, *Camp and Bourimi v. the Netherlands*, No. 28369/95; ECtHR, 13 July 2004, *Pla and Puncernau v. Andorra*, No. 69498/01; ECtHR, 28 May 2009, *Brauer v. Germany*, No. 3545/04; 9 February 2017, *Mitzinger v. Germany*, No. 29762/10).

69 Benedetta Liberali, "L'importanza delle parole e della tecnica decisoria in due recenti pronunce della Corte costituzionale in materia di omogenitorialità", *Studium Iuris*, no. 1, 2021, pp. 1190–1201, spec. 1201. As regards surrogacy and Article 8 ECHR on the right to respect for private and family life, according to the ECtHR the recognition of the legal parent-child relationship is due only where a biological link exists, whereas the relationship with the intended parent remains within the States' margin of appreciation (on this issue, see: Maria Caterina Baruffi, "Surrogacy in the recent 'multilevel' case law", in Cécile Corso and Patrick Wautelet (eds.), *L'accès aux droits de la personne et de la famille en Europe*, Bruxelles, Bruylant, 2022, pp. 85–111, especially concerning ECtHR, 26 June 2014, *Mennesson v. France*, No. 65192/11, and ECtHR, *Labassee v. France*, No. 65941/11; ECtHR, 24 January 2017, *Paradiso and Campanelli v. Italy*, No. 25358/12; and advisory opinion P16-2018-001, 10 April 2019). On the intra-EU recognition of parenthood established in a Member State, see the 2022 Commission Proposal for a Council Regulation on jurisdiction, applicable law, recognition of decisions and acceptance of authentic instruments in matters of parenthood and on the creation of a European Certificate of Parenthood, *cit.* (for a comment, see: Lenka Válková, "The Commission Proposal for a Regulation on

According to Article 17 RESC a child has, in principle, the right to know his or her origins. The ECSR has examined the procedures available for the establishment of maternity and paternity and, in particular, those situations where such assessment is not possible and where the right of a child to know his or her origins is restricted.[70] From a general perspective, legitimate and justified grounds should be submitted whenever the right to know the origins is limited so as to grant protection of the rights of the child against the rights of the other persons involved. For instance, it found that the right of the child to know his or her origins was not adequately protected under French legislation, where the mother of a child has requested that her identity should be kept secret during the birth and declaration of the birth, and where parents who place their child in care request that their identity remain secret.[71] As regards Ukraine, the ECSR noted that a child is entitled to information about his or her "absent parents", if such information is not harmful to the child's mental or physical health. In this respect, it requested further information on the grounds of considering the harmful effect on the child. Moreover, discrimination would occur in a case where adopted children have no right to information about their birth parents.[72]

As regards the minimum age for marriage, questions have been raised where there is a difference in the minimum age for marriage for males and females, on the grounds that this may be discriminatory, and that where the age is low for females, this may not adequately protect them.[73] The ECSR found that

---

the Recognition of Parenthood and Other Legislative Trends Affecting Legal Parenthood", *Rivista di diritto internazionale privato e processuale*, no. 4, 2022, pp. 854–899).

70 See ECSR, Conclusions 2011, Ukraine. The protection recognised by the Committee is similar to that of the ECtHR, which protects the right to know the origins pursuant to Article 8 ECHR (see, *inter alia*, ECtHR, 7 July 1989, *Gaskin v. the United Kingdom*, No. 10454/83; ECtHR, 13 July 2006, *Jäggi v. Switzerland*, No. 58757/00; ECtHR, 14 February 2012, *A. M. M. v. Romania*, No. 2151/10; ECtHR, 25 September 2012, *Godelli v. Italy*, No. 33783/09; ECtHR, 6 December 2022, *Scalzo v. Italy*, No. 8790/21).

71 ECSR, Conclusions 2003, France.

72 ECSR, Conclusions 2011, Ukraine.

73 ECSR, Conclusions 2003, France; ECSR, Conclusions 2011, Ukraine. In this regard, the ECSR approach appears more protective then the ECHR to the extent that it requires to avoid any discrimination based on gender whenever children are concerned. Though, the requirements for contracting marriage fall within national sovereignity, as emerges from the ECtHR case law. Article 12 ECHR indeed provides for the right to marry for those of "marriageable age" according to national laws (ECmHR, 7 July 1986, *Khan v. the United Kingdom*, No. 11579/85 on an Islamic marriage; ECtHR, 8 December 2015, *Z.H. and R.H. v. Switzerland*, No. 60119/12, where it considered that neither Articles 8 nor 12 ECHR could be interpreted as imposing on any State party to the Convention an obligation to recognise a marriage, religious or otherwise, contracted by a 14-year-old child).

French legislation was not in conformity with the Charter to the extent that it provided the minimum age of marriage for females of 15 years but 18 years for males.[74]

Another aspect examined under Article 17 § 1 RESC concerning the legal status of the child is the issue of statelessness.[75] In this regard, it can be noted that, in its Conclusions of 2019, the Committee asked the Parties what actions had been taken to reduce statelessness. This included such measures as ensuring that every stateless migrant child is identified, simplifying procedures for obtaining nationality, taking measures to identify children unregistered at birth as well as to facilitate birth registration.[76] Indeed, pursuant to its 2013 Statement of Interpretation on the rights of stateless persons under the Charter, "stateless persons must be guaranteed the protection of the Charter on an equal footing with nationals of other States Parties to the Charter".[77]

2 Rights of Children in Public Care

According to the Committee's interpretation of the rights of children in public care under Article 17 RESC,[78] the main criterion is that "placement must be an exceptional measure, and is only justified when it is based on the needs of the child, namely if remaining in the family represents a danger for the child".[79] For this purpose, "[t]he financial conditions or material circumstances of the family should not be the sole reason for placement".[80] In any case, the Committee

---

74 ECSR, Conclusions 2003, France.

75 See Appendix, *cit.*, § 3.

76 ECSR, Conclusions XXI-4 (2019), General Introduction, March 2020, spec. General question on Article 17.

77 ECSR, Conclusions 2013, Statement of Interpretation on the rights of stateless persons under Charter; Effrosyni Bakirtzi, "The European Social Charter and the International Covenant on Economic, Social and Cultural Rights", in Stefano Angeleri and Carole Nivard (eds.), *The European Social Charter: A Commentary*, vol. I: *Cross-cutting Themes*, *cit.*, pp. 425–464, spec. p. 439; Lukas Karin, *cit.*, p 361 ff.

78 CoE, *Digest of the Case Law of the European Committee of Social Rights*, *cit.*, p. 149 ff.

79 ECSR, Conclusions 2011, Statement of Interpretation on Article 16 and 17 § 1. The ECSR approach is similar to the ECtHR case law, where the latter considered that pursuant to Article 8 ECHR the best interests of the children must be taken into consideration by the authorities when placing them in institutions (see: ECtHR, 7 June 2022, *I.G.D. v. Bulgaria*, No. 70139/14).

80 ECSR, Conclusions 2011, Statement of Interpretation on Article 16 and 17 § 1. Similarly, according to the ECtHR, the mere existence of economic difficulties does not justify the children's placement in institution (ECtHR, 13 October 2015, *S.H. v. Italy*, No. 52557/14), while the risk for the minors to be illtreated or abandoned imposes the authorities to place children in institution (ECtHR, 10 May 2001, *Z. and Others v. the United Kingdom*, No. 29392/95, according to which the failure by UK authorities to provide children with

affirmed that "appropriate alternatives to placement should be explored first, taking into account the views and wishes expressed by the child, his or her parents and other members of the family".[81]

Indeed, any restrictions to the custodial rights of parents should be based upon adequate and reasonable criteria laid down in legislation and should not go beyond what is necessary for the protection and best interests of the child and the rehabilitation of the family,[82] because "the family is the natural environment for the growth and well-being of the child" and "parents have the primary responsibility for the upbringing and development of the child".[83]

In its 2011 Statement,[84] the ECSR specified that the placement, when necessary, should be considered as a temporary solution, during which continuity of the relationship with the family should be maintained. Indeed, "[t]he child's re-integration within the family should be aimed at, and contacts with the family during the placement should be provided for, unless contrary to the best interest of the child". Placement of children outside their home, in a foster family or in a family-type environment, should have preference over placement in an institution. In any case, fundamental rights and freedoms such as the right to integrity, privacy, property and to connect with persons close to the child, must be adequately guaranteed for children living in institutions.[85]

In the 2020 decision in the *European Roma Rights Centre (ERRC) and Mental Disability Advocacy Centre (MDAC) v. Czech Republic* case, the Committee addressed the practice of placing young children under the age of three in child centres, and the alleged failure to put in place non-institutional and

---

appropriate protection against serious, long-term neglect and abuse amounted to inhuman and degrading treatment in breach of Article 3 ECHR).

81 ECSR, Conclusions 2011, Statement of Interpretation on Article 16 and 17 § 1. See also: ESCR, *European Roma Rights Centre (ERRC) and Mental Disability Advocacy Centre (MDAC) v. Czech Republic*, complaint No. 157/2017, decision on the merits of 17 June 2020, § 140 ff.

82 ECSR, Conclusions XV-2 (2001), Statement of Interpretation on Article 17 § 1.

83 ECSR, *European Roma Rights Centre (ERRC) and Mental Disability Advocacy Centre (MDAC) v. Czech Republic, cit.*, § 135; ECSR, Conclusions 2011, Statement of Interpretation on Article 16 and 17§1, ECSR, Conclusions XV-2, Statement of Interpretation on Article 17 § 1.

84 ECSR, Conclusions 2011, Statement of Interpretation on Articles 16 and 17 § 1.

85 See: Information Document prepared by the Secretariat of the ESC, *Children's rights under the European Social Charter, cit.*, p. 8. Also according to the ECtHR, placement should be temporary and aimed at facilitating the family reunification in the light of Article 8 ECHR (ECtHR, 13 July 2000, *Scozzari and Giunta v. Italy*, No. 39221/98 and No. 41963/98, concerning the placement of children in community where certain personnel had convictions for paedophilia).

family-like alternative forms of care. It evaluated this under Article 17 of the 1961 Charter, which refers to "the establishment or maintenance of appropriate [in the RESC, 'sufficient and adequate'] institutions or services".[86] According to the Committee, the Czech Republic's legislation on institutional care for children under the age of three years neither offered guarantees that the placement in institutions of children below the age of three was based on the needs of the child and served his or her best interests, nor ensured that appropriate available alternatives to placement were given prior consideration and applied accordingly. Thus, such legislation could not *per se* be regarded as being in conformity with the obligation to ensure the effective exercise of the right to protection of young children.[87]

Stemming from the Conclusions of 2005 regarding Moldova, children placed in institutions should be entitled to the highest degree of satisfaction of their emotional needs and physical well-being, as well as to special protection and assistance.[88] Such institutions must provide conditions promoting all aspects of children's development. The Committee concluded that "a unit in a child welfare institution shall resemble the home environment and shall not accommodate more than 10 children".[89]

It is therefore necessary that domestic law provide for the possibility to lodge an appeal against a decision to restrict parental rights, to take a child into public care, or to limit the right of access to the child's closest family.[90] Remedies for children living in institutions, or for their guardians, to complain about the conditions in the institution should be provided.[91] Finally, States Parties must ensure adequate supervision of the child welfare system and in particular of the institutions involved.[92]

86 ESCR, *European Roma Rights Centre (ERRC) and Mental Disability Advocacy Centre (MDAC) v. Czech Republic*, complaint No. 157/2017, decision on the merits of 17 June 2020, § 131 ff.

87 *Ibid.*, §§ 148–156.

88 See also: ECSR, Conclusions XV-2 (2001), Statement of Interpretation on Article 17 § 1. Similarly, on the consideration of children's needs when placed in institutions, see: ECtHR, 18 July 2019, *R.V. and Others v. Italy*, No. 37748/13, where the Court found that the various delays in the decision-making process, which resulted in the children's uninterrupted placement in care for over ten years, were incompatible with the requirements of Article 8 ECHR.

89 ECSR, Conclusions 2005, Republic of Moldova.

90 ECSR, Conclusions XV-2 (2001), Statement of Interpretation on Article 17 § 1.

91 *Ibid.*

92 *Ibid.* See also: ECSR, Conclusions 2005, Lithuania.

3 Protection of Children from Violence, Ill-Treatment and Abuse

According to the Committee's interpretation, Article 17 § 1 RESC entails the prohibition and penalisation of all forms of violence against children, including all forms of corporal punishment,[93] both in the home and in all educational settings, public and private, and in alternative care. These forms consist of acts or behaviours likely to affect the physical integrity, dignity, development or psychological well-being of children. The relevant legislation must be sufficiently clear, binding and precise, so as to preclude the courts from refusing to apply it to violence against children. Moreover, States must act with due diligence to ensure that such violence is eliminated in practice.[94]

In its decisions on the complaints submitted by the *World Organisation against Torture* (OMCT) against *Italy, Portugal, Ireland, Greece* and *Belgium*,[95] the ECSR clarified the scope of application of Article 17 by taking into consideration the nature of the Charter as a living instrument to be interpreted in light of the developments in the national law and the relevant international conventions.[96] According to the Committee's case-law, "the prohibition of all forms of violence must have a legislative basis".[97] This "must cover all forms of violence regardless of where it occurs or to the identity of the alleged perpetrator", and "the sanctions available must be adequate, dissuasive and proportionate".[98]

93 ECSR, Conclusions 2011 (XIX-4), Statement of Interpretation on Articles 16 and 17.

94 ECSR, *World Organisation against Torture* (OMCT) *v. Portugal*, complaint No. 34/2006, decision on the merits of 6 December 2006, §§ 19–21.

95 ECSR, *World Organisation against Torture* (OMCT) *v. Greece* (complaint No. 17/2003), *Italy* (complaint No. 19/2003), *Ireland* (complaint No. 18/2003), *Portugal* (complaint No. 20/2003) and *Belgium* (complaint No. 21/2003), decisions on the merits of 7 December 2004.

96 See, for all, *World Organisation against Torture* (OMCT) *v. Italy, cit.*, §§ 40–41. The Committee referred to the following sources: Article 19 of the UNCRC as interpreted by the Committee on the Rights of the Child; Article 3 of the ECHR as interpreted by the European Court of Human Rights (inter alia ECtHR, 25 April 1978, *Tyrer v. the United Kingdom*, No. 5856/72, as regards judicial birching of children; ECtHR, 25 February 1982, *Campbell and Cosans v. the United Kingdom*, Nos. 7511/76 and 7743/76, as regards corporal punishment inflicted at school and ECtHR, 23 September 1998, *A v. the United Kingdom*, No. 25599/94, as regards parental corporal punishment); Rec. No. R (93) 2 on the medico-social aspects of child abuse adopted by the Committee of Ministers on 22 March 1993; Rec. R(90) 2 on social measures concerning violence within the family adopted by the Committee of Ministers on 15 January 1990; Rec. No. R(85)4 on violence within the Family adopted by the Committee of Ministers on 26 March 1985; Rec. 1666 (2004) "Europe-wide ban on corporal punishment of children" adopted by the Parliamentary Assembly on 24 June 2004.

97 ECSR, *World Organisation against Torture* (OMCT) *v. Italy, cit.*, § 42.

98 *Ibid.* The lack of clear legislation and positive actions undertaken by the authorities to prevent domestic violation and abuse, as well as the failure to protect children, may amount to a violation of Article 3 ECHR on the prohibition of torture, inhuman or

In this same case concerning Italy, the applicant complained about the possibility, under national legislation and practice, that parents or other persons with children under their charge may be authorised to use "correctional measures" involving a certain degree of violence. However, the Committee did not find any violation of Article 17 RESC since, based on the submitted domestic case law regarding the relevant rules, no ambiguity emerged about the lawfulness of the use of any degree of violence against children by any person, even in circumstances traditionally regarded as justifying such conduct.[99] On the contrary, in another case regarding Ireland, the Committee noted that the corporal punishment of children within the home was permitted by virtue of the existence of the common law defence of reasonable chastisement. Although the domestic criminal law protects children from very serious violence within the home, the Committee held that certain forms of violence are in fact permitted and that the situation was in violation of Article 17.[100]

In the 2006 decision involving Portugal,[101] the Committee upheld the OMCT arguments affirming that under national legislation and case law no explicit or effective prohibition of all corporal punishment of children, either by their parents or by others, is provided. Therefore, the absence of an explicit statutory ban in the legislation entailed a violation of Article 17.[102] Similarly, in the cases introduced by *Association for the Protection of All Children* (*APPROACH*) against *France*, *Ireland*, *Italy*, *Slovenia*, *Belgium* and *Czech Republic*,[103] the

degrading treatment or punishment, occasionally in conjunction with Article 8 ECHR on the right to private and family life (see: ECtHR, 10 May 2001, *Z. and Others v. the United Kingdom*, No. 29392/95; ECtHR, 15 September 2009, *E.S. and Others v. Slovakia*, No. 8227/04; ECtHR, 3 September 2015, *M. and M. v. Croatia*, No. 10161/13; ECtHR, 3 October 2017, *D.M.D. v. Romania*, No. 23022/13).

99 ECSR, *World Organisation against Torture* (*OMCT*) *v. Italy*, *cit.*, § 46.

100 ECSR, *World Organisation against Torture* (*OMCT*) *v. Ireland*, *cit.*, § 57.

101 ECSR, *World Organisation against Torture* (*OMCT*) *v. Portugal*, *cit.*

102 *Ibid.*, § 22.

103 ECSR, *Association for the Protection of All Children* (*APPROACH*) *Ltd. v. France*, complaint No. 92/2013, decision on the merits of 12 September 2014; *Ireland*, complaint No. 93/2013, decision on the merits of 2 December 2014; *Italy*, complaint No. 94/2013, decision on the merits of 5 December 2014; *Slovenia*, complaint No. 95/2013, decision on the merits of 5 December 2014; *Belgium*, complaint No. 98/2013, decision on the merits of 20 January 2015; *Czech Republic*, complaint No. 96/2013, decision on the merits of 20 January 2015. The findings of the ECSR are in line with the protection afforded within the ECHR context. According to the ECtHR, as regards France, the malfunctioning of its justice system amounted to a breach of Article 3 ECHR since it failed to protect the child from the severe abuse by her parents which had led to her death (ECtHR, 4 June 2020, *Association Innocence en Danger v. France* and *Association Enfance et Partage v. France*, No. 15343/15 and No. 16806/15; ECtHR, 3 November 2022, *Loste v. France*, No. 59227/12 regarding the failure to protect the child from ill-treatment while in the foster care). The ECtHR found

complainant organisation alleged that they were in breach of Article 17 § 1 RESC because of the lack of explicit and effective prohibition of all corporal punishment of children within the family, schools and other settings, and because the States in question had failed to act with due diligence to eliminate such punishment in practice. The Committee confirmed that they violated the provision on the grounds that the respective State legislation did not set out an "express and comprehensive prohibition on all forms of corporal punishment of children"[104] and there was no case law by superior courts showing that the respective legislation had been interpreted as prohibiting all forms of violence against children.[105]

It must be recalled that Article 17 RESC is closely linked with Article 7 § 10.[106] The States Parties having accepted both provisions must respect, under Article 7 § 10, the following issues: the protection of children against moral dangers at work and outside work and the involvement of children in the sex industry and in begging. On the other hand, the issues dealt with under Article 17 are, in particular, the protection of children from ill-treatment, including corporal punishment. As regards the coordination of the above noted articles, in the *APPROACH v. Cyprus*[107] complaint the Committee recalled that the Charter was conceived as a whole and in some cases its provisions complement each other, as well as overlap in part, and this is the case of the protection of children from ill-treatment and abuse.[108] The ECSR pointed out that "the fact that the right of children and young persons to social, legal and economic protection is guaranteed under Article 17 of the Charter does not exclude the examination of certain relevant issues relating to the protection of children under Article 7 § 10".[109] Thus, a State that has not accepted Article 17 may be

---

a violation of Article 3, as well as of Article 13 on the right to an effective remedy, in a case concerning the Irish State's failure to protect the applicant from sexual abuse and her inability to obtain recognition at national level of that failure (ECtHR, 28 January 2014, *O'Keeffe v. Ireland*, No. 35810/09). Furthermore, the ECtHR stated that the deficient investigation due to the authorities' failure to effectively apply the criminal-law system for punishing all forms of rape and sexual abuse was in breach of Articles 3 and 8 ECHR (ECtHR, 24 May 2016, *I.C. v. Romania*, No. 36934/08; similarly, ECtHR, 22 June 2021, *R.B. v. Estonia*, No. 22597/16).

104 See ECSR, *Association for the Protection of All Children* (*APPROACH*) *Ltd. v. Belgium*, *cit.*, § 51.

105 *Ibid.*, §§ 54–55.

106 See also the comment of Article 7 in this volume.

107 ECSR, *Association for the protection of All Children* (*APPROACH*) *Ltd. v. Cyprus*, complaint No. 97/2013, decision on admissibility of 2 July 2013.

108 See ECSR, Conclusions XV-2, vol. 1, Statement of Interpretation on Article 7 § 10.

109 ECSR, *Association for the protection of All Children* (*APPROACH*) *Ltd. v. Cyprus*, *cit.*, §10.

examined under Article 7 § 10 whenever the subject matter deals with ill-treatment and abuse.[110]

4 Young Offenders

Regarding young offenders, or children in conflict with the law, the ECSR stated that the age of criminal responsibility must not be excessively low even for very serious crimes.[111] The criminal procedure relating to children and young persons must be adapted to their age and they must be afforded the same procedural guarantees as adults, although proceedings involving minors should be conducted rapidly, as set out in the 2001 Statement of Interpretation on Article 17 RESC.[112] Moreover, minors should not normally be held in custody on remand, and if so, only for serious offences and for a short duration.[113] In such cases, minors should be separated from adults. In this last regard, in *EUROCEF v. France* the Committee declared that the detention of a minor in waiting areas, together with adults, and/or accommodated in hotels, deprived of the assistance of a guardian, cannot be in the best interests of the child and was in violation of Article 17 § 1 RESC.[114]

---

110 ECSR, Conclusions XV-2 (2001), Statement of Interpretation on Article 17, 7 § 10; CoE, *Digest of the Case Law of the European Committee of Social Rights, cit.*, p. 99.

111 ECSR, Conclusions 2011, Ireland; ECSR, Conclusions XIX-4 (2011), United Kingdom, where the Committee held that the age of criminal responsibility at 10 years remains manifestly too low and therefore it is not in conformity with the Charter; see also ECSR, *International Commission of Jurists (ICJ) v. Czech Republic*, Complaint No. 148/2017, decision on the merits of 20 October 2020.

112 ECSR, Conclusions XV-2 (2001), Statement of Interpretation on Article 17. Also the ECtHR found a violation of Article 6 ECHR on the right to fair trial when no procedural guarantees are afforded to minors (ECtHR, 2 March 2010, *Adamkiewic v. Poland*, No. 54729/00) or due to the failure to provide legal assistance (ECtHR, 27 November 2008, *Salduz v. Turkey*, No. 36391/02).

113 ECSR, Conclusions 2005, France; ECSR, Conclusions XIX-4 (2011), Denmark, where the Committee found that 8 months, extendable, of pre-trial detention is excessive and therefore not in conformity with the Charter.

114 ECSR, *European Committee for Home Based Priority Action for the Child and the Family (EUROCEF) v. France, cit.*, §§ 99–101. In general on migration and detention procedures concerning children, see also: CoE, *A handbook for frontline professionals, How to convey child-friendly information to children in migration*, 2019, available online at <https://edoc.coe.int/en/migration/7998-how-to-convey-child-friendly-information-to-children-in-migration-a-handbook-for-frontline-professionals.html>; CoE, *A study of immigration detention practices and the use of alternatives to immigration detention of children*, 2017, available online at <https://edoc.coe.int/en/migration/7533-a-study-of-immigration-detention-practices-and-the-use-of-alternatives-to-immigration-detention-of-children.html>; CoE, *Visiting places where children are deprived of their liberty as a result of immigration procedures*, Guide for Parliamentarians, 2017, available online at

Moreover, prison sentences should only exceptionally be administered to young offenders and various alternative measures, such as those mentioned in Recommendation No. R(87)20,[115] should be considered.[116] Prison sentences for young offenders should in any case only be for a short duration[117] and the length of the sentence must be laid down by a court. As noted in its Conclusions of 2011 regarding Belgium, the Committee required that young offenders should not serve their sentence together with adult prisoners, and thus observed that the possibility of relinquishment of a youth jurisdiction which would allow for minors to be treated as adults and serve their sentence with adults is contrary to the Charter.[118]

Finally, in its 2001 Statement, the ECSR underlined "the importance of enabling young offenders to maintain contact with their family, *inter alia* by placing them as close to the family as possible and by allowing them to receive correspondence and visits".[119] It follows that young persons in conflict with the law should also be provided with specific protective measures that are aimed at ensuring their full development, physically and mentally, as well as at ultimately safeguarding their best interests.

5 Right to Assistance and the Situation of Children in Poverty

According to the Committee's interpretation, Article 17 § 1 RESC guarantees the right of children and young persons – including minors in an irregular situation and unaccompanied, as observed above – to care and assistance, which also covers medical assistance,[120] social assistance and appropriate accommodation.

<https://edoc.coe.int/en/migration/7526-visiting-places-where-children-are-deprived-of-their-liberty-as-a-result-of-immigration-procedures-guide-for-parliamentarians.html>.

115 Rec. No. R(87)20 on social reactions to juvenile delinquency adopted by the Committee of Ministers on 17 September 1987.

116 ECSR, Conclusions XV-2 (2001), Statement of Interpretation on Article 17.

117 ECSR, Conclusions 2011, Norway, where the Committee considered that the maximum penalty of imprisonment for a term of 21 years for minors is excessive and therefore not in conformity with the Charter.

118 ECSR, Conclusions 2011, Belgium.

119 ECSR, Conclusions XV-2 (2001), Statement of Interpretation on Article 17.

120 In *International Federation of Human Rights Leagues (FIDH) v. France*, complaint No. 14/2003, decision on the merits of 8 September 2004, § 36, the ECSR noted that medical assistance to unaccompanied minors in France was limited to situations that involve an immediate threat to life, and that children of illegal immigrants were only admitted to the medical assistance scheme after a certain time; and thus such situation was not in conformity with Article 17.

Under this provision, States are obliged to take the necessary measures to provide the required protection and special aid to children temporarily or definitively deprived of their family's support. It follows that, as the ECSR found in *Defence for Children International* (*DCI*) *v. the Netherlands*,[121] when children are unlawfully present in the territory and when, according to the relevant national legislation, they may not claim entitlement to the benefits or facilities which would *inter alia* secure them shelter, they are deprived of their family's support.[122] Such a situation is not in conformity with Article 17 § 1 RESC. In that decision, the Committee also affirmed that "the obligations related to the provision of shelter under Article 17 § 1 (c) are identical in substance to those related to the provision of shelter under Article 31 § 2" RESC on the right to housing, and may thus be violated on that same ground.[123]

The obligation of States Parties to provide assistance also implies the protection of children and young persons from negligence, violence or exploitation. In *Defence for Children International* (*DCI*) *v. Belgium*, the Committee referred to the content of Article 17 concerning the aid to be provided by the State where the minor is unaccompanied or if the parents are unable to provide such aid. It recalled the importance of Article 17 § 1(b) RESC, "because failure to apply it would obviously expose a number of children and young persons to serious risks to their lives or physical integrity"[124] as well as to a threat "to respect for human dignity".[125] In this respect, a violation of Article 17 § 1 may occur when medical age assessments are based on the use of bone testing because this can have serious consequences for the unaccompanied foreign minors and "is inappropriate and unreliable", as acknowledged by the ECSR in the complaint *EUROCEF v. France*.[126] Regarding age assessment in the

---

121 ECSR, *Defence for Children International* (*DCI*) *v. The Netherlands*, *cit.*, §§ 70–71.

122 *Ibid.*

123 *Ibid.*, § 71. In this sense, see: ECSR, *European Federation of National Organisations working with the Homeless* (*FEANSA*) *v. the Netherlands*, complaint No. 86/2012, decision on the merits of 2 July 2014, § 50. See also *Digest of the Case Law of the European Committee of Social Rights*, *cit.*, p. 153 and the comment under Article 31 in this volume.

124 ECSR, *Defence for Children International* (*DCI*) *v. Belgium*, *cit.*, § 73.

125 *Ibid.*, § 82.

126 ECSR, *European Committee for Home Based Priority Action for the Child and the Family* (*EUROCEF*) *v. France*, *cit.*, §§ 106 and 113. In this regard, see: CoE, *We are children, hear us out! – Children speak out about age assessment*, Report on consultations with unaccompanied children on the topic of age assessment, 2019, available online at <https://edoc.coe.int/en/migration/7996-we-are-children-hear-us-out-children-speak-out-about-age-assessment.html>; CoE, *Age assessment for children in migration – A human rights-based approach*, A guide for policy makers, 2019, available online at <https://rm.coe.int/ageassessmentchildrenmigration/168099529f>.

context of migration, the Committee of Ministers has recently adopted a new Recommendation to member States establishing human rights principles and guidelines based on the principle of the "presumption of minority" for persons undergoing age assessment, and requiring states to implement multidisciplinary and evidence-based procedures.[127]

The ECSR also assesses the situation of foreign migrant children in poverty and their need of care and assistance. It conducts its evaluation on the basis of the UN Guiding Principles on extreme poverty and human rights.[128] According to these Guiding Principles, "[e]ven short periods of deprivation and exclusion can dramatically and irreversibly harm a child's right to survival and development. To eradicate poverty, States Parties must take immediate action"[129] and "promote the rights of children living in poverty, including by strengthening and allocating the necessary resources to child protection strategies and programmes, with a particular focus on marginalized children".[130] Thus, since "unaccompanied foreign minors must be placed as quickly as possible in an appropriate reception structure and their needs must be meticulously assessed in order to keep any changes to a minimum", compliance with Article 17 RESC requires that States ensure immediate assistance, in light of the fact that such prompt support allows meeting the material needs of young people and the demand for medical or psychological care in order to set up a child support plan.[131]

Yet, the Committee has not formally dealt with child poverty in the context of Article 17 RESC. Rather, it addressed the issue under Article 30 which deals

---

127 Rec. CM/Rec(2022)22 on human rights principles and guidelines on age assessment in the context of migration and its Explanatory Memorandum, adopted by the Committee of Ministers on 14 December 2022 at the 1452nd meeting of the Ministers' Deputies. This Recommendation refers also to the ECtHR case law, according to which failure to take into consideration the vulnerability of children in this context may amount to a violation of Articles 3, 8 and 13 ECHR. See: ECtHR, 21 July 2022, *Darboe and Camara v. Italy*, No. 5797/17, where it recalled the existing domestic and EU law on guarantees for unaccompanied minor asylum-seekers, as well as the Resolution of the Council of the European Union of 26 June 1997 and the Council of Europe's Parliamentary Assembly Resolution 1810 (2011) on the primary importance of the best interests of the child and of the principle of presumption of minority in respect of unaccompanied migrant children, who require special protection and should be assigned a guardian and be assisted during the asylum proceedings.

128 Magdalena Sepúlveda Carmona, *Guiding principles on extreme poverty and human rights*, adopted by the United Nations Human Rights Council on 27 September 2012, A/HRC/21/39. See also: ECSR, *Defence for Children International (DCI) v. Belgium*, *cit.*, § 81.

129 *UN Guiding principles*, *cit.*, § 32.

130 *Ibid.*, § 34.

131 ECSR, *Defence for Children International (DCI) v. Belgium*, *cit.*, § 81.

with the right to protection against poverty and social exclusion.[132] However, the obligations upon member States to ensure that children have the assistance they need may also include measures directed towards the amelioration and eradication of child poverty and social exclusion, since Article 17 RESC clearly refers to economic protection.[133] In its Conclusions of 2019, the ECSR submitted a general question on Article 17 regarding the right to assistance[134] and underlined that the obligation upon States Parties to take all measures to ensure care and assistance are provided to children and young persons "is strongly linked to measures directed towards the amelioration and eradication of child poverty and social exclusion". Therefore, child poverty levels will be taken into account when considering the State's obligations in terms of Article 17 RESC. Measures that States may adopt to reduce child poverty include non-monetary measures, such as ensuring access to quality and affordable services in the cases of health, education, housing etc. This may also include measures focused on combatting discrimination against, and promoting equal opportunities for, children, particularly from vulnerable groups such as ethnic minorities, Roma children, children with disabilities, and children in care; as well as the extent to which child participation is ensured in work directed towards combatting child poverty and social inclusion.[135]

6 Right to Education

Both paragraphs 1(a) and 2 of Article 17 RESC guarantee the right of children and young persons to education.[136] According to the Committee's interpretation,

---

132 In this regard, see Aoife Nolan, *Protecting the Child from Poverty: The Role of Rights in the Council of Europe*, 2019, p. 10, where the Author observes that "[w]hile the ECSR has made extensive reference to provisions that have implications for child poverty, it has made relatively little reference to child poverty specifically in its Article 30 conclusions work. This omission is striking and regrettable given the ongoing problem of child poverty in the CoE. It is also surprising given the heavy focus on children within the Charter itself – particularly in Article 17", available online at <https://rm.coe.int/protecting-the-child-from-poverty-the-role-of-rights-in-the-council-of/168098c54c>.

133 Aoife Nolan, *cit.*, p. 46. See also: ECSR, Conclusions 2013, Statement of Interpretation on Article 30; and the comments under Articles 30 and 31 in this volume.

134 ECSR, Conclusions 2019, General introduction, General Question on Article 17§1, March 2020.

135 *Ibid.*

136 It must be noted that the ESC of 1961 does not contain a provision on the right to education. The right to education is also protected indirectly pursuant to Article 7 RESC, imposing restrictions on children's employment rights with a view to enabling them to obtain the full benefts of compulsory education (see *Handbook on European law relating to the rights of the child, cit.*, p. 172 ff., spec. p. 180). On this right, see: *Digest of the Case Law of the European Committee of Social Rights, cit.*, p. 155 ff.; CoE, Information Document

this provision as a whole places positive obligations upon States to establish and maintain an education system that is both accessible and effective. For a system of education to be accessible and effective, "there must be *inter alia* a functioning system of primary and secondary education; which includes an adequate number of schools fairly distributed over the geographical area (in particular between rural and urban areas); the number of children enrolled in school should reach 100% of those of the relevant age; class sizes and the teacher pupil ratio must be reasonable; there must be a mechanism to control the quality of teaching and the methods used; education must be compulsory until the minimum age for admission to employment".[137]

In assessing whether the system is effective, the Committee will examine if, considering that equal access to education should be guaranteed for all children, "particular attention is paid to vulnerable groups such as children from minorities, children seeking asylum, refugee children, children in hospital, children in care, pregnant teenagers, teenage mothers, children deprived of their liberty etc. and whether necessary special measures have been taken to ensure equal access to education for these children".[138]

In general, the ECSR observed that all education provided by States must fulfil the criteria of availability, accessibility, acceptability and adaptability.[139] It also specified that the criteria of accessibility and adaptability relate to educational institutions and curricula that have to be accessible to everyone, without discrimination, and that teaching must be designed to respond to children with special needs.[140]

In the Committee's decisions in the complaints *Mental Disability Advocacy Centre (MDAC) v. Bulgaria*[141] and *International Association Autism-Europe*

---

prepared by the Secretariat of the ESC, *The right to education under the European Social Charter*, 2006, available online at <https://www.right-to-education.org/sites/right-to-education.org/files/resource-attachments/ESC_The_Right_to_Education_under_the_European_Social_Charter_2006_en.pdf>.

137 ECSR, Conclusions 2003, Statement of Interpretation on Article 17.

138 ECSR, *Mental Disability Advocacy Centre (MDAC) v. Bulgaria*, complaint No. 41/2007, decision on the merits of 3 June 2008, § 34; ECSR, Conclusions 2003, Bulgaria, Article 17 § 2; Conclusions 2005, Bulgaria, Article 17 § 2.

139 ECSR, *Mental Disability Advocacy Centre (MDAC) v. Bulgaria, cit.*, § 37, where the Committee referred to the General Comment No. 13 of the Committee on Economic, Social and Cultural Rights of the United Nations International Covenant on Economic, Social and Cultural Rights on the right to education (document E/C.12/1999/10 of 8 December 1999, §6).

140 ECSR, *Mental Disability Advocacy Centre (MDAC) v. Bulgaria, cit.*, § 37.

141 *Ibid.*

v. France,[142] it stated that, while a distinction between children with and without disabilities in the application of Article 17 § 2 RESC is acceptable, "the integration of children with disabilities into mainstream schools in which arrangements are made to cater [to]their special needs should be the norm and teaching in specialised schools must be the exception".[143] Any special education should provide the children concerned with sufficient instruction and training and complete their schooling in equivalent proportions to those of children in mainstream schools.[144] However, the Committee pointed out that the right to education of children with disabilities is also guaranteed by Articles 15 § 1 and 10 of the RESC, and that Article 15 applies as *lex specialis*.[145]

In the Conclusions of 2011 regarding Slovakia, the ECSR observed that special measures for Roma children should not involve the establishment of separate schools or classes only for this group, which may otherwise lead to segregation. The fact that Roma children are disproportionately represented in special classes was not in conformity with Article 17 § 2 RESC.[146] In *European Roma and Travellers Forum (ERTF) v. France*,[147] the Committee observed that "educational policies for Roma children may be accompanied by flexible structures to meet the diversity of the group and may take into account the fact that some groups lead an itinerant or semi-itinerant lifestyle".[148]

142 ECSR, *International Association Autism-Europe v. France*, complaint No. 13/2002, decision on the merits of 4 November 2003.

143 ECSR, *Mental Disability Advocacy Centre (MDAC) v. Bulgaria, cit.*, § 35; *International Association Autism-Europe v. France, cit.*, § 49.

144 ECSR, *Mental Disability Advocacy Centre (MDAC) v. Bulgaria, cit.*, § 36. Also within the ECHR context, the need to educate disabled children, whenever possible, with other children of their own age has been stressed (ECtHR, 4 July 1995, *Klerks v. the Netherlands*, No. 25212/94; ECtHR, 21 October 1998, *McIntyre v. United Kingdom*, No. 29046/95).

145 ECSR, *European Action of the Disabled (AEH) v. France*, complaint No. 81/2012, decision on the merits of 11 September 2013, §§ 24–30; ECSR, Conclusions 2003, Bulgaria; CoE, *Digest of the Case Law of the European Committee of Social Rights, cit.*, p. 156. For a comment, see: Shivaun Quinlivan, "Emerging Jurisprudence on Inclusive Education under the European Social Charter (Revised)", in Gauthier De Beco, Shivaun Quinlivan and Janet E. Lord (eds.), *The Right to Inclusive Education in International Human Rights Law*, Cambridge University Press, 2019, pp. 447–472.

146 ECSR, Conclusions 2011, Slovakia, Article 17 § 2.

147 ECSR, *European Roma and Travellers Forum (ERTF) v. France*, complaint No. 119/2015, decision on the merits of 5 December 2017.

148 *Ibid.*, § 69. In this regard, the ECSR findings are in line with the right to education granted by Article 2 of Protocol No. 1 to the ECHR, that states: "No person shall be denied the right to education. In the exercise of any functions which it assumes in relation to education and to teaching, the State shall respect the right of parents to ensure such education and teaching in conformity with their own religious and philosophical convictions". According to the ECtHR, the disproportionately prejudicial effect on Roma children by

As stems from the Statement of Interpretation on Article 17 § 2,[149] access to education is crucial for the life and development of every child and its denial would thus exacerbate the vulnerability of a child irregularly present in the territory of one State Party. It implies that children, whatever their residence status, who fall within the personal scope of the Charter – in the light of the Committee's case law[150] – and thus of Article 17 § 2, must be granted as effective access to education as any other child, even for those over the age of compulsory education.[151]

Under paragraph 2, the Parties undertake to adopt all appropriate and necessary measures designed to provide children and young persons with a free primary and secondary education as well as to encourage their regular attendance at school. As observed above, the right of all children to education is also guaranteed by Article 17 § 1 RESC where, however, there is no question of free education.[152] Primary and secondary education, which covers the basic education system, must be free of charge.[153] In addition, hidden costs such as books or uniforms must be reasonable and assistance must be available to limit their impact on the most disadvantaged groups in order not to impinge

---

national law is in breach of such Article 2 taken in conjunction with Article 14 ECHR on the prohibition of discrimination (ECtHR,13 November 2007, *D.H. and Others v. the Czech Republic*, No. 57325/00; ECtHR, 16 March 2010, *Oršuš and Others v. Croatia*, No. 15766/03; ECtHR, 13 December 2022, *Elmazova and Others v. North Macedonia*, Nos. 11811/20 and 13550/20). As to the specification regarding the respect for parents' convictions, the ECtHR stated that "the setting and planning of the curriculum fall in principle within the competence" of the State (ECtHR, 29 June 2007, *Folgerø and Others v. Norway*, No. 15472/02). In any case, for the purpose of safeguarding pluralism and differences in teaching, a particular religion or philosophy must be balanced by offering parents the possibility of either partially or fully exempting their children from such teaching – such as the possibility not to attend certain classes or the religious course as a whole (*ibid.*).

149 ECSR, Statement of Interpretation on Article 17 § 2, 2011.

150 See *supra*.

151 ECSR, Conclusions 2015, Slovenia; ECSR, Conclusions 2015, ECSR, Netherlands; *Médecins du Monde – International v. France*, complaint No. 67/2011, decision on the merits of 11 September 2012, § 128.

152 Katarzyna Dunaj and Joanna Ryszka, *cit.*, p. 331.

153 This provision differs from Article 2 of Protocol No. 1 to the ECHR on the right to education. According to the ECtHR, this Article does not oblige States to make education available; it provides "a right of access to educational institutions existing at a given time" (ECtHR, 23 July 1968, *"Relating to certain aspects of the laws on the use of languages in education in Belgium" v. Belgium*, Nos. 1474/62, 1677/62, 1691/62, 1769/63, 1994/63 and 2126/64, section "The law", part B, § 4). This is not however an absolute right; limitations must be foreseeable for those concerned, must pursue a legitimate aim and may not result in a denial of the right to education (ECtHR, 6 September 2016, *C.P. v. United Kingdom*, No. 300/11).

upon the goal being pursued.[154] As stated in the Appendix, this paragraph does not imply an obligation to provide compulsory education up to the age of majority.[155] The Explanatory Report specifies that the reason for this approach is that in some States only primary education is compulsory, whereas in others secondary education is also compulsory.[156]

The Explanatory Report then clarified that this paragraph does not imply that children and young persons have a right to exercise this right in a private school.[157] However, in its Conclusions of 2019, the ECSR adopted a "Statement of Interpretation on Article 17 § 2 – Private sector involvement in education",[158] where it reiterated that the Charter provides that the obligations under this provision may be met directly or through the involvement of private actors, and observed that, in fact, in many States private education is also available.[159]

Although States respect the freedom of parents to choose an educational institution other than a public institution, the State must provide free quality public education.[160] The Committee then added that even the offer of educational alternatives by private actors must not be detrimental to the allocation of resources towards, or otherwise undermine the accessibility and quality of, public education. Moreover, States are required to strictly regulate and supervise private sector involvement in education, making sure that the right to education is not undermined. Thus, appropriate measures should ensure that State allocation of resources to private education does not negatively impact upon the right of all children to access free, quality public education.[161]

According to a number of CoE documents on the increasing importance of the digital environment, States are invited to ensure that children have access to the digital environment and which must be inclusive and take into account

154 ECSR, Conclusions 2003, Bulgaria; ECSR, *European Committee for Home-Based Priority Action for the Child and the Family (EUROCEF) v. France, cit.*, § 31.

155 Appendix, *cit.*, on Article 17.

156 Explanatory Report, *cit.*, § 74.

157 *Ibid.*, § 73.

158 ECSR, Conclusions 2019, General introduction, Statement of Interpretation on Article 17 § 2 – Private sector involvement in education.

159 In this regard, the ECSR also considered the "Abidjan Guiding Principles on the human rights obligations of States to provide public education and to regulate private involvement in education".

160 See ECSR, Conclusions 2019, General introduction, Statement of Interpretation on Article 17 § 2 – Private sector involvement in education.

161 *Ibid.*

children's developing capacities and the particular circumstances of children in vulnerable situations.[162]

As concerns school attendance, measures must be taken to encourage children's attendance at school as well as to actively reduce the number of children dropping out or not completing compulsory education as well as the rate of absenteeism.[163] States Parties have a margin of discretion in developing and implementing concrete measures to combat absenteeism, depending upon the causes and their national situations.[164]

In the assessment of national actions regarding educational systems, as set out in the Conclusions of 2019, States are also expected to adopt actions to introduce anti-bullying policies in schools, i.e. measures relating to awareness raising, prevention and intervention,[165] as well as measures to facilitate child participation across a broad range of decision-making and activities related to education (including within the context of children's specific learning environments).[166]

Concluding Remarks

Article 17 RESC represents a fundamental provision aimed at promoting respect for the rights of children, that contributes to the concrete and effective pursuit of the general principle of the protection of the best interests of the child being embraced at international and European level under different perspectives. This Charter provision requires States Parties to provide practical actions and measures fit-for-purpose. It can also be regarded as a minimum standard with which national legislation and practice must comply. Children's rights are increasingly demanding attention in relation to the various situations analysed above, and indeed in relation to contemporary child protection issues, such as trafficking, migration, poverty, exploitation in work, gender

162 Rec. CM/Rec(2018)7 on guidelines to respect, protect and fulfl the rights of the child in the digital environment, 4 July 2018; Rec. CM/Rec(2019)10 on developing and promoting digital citizenship education, 21 November 2019; Rec. CM/Rec(2016)2 on the Internet of citizens, 10 February 2016. See also: *Handbook for policy makers on the rights of the child in the digital environment*, 2020, available online at <https://rm.coe.int/publication-it-handbook-for-policy-makers-final-eng/1680a069f8>.

163 ECSR, Conclusions 2011, Republic of Moldova; Conclusions 2003, Bulgaria.

164 CoE, *Digest of the Case Law of the European Committee of Social Rights*, *cit.*, p. 156.

165 ECSR, Conclusions 2019, General question on Article 17 § 2, on "Measures to combat bullying in the context of education".

166 *Ibid.*, on "Voice of the child in education".

identity challenges, and child pornography, as well as the legacy of the COVID-19 pandemic and the conflict in Ukraine.

As underlined by the Committee in its Statement on COVID-19 and social rights,[167] the necessity to ensure guarantees for the protection of social rights is overwhelming, especially towards most socially vulnerable groups. The COVID-19 pandemic led to the closures of schools and other educational institutions which "exacerbated pre-existing inequalities in education", and that the necessary recourse to remote learning during lockdown periods has highlighted the issue of digital exclusion. It also recognised that, under Article 17 § 2, equal access to education should have been ensured for all children during the COVID-19 crisis. Other observations concerned child poverty and social exclusion, also exacerbated by the public health crisis, as well as the increased physical, psychological and sexual violence against children during the lockdown.

In its Statement on the crisis caused by the Russian Federation's military aggression against Ukraine,[168] adopted on 24 March 2022, the ECSR stressed, in general, that the conflict should not prejudice the protection of the rights recognised by the Charter, both within Ukraine and beyond its borders, and that the States Parties to the Charter have obligations to effectively guarantee them at all times. This is particularly relevant in the context of the millions of children seeking international protection across Europe.

States Parties are invited to report on the rights of children, families and migrants by 31 December 2022.[169] Among the requested information, which essentially refer to the Conclusions of 2019, States are also to report on measures taken to protect and assist children in crisis situations and emergencies, including arrangements regarding their education.

167 ECSR, Statement on COVID-19 and social rights, adopted on 24 March 2021.

168 ESCR, Statement on the crisis caused by the Russian Federation's military aggression against Ukraine, adopted on 24 March 2022.

169 The ESCR transmitted on 8 July 2022 the Questions on Group 4 provisions (Conclusions 2023), Children families and migrants. States' reports will be examined in 2023. Consequently, trade unions, employers' organisations, non-governmental organisations, national human rights institutions and national equality bodies are invited to submit their comments on national reports by 30 June 2023.

ARTICLE 18

The Right to Engage in Gainful Occupation in the Territory of Other Parties

Elisabeth David and Sébastien Van Drooghenbroeck

With a view to ensuring the effective exercise of the right to engage in a gainful occupation in the territory of any other Party, the Parties undertake:

1. to apply existing regulations in a spirit of liberality;
2. to simplify existing formalities and to reduce or abolish chancery dues and other charges payable by foreign workers or their employers;
3. to liberalise, individually or collectively, regulations governing the employment of foreign workers; and recognise
4. the right of their nationals to leave the country to engage in a gainful occupation in the territories of the other Parties.

Introduction

Article 18 of the Revised European Social Charter provides for the right to engage in gainful occupation in the territory of other parties. It contains a set of rights regarding certain aspects of emigration and immigration of migrant workers. This provision of the Charter is, compared to the others, relatively *discreet* and *modest* in its ambitions. This *discretion* is demonstrated by the modest amount of commentary devoted to it in the legal literature[1] and by the

1 See for instance: Karin Lukas, *The Revised European Social Charter: An Article by Article Commentary*, Elgar Commentaries series, 2021, pp. 235–240; Elaine Dewhurst, "Article 18 RSCE. The right to engage in gainful occupation in the territory of other Parties", in Edoardo Ales *et al.* (eds.), *International and European Labour Law: A commentary*, Nomos Verlagsgesellschaft mbH and Co. KG, 2017, pp. 310–313; Colm O'Cinneide, "Migrant Rights under the European Social Charter", in Cathryn Costello and Mark Freedland (eds.), *Migrants at Work: Immigration and Vulnerability in Labour Law*, Oxford, 2014, pp. 282–302; David Harris and John Darcy, *The European Social Charter. 2nd edition. (Procedural Aspects of International Law Monograph Series; vol. 25)*, New York, Transnational Publishers, 2001, pp. 200–210; Yannis Ktistakis, *Protecting Migrants under the European Convention on Human Rights and the European Social Charter: A Handbook for Legal Practitioners*, 2nd edition, Strasbourg,

DOI:10.1163/9789004434141_009

European Committee of Social Rights (ECSR):[2] the latest version of the *Digest*,[3] published in December 2022, devotes only a handful of pages to Article 18, which do not fundamentally differ from the equally small number of pages that could already have been read in the 2018 version of the *Digest*. Discretion is also evident when reviewing the *travaux préparatoires* for this provision: neither its initial adoption nor its inclusion in the Revised Charter gave rise to extensive discussions (I). *Modesty* is explicable, firstly, when one considers the normative environment in which Article 18 of the Charter operates – its added value is not obvious, particularly with regard to the acquis of Union law (II) – and, secondly, its limited scope of application, which has to do with its non-inclusion in the 'hard core' of the Charter (III). In terms of substance, the rights guaranteed by Article 18 are characterized by their 'dynamism', which is quite significant considering the socio-economic context in which they were formulated. This characteristic certainly makes the rights contained in Article 18 valuable, but it also explains the limited nature of their performance (IV).

1 Drafting History[4]

The actual text of Article 18 of the Revised Charter has not been amended[5] since it was first introduced in the Charter of 1961. In 1959, when this Article was drafted, attention was drawn to the initial wording of the provision and the fact that it might give the impression that the regulation and formalities mentioned in the different paragraphs "relate only to the right to leave the country to engage in gainful activity abroad".[6] In order to avoid this misinterpretation, the wording was changed.

Council of Europe Publishing, 2016; Matti Mikkola, "Social Human Rights of Migrants under the European Social Charter", *European Journal of Social Security*, vol. 10, no. 1, 2008, pp. 25–59 and sp. 39–40; L. Samuel, *Droit sociaux fondamentaux. Jurisprudence de la Charte sociale européenne,* Strasbourg, 2nd ed., ed. du Conseil de l'Europe, 2002, pp. 399–420. See also the references mentioned punctually in other footnotes.

2 There is only one "contentious" case concerning Article 18: ECSR, *European Federation of Public Service Employees (EUROFEDOP) v. Greece,* complaint No. 115/2015, decision on the merits of 13 September 2017.

3 *Digest of the case law of the European Committee of Social Rights,* December 2022, available at https://www.coe.int/en/web/european-social-charter/case-law# (last accessed 17 february 2023).

4 See also Karin Lukas, *cit.*, p. 236.

5 See Explanatory Report to the European Social Charter (Revised), p. 8.

6 Seventh session – European Social Charter – Points to be remembered in connection with the final checking of text (6 January 1958), Doc. CE/Soc (58) 1, point 9.

Moreover, different points were raised by various delegations regarding the scope of application of this provision. One the one hand, the Delegation of Belgium did not agree with the initial draft, which only referred to the employment of foreign workers, and indicated that this Article should apply not only to employees but also to self-employed workers.[7] On the other hand, the Delegation of the Netherlands considered that it should be stipulated that this Article only applies to nationals of the contracting parties, as in Part I, paragraph 18.[8] It was pointed out, however, that this was clarified by the Article heading which mentioned "member countries".[9]

II Article 18 in Its International and European Normative Environment

Article 18 of the Charter is part of a larger international and regional body of law dedicated to labour[10] and migration law.[11] However, this instrument is not the one offering most protection to migrant workers. On the international scene, we should first note the similarities with Conventions 97 and 143 concluded within the International Labour Organisation.[12] The first one[13] – the *Migration for Employment Convention* (Revised), dated 1949 – is limited in its scope to regular labour migration.[14] It provides in particular for the obligation of State parties to take measures "to facilitate the departure, journey and reception of migrants for employment" (art. 4), as well as the obligation to grant immigrants lawfully within its territory, "treatment no less favourable than that which it applies to its own nationals" in respect of several matters (e.g., remuneration and social security – art. 6). As Cholewinski notes, "Article 6 is a progressive provision that subsequently influenced similar provisions elsewhere,

---

7 ESC, Collected travaux préparatoires, Vol. 5, 1958, p. 110.

8 *Ibid.*

9 *Ibid.* The formulation of the heading finally adopted mentions "other Contracting Parties" (original Charter) "other Parties" (Revised Charter).

10 Edoardo Ales *et al.* (eds.), *International and European Labour Law: A commentary*, Nomos Verlagsgesellschaft mbH and Co. KG, 2017.

11 See Ryszard Cholewinski, *Migrant Workers in International Human Rights Law: Their Protection in Countries of Employment*, Oxford, Clarendon Press, 1997.

12 For a more extensive discussion of these conventions, see Edoardo Ales *et al.* (eds.), *cit.*, pp. 848 ff.; Ibrahim Awad, "Les travailleurs migrants", in Jean-Marc Thouvenin et Anne Trebilcock (eds.), *Droit international social. Droits économiques, sociaux et culturels*, tome 2, *Règles de droit international social*, Bruxelles, Brulant, 2013, pp. 1319 ff.

13 To this date, the convention has been ratified by 53 states.

14 Edoardo Ales *et al.* (eds.), *cit.*, p. 849.

including the Equality of Treatment provisions of European (EU) free movement provisions".[15] Convention 143 – *Migrant Workers (Supplementary Provisions) Convention* (1975) – is broader in scope,[16] as it also addresses the issue of irregular migration, and the fight against its exploitation, while guaranteeing migrant workers – regardless of their status – a number of fundamental rights borrowed from other international human rights instruments. This is the purpose of Part I of the Convention. Part II sets out specific rights for migrant workers in a regular situation,[17] which also overlap with the provisions of Article 18 of the Charter, while going beyond them on certain points. In particular, we ought to mention equality and non-discrimination (Article 10) and the positive obligations associated with this principle (Article 12), as well as the adoption of "all necessary measures" (including collaboration with other Members) "to facilitate the reunification of the families of all migrant workers legally residing in its territory" (Article 13). Article 14 is dedicated to "free choice of employment" and the restrictions to which it may be subject.

Still at the international level, but this time within the UN sphere, the Charter's environment also consists of the *International Convention on the Protection of the Rights of All Migrant Workers and Members of Their Families* ICRMW (1990),[18] which has been ratified by 58 states. However, among those states, only 4[19] are also parties to the – original or revised – European Social Charter,[20] which renders the practical intersections between the two instruments very limited.[21] The purpose of this particularly long and detailed convention[22] is to enshrine a series of 'classic' rights and freedoms to the benefit of all migrant workers and members of their families, whether legally resident

15 *Ibid.*, p. 852.

16 *Ibid.*, p. 850.

17 See definition of this notion in Article 11 of the Convention.

18 Paul De Guchteneire and Antoine Pécoud, "Introduction: The UN Convention on Migrant Workers' Rights", in Ryszard Cholewinski, Paul De Guchteneire and Antoine Pecoud (eds.), *Migration and Human Rights: The United Nations Convention on Migrant Workers' Rights*, Cambridge, Cambridge University Press, 2010.

19 Albania, Azerbaijan, Bosnia and Herzegovina and Turkey.

20 Armenia, which has ratified the Charter, has however only signed the Convention. The same applies to Serbia.

21 Significantly, no EU Member State has ratified the ICRMW. For an overview of this situation, its explanation and critical analysis, see Marie D'auchamp, *Rights of migrant workers in Europe*, published by the Regional Office for Europe of the UN High Commissioner for Human Rights, 2011, available at https://europe.ohchr.org/Documents/Publications/Migrant_Workers.pdf.

22 Ibrahim Awad, *cit.*, pp. 1329 ff.

or not.[23] In contrast to the above-mentioned Convention No. 143, these are listed *in extenso* and, where appropriate, compared to their classic formulation in 'universal' human rights protection instruments, 'concretized' to be better adapted to the situation of these workers.[24] A series of additional rights are provided for, but this time only for the benefit of migrant workers and members of their families who are documented or in a regular situation: a.o. freedom to choose their residence (Article 39), equality of treatment with nationals of the State of employment in relation to access to educational institutions, access to vocational guidance and placement services; access to housing, ... (Article 43).

Council of Europe law also includes, alongside the European Social Charter, a number of instruments specifically dedicated to the protection of migrant workers' rights.[25] The *European Convention on Establishment* (1955), ratified by 12 Council of Europe member states, operates, like the European Social Charter, on a model of reciprocity *ratione personae*: only nationals of other State parties benefit from the rights it enshrines. Among these, we would point specifically to those in Chapter IV, dedicated to the right "to engage in its territory in any gainful occupation on an equal footing with its own nationals", and to its possible limitations.

Last but not least, European Union law plays an important role in the normative environment of Article 18 of the Charter. The free movement of workers is a foundational principle of the European Union, enshrined in Article 15(3) of the EUCFR and Article 45 of the TFEU. More specifically, those provisions entail the rights of movement and residence for workers, the rights of entry and residence for family members, the right to work in another Member State and to be treated equally with nationals of that Member State.

Over the years, the European institutions have substantiated this freedom by adopting several legislative acts. Regulation 1612/68,[26] the founding

23 See, for the particular situation of the latter, Committee on the Protection of the Rights of All Migrant Workers and Members of Their Families, *General Comment no. 2 on the rights of migrant workers*, 2013, CMW/C/GC/2.

24 Marie D'auchamp, *cit.*, p. 11: "The ICRMW does not create 'new rights' for migrant workers and their families. It features rights that have been recognized to all under other core human rights treaties, in particular the InternationalCovenants on Civil and Political Rights and on Economic, Social and Cultural Rights. The ICRMW does however address specific protection needs of migrant workers and members of their families through the formulation of previously recognized rights, and through additional guarantees that are necessary due to the particular vulnerability of migrant workers".

25 See also *European Convention on the Legal Status of Migrant Workers* (ETS No. 093) (1977), ratified by 11 states.

26 Regulation 1612/68/EEC of the Council of 15 October 1968 on freedom of movement for workers within the Community.

regulation on freedom of movement of workers and Directive 68/360,[27] its complementing directive on the abolition of restrictions on movement and residence, have been modernized several times. Currently, the relevant legislative acts are Directive 2004/38[28] on the right of movement and residence and Regulation 492/2011[29] on free movement of workers.

At the time, Regulation 1612/68 already stood out in contrast to the ambiguous wording of Article 18 of the Charter.[30] The first article of the Regulation already clearly provided that "any national of a Member State, shall, irrespective of his place of residence, have the right to take up an activity as an employed person, and to pursue such activity, within the territory of another Member State". Moreover, Article 3 and 4 imposed the abolition of any national rule or measures aiming at protecting the nationals of that State with respect to access to employment.[31] Article 5 guaranteed equal treatment between workers of EU member states in respect of assistance in seeking employment and Article 10 already extended the right of equal access to employment with nationals throughout the territory of the host country to the worker's spouse and descendants under 21 years of age or to his dependent relatives in the ascending line.

These rights can be found today in Regulation 492/2011 on the free movement of workers. Similarly to Regulation 1612/68, the regulation currently in force sets rules for employment, equal treatment and workers' families. In accordance with the first article of the Regulation, any national of a Member State has the right to take up an activity as an employed person within the territory of another Member State. Those workers should not be treated differently from national workers in respect of any condition of employment and work.[32] Furthermore, migrant workers covered by the Regulation are entitled

27 Directive 68/360/EEC of the Council of 15 October 1968 on the abolition of restrictions on movement and residence within the Community for workers of Member States and their families.

28 Directive 2004/38/EC of the European Parliament and of the Council of 29 April 2004 on the right of citizens of the Union and their family members to move and reside freely within the territory of the Member States amending Regulation (EEC) No 1612/68 and repealing Directives 64/221/EEC, 68/360/EEC, 72/194/EEC, 73/148/EEC, 75/34/EEC, 75/35/EEC, 90/364/EEC, 90/365/EEC and 93/96/EEC.

29 Regulation 492/2011/EU of the European Parliament and of the Council of 5 April 2011 on freedom of movement for workers within the Union.

30 Ryszard Cholewinski, *cit.*, p. 299.

31 *Ibid.*

32 Article 7 of Regulation 492/2011/EU of the European Parliament and of the Council.

to receive the same social and tax advantages as national workers,[33] and the same rights and benefits accorded to national workers in matters of housing.[34]

This Regulation,[35] combined with other legislative acts and initiatives[36] in the area of free movement of workers, provide migrant workers[37] with a comprehensive set of enforceable rights. In light of this, the added value of Article 18 of the Charter, particularly for those State parties to the Charter which are also EU Member States, has been very limited.[38]

By contrast, non-EU citizens' right to move freely within the Union in order to work is very limited. It should be noted that specific categories of third country nationals do, by exception, benefit from the right to work in an EU country and enjoy the same working conditions as EU citizens either when they are considered as an EU citizen's family member or because they are nationals of a particular state.[39]

Several legislative acts have been adopted which aim at regulating the status of third country nationals who wish to work in the EU but do not fall into these categories. For example, Directive 2003/109[40] concerns third

33 *Ibid.*

34 Article 9 of Regulation 492/2011/EU of the European Parliament and of the Council.

35 Although it does not provide for additional rights, Directive 2014/54 (Directive 2014/54/EU of the European Parliament and of the Council of 16 April 2014 on measures facilitating the exercise of rights conferred on workers in the context of freedom of movement for workers) was adopted in order to facilitate free movement of EU workers and their family members and enhance the effectiveness of the rights contained in the above-mentioned directives. This is namely illustrated by Article 4 of the Directive which stipulates that "each Member State shall designate one or more structures or bodies (…) for the promotion, analysis, monitoring and support of equal treatment of Union workers and members of their family without discrimination on grounds of nationality (…) and shall make the necessary arrangements for the proper functioning of such bodies".

36 See *infra*.

37 Who are nationals of an EU Member state and exercise their right to free movement.

38 David Harris and John Darcy, *cit.*, p. 201 ff.

39 For nationals of Island, Norway and Lichtenstein, the EEA Agreement guarantees equal rights and obligations within the Internal Market for individuals and economic operators in the EEA. Another example is the EU-Swiss agreement on free movement of persons according to which Swiss nationals can live and work freely in the EU. Lastly, according to the EU-Turkey agreement, Turkish workers who are legally employed in an EU country and who are duly registered have, after some fixed time periods, the right to the renewal of their work permit for the same employer, the right to change employers and respond to any other offer of employment for the same occupation and the right to enjoy free access to any paid employment in that EU country. Moreover, Turkish nationals working legally in an EU country are entitled to the same working conditions as the nationals of that country.

40 Directive 2003/109/EC of the Council of 25 November 2003 concerning the status of third-country nationals who are long-term residents.

country long-term residents, who may apply for a residence permit in a second Member State only after they have acquired long-term residence status in the first Member State.[41] Directive 2009/50[42] sets out the entry and residence conditions for highly qualified non-EU nationals and their families wishing to work in a highly qualified job in an EU Member state and Directive 2016/801[43] aims at facilitating the free movement of researchers and students.

The international and European normative environment of Article 18 of the Charter is, as one can notice, particularly dense. The interaction between all these provisions is complex, given the 'variable geometry' of states that are subject to them – the circles do not overlap–, the variable geometry of their commitments – partial commitments (see *infra*) and *réserves* are numerous – and the fact that some, but not all,[44] of these instruments operate on the basis of reciprocity with regard to their scope *ratione personae* (see *infra*). In spite of this complexity, it appears that, overall, Article 18 of the Charter is not the most generous instrument in this *corpus juris*. In the relations between Member states of the European Union and workers who are nationals of those states or of an EEA state, the added-value of the Charter in relation to European Union law appears to be very limited,[45] although – as emphasized by O'Cinneide[46] – not totally non-existent. The subsidiarity clause contained in Article H of Part III of the Revised Charter is therefore particularly relevant in this context: "The provisions of this Charter shall not prejudice the provisions of domestic law or of any bilateral or multilateral treaties, conventions or agreements which are already in force, or may come into force, under which more favourable treatment would be accorded to the persons protected." The Appendix to the Revised Charter expressly confirms that Article 18 does "not prejudice the provisions of the European Convention on Establishment, signed in Paris on 13 December 1955".

---

41 According to Article 4 of the Directive, "Member States shall grant long-term resident status to third-country nationals who have resided legally and continuously within its territory for five years".

42 Directive 2009/50/EC of the Council of 25 May 2009 on the conditions of entry and residence of third-country nationals for the purposes of highly qualified employment.

43 Directive 2016/801/EU of the European Parliament and of the Council of 11 May 2016 on the conditions of entry and residence of third-country nationals for the purposes of research, studies, training, voluntary service, pupil exchange schemes or educational projects and au pairing (recast).

44 Reciprocity does not apply, for example, to ILO Conventions no. 97 and no. 143 (see, Ibrahim Awad, *cit.*, p. 1337).

45 See Andrzej Marian Swiatkowski, *Labour Law: Council of Europe,* 2nd edition, Kluwer, 2016, p. 49; David Harris and John Darcy, *cit.*, p. 202.

46 Colm O'cinneide, *cit.*, p. 292.

III Scope of Application

A *Member States' Ratification*

The system of 'à la carte commitments' set up by the original 1961 Charter (Art. 20) and taken over by the Revised Charter (Part III, Article A, 1, b) did not include Article 18 in the list of rights around which the freedom of acceptance of States is restricted. Its status therefore differs from that of Article 19, which is indeed included in the said list. This difference in regime raises questions, as these provisions, although having distinct scopes, do overlap, notably around the principle of equal treatment *vis-à-vis* national workers. In any case, this situation has resulted in a rather modest acceptance rate for Article 18. Of the 35 states that have ratified the Revised Charter, only 16 have subscribed to the whole of Article 18. Five states, on the other hand, have not included any of the paragraphs of Article 18 in their commitments. The remainder of the states have made partial commitments.[47] Article 18(3), which is arguably the most 'intrusive' regarding states' migration policies, is frequently not included in these partial commitments. Conversely, paragraph 4 – which, as we shall see, largely duplicates the achievements of 'ordinary' human rights law – is favoured within these 'partial' commitments.

B *Personal Scope of Application*

Unlike the corresponding rights in the International Covenant on Economic, Social and Cultural Rights, which does not contain such a *ratione personae*[48] restriction, Article 18 of the Charter applies only to employees and the self-employed[49] who are *nationals* of Charter-party States.[50] Indeed, the Appendix to the Revised Charter provides that "the persons covered by Articles 1 to 17 and 20 to 31 include foreigners only in so far as they are nationals of other Parties lawfully resident or working regularly within the territory of the Party concerned, subject to the understanding that these articles are to be interpreted in the light of the provisions of Articles 18 and 19". Hence, it cannot be

---

47 This poses difficulties because of the 'overlap' of these paragraphs (see below).

48 The Covenant applies to everyone within the jurisdiction of the member state, and the migrant worker can therefore derive rights from it. See UN CESCR, *General Comment no. 18 on the right to work*, 2005, E/C.12/GC/18, pt. 18 ; UN CESCR, *General Comment no. 23 on the right to just and favourable conditions of work (article 7 of the International Covenant on Economic, Social and Cultural Rights)*, 2016, E/C.12/GC/23, pt. 47 ; UN CESCR, *Statement on Duties of States towards refugees and migrants under the International Covenant on Economic, Social and Cultural Rights*, 2017, E/C.12/2017/1, pt. 16.

49 David Harris and John Darcy, *cit.*, p. 203.

50 Digest of the case law of the European Committee of Social Rights, December 2022, p. 157.

deduced from an *a contrario* interpretation of this Article that non-nationals of State parties to the Charter would enjoy the rights set forth by Article 18.[51] Of course, it is known that the ECSR has given a very dynamic interpretation[52] of the Charter, and has, in substance, affirmed that the rights relating to the 'minimum core' essential to the preservation of human dignity[53] could benefit persons who are illegally resident in the State concerned. The ECSR has not yet had the opportunity to enumerate exhaustively the rights included in this category. However, in light of what has been said above (A), it is doubtful whether Article 18 could be included in this list.

In addition to the nationals of the State parties,[54] persons who have been recognized as refugees[55] in the State parties and stateless persons[56] must also be included as beneficiaries of rights guaranteed by Article 18. Asylum seekers who are not nationals of a State party are, in principle, not covered.[57]

It should also be noted, as mentioned by Swiatkowski,[58] that a person who is a national of a State that has ratified the Charter may invoke Article 18 with

---

51 Stefan Clauwaert, "Article 19, § 4. The right of migrants workers and their families to protection and assistance", in Niklas Bruun *et al.* (eds.), *The European Social Charter and the Employment Relation*, Oxford, Hart Publishing, 2017, p. 346.

52 See ECSR, *International Federation of Human Right League* (FIDH) *v. France*, collective complaint No. 14/2003, 8 September 2004.

53 Colm O'cinneide, *cit.*, p. 291.

54 See Matti Mikkola, "Migrants", in Matti Mikkola (ed.), *Social Human Rights of Europe*, Porvoo, Karelactio Legisactio, 2010, pp. 563–564 and pp. 568–569.

55 See Appendix to the Charter: "Each Party will grant to refugees as defined in the Convention relating to the Status of Refugees, signed in Geneva on 28 July 1951 and in the Protocol of 31 January 1967, and lawfully staying in its territory, treatment as favourable as possible, and in any case not less favourable than under the obligations accepted by the Party under the said convention andunder any other existing international instruments applicable to those refugees". See also ECSR, Conclusions 2015 (Andorra, Armenia, Austria, Azerbaijan, Belgium, Bosnia and Herzegovina, Bulgaria, Cyprus, Estonia, Finland, France, Georgia, Hungary, Latvia, Lithuania, Malta, Republic of Moldova, Montenegro, The Netherlands, Norway, Portugal, Romania, Russian Federation, Serbia, Slovak Republic, Slovenia, Sweden, "The Former Yugoslav Republic of Macedonia", Turkey, Ukraine), Articles 7, 8, 16, 17, 19, 27 and 31 of the Charter, p. 11.

56 See Appendix to the Charter: "Each Party will grant to stateless persons as defined in the Convention on the Status of Stateless Persons done in New York on 28 September 1954 and lawfully staying in its territory, treatment as favourable as possible and in any case not less favourable than under the obligations accepted by the Party under the said instrument and under any other existinginternational instruments applicable to those stateless persons".

57 See Lieneke Slingenberg, *The Reception of Asylum Seekers under International Law. Between Sovereignty and Equality*, Oxford, Hart Publishing, 2014, p. 224.

58 Andrzej Marian Swiatkowski, *cit.*, p. 330; David Harris and John Darcy, *cit.*, p. 203.

regard to the State that has subscribed to this provision, even if his or her State of nationality has not consented to it. It is necessary, but also sufficient, that the State of nationality has ratified the Charter, without further specification.

Lastly, Article 18 includes any of the migrant worker's family members[59] who are admitted to the country for the purposes of family reunification.[60] Furthermore, this Article applies *ratione loci*[61] to both workers who are already on the territory of the State in question as well as to workers who are outside the country and request a permit to work inside the territory of that State.[62] Finally, it is accepted that posted workers[63] also fall within the scope of Article 18.

IV Content

A *General Considerations*

As François Vandamme points out,[64]

> The economic and political context at the time of the negotiation of the Charter at the end of the 1950s, which to some extent favoured the international immigration of much-needed labour, has permeated (Articles 18 and 19 of the Charter); this can be felt in the encouragement of employment or gainful activity, the assistance to which these workers and their families are entitled, the principle of equal treatment with

59 The Appendix to the revised Charter specifies, regarding the notion of 'family of the foreign worker' that "(this term) is understood to mean at least the worker's spouse and unmarried children, as long as the latter are considered to be minors by the receiving State and are dependent on the migrant worker". In our opinion, the notion of 'spouse' should be interpreted in an evolutionary manner, as including also the same-sex partner (see, by analogy, ECJ, 5 June 2018, *Relu Adrian Coman and Others v Inspectoratul General pentru Imigrări and Ministerul Afacerilor Interne*, C-673/16).

60 Digest of the case law of the European Committee of Social Rights, December 2022, p. 157; ECSR, Conclusions X-2 (1990), Austria.

61 According to Swiatkowski, the terms 'a different member state' in Article 18 "is understood by the Committee to be the territory of that state as well as structures located beyond territorial waters being the property of that given member state such as for example oil rig platforms in the north sea" (Andrzej Marian Swiatkowski, *cit.*, p. 49).

62 ECSR, Conclusions XIII-1 (1993), Sweden.

63 ECSR, Conclusions 2015, Statement of interpretation on Article 19 § 4.

64 François Vandamme, "Les droits protégés par la Charte sociale. Contenu et portée", in Stéphane Leclerc et Jean-François Akandji-Kombé (eds.), *La Charte sociale européenne*, Bruxelles, Bruylant, 2001, pp. 31–32 (own translation).

national workers in a variety of fields (…) and the invitation to collaboration between the emigration and immigration services of the sending and receiving countries.

This original inspiration, which the authors of the Revised Charter have not called into question, can be seen in the 'dynamic' character of Article 18, which is often[65] emphasized:[66] it sets a series of objectives to be pursued by the States which subscribe to it, a horizon towards which it should be aimed, and a threshold to be reached which, once crossed, must be maintained.[67] The *Digest* stresses this particular dimension of the obligations generated by Article 18, despite its limited ambition, and the guidelines for interpretation that must therefore be observed in its implementation:

> Whilst the provisions of Article 18 do not cover regulations governing the entry of foreigners to the territory of the State Party, the Committee cannot accept an interpretation which would undermine its aim, which is "to ensure the effective exercise of the right to exercise a gainful activity in the territory of another State Party," by restricting the benefits of liberalisation to only those nationals of other States Parties already in the country.[68]

Earlier, the same Committee stressed that:

> The letter and spirit of Article 18 mean that the situation of nationals of States bound by the Charter should gradually become as far as possible like that of nationals.[69]

---

65 ECSR, Conclusions II (1968), Statement of interpretation on Article 18: "The very wording of these provisions gives them, as was stressed (see Conclusions I (1969), General Introduction, para. 13), a dynamic character, implying an evolution of the provisions and of their application, which should be shown in every biennial report".

66 Andrzej Marian Swiatkowski, *cit.*, p. 49.

67 Andrzej Marian Swiatkowski, *cit.*, p. 55 and references to the case law of the ECSR; ECSR, Conclusions II (1968), Statement of interpretation on Article 18: "For instance, as already recognised in the Committee's Conclusions I (United Kingdom, Article 18), where no specific regulation exists, there can obviously be no question of liberalising its application".

68 See also, among others, ECSR, Conclusions XIII-1 (1993), Sweden.

69 ECSR, Conclusions II (1968), Statement of interpretation on Article 18.

This originality of Article 18 – its dynamism,[70] its gradual nature – also constitutes its limit: its concretisation, in its logic of 'more or less' rather than 'all or nothing', is certainly not palpable, and leaves room for a wide margin of appreciation to the benefit of states.

A final, but important, clarification is needed. Like any human rights instrument, the Charter must be interpreted as a 'coherent whole'. This holistic interpretation implies obvious alliances and symbioses – notably with Article 19[71] – but also the avoidance of conflicts. From the latter point of view, it goes without saying that States could not use Article 18 to justify such deregulation that they would fail to meet their other obligations to protect foreign workers under the Charter – including domestic workers, who are particularly vulnerable to trafficking and economic exploitation.

B *Article 18 § 1: Applying Regulations in a Spirit of Liberality*

According to the first paragraph of Article 18, State parties undertake to apply the regulations to the citizens of other State parties to the Charter 'in a spirit of liberality'. The boundaries to be drawn between the obligations under Article 18 § 1 and those under Article 18 § 3 are not always easy to define. However, the issue at stake is not purely theoretical, since, as we have seen (*supra*), some States have undertaken to comply with § 1, but not with § 3.

However, it is generally accepted[72] that Article 18 § 1 concerns the application of standards and the administrative practices followed in this respect, whereas Article 18 § 3 concerns the enactment of standards and their actual content, which is not the same thing.[73] As stated by Swiatkowski, "even strict legislation interpreted in accordance with the guidelines of the article in question does not provide the Committee with a legal basis for issuing decisions on the failure of member states to comply with the standards set out in Article 18(1) of the Charter".[74]

---

70 This dynamic character would be associated with a non-regression obligation. According to Cholewinski, "It is arguable that Article 18 § 1 operates as an implicit standstill clause precluding contracting parties from making their rules more restrictive", Ryszard Cholewinski, *The Legal Status of Migrants admitted for Employment. Committee of experts on the legal status and rights of immigrants. A comparative study of law and practice in selected European states*, Strasbourg, Council of Europe Publishing, 2004, p. 11.

71 On this article, see next chapter.

72 ECSR, Conclusions 2012, Serbia: "Article 18 § 1 is concerned with administrative practice rather than legal aspects".

73 Andrzej Marian Swiatkowski, *cit.*, p. 52.

74 *Ibid.* However, this distinction between the content of the standard and its application is not always very clear in the ECSR's case law. In the Digest, the ECSR states that "regulations preventing nationals of another State Party from applying for work permit, due

The assessment of compliance with Article 18 § 1 will therefore be based primarily on the analysis of factual and statistical data. The acceptance and refusal rates for work permits are the main criteria for the ECSR's assessment of this 'spirit of liberality'.[75] To do so, the ECSR requires that data be organized by country of origin and that they be differentiated between initial and renewal applications.[76] In addition, the ECSR takes into account the formalities, fees and other costs associated with work permits. Although these elements are specifically mentioned in § 2 of Article 18, the ECSR also considers them as indicators of 'liberality' in the sense of § 1.[77]

Due to the wording of this article, State parties have a wide margin of appreciation and can restrict the access of foreign workers to their labour market by providing economic or social justifications. This could happen, for example, in order to re|solve the problem of national unemployment by promoting the employment of national workers. However, the implementation of such rules restricting the access of third-country nationals to the national labour market must not result in a total exclusion of non-EU (or EEA) Charter nationals from the national labour market, nor in a significant restriction of their ability to access the national labour market.[78]

---

to the combined effects of the various rules on entry, length of stay, residence and the exercise of a gainful activity would not be in keeping with this provision of the Charter". It seems that the criticism here relates directly to the content of the applied standards. See also David Harris and John Darcy, *cit.*, p. 205: "it should be noted that the Committee has not always been consistent in its allocation of issues to particular paragraphs of Article 18 and would sometimes appear to have treated an issue under the wrong paragraph".

75 ECSR, Conclusions 2012, Serbia: "a high percentage of successful applications by nationals of States Parties to the Charter for work permits and for renewal of work permits and a low percentage of refusals has been regarded by the Committee as a clear sign that existing regulations are being applied in a spirit of liberality".

76 ECSR, Conclusions XVII-2 (2005), Spain.

77 ECSR, Conclusions IX-1 (1990), United Kingdom.

78 ECSR, Conclusions 2012, Statement of interpretation of article 18 § 1 and 18 § 3. The ECSR uses this principle to criticize the 'priority rule' then in force in the European Union: "this (EU Council Resolution of 20 June 1994 on limitation on admission of third-country nationals to the territory of the Member States for employment) states *inter alia* that EU Member States will consider requests for admission to their territories for the purpose of employment only where vacancies cannot be filled by national and Community manpower, or by non-Community manpower lawfully resident on a permanent basis in that Member State and already forming part of the Member State's regular labour market. In this regard the Committee notes, however, that in order not to be in contradiction with Article 18 of the Charter, the implementation of such policies limiting access of third-country nationals to the national labour market, should neither lead to a complete exclusion of nationals of non-EU (or non-EEA) States parties to the Charter from the national labour market, nor substantially limit the possibility for them of acceding the national

C *Article 18 § 2: Simplify Existing Formalities and Reduce or Abolish Chancery Dues and Charges*

Once again, the boundaries between the obligations contained in Article 18 § 2 and those resulting from Article 18 § 3 are not easy to draw. As Swiatkowski[79] points out, the liberalisation of rules governing the employment of foreign workers, as referred to in Article 18 § 3, will often, if not necessarily, result in a simplification of existing formalities within the meaning of Article 18 § 2. There is therefore an overlap, which, as with Article 18 § 1, raises a difficulty with regard to States which have entered into partial commitments. The ECSR assumes and resolves this difficulty – at least on a theoretical level – by recalling, in the latest edition of the *Digest*, that "(f)ormalities and dues and other charges are one of the aspects of regulations governing the employment of workers also covered by Article 18 § 3 but are dealt with specifically under (Article 18, § 2)".[80]

According to the ECSR, "conformity with Article 18 § 2 presupposes the possibility of completing formalities related to the employment of foreign workers in the country of destination as well as in the country of origin and obtaining the residence and work permits at the same time and through a single application".[81] It also implies that "waiting times for requisite permits (residence and work) must be reasonable".[82] In its recent conclusions on Ukraine,[83] the ECSR thus concluded that the existence of a "dual procedure for obtaining work and residence permits" does not fit in with the simplification horizon set by Article 18 § 2. In another example,[84] Greece was "condemned" for violating Article 18 § 2, the ECSR having concluded that "the procedure for issuing work permits was very complex and that all the formalities it had previously criticised continued to apply".[85] In this case, Greece relied on its duty to safeguard

labour market. Such a situation, deriving from the implementation of 'priority rules' of the kind just mentioned, would not be in conformity with Article 18 § 1, of the Charter, since it would prove an insufficient degree of liberality in applying existing regulations with respect to the access to the national labour market of foreign workers of a number of States Parties to the Charter. It would also be contrary to Article 18 § 3, since the State in question would not comply with its obligation to progressively liberalise regulations governing the access to the national labour market with respect to foreign workers of a number of States Parties to the Charter".

79 Andrzej Marian Swiatkowski, *cit.*, p. 53; Lenia Samuel, *cit.*, p. 410.

80 Digest of the case law of the European Committee of Social Rights, December 2022, p. 158.

81 ECSR, Conclusions 2016, Armenia.

82 *Ibid.*

83 ECSR, Conclusions 2020, Ukraine.

84 For other examples of 'simplification', see Andrzej Marian Swiatkowski, *cit.*, p. 54.

85 ECSR, Conclusions XIII-2 (1994), Greece.

the rights of foreigners legally residing in the country and to combat illegal immigration to justify not simplifying its procedures for granting and renewing work permits.[86]

Moreover, these permits must be distributed within a reasonable time.[87]

Article 18 § 2 imposes an obligation on States that have subscribed to it to reduce or abolish chancery fees and other charges paid either by foreign workers or by their employers. The obligation imposed is, like Article 18 as a whole, dynamic in nature: State parties must make concrete efforts to *progressively reduce* the level of fees and other charges imposed.[88] To this end, they must demonstrate that they have taken steps in this direction.[89] The obligation of *progression* is logically accompanied by an obligation of *non-regression*: unless there is a 'good reason' (e.g. to cover the increase in treatment costs or inflation), an increase is not conceivable.[90] Beyond this dynamic obligation, the assessment of which remains in essence relative, the ECSR sometimes provides figures, in absolute terms, on admissible or inadmissible financial costs under Article 18 § 2. Extrapolating data from some of the most recent findings, the *Digest*[91] mentions that the fee of €48 charged to employers for obtaining a work permit for a foreign worker, and of €108 for a temporary stay or €264 for a permanent stay, is excessive. The same applies to fees ranging from €266 to €1536 for work permits.

D *Article 18 § 3: Liberalize Regulations Governing the Employment of Foreign Workers*

Paragraph 3 of Article 18 requires the parties to the Charter to progressively liberalise, individually or collectively, regulations relating to the employment of foreign workers.

The obligation thus imposed is divided into two areas. The first area is *access to the national labour market*. According to the ECSR, restrictions on the access of foreign workers to the national labour market do not have to be abolished overnight[92] – the obligation is only gradual – but they should not be too burdensome, especially with regard to the specificities determining the geographical area in which these activities can be carried out and the requirements to

86 *Ibid.*

87 ECSR, Conclusions XVII-2 (2005), Portugal; ECSR, Conclusions 2020, Ukraine.

88 ECSR, Conclusions 2012, Statement of interpretation of article 18 § 2.

89 *Ibid.*

90 Digest of the case law of the European Committee of Social Rights, December 2022, p. 159.

91 *Ibid.*, p. 158.

92 Andrzej Marian Swiatkowski, *cit.*, p. 56.

be met.[93] In its recent conclusions on Ukraine, the ECSR recalls "that a person who has been legally resident for a given length of time on the territory of another Party should be able to enjoy the same rights as nationals of that country. The restrictions initially imposed with regard to access to employment (which can be accepted only if they are not excessive) must therefore be gradually lifted".[94]

Of course, State parties may continue to require work permits for foreigners seeking employment in their territory, but they may not prevent nationals of State parties from obtaining employment for reasons other than those set out in Article G of the Charter.[95] According to Article G, only restrictions "prescribed by law and [...] necessary in a democratic society for the protection of the rights and freedoms of others or for the protection of public interest, national security, public health, or morals"[96] are permitted. Therefore, the only occupations from which foreigners may be excluded are those directly related to the protection of public interest or national security and which require the exercise of public authority.[97]

In European law, Article 45(4) TFEU contains a similar exception. According to this provision, Member States may reserve access to employment in the public service to their nationals. The Court of Justice of the European Union has interpreted this derogation restrictively. According to the Court's established case law, this exception concerns "posts involving direct or indirect participation in the exercise of powers conferred by public law or duties designed to safeguard the general interests of the State or of other public authorities"[98] such as internal or external security of that State. The Court has also stated that these criteria must be assessed on a case-by-case basis in light of the nature of the tasks and responsibilities of the post concerned.[99]

---

93 Digest of the case law of the European Committee of Social Rights, December 2022, citing ECSR, Conclusions V (1977), Germany.

94 ECSR, Conclusions 2020, Ukraine.

95 The wording of the commitment in point 18 of Part I is quite explicit: "The nationals of any one of the Parties have the right to engage in any gainful occupation in the territory of any one of the others on a footing of equality with the nationals of the latter,subject to restrictions based on cogent economic or social reasons".

96 ECSR, Conclusions XI-1 (1989), Netherlands; ECSR, Conclusions 2005, Cyprus.

97 Digest of the case law of the European Committee of Social Rights, December 2018, p. 176.

98 See ECJ, 2 July 1996, *Commission of the European Communities v Hellenic Republic*, C-290/94, and more recently ECJ, 10 September 2014, *Iraklis Haralambidis v Calogero Casilli*, C-270/13.

99 *Ibid.*

In order to avoid conflict with Article 18 of the Charter, the implementation of such policies restricting access of third-country nationals to the national labour market should neither result in the total exclusion of nationals of non-EU (or non-EEA) State parties to the Charter from the national labour market nor substantially impede upon their ability to access the national labour market. Such a situation, resulting from the application of rules prioritizing nationals of that state, would not be compliant with Article 18, §3, as the state in question would be failing to fulfil its obligation to gradually liberalize regulations governing the access of foreign workers from a number of State parties to the Charter to the national labour market.[100]

A *second area* concerns the *recognition of certificates, qualifications and diplomas*.[101] To guarantee the effectiveness of the right set forth in Article 18 § 3, State parties must provide for rules governing the recognition of foreign diplomas and professional certifications, to the extent that such qualifications are required to engage in a gainful occupation as an employee or self-employed worker.[102]

A requirement for foreign workers to possess certificates, professional qualifications, or diplomas that have only been issued by national authorities or educational and training institutions of the host State, without allowing for the recognition of such certifications obtained as a result of substantially equivalent qualifications issued by the same kind of institution in other State parties, would constitute a serious obstacle to access the national labour market, and a violation of the principle of non-discrimination.[103] Once again, there is a parallel here with the case law of the Court of Justice of the European Union on free movement of workers,[104] it being understood, however, that EU law has reached a level of harmonisation on this point which goes beyond what can be expected from the application of the Charter. The European Union has indeed taken several complementary initiatives in order to facilitate mobility of workers amongst Member states. A first example is the development of a system of recognition of professional qualifications completed in other EU Member States. In this context, Directive 2005/36[105] (amended by Directive 2013/55) provides for the automatic recognition of a number of professions

100 ECSR, Conclusions 2012, Statement of interpretation of article 18 § 1 and 18 § 3.

101 Digest of the case law of the European Committee of Social Rights, December 2022, p. 159.

102 ECSR, Conclusions 2012, Statement of interpretation of article 18 § 1 and 18 § 3.

103 Digest of the case law of the European Committee of Social Rights, December 2022, p. 160.

104 ECJ, 5 February 2015, *European Commission v Kingdom of Belgium*, C-317/14.

105 Directive 2005/36/EC of the European Parliament and of the Council of 7 September 2005 on the recognition of professional qualifications.

namely in the health sector. The European Professional Card, introduced in 2016, constitutes a second example. Through an electronic procedure, workers can now apply to have their regulated profession recognized in another Member state.[106]

One final and very important question concerns the migrant worker's rights *in the event of loss of employment*. The ECSR considers that a worker's residence permit cannot be revoked on the sole ground of loss of employment, forcing him/her to leave the country.[107] Additional 'exceptional circumstances' must be invoked to carry out an expulsion of a migrant worker.[108] The recent conclusions on the Netherlands put it this way: "in cases where a work permit is revoked before the date of expiry, either because the work contract is prematurely terminated, whether or not through the fault of the worker, or because the worker no longer meets the conditions under which the work permit was granted, it would be contrary to the Charter to automatically deprive such worker of the possibility to continue to reside in the state concerned and to seek another job and a new work permit, unless there are exceptional circumstances which would authorise expulsion of the foreign worker concerned, within the meaning of Article 19 § 8".[109] The same conclusions add that the "automatic withdrawal of that person's residence permit with no possibility of seeking new employment" based on "early termination of the employment relationship of a foreign national (for professional misconduct)" is not in conformity with Article 18 § 3 of the Charter.[110]

In March 2021, the ECSR issued a statement on Covid-19 and social rights[111] highlighting that the pandemic is seriously affecting a number of the rights guaranteed by the Charter such as the rights to employment, work and social security. More precisely, the ECSR addressed unemployment caused by Covid-19 and emphasized the fact that migrant workers are often among the first to lose their jobs and face many obstacles when seeking new ones.[112] The ECSR thus seizes the opportunity of the pandemic to recall the importance of respecting Article 18 § 3 of the Charter, which "requires that the loss of a job

---

106 Commission Implementing Regulation (EU) 2015/983 on the procedure for issuance of the European Professional Card and the application of the alert mechanism pursuant to the Professional Qualifications Directive.

107 ECSR, Conclusions XI-1 (1989), Netherlands.

108 ECSR, Conclusions 2012, Statement of interpretation of article 18 § 1 and 18 § 3.

109 ECSR, Conclusions 2020 – Netherlands – Article 18–3. See also ECSR, Conclusions 2012, Statement of interpretation of article 18 § 1 and 18 § 3, and Elaine Dewhurst, *cit.*, p. 312.

110 ECSR, Conclusions 2020 – Netherlands – Article 18–3.

111 ECSR, Statement on COVID-19 and social rights adopted on 24 March 2021.

112 *Ibid.*, p. 7.

does not automatically lead to the withdrawal of a foreign worker's residence permit".[113]

E *Article 18 § 4: Recognize the Right of Nationals to Leave the Country to Engage in a Gainful Occupation in Other Parties to the Charter*

States are obligated under this provision to refrain from limiting their citizens' ability to work legally in other states that are Charter parties after they leave their own country. The ECSR has determined that restrictions are in line with the Charter only when they give due consideration to how important travel is in terms of the person's family relations, health, income, occupation, and other similar circumstances.[114]

As determined by Article 18(3) of the Charter,[115] the ECSR has also considered restrictions authorized under Article G of the Charter.[116] Compliance with Article G involves, first of all, *substantive* requirements relating to the pursuit of a legitimate aim and compliance with the principle of proportionality.

In terms of substantive requirements, this Article must be interpreted in accordance with Article 2 of the Fourth Protocol to the European Convention on Human Rights[117] and Article 12 of the International Covenant on Civil and Political Rights.[118] In its General Comments on Article 12 of the International Covenant on Civil and Political Rights,[119] the Human Rights Committee has stated that "a major source of concern are the manifold legal and bureaucratic barriers unnecessarily affecting the full enjoyment of the rights of the individuals to move freely, to leave a country, including their own, and to take

113 *Ibid.*, p. 7.

114 ECSR, Conclusions 2016, Finland.

115 ECSR, Conclusions 2012, Georgia.

116 ECSR, Conclusions 2016, Georgia; ECSR, Conclusions 2020, Serbia. See also Decision on the merits: ECSR, *European Federation of Public Service Employees* (*EUROFEDOP*) *v. Greece*, complaint No. 115/2015, decision on the merits of 13 September 2017.

117 This Article provides that: "§ 2 Everyone shall be free to leave any country, including his own. § 3 No restrictions shall be placed on the exercise of these rights other than such as are in accordance with law and are necessary in a democratic society in the interests of national security or public safety, for the maintenance of order public, for the prevention of crime, for the protection of health or morals, or for the protection of the rights and freedoms of others."

118 This Article provides that: "2. Everyone shall be free to leave any country, including his own. 3. The above-mentioned rights shall not be subject to any restrictions except those which are provided by law, are necessary to protect national security, public order (ordre public), public health or morals or the rights and freedoms of others, and are consistent with the other rights recognized in the present Covenant."

119 Human Rights Committee, *General Comment no. 27 on freedom of movement (article 12)*, 1999, CCPR/C/21/Rev.1/Add.9.

up residence".[120] The Committee adds that, regarding the right to movement within a country, it "has criticized provisions requiring individuals to apply for permission to change their residence or to seek the approval of the local authorities of the place of destination, as well as delays in processing such written applications. States' practice presents an even richer array of obstacles making it more difficult to leave the country, in particular for their own nationals".[121]

In practice, restrictions may be permissible if enabling free emigration would run contrary to the public interest or pose a threat to the security of the country. For example,[122] in its conclusions on the Netherlands,[123] the ECSR found that restrictions based upon the following grounds were in conformity with Article 18 § 4: "cases of criminal delinquency, maintenance obligations, debts to the State, bankruptcy, military obligations and security, and are founded on the presumption that the person's departure from the country might permit the person concerned to evade his obligations or might jeopardise the security of the Netherlands or allied States."

The ECSR's contentious case law shows that there are subtle boundaries to be drawn in this respect. In collective complaint no. 116/2016, EUROFEDOP alleged that during the period of compulsory military service in Greece, medical army officers are deprived of the right to leave the country to engage in a gainful occupation in the territory of another contracting Party to the Charter and that this would constitute a breach of Article 18 § 4. However, the ECSR did not follow this conclusion: "during the period of service (either voluntary or obligatory) medical officers cannot leave Greece in order to engage in a gainful occupation abroad. However, once they are free of their obligations,

120 *Ibid.*, § 17.

121 According to the UN Human Rights Committee, "these rules and practices include, *inter alia*, lack of access for applicants to the competent authorities and lack of information regarding requirements; the requirement to apply for special forms through which the proper application documents for the issuance of a passport can be obtained; the need for supportive statements from employers or family members; exact description of the travel route; issuance of passports only on payment of high fees substantially exceeding the cost of the service rendered by the administration; unreasonable delays in the issuance of travel documents; restrictions on family members travelling together; requirement of a repatriation deposit or a return ticket; requirement of an invitation from the State of destination or from people living there; harassment of applicants, for example by physical intimidation, arrest, loss of employment or expulsion of their children from school or university; refusal to issue passport because the applicant is said to harm the good name of the country" (*Ibid.*, § 17).

122 Earlier, for other examples, see Lenia Samuel, *cit.*, pp. 419–420.

123 ECSR, Conclusions XI-1 (1986), Netherlands.

there is no restriction on them exercising their right under Article 18 § 4 of the 1961 Charter". The ECSR concludes, on this basis, that "the complaint made by EUROFEDOP concerns exclusively Article 1 § 2 of the 1961 Charter, and consequently holds that there is no violation of Article 18 § 4".[124]

In addition to *substantive* requirements, the existence of *procedural* protection is also necessary for restrictions to the right guaranteed by Article 18 § 4 to be in conformity with Article G. The recent conclusions on Latvia[125] indicate that such restrictions must be based on a "legislative framework", and that there must be "legal remedies to challenge such decisions".

Concluding Remarks

As set out in the introduction, the impact of Article 18 for State parties to the Charter – when they have subscribed to it – is rather discreet. Its scope of application *ratione personae* is not very generous, and is often overshadowed by its normative environment. Its strength lies in its dynamic character – it requires constant progress – but this is also its weakness. It does not generally impose clear and immediate results that can be used as 'benchmarks' against which compliance or non-compliance can be identified. Even when this is the case, deviations from these expected results can be justified by Article G, in the implementation of which states also enjoy – according to Karin Lukas' observations[126] – a wide margin of discretion. Dated 2021, the final words of the former Chair of the ECSR are particularly symptomatic of the discretion that we have tried to highlight: "the Committee's case law on this article is not very elaborate, and State parties have had few difficulties in implementing Article 18".[127]

---

124 See Decision on the merits: ECSR, *European Federation of Public Service Employees (EUROFEDOP) v. Greece*, complaint No. 115/2015, decision on the merits of 13 September 2017.

125 ECSR, Conclusions 2020, Latvia.

126 Karin Lukas, *cit.*, p. 240.

127 *Ibid.*

ARTICLE 19

The Right of Migrant Workers and Their Families to Protection and Assistance

Ana Teresa Ribeiro, Milena Rouxinol and Inês Pereira de Sousa

With a view to ensuring the effective exercise of the right of migrant workers and their families to protection and assistance in the territory of any other Party, the Parties undertake:

1. to maintain or to satisfy themselves that there are maintained adequate and free services to assist such workers, particularly in obtaining accurate information, and to take all appropriate steps, so far as national laws and regulations permit, against misleading propaganda relating to emigration and immigration;
2. to adopt appropriate measures within their own jurisdiction to facilitate the departure, journey and reception of such workers and their families, and to provide, within their own jurisdiction, appropriate services for health, medical attention and good hygienic conditions during the journey;
3. to promote cooperation, as appropriate, between social services, public and private, in emigration and immigration countries;
4. to secure for such workers lawfully within their territories, insofar as such matters are regulated by law or regulations or are subject to the control of administrative authorities, treatment not less favourable than that of their own nationals in respect of the following matters:
   a) remuneration and other employment and working conditions;
   b) membership of trade unions and enjoyment of the benefits of collective bargaining;
   c) accommodation;
5. to secure for such workers lawfully within their territories treatment not less favourable than that of their own nationals with regard to employment taxes, dues or contributions payable in respect of employed persons;
6. to facilitate as far as possible the reunion of the family of a foreign worker permitted to establish himself in the territory;

 | DOI:10.1163/9789004434141_010

7. to secure for such workers lawfully within their territories treatment not less favourable than that of their own nationals in respect of legal proceedings relating to matters referred to in this Article;
8. to secure that such workers lawfully residing within their territories are not expelled unless they endanger national security or offend against public interest or morality;
9. to permit, within legal limits, the transfer of such parts of the earnings and savings of such workers as they may desire;
10. to extend the protection and assistance provided for in this Article to self-employed migrants insofar as such measures apply;
11. to promote and facilitate the teaching of the national language of the receiving state or, if there are several, one of these languages, to migrant workers and members of their families;
12. to promote and facilitate, as far as practicable, the teaching of the migrant worker's mother tongue to the children of the migrant worker.

Introduction

The purpose of Article 19 ESC, along with Article 18, is to ensure "certain minimum safeguards for migrant workers and their families".[1] This commentary focuses on each provision of Article 19, as preceded by a contextualization of sources and some clarifications on its personal scope.

This Article, which is one of the so-called *core provisions* of the Charter,[2] deals with with one of the main challenges of 21st century,

1 Pascale Boucaud, *Migrant workers and their Families Protection within the European Social Charter*, Strasbourg, Council of Europe Publishing, 1996, p. 8; Stefan Clauwaert, «The Right of Migrant Workers and Their Families to Protection and Assistance», in Niklas Bruun *et al.* (eds.), *The European Social Charter and The Employment Relation*, Oxford/Portland (Oregon), Hart Publishing, 2017, pp. 340–357, p. 340. According to this last Author, the intention of both provisions was to liberalise the conditions of migration, ensure the rights of migrant workers and their families, and to ensure equal treatment of migrants.

2 See Article 20 of the ESC and Article A(1)(b) of the revised ESC. For an overview of the States Parties that have accepted (or not) the several provisions of Article 19, see: <https://rm.coe.int/country-by-country-table-of-accepted-provisions/1680630742>. This is also one of the longest and one of the most complex Articles of the Charter, referring to the protection and assistance of migrant workers and their families in a wide sense – see Karin Lukas,

migration.[3] It is a phenomenon that, albeit global, due to the actors involved and to the sort of action it requires (indeed, despite recent nationalist tendencies, it cannot be dealt with in an individualized way), also concerns all the elements that define a State (its sovereignty, its territory, and its population).[4] And even though migrations are as ancient as humanity, with globalization they have become more complex, diversified, and intense, affecting every continent and, in particular, Europe. Particularly, the ethnic, racial, and religious diversity that migration has brought has fed tensions, due to idea that it presents a threat to national identity, leading to emotional and heated debates.[5]

In this context, Article 19 focuses on assistance for migrant workers who already have jobs or who are seeking employment. It covers emigrant and immigrant workers and protects members of their families as well as themselves. In the case of immigrant workers, it calls to some extent for preferential treatment, not just equality of treatment with nationals.[6]

As noted by Colm O'Cinnéide,[7] the ESC provisions on migrant workers are often overlooked, since, in contrast with EU law, they do not grant a right to entry as such, except for family reunification purposes. In addition, as explained below, the scope of these guarantees is restricted to nationals of contracting Parties who are lawfully present or regularly working in the territory of the host state. Nevertheless, since these provisions encompass non-EU states, they still have some *bite*.

The Revised European Social Charter. An Article by Article Commentary, Cheltenham (UK)/ Northampton (USA), Edward Elgar Publishing, 2021, p. 243.

3 Being the key provision of the Charter, where it comes to migrants' rights – see Colm O'Cinnéide, «Migrant Rights under the European Social Charter», in Cathryn Costello and Mark Freedland (eds.), *Migrants at Work – Immigration and Vulnerability in Labour Law*, Oxford, Oxford University Press, 2014, p. 294.

4 María Reyes Fernandez, «El Pacto Mundial para una Migración Segura, Ordenada e Regular desde la Perspectiva del Ministerio de Trabajo, Migraciones y Seguridad Social», *Revista del Ministerio de Trabajo, Migraciones y Seguridad Social*, 2019, no. 140, pp. 67–88, p. 67. As the Author stresses, it has become a key-element of the political discourse, and not always under objective and realistic lenses.

5 Constança Urbano de Sousa, «A Securitização da Imigração e o Imperativo de uma Gestão da Migração Baseada no Respeito pelos Direitos Humanos», *Revista del Ministerio de Trabajo, Migraciones y Seguridad Social*, 2019, no. 140, pp. 35–66, p. 35.

6 See Donna Gomien, David Harris and Leo Zwaak, *Law and Practice of the European Convention on Human Rights and the European Social Charter*, Strasbourg, Council of Europe Publishing, 1996, p. 406; David Harris and John Darcy, *The European Social Charter*, 2nd ed., Ardsley (NY), Transnational Publishers Inc., 2001, p. 211.

7 Colm O'Cinnéide, «Migrant Rights under the European Social Charter», *cit.*, p. 282. The Author adds (*ibidem*, p. 287) that the situation of migrants under the original Charter and the revised version is more or less identical, being also complex, nuanced, and controversial.

1 Scope of Application

A *Contextualization of Sources*

Aside from Article 19 ESC, several other sources of international law address the issue of migration and migrants' rights. At United Nations level, this is the case of Article 13 of the International Covenant on Civil and Political Rights, as well as the International Convention on the Protection of the Rights of all Migrant Workers and their Families[8] and the New York Declaration for Refugees and Migrants.

Within the ILO, several conventions and recommendations relate to this issue, such as Convention No. 19 and Recommendation No. 25, on equality of treatment; Convention No. 48, on the maintenance of migrants' pension rights; Convention No. 82, on social policy; Convention No. 97[9] (revised) and Recommendation No. 86 (revised), on migration for employment; Recommendation No. 100, on the protection of migrant workers (undeveloped countries); Convention No. 117, on social policy;[10] Convention No. 143 and Recommendation No. 151, on migrant workers.

Within the Council of Europe, aside from the ESC,[11] there is the Convention for the Protection of Human Rights and Fundamental

8 As stressed by Stefan Clauwaert, «The Right of Migrant Workers and their Families to Protection and Assistance», *cit.*, p. 341, from a United Nations' perspective, there are several texts that have relevance for the protection of the rights of migrants, such as the Universal Declaration of Human Rights, the International Convention on the Elimination of All Forms of Racial Discrimination, the International Covenant on Economic, Social and Cultural Rights. However, only the International Convention on the Protection of the Rights of all Migrant Workers and their Families deals directly with the rights of migrants and their families. Still, as noted by the Author (p. 342, ft. 6), although this convention alludes, in its general considerations, to several ILO conventions, it does not mention Article 19 of the ESC, despite it being already in force at the time of its adoption.

9 Literature confirms that several norms of Article 19 are largely based on the provisions of Convention No. 97 – see Stefan Clauwaert, «The Right of Migrant Workers and their Families to Protection and Assistance», *cit.*, p. 342, and the references mentioned on ft. 9.

10 Whose part III has provisions on migrant workers.

11 Aside from Articles 18 and 19, and despite not being expressly alluded in these provisions, migrant workers and their families are also protected by Articles 1 to 17 ESC – see Pascale Boucaud, *Migrant Workers and their Families Protection within the European Social Charter, cit.*, p. 9; Stefan Clauwaert, «The Right of Migrant workers and their Families to Protection and Assistance», *cit.*, p. 344 and ft. 22; Matti Mikkola, «Social Human Rights of Migrants under the European Social Charter», *European Journal of Social Security*, 2008, vol. 10, no. 1, pp-25–59, p. 29; *Fourth Report on Certain Provisions of the Charter Which Have Not Been Accepted*, 1995, pp. 18–19, available at https://rm.coe.int/09000016809137b7. Stefan Clauwaert, «The Right of Migrant Workers and their Families to Protection and

Freedoms,[12] the European Convention on Establishment, the European Convention on the Legal Status of Migrant Workers, and the European Code of Social Security.

Finally, in the context of EU law, there are several primary and secondary law provisions connected to migration, such as Articles 21, and 45–49 of the Treaty on the Functioning of the European Union, Article 15 of the Charter of Fundamental Rights of the European Union (CFREU), and, among others, Directives 2000/43/EC, of 29 June, implementing the principle of equal treatment between persons irrespective of racial or ethnic origin; 2000/78/EC, of 27 November, establishing a general framework for equal treatment and occupation; 2002/73/EC, of 23 September, amending Directive 76/207/EEC, on the implementation of the principle of equal treatment for men and women as regards access to employment, vocational training and promotion, and working conditions; 2003/86/EC, of 22 September 2003, on the right to family reunification; 2003/8/EC, of 27 January, to improve access to justice in cross-border disputes by establishing minimum common rules relating to legal aid for such disputes; 2004/113/EC, of 13 December, implementing the principle of equal treatment between men and women in the access to, and supply of, goods and services; 2006/123/EC, of 12 December, on services in the internal market; 2008/104/EC, of 19 November, on temporary agency work; and 96/71/EC, 16 December (amended by (EU) 2018/957, of 28 June 2018), concerning the posting of workers in the framework of the provision of services.[13]

B *Personal Scope*

Article 19 of the ESC does not grant foreign nationals any right of entry to the territory of other Parties nor any free movement right – in contrast to the EU regime. Indeed, the protection provided to migrants by the ESC has little

Assistance», *cit.*, p. 344, also stresses the connection between Article 19 and horizontal Article E on non-discrimination.

12 Article 6 protects the right of every person to a fair and public hearing within a reasonable time by an independent and impartial tribunal established by law; while Article 2, par. 2, of Protocol no. 4, enshrines the freedom of every person to leave any country, including his own; Article 4, of Protocol no. 4, establishes the prohibition of collective expulsion of aliens, and, finally, Article 1 of Protocol no. 7, states guarantees concerning expulsion.

13 Several of these sources of law are referenced at ECSR, *The Relationship between European Union Law and the European Social Charter*, Working document, 2014, pp. 116 and ff. See also: Regulation (EU) No. 492/2011 of the European Parliament and of the Council of 5 April 2011 on freedom of movement for workers within the Union. Particularly, regarding migration from non-EU nationals, see: https://www.europarl.europa.eu/factsheets/en/sheet/152/immigration-policy.

significance for those ESC Member States that are also Member States of the European Union or Parties to the Agreement on the European Economic Area in connection with their employment in other States in the same situation. A weakness frequently reported in relation to this concerns the ESC personal scope, which excludes an important number of migrants in need of protection. In fact, according to the Appendix, the Charter applies to foreigners "only in so far as they are nationals of other Parties lawfully resident or working regularly within the territory of the Party concerned".[14] This means that the protection and control of social rights provided by the Charter apply neither to foreigners who, although being within the jurisdiction of the contracting Parties, are third State nationals, nor to nationals of contracting Parties who do not lawfully reside and/or work regularly within the territory of the Party concerned (*irregular migrants*).[15] However, in accordance with the general rule in the Appendix, Article 19 applies to refugees, as far as it is necessary to secure a "treatment as favourable as possible", as well as to stateless persons.[16]

Literature emphasizes that these restrictions are hardly coherent with the nature of the Charter, an instrument intended to protect human dignity and the essential rights that uphold such dignity.[17] It is also hardly consistent with the relevance given to migrant protection, that is reflected by the fact that Article 19 belongs to the *core provisions* of the ESC whose ratification is mandatory in order for a State to be accepted as a contracting Party. In what concerns, particularly, the exclusion of third state nationals, two points must be underlined: firstly, the fact that migratory movements from non-European States

---

14 According to Stefan Clauwaert, «The Right of Migrant Workers and their Families to Protection and Assistance», *cit.*, p. 345, no distinction shall be made between permanent or temporarily lawful migrants.

15 Stressing that the conditions of application of each paragraph are not exactly coincident, David Harris and John Darcy, *The European Social Charter*, *cit.*, p. 212.

16 Marie-Françoise Valette, «Protection et Promotion des Droits Sociaux des Migrants par le Comité Européen des Droits Sociaux», *Revue Européenne des Migrations Internationales*, 2016, vol. 32, no. 3–4, p. 339–340.

17 For example: Giuseppe Palmisano, «Overcoming The Limits of The European Social Charter in Terms of Persons Protected: The Case of Third State Nationals and Irregular Migrants», in Marilisa D'amico and Giovanni Guiglia (eds.), *European Social Charter and The Challenges of the XXI Century/La Charte Sociale Européenne et Les Défis du XXIe Siècle*, Napoli, Edizione Scientifiche Italiane, 2014, pp. 175 ff.; Giuseppe Palmisano, «Sui Limiti di Applicazione Della Carta Sociale Europea in Termini di Persone Protette», in Marilisa D'amico, Giovanni Guiglia and Benedetta Liberali (eds.), *La Carta Sociale Europea e La Tutela Dei Diritti Sociali. Atti Del Convegno del 18 Gennaio 2013 Università degli Studi di Milano*, Napoli, Edizioni Scientifichi Italiane, 2013, pp. 41 ff.

(eg. from Africa or Latin America) to Europe are increasing, which makes the inadequacy of that restriction more evident; and secondly, the system of the ESC contrasts with instruments such as the 1966 International Covenant on Economic, Social and Cultural Rights, several conventions on labour standards adopted by the ILO, and the CFREU, which were given a legally binding character by the Treaty of Lisbon. In conclusion, "on the one hand, the exclusion of third State nationals from the scope of the European Social Charter represents a real anomaly in the framework of international instruments dealing with human rights; (…) on the other hand, the same States Parties to the Charter have in fact already committed themselves, in legal contexts other than the Social Charter, to guaranteeing social rights in their territory beyond the limited personal scope set out in the Appendix to the Social Charter".[18]

In what concerns the so-called *irregular migrants*, the ECSR's case law has been mitigating the consequences of a literal interpretation of the Appendix, which would lead to denying any protection to those migrants not lawfully residing and/or not legally working within the territory of a contracting State. The most well-known ECSR decision, clarifying former precedents[19] and also replicated in 2014,[20] is in response to Collective Complaint No. 69/2011 (23 October 2012). The case concerns a group of accompanied and unaccompanied minors unlawfully residing in Belgium. According to the complaint, filed by the international non-governmental organization Défense des Enfants International, the Belgian State was denying those minors indispensable medical and social assistance, which would be in breach of Articles 7, 11, 13, 17, and E of the ESC. Following a systematic and teleological interpretation of the Charter and taking into account other international instruments, namely the United Nations Convention on the Rights of the Child, the ECSR stated that "the restriction of the personal scope included in the Appendix should not be read in such a way as to deprive foreigners coming within the category of unlawfully

18 Giuseppe Palmisano, «Overcoming the Limits of the European Social Charter in Terms of Persons Protected: The Case of Third State Nationals and Irregular Migrants», *cit.*, p. 178.

19 ECSR, *International Federation of Human Rights Leagues v. France*, collective complaint No. 14/2003, decision on the merits of 8 September 2004; ECSR, *Defense of Children International v. the Netherlands*, collective complaint No. 47/2008, decision on the merits of 20 October 2009. During a debate between the Governmental Committee and the ECSR, that took place in Turin in October 2014, the ECSR had the opportunity of highlighting the consistency of its case law. For further developments, see: Stefan Clauwaert, «The Right of Migrant Workers and their Families to Protection and Assistance», *cit.*, p. 347.

20 ECSR, *European Federation of National Organisations Working with the Homeless (FEANTSA) v. the Netherlands*, collective complaint No. 86/2012, decision on the merits of 2 July 2014.

present migrants of the protection of the most basic rights enshrined in the Charter or to impair their fundamental rights such as the right to life or physical integrity or the right to human dignity".[21] However, the ECSR underlined that this extensive application of the Charter is exceptional and justified only if the exclusion of unlawfully present foreigners puts them in an unacceptable situation regarding the right to life, preservation of human dignity, psychological and physical integrity, and health; therefore, unlawfully present foreigners, including minors, are not covered by all the provisions of the Charter, but only by those fundamental to secure the rights mentioned above.[22] This *minimum core* includes emergency health care, shelter, and social assistance, but, as Colm O'Cinnéide notes, "it is possible to identify other situations where the Committee's logic may also apply", such as the protection against forms of forced labour that constitute slavery.[23]

Finally, it is important to point out, as stated by Stefan Clauwaert,[24] that, as the Appendix uses the term "person" and not "worker", the rights provided in this provision apply to all sorts of workers – cross-border workers, namely posted workers,[25] seasonal workers, wage-earners or self-employed, and jobseekers.

II Article 19 § 1: the Right to Adequate and Free Services to Assist Migrant Workers and to Action against Misleading Propaganda Relating to Emigration and Immigration

This provision applies both to immigrant and emigrant workers[26] and enshrines two different obligations:[27] the need to ensure adequate and free services that

21 § 28. See also §§ 29–33.

22 §§ 35 and 36.

23 Colm O'Cinnéide, «Migrant Rights under the European Social Charter», *cit.*, p. 291.

24 Stefan Clauwaert, «The Right of Migrant Workers and their Families to Protection and Assistance», *cit.*, p. 345.

25 ECSR, Conclusions 2015, Statement of Interpretation of Article 19 § 4. For posted workers, see Colm O'Cinnéide, «Migrant Rights under The European Social Charter», *cit.*, pp. 290 and 291/292, and Stefan Clauwaert, «The Right of Migrant Workers and their Families to Protection and Assistance», *cit.*, pp. 348–349.

26 ECSR, Conclusions I (1969), Statement of Interpretation of Article 19§1.

27 As noted by David Harris and John Darcy, *The European Social Charter*, *cit.*, p. 213, these obligations are taken, almost word for word, from the equivalent provisions of the ILO Migration for Employment Convention (Revised).

assist migrant workers, particularly with obtaining accurate information, and to take all appropriate steps against misleading propaganda relating to emigration and immigration.

The first obligation implies the provision of reliable and objective information on issues of concern such as the formalities that should be completed, as well as the living and working conditions found in the country of destination (such as vocational guidance and training, social security, trade union membership, housing, social services, education, and health).[28]

Contracting Parties shall provide the necessary public services or ensure that they are being privately delivered.[29] These services must be offered before and after migration and their adequacy will be determined by their ability to meet the demands placed upon them and by the kind of assistance that is being given.[30] More precisely, if they are appropriate to the prevailing patterns of emigration and immigration that will be sufficient (contracting Parties do not have to ensure that the services in question exist in respect to immigration from all other contracting Parties).[31]

It should be stressed that this obligation includes not only the provision of information, but also of all the services of advice and assistance to migrant workers, except those covered by the most specific provisions of §§ 2–9 of Article 19.[32] Finally, the Committee stressed that, in order to be effective, free information and assistance services for migrants must be accessible. And while the provision of online resources is a valuable service, due to the potential restricted access of migrants, other means of information are necessary, such as helplines and drop-in centres.[33]

Regarding the obligation to take steps against misleading propaganda, contracting Parties must prevent the communication of deceitful information

---

28 ECSR, Conclusions III (1973), Cyprus and *Digest of the Case Law of the European Committee of Social Rights*, 2018, p. 179.

29 David Harris and John Darcy, *The European Social Charter*, *cit.*, p. 213. According to the ECSR, the information does not necessarily have to be provided by public services. Therefore, entrusting this task to non-governmental institutions should be deemed acceptable – see ECSR, Conclusions IV (1975), Germany.

30 David Harris and John Darcy, *The European Social Charter*, *cit.*, p. 214.

31 David Harris and John Darcy, *The European Social Charter*, *cit.*, p. 214; ECSR, Conclusions II (1971), Italy, Conclusions XIII-2 (1994), Ireland, and Conclusions XIII-3 (1995), Turkey.

32 ECSR, Conclusions IV (1975), Germany.

33 ECSR, Conclusions 2015, Armenia. Similarly see Karin Lukas, *The Revised European Social Charter*, *cit.*, p. 246.

to nationals leaving the country and act against false information targeted at migrants seeking to enter.[34] In order to be effective, this undertaking should include legal and practical measures to tackle racism and xenophobia, as well as trafficking of women.[35] As stated by the ECSR, such measures, which should be aimed at the whole population, are necessary *inter alia* to counter the spread of stereotyped assumptions that migrants are inclined to crime, violence, drug abuse, or disease.[36] This is an awareness that must be particularly cultivated amongst law enforcement officials, namely through the training of officials who are in first contact with migrants.[37]

Furthermore, in order to combat misleading propaganda, there must be an effective system to monitor discriminatory, racist or hate-inciting speech, particularly in the public sphere.[38] Finally, as stressed by David Harris and John Darcy, even though this provision refers to "propaganda relating to emigrations and immigration" without qualification, it should be read as being limited to misleading information that might affect a person intending to migrate for employment purposes to the territory of a contracting Party. Furthermore, the wording "so far as national law and regulations permit" makes allowance for constitutional or infra-constitutional laws in contracting Party's legal systems protecting freedom of speech, although it does not permit laws

34 ECSR, Conclusions XIV-1 (1998), Greece and *Centre on Housing Rights and Evictions (COHRE) v. Italy*, complaint No. 58/2009, decision on the merits of 25 June 2010, §§ 138–140. In this decision, the Committee also stresses that statements by public actors are capable of creating a discriminatory atmosphere. And racist misleading propaganda indirectly allowed or directly emanating from the state authorities constitutes a violation of the Charter. The Committee's establishment of the doctrine of "aggravated violation" sends a clear message of "zero tolerance" in relation to (a) state commission of, (b) state failure to address, and (c) state collusion in, discrimination and violence suffered by vulnerable groups. Given the strong evidence from a range of jurisdictions of state participation in, or tolerance of, discrimination against Roma and Sinti, the scope for future employment of the aggravated violation by the Committee seems highly probable – see Aoife Nolan, «'Aggravated Violations', Roma Housing Rights, and Forced Expulsions in Italy: Recent Developments under the European Social Charter Complaints System», *Human Rights Law Review*, 2011, vol. 11, issue 2, pp. 343–361 and sp. 353–354.

35 *Digest of The Case Law of the European Committee of Social Rights*, *cit.*, p. 170. Naturally, they should also prevent human trafficking in general – see Colm O'Cinnéide, «Migrant Rights under the European Social Charter», *cit.*, p. 295.

36 ECSR, Conclusions XV-1 (2000), Austria.

37 *Digest of The Case Law of the European Committee of Social Rights*, *cit.*, p. 179. Immigration and border control authorities must receive adequate guidance in equal treatment – see Matti Mikkola, «Social Human Rights of Migrants under The European Social Charter», *cit.*, p. 40.

38 ECSR, Conclusions 2006, Slovenia.

that substantially limit or undermine the obligation to control misleading propaganda.[39]

III Article 19 § 2: Right to Health and Medical Services in Transit and Reception Facilities for Migrant Workers

Once again, this provision applies to both emigrant and immigrant workers and contains two obligations which were taken, in substance, from the ILO Migration for Employment Convention (revised).[40]

The first obligation requires contracting Parties to adopt appropriate measures[41] to facilitate the departure, journey, and reception of such workers and their families and it applies both to organized migration and to migration by individuals.[42] According to the ECSR, this provision demands the adoption of special measures for the benefit of migrant workers, beyond the ones provided for nationals[43] and States must provide explicitly for assistance in matters of basic need, or demonstrate that the authorities are adequately prepared to afford it to migrants when necessary.[44]

The ECSR has clarified that *reception*[45] refers to the period of weeks which follows immediately from the arrival of migrant workers, during which they and their families most often find themselves in situations of particular difficulty,[46] and that the measures in question must include not only assistance

---

39 David Harris and John Darcy, *The European Social Charter*, *cit.*, p. 215. The Authors add that, as in the case of the first obligation enshrined in this paragraph, the wording "appropriate" supports an interpretation that looks at the existing patters of migration when determining what steps need to be taken.

40 David Harris and John Darcy, *The European Social Charter*, *cit.*, p. 215–216; ECSR, Conclusions XII-2 (1992), Spain.

41 ECSR, Conclusions III (1973), Cyprus.

42 ECSR, Conclusions I (1969), Germany. And, as noted by David Harris and John Darcy, *The European Social Charter*, *cit.*, p. 213, by "jurisdiction", the Charter means the contracting Parties' "territorial jurisdiction".

43 ECSR, Conclusions III (1973), Cyprus.

44 ECSR, Conclusions XX-4 (2015), Poland.

45 Reception must be regulated by law, enjoy sufficient resources, and be effective, in order to ensure dignified treatment, security, and necessary assistance to migrants, both during the journey to the immigration country and at the start of resettling in that country – see Matti Mikkola, «Social Human Rights of Migrants under The European Social Charter», *cit.*, p. 43.

46 ECSR, Conclusions IV (1975), Statement of Interpretation of Article 19 § 2. This assistance does not require the creation of specific services, since it may be rendered by commonly operating social services – see Conclusions XIII-5 (1997), Finland.

with regard to placement and integration in the workplace, but also in overcoming problems, such as short-term accommodation, illness, shortage of money, and adequate health measures, as well as ensuring an appropriate reception in educational establishments for the children of such workers.[47]

Since the ILO Migration for Employment Convention was the inspiration behind this provision, David Harris and John Darcy suggest that an indication of what these appropriate measures constitute may also be found at Article 6 of Annex I of that convention,[48] which alludes to the simplification of administrative formalities; the provision of interpretation services; the provision of any necessary assistance during an initial period in the settlement of the migrants and members of their families authorised to accompany or join them; and the safeguarding of the welfare, during the journey and in particular while on board a ship, of migrants and members of their families authorised to accompany or join them.

The second obligation present hereby determines that contracting Parties shall provide migrant workers and their families, within their own jurisdiction, appropriate services for health, medical attention, and good hygienic

47 ECSR, Conclusions IV (1975), Germany; ECSR, Conclusions IV (1975), United Kingdom. As pointed out by Pascale Boucaud, *Migrant Workers and their Families Protection within The European Social Charter*, *cit.*, p. 13, these measures include very wide aspects. Furthermore, although information and advice are generally treated as coming within par. 1, it seems likely that they are encompassed by par. 2, as far as the reception period is concerned – see David Harris and John Darcy, *The European Social Charter*, *cit.*, p. 217. Article 19 encompasses the unmarried children of migrant workers as long as they are dependent on the aforementioned workers and they are considered minors by the host country – see Karin Lukas, *The Revised European Social Charter*, *cit.*, p. 245.

48 David Harris and John Darcy, *The European Social Charter*, *cit.*, p. 216. The ILO Migration for Employment Recommendation (Revised) is more detailed. Its Article 10 lists, as appropriate measures, providing migrants, in case of necessity, with adequate accommodation, food, and clothing on arrival in the country of immigration; ensuring, where necessary, vocational training to enable migrants for employment to acquire the qualifications required in the country of immigration; allowing, taking into account the limits imposed by national laws and regulations concerning export and import of currency, the transfer of earnings and savings of migrants as they may desire; arranging, in the case of permanent migration, for the transfer, where desired, to the country of immigration, of the capital of migrants for employment, within the limits allowed by national laws and regulations concerning export and import of currency; providing access to schools for migrants and members of their families. Article 11 also states that migrants and the members of their families should be assisted in obtaining access to recreation and welfare facilities, and steps should be taken where necessary to ensure that special facilities are made available during the initial period of settlement in the country of immigration.

conditions during the journey.[49] And, according to the ECSR, this applies to people travelling either collectively or under the public or private arrangements for collective recruitment. It does not apply to forms of individual migration for which the State is not responsible.[50]

As with part 1, the ECSR takes into account the actual patterns of emigration and immigration between the contracting Parties for employment purposes, meaning that the lower the level of immigration or emigration, the lower are the expectations of a contracting Party.[51] And it should be noted that these services do not always have to be provided by the State. In fact, when the United Kingdom reported that employers were charged with ensuring the social aspects of the reception of migrants and their families and that special official arrangements were unnecessary, the Committee stated that this situation complied with the Charter, provided that the country could confirm that, where such arrangements broke down or where emergencies or special problems arose, appropriate assistance was made available.[52]

Finally, in its assessment of this paragraph, the ECSR has stressed the importance of treating persons in transit with humanity. In fact, in the first cycle of national reports, the Committee complained that the documents provided related almost exclusively to purely administrative measures and often did not make any reference to the social and human aspect of the problem which, in its view, is of capital importance.[53]

IV Article 19 § 3: Cooperation between the Public and Private Social Services of Emigration and Immigration Countries

As in the two previous paragraphs, this provision is applicable both to emigrant and immigrant workers[54] and it establishes the need for contracting Parties to

49 Since this obligation applies only during the voyage, it does not require the contracting Parties to take any measures either before or after such journeys – see David Harris and John Darcy, *The European Social Charter*, *cit.*, p. 218.

50 ECSR, Conclusions IV (1975), Statement of Interpretation of Article 19 § 2. Still, the ECSR recognized that, in those cases, the need for reception facilities is all the greater.

51 David Harris and John Darcy, *The European Social Charter*, *cit.*, p. 218; ECSR, Conclusions III (1973), Ireland, and IV (1975), Cyprus. And if the migration patterns change, so will the Committee's expectations – see David Harris and John Darcy, *The European Social Charter*, *cit.*, p. 218; ECSR, Conclusions IV (1975), Cyprus.

52 ECSR, Conclusions IV (1975), United Kingdom.

53 ECSR, Conclusions I (1969), Statement of Interpretation of Article 19 § 2.

54 *Digest of the Case Law of The European Committee of Social Rights*, *cit.*, p. 180.

foster cooperation between social services, private and public, in emigration and immigration countries to ensure the assistance and protection of migrant workers and their families.

The concept of *social services* encompasses not only employment services, but services by all public or private organizations which facilitate the life of emigrants and their families, their adjustment to their new environment, and their relations with members of their families who have remained in the country of origin.[55] And, in order to achieve such goals, contacts and information exchanges should be established between these entities.[56] This kind of cooperation is useful in situations such as where the migrant worker, who has left his or her family in the home country, fails to send money back[57] or needs to be contacted for family reasons, or where the worker has returned to his or her country but needs to claim unpaid wages or benefits or must deal with various issues in the country in which he was employed.[58]

As with the previous paragraphs of the present Article, the Committee takes into account the influx of migratory movements, stating that formal arrangements are not necessary if there is little migratory movement in a given country. In such cases, the provision of practical cooperation on an as-needed basis may be sufficient.[59] However, where no systematic cooperation has been established, it is necessary to provide information about any form of cooperation suited to individual circumstances, even through private agencies.[60]

As stressed by David Harris and John Darcy, even though this obligation is stated without qualification, it follows from the provisions' context that a contracting Party is expected to promote cooperation only between social services established in its own country or in those of other contracting Parties.[61] Still, when Ireland tried to argue that the wording *as appropriate* meant that each contracting Party was free to decide which steps should be taken to promote

---

55 ECSR, Conclusions III (1973), Ireland. The cooperation required entails a wider range of social and human problems facing migrants and their families than social security – see ECSR, Conclusions VII, (1981), Ireland.

56 ECSR, Conclusions XIV-1 (1998), Belgium and *Digest of the Case Law of the European Committee of Social Rights, cit.*, 180.

57 The right to transfer earnings and savings to the country of origin is also provided by Article 19 § 9.

58 ECSR, Conclusions XV-1 (2000), Finland.

59 *Digest of the Case Law of the European Committee of Social Rights, cit.*, p. 180. Nevertheless, a state that experiences very small overall migrations flows must still undertake some actions towards cooperation between social services – see ECSR, Conclusions XIV-I (1998), Norway.

60 ECSR, Conclusions VII (1981), Sweden.

61 David Harris and John Darcy, *The European Social Charter, cit.*, p. 220.

cooperation, the ECSR rejected this interpretation. It noted that such expression should be understood as applying not to the undertaking as such, but to the ways of implementing it, organizing *as appropriate* either between public services or between private services, or both, depending on the structure of the social services of the country concerned.[62]

V Article 19 § 4:[63] Right to an Equal Treatment on Remuneration and Other Employment and Working Conditions, Membership of Trade Unions and Enjoyment of the Benefits of Collective Bargaining, and Accommodation

This provision is closely modelled on Article 6(1)a of the ILO Migration for Employment Convention (revised) and it ensures the right of migrant workers to a treatment no less favourable than that of nationals concerning remuneration and other employment[64] and working conditions, trade union membership and the enjoyment of benefits of collective bargaining, and accommodation.[65]

It should be noted that, regarding the territory of the contracting Parties, all rights situated beyond territorial waters, but under the supervision of such Parties, are encompassed as well as, presumably, employment aboard ships and aircraft registered under the law of a contracting Party.[66]

---

62 ECSR, Conclusions III (1973), Ireland.

63 According to Stefan Clauwaert, «The Right of Migrant Workers and their Families to Protection and Assistance», *cit.*, p. 355, given the importance of this Article and the issue of migration and migrant workers, it would be worthwhile for the ECSR to elaborate on the enforcement aspect, remedies, and sanctions, of this provision. Particularly, since it begins by saying that equal treatment is subject to control of administrative authorities and national governments often report on controls made by inspectorate services to ensure compliance in practice.

64 This provision also applies to provisions in law guaranteeing the employment of persons who are obliged to return to their own country to perform military service – see ECSR, Conclusions XIII-2 (1994), Germany.

65 Stefan Clauwaert, «The Right of Migrant Workers and their Families to Protection and Assistance», *cit.*, p. 352, notes that, regarding access to employment, the ECSR case law seems to have shifted. At first, this matter was considered to be subject to Article 18, whereas, more recently, the Committee found cases of non-conformity under Article 19 § 4. See, for instance: ECSR, Conclusions 2011, Turkey. Finally, David Harris and John Darcy, *The European Social Charter*, *cit.*, p. 221, explain that, as with the previous paragraphs, this one is also dependent on migration patterns.

66 Stefan Clauwaert, «The Right of Migrant Workers and their Families to Protection and Assistance», *cit.*, p. 351; David Harris and John Darcy, *The European Social Charter*, *cit.*, p. 220 and 212, ft. 1360; see for instance: ECSR, Conclusions IV (1975), Germany; ECSR, Conclusions VI (1979), Germany.

The equal treatment obligation enshrined in this provision is not conditional on reciprocity. It applies to nationals of all other Charter Parties, regardless of whether they have accepted it and of any limitations in their national law.[67] Furthermore, according to the ECSR, this provision also applies to posted workers since, even though their situations differ, for the period of stay and work within the territory of the host State, posted workers are workers coming from another State and lawfully within the territory of the host State.[68]

Concerning the issue of remuneration and other employment and working conditions, the Charter determines that the States Parties are required to eliminate all legal and *de facto* discrimination, namely in the domains of in-service training, promotion, and vocational training.[69] The Committee also stressed that any restriction to the access of migrant workers to employments in some fields shall be objectively justified by reference to the sovereign prerogatives of the state.[70]

Following this provision, migrant workers should enjoy certain benefits granted to national workers when changing jobs or taking up a first job, such as removal or settling-in allowances, or regarding receiving guaranteed wages to

67 ECSR, Conclusions VIII (1984), Spain.

68 ECSR, Conclusions 2015, Statement of Interpretation of Article 19 § 4. Therefore, in order to conform with the requirements of the Charter, any restrictions on the right to equal treatment for posted workers, which are imposed due to the nature of their sojourn, must be objectively justified by reference to the specific situations and status of posted workers, having regard to the principles of Article G of the Revised Charter (Article 31 of the 1961 Charter) – *idem, ibidem*. Karin Lukas, *The Revised European Social Charter, cit.*, p. 249, adds that, also during such period, foreign undertakings should be treated equally when providing services through posted workers. In fact, as stressed by the Author, the Committee has deemed that limiting or excluding the right to collective bargaining or collective action with respect to foreign undertakings, for the sake of enhancing free cross-border movement of services and advantages in terms of competition within a common market zone, constitutes discriminatory treatment on the grounds of nationality (see *Swedish Trade Union Confederation (LO) and Swedish Confederation of Professional Employees (TCO) v. Sweden,* complaint No. 85/2012, decision on the merits of 3 July 2013, §§ 140–142).

69 *Digest of the Case Law of The European Committee of Social Rights, cit.*, p. 181; ECSR, Conclusions VII (1981), United Kingdom. The Committee recalled that these issues also concern Articles 1 (right to work), 4 (rights to remuneration), 2, 3 (rights to just conditions of work and to safe and healthy working conditions), 9, 10, and 15 (rights to vocational guidance, training, and rehabilitation, respectively) – see *Fourth Report on Certain Provisions of the Charter Which Have Not Been Accepted, cit.*, p. 20. The ECSR also considers that any denial of access to vocational training, which reflects discrimination against migrant workers who are nationals of other Parties, is incompatible with the Charter, even if it just affects some migrants – see ECSR, Conclusions VII (1981), United Kingdom.

70 ECSR, Conclusions 2019, Turkey.

which they are entitled after contract termination.[71] And, according to Stefan Clauwaert, it is crystal-clear from the case law that, both in relation to equality of employment and working conditions, any length of residence requirement is contrary to the Charter.[72]

The ECSR has also noted that it is not sufficient for a government to prove the absence of discrimination merely in terms of the law. It must also show that there is no discrimination in practice or inform the supervisory organs of any practical measures taken to remedy cases of discrimination.[73] In particular, the Committee stressed that in order to monitor and ensure that no discrimination occurs in practice, States Parties should have in place sufficient effective monitoring procedures or bodies to collect information, for example disaggregated data on remuneration or information on cases in employment tribunals.[74]

Finally, the Committee stressed that the need to ensure equality of treatment with regard to employment is increasing in importance and poses particular problems during periods when most contracting Parties are suffering from economic recession. In that case, the concerned countries should take specific action to avoid discrimination to the extent that an increase in the level of unemployment is likely to have a particular impact on this category of workers.[75]

Concerning the right to equal treatment regarding the membership of trade unions and the enjoyment of the benefits of collective bargaining, the Charter requires States Parties to take action to eliminate all legal and *de facto* discrimination concerning trade union membership and the enjoyment of the benefits of collective bargaining, including the right to be a founding member and to access administrative and managerial posts in trade unions.[76]

Particularly concerning collective bargaining, countries shall act to ensure that migrant workers enjoy equal treatment when it comes to benefiting from

71 Stefan Clauwaert, «The Right of Migrant Workers and their families to Protection and Assistance», *cit.*, p. 352.

72 *Ibid.*, p. 353.

73 ECSR, Conclusions III (1973), Statement of Interpretation of Article 19 § 4.

74 ECSR, Conclusions XX-4 (2015), Germany.

75 ECSR, Conclusions IV (1975), Statement of Interpretation of Article 19 § 4.

76 ECSR, Conclusions XIII-3 (1995), Turkey; ECSR, Conclusions 2011, Statement of Interpretation of Article 19 § 4b; ECSR, Conclusions XIX-4 (2011), Luxembourg. The Committee has stressed that these issues also concern Article 5 (right to organize) and Article 6 (right to collective bargaining – particularly, paragraph 2). Therefore, discrimination observed in one of these matters may lead to a negative conclusion on Article 19 § 4 and Article 5 (and, even though the document does not allude to it, also regarding Article 6) – see *Fourth Report on Certain Provisions of the Charter Which Have Not Been Accepted*, *cit.*, p. 21.

collective agreements aimed at implementing the principle of equal pay for equal work for all workers at the workplace, or from legitimate collective action in support of such an agreement, in accordance with domestic laws or practice.[77] The same non-discrimination requirement is also valid for eligibility criteria regarding work councils and other official bodies involving both management and labor, such as employment tribunals, social security institutions, public bodies representing trades and professions, among others.[78]

Finally, on the matter of accommodation,[79] the contracting Parties should undertake to eliminate all legal and *de facto* discrimination concerning access to public and private housing,[80] regarding home–

77 *Digest of the Case Law of the European Committee of Social Rights*, *cit.*, p. 182.

78 Stefan Clauwaert, «The Right of Migrant Workers and their Families to Protection and Assistance», *cit.*, p. 354; ECSR, Conclusions, XV-1 (2000), Luxembourg. And, as noted by the Author, any length of residence requirement is contrary to the Charter. Furthermore, on the *Laval* decision (ECSR, *Swedish Trade Union Confederation (LO) and Swedish Confederation of Professional Employees (TCO) v. Sweden*, complaint No. 85/2012, decision on the merits of 3 July 2007), the ECSR stated that withdrawing the requirement of foreign companies to appoint a contact person to negotiate and conclude collective agreements with Swedish trade unions is a violation of Article 19 § 4 (since foreign companies should be treated equally by the host country when using posted workers). This provision is also encroached when collective action is forbidden due to the fact that employers provide posted workers with conditions as favourable as the minimum ones contained in a collective agreement concluded at central level. In fact, as stressed by Stefan Clauwaert, «The Right of Migrant Workers and their Families to Protection and Assistance», *cit.*, p. 354, when posted workers are applied a limited scope of working conditions, that could be regulated through collective agreement, preventing collective action will make it unlikely that employers will grant posted workers more favourable conditions, since there will be no effective negotiating method within the employees' reach to persuade the employer. However, as stressed by the Author, in another case, the ECSR found no violation of Article E (on non-discrimination) in conjunction with Article 19 § 4, when French authorities refused to grant civilian officials of the French military forces stationed in Germany a certain benefit in the career structure of public officials for the sole reason that their former contracts were private law contracts under German labour legislation. Using the criterion "other status", mentioned in Article E, the Committee considered that, although they all were working abroad, there was no discrimination because of the different conditions of their recruitment and the legal status which applied to them – see ECSR, *Confédération française démocratique du travail (CFDT) v. France*, complaint No. 50/2008, decision on the merits of 9 September 2009.

79 The Committee has noted that this matter also concerns Article 16 (right of the family to social, legal, and economic protection) – see *Fourth Report on Certain Provisions of the Charter Which Have Not Been Accepted*, *cit.*, p. 21.

80 See ECSR, *European Roma Rights Centre (ERRC) v. France*,complaint No. 51/2008, decision on the merits of 19 October 2009, §§ 111–113; ECSR, *Centre on Housing Rights and Evictions (COHRE) v. Italy*, complaint No. 58/2009, decision on the merits of 25 June 2010, §§ 145–147 (finding of violation of Article E taken in conjunction with Article 19 § 4c).

buying,[81] house renting, or access to subsidised housing or housing aids, such as loans or other allowances.[82] Consequently, a legal restriction regarding the acquisition or renting of accommodation by a migrant worker would be contrary to Article 19 § 4.[83] So too would the limitation of financial assistance for housing to nationals of the host state or to nationals of Charter Parties that are EU or European Economic Area (EEA) agreement Parties.[84]

Furthermore, the ECSR has stated that economic obstacles to achieving full provision of social housing to those eligible do not provide a valid reason to discriminate against nationals of non-EU States.[85]

As stated by Pascale Boucaud,[86] the main difficulty regarding equal treatment in respect of housing is the existence of length of residence requirements which are the same for nationals and foreigners.In fact, even though, in appearance, both categories receive the same treatment, in practice, this kind of requirement is harder for foreigners to comply with.[87]

81 ECSR, Conclusions IV (1975), Norway.

82 Matti Mikkola, «Social Human Rights of Migrants under the European Social Charter», *cit.*, p. 49; ECSR, Conclusions III (1973), Italy. And the right to equal treatment provided in Article 19 § 4(c) can only be effective if there is a right of appeal before an independent body against the relevant administrative decisions – see ECSR, *European Federation of National Organisations working with the Homeless* (FEANTSA) *v. the Netherlands*, complaint No. 86/2012, decision on the merits of 2 July 2014, § 204. However, Matti Mikkola, «Social Human Rights of Migrants under The European Social Charter», *cit.*, p. 49, notes that the Committee has not aligned itself clearly in respect of what the States may require of migrant's work and residence permits before allowing equal access to the queue for social housing. This issue was addressed in 2004 and 2006, in the context of the reporting procedures, but the ECSR did not conclude negatively on the Italian legislation that demanded that a person should have a longer-term residence permit before being eligible to queue for rental housing. For those ineligible, the law guaranteed temporary shelter, usually at a reception centre.

83 ECSR, Conclusions V (1977), Norway. A restriction on the location of a migrant worker's residence would also infringe on this provision – see ECSR, Conclusions VI (1979), Germany. According to David Harris and John Darcy, *The European Social Charter*, *cit.*, p. 224, in recent cycles, the Committee has concerned itself with the quality of housing provided for immigrant workers on the basis that the provision of unhealthy, unsafe, or otherwise low-level housing might be demonstrably unequal when compared with the housing afforded to nationals – see also ECSR, Conclusions IX-2 (1986), France and ECSR, Conclusions XIII-2 (1994), Belgium.

84 ECSR, Conclusions XIII-3 (1995), Portugal; ECSR, Conclusions XIV-1 (1998), UK.

85 ECSR, Conclusions 2015, Slovenia.

86 Pascale Boucaud, *Migrant Workers and their Families Protection within The European Social Charter*, *cit.*, p. 38.

87 ECSR, Conclusions V (1975), Norway.

In turn, the requirement of a period of residence in the state or geographical area as condition of eligibility for public housing has been considered, by the ECSR, as indirect discrimination, since it is more difficult for non-national migrant workers to comply with it and it cannot be justified by reasons of good public interest.[88] However, there are some indications that the Committee will not find a breach where the number of contracting Party nationals affected by the requirement is *de minimis*.[89]

Furthermore, concerning the passage "in so far as such matters are regulated by law or regulations or are subject to the control of administrative authorities", the Committee made it clear that if in a given state these matters are not regulated by law or regulations, nor subject to the control of the state's administrative authorities, the contracting Party cannot be regarded as failing to comply with the provisions of said paragraph.[90]

VI Article 19 § 5: Right to an Equal Treatment with Regard to Employment Taxes, Dues or Contributions Payable in Respect of Employed Persons

Following this paragraph, migrant workers are entitled to an equal treatment in law and in practice concerning the payment of employment taxes, dues, or contributions.[91] What is more, according to the ECSR, a tax allowance for dependent children that is limited to those habitually resident in the state concerned is a *de facto* discrimination, encroaching on Article 19 § 5, *vis-à-vis* migrant workers who are nationals of other Charter Parties.[92]

88 David Harris and John Darcy, *The European Social Charter*, *cit.*, p 223; ECSR, Conclusions V (1975), Norway; ECSR, Conclusions XI-1 (1989), Norway, among others. The Authors stress that, while earlier, the Committee had, incorrectly, referred to a *de facto* discrimination, it now uses the established discrimination law term "indirect discrimination" (*cit.*, p. 223, ft. 1442).

89 David Harris and John Darcy, *The European Social Charter*, *cit.*, p. 224; Conclusions XIII-2 (1994) Norway; Conclusions XIII-2 (1994), Spain.

90 ECSR, Conclusions II (1971), Statement of Interpretation of Article 19 § 4.

91 ECSR, Conclusions II (1971), Norway; ECSR, Conclusions XIX-4 (2011), Greece.

92 ECSR, Conclusions XI-2 (1990), Germany. Similarly, the obligation imposed on an employer to contribute substantially to the cost of language of a migrant worker is in breach of Article 19 § 5, constituting a *de facto* discrimination, as it leads employers to prefer local employees – see ECSR, Conclusions VII (1981), Sweden.

VII Article 19 § 6: Right of Reunion of the Families of Migrant Workers

Similarly to the ILO Migrant Workers Convention (Supplementary Provisions), of 1975, § 6 of Article 19 of the ESC provides that contracting Parties shall adopt measures "to facilitate as far as possible the reunion of the family of a foreign worker permitted to establish himself in the territory".

The Appendix clarifies the significance of the expression *family of a foreign worker* for these effects: the "worker's spouse and unmarried children, as long as the latter are considered to be minors by the receiving State and are dependent on the migrant worker".[93] According to the ECSR, dependent children are understood as being those who have no independent existence outside the family group, particularly for economic or health reasons, or because they are pursuing unpaid studies.[94]

The right to family reunion seems to apply to a narrower circle of cases than the rest of Article 19. In fact, this right is applicable only when the worker is "permitted to establish himself in the territory", which, apparently, indicates that he/she has to be *settled*.[95] This right to settlement may differ from one Party to another.

While the term *facilitate* signifies that any legal obstacle to family reunion shall be removed,[96] it is also true that contracting Parties are only obliged to promote that reunion "as far as possible"; they are not obliged to ensure that result.

The establishment of a reasonable[97] waiting period for the family to be allowed to join the worker within the territory is admissible, if legally provided.[98]

The requirement that the migrant has an accommodation was already found admissible.[99] However, the general rule is that the requirement of having

---

93 The original version of the Charter mentioned children under twenty-one years, which was not in accordance with the national systems of several Parties that reduced the age of majority below twenty-one after having ratified the Charter. See David Harris and John Darcy, *The European Social Charter*, *cit.*, p. 226. That same original version referred to the worker's *wife*, instead of *spouse*, which obviously was not adequate to gender equality requirements (was the husband of a female worker covered by the provision?).

94 ECSR, Conclusions VIII (1984), Statement of Interpretation of Article 19 § 6.

95 *Idem*, pp. 226–227.

96 ECSR, Conclusions II, Cyprus.

97 A one-year period is acceptable, but a period of eighteen months or more constitutes a breach of the ESC (ECSR, Conclusions I (1969), Germany; ECSR, Conclusions (2011), Statement of Interpretation of Article 19 § 6; ECSR, Conclusions (2011), France; ECSR, Conclusions (2011), Cyprus).

98 ECSR, Conclusions VI (1979), Germany.

99 ECSR, Conclusions X (1988), Italy.

sufficient or suitable accommodation to house the family or certain family members should not be so restrictive as to prevent any family reunion;[100] States are entitled to impose such accommodation requirements in a proportionate manner so as to protect the interests of the family and in consideration of individual circumstances.[101]

Similarly, the requirement of the worker to be financially able to support the family may be admissible, but the level of means required by States Parties to bring in the family or certain family members should not be so restrictive as to prevent any family reunion.[102] On the contrary, requiring that both parents of a dependent child be resident is not permitted,[103] nor is the exclusion on grounds of a disease, even if contagious, unless in particularly serious cases that endanger public health.[104]

Although Parties may take measures to encourage the integration of migrant workers and their family members, requirements that family members pass language and/or integration tests or complete compulsory courses, whether imposed prior to or after entry to the State, may impede family reunion and are therefore contrary to Article 19 § 6 of the Charter where they: a) have the potential effect of denying entry or the right to remain to family members of a migrant worker, or b) otherwise deprive the right guaranteed under Article 19 § 6 of its substance, for example by imposing prohibitive fees, or by failing to consider specific individual circumstances such as age, level of education or family or work commitments.[105]

Besides eliminating obstacles to family reunion, the Parties are also bound by the obligation to provide "appropriate practical administrative and social measures" and to facilitate reunion, "particularly in regard of housing".[106]

100 ECSR, Conclusions IV (1975), Norway.

101 ECSR, Conclusions (2015), Statement of Interpretation of Article 19 § 6.

102 ECSR, Conclusions XVII-1 (2004), the Netherlands; ECSR, Conclusions (2011), Statement of Interpretation of Article 19 § 6.

103 ECSR, Conclusions XIII (1994), Germany.

104 Diseases requiring quarantine which are stipulated in the World Health Organisation's International Health Regulations of 1969, or other serious contagious or infectious diseases such as tuberculosis or syphilis. Very serious drug addiction or mental illness may justify refusal of family reunion, but only where the authorities establish, on a case-by-case basis, that the illness or condition constitutes a threat to public order or security. ECSR, Conclusions III (1973), Austria; ECSR, Conclusions X-1 (1987), Greece; ECSR, Conclusions XIII-2 (1994), Spain; ECSR, Conclusions VIII (1984) and IX-1 (1985), the Netherlands; ECSR, Conclusions XVI-1 (2003), Greece; ECSR, conclusions XV-1 (2000), Finland.

105 ECSR, Conclusions (2015), Statement of Interpretation of Article 19 § 6.

106 ECSR, Conclusions I (1969), Norway; ECSR, Conclusions II (1971), Cyprus; ECSR, Conclusions III (1973), Cyprus, ECSR, conclusions V (1977), Austria; ECSR, conclusions V (1977), France.

Migrant worker's family members, who have joined him or her through family reunion, may not be expelled as a consequence of his or her own expulsion, since these family members have an independent right to stay in the territory. As long as a migrant worker's family members hold a right of residence, it must not be possible to remove them, even if the migrant worker has personally lost this right, except where they endanger national security or offend against public interest or morality.[107]

Restrictions on the exercise of the right to family reunion should be subject to an effective mechanism of appeal or review, which provides an opportunity for consideration of the individual merits of the case consistent with the principles of proportionality and reasonableness.[108]

VIII Article 19 § 7: Right of Access to Legal Proceedings Relating to Matters Referred to in This Article

According to this paragraph, the Parties are obliged to secure for migrant workers lawfully within their territories treatment no less favourable than that of their own nationals in respect of legal proceedings relating to matters referred to in Article 19. States must grant access to courts, lawyers, and legal support upon the same conditions as nationals,[109] concerning all legal proceedings regarding the rights provided in Article 19.[110]

Any migrant worker residing or working lawfully within the territory of a State Party who is involved in legal or administrative proceedings and does not have counsel of his or her own choosing should be advised that he/she may appoint counsel and, if necessary, be provided with counsel, free of charge if he/she does not have sufficient means, as is the case for nationals or should be by virtue of the ESC. Under the same conditions (involvement of a migrant worker in legal or administrative proceedings), whenever the interests of justice so require, a migrant worker must have the free assistance of an interpreter if he or she cannot properly understand or speak the national language used in the proceedings and have any necessary documents translated. Such legal assistance should be extended to obligatory pre-trial proceedings.[111]

107 ECSR, Conclusions XVI-1 (2003), the Netherlands (Article 19 § 8); ECSR, conclusions 2015, Statement of Interpretation of Articles 19 § 6 and 19 § 8.

108 ECSR, Conclusions (2015), Statement of Interpretation of Article 19 § 6.

109 ECSR, Conclusions I (1969), Italy, Norway, United-Kingdom.

110 ECSR, Conclusions I (1969), Germany.

111 ECSR, Conclusions (2011), Statement of Interpretation of Article 19 § 7.

IX Article 19 § 8: Right of Not Being Expelled Unless under Exceptional Circumstances

This paragraph obliges contracting Parties to legally prohibit the expulsion of migrants lawfully residing within their territories, unless they are a threat to national security or offend against public interest or morality.[112]

This right only applies to migrant workers *lawfully residing* within the territory of a contracting Party, that is, workers "in possession of all papers legally required by the country of residence for regular residence, including, if need be, a resident permit and a work permit".[113] However, national legislation shall reflect the implications of Articles 18 § 1 and 19 § 8, as well as the case law of the ECHR: foreign nationals who have been resident for a sufficient length of time in a state, either legally or with the tacit acceptance of their illegal status by the authorities in view of the host country's needs, should be covered by the rules protecting from deportation.[114]

As David Harris and John Darcy[115] explain, the expression *public interest* shall be understood as meaning the equivalent to *ordre public*, the term used in the French version, which has a reasonably clear scope – the protection of the existing State institutions and social order.[116] The reference to morality has the significance of compliance with *bonnes moeurs*, that is a legal term, whereas *morality* is not.

According to the ECSR's case law, such expulsions can only be in conformity with the Charter if they are ordered by a court or a judicial authority, or by an administrative body whose decisions are subject to judicial review. These sorts of rulings shall not occur unless the individual concerned has been convicted of a serious criminal offence, or has been involved in activities which constitute a substantive threat to national security, the public interest or public morality. Furthermore, expulsion orders must be proportionate, taking into account all aspects of the non-nationals' behaviour, as well as the circumstances and the length of time of his/her presence in the territory of the State, and the individual's connection or ties with both the host state and the state of origin. Furthermore, the strength of any family relationships that he/she may have

112 ECSR, Conclusions VI (1979), Cyprus.
113 ECSR, Conclusions II (1971), Cyprus.
114 ECSR, Conclusions (2011), Statement of Interpretation of Article 19 § 8.
115 *The European Social Charter*, *cit.*, p. 231–232.
116 Examples can be found in ECSR, Conclusions XIV-1 (1998), Italy; ECSR, Conclusions XIV-1 (1998), Germany; ECSR, Conclusions XIII-4 (1996), the Netherlands; ECSR, Conclusions XIII-1 (1993), Turkey, or ECSR, Conclusions XIII-1 (1993), Sweden.

formed during this period, must also be considered in determining whether expulsion is proportionate.[117]

Risks to public health cannot constitute a ground for expulsion, unless the person refuses to undergo suitable treatment.[118] Also, the fact that a migrant worker is dependent on social assistance shall not be regarded as a threat against public order and is not a ground for expulsion.[119] Unemployment or a general situation of high unemployment are not reasonable reasons for expulsion.

The Committee considers that there is no compliance with the Charter if, according to the national regime, a migrant worker's family members who have settled in a Contracting Party's territory as a result of family reunion may be expelled when the migrant worker is expelled.[120] However, according to the most recent case law, this situation is to be assessed in the context of § 6 and not at the level of § 8.[121]

States Parties must ensure that foreign nationals served with expulsion orders have a right of appeal to a court or other independent body, even in cases where national security, public order or morality are at stake.[122] Furthermore, the Committee stressed that an appeal must be available and exercisable prior to deportation.[123]

---

117 ECSR, Conclusions (2015), Statement of Interpretation of Article 19 § 8.

118 ECSR, Conclusions V (1977), Germany; ECSR, Conclusions XIII-2 (1994), Germany; ECSR, Conclusions XIII-3 (1995), Finland; ECSR, Conclusions XIV-1 (1998), Turkey; ECSR, Conclusions XIV-1 (1998), Germany. See David Harris and John Darcy, *The European Social Charter*, *cit.*, p. 233–234.

119 ECSR, Conclusions V (1977), Italy. If a decision of expulsion from the territory of a State Party, which is also a member of the European Union, may be taken against citizens of the European Union (as well as nationals of another State Party to the Charter), in the situation where, through lack of resources, these persons are likely to become a burden on the social assistance system, it is necessary – in application of the principle of proportionality – that the burden of coverage of the persons concerned by the system of social assistance be excessive, even unreasonable, such that it could render expulsion necessary so as to relieve the State of this burden (ECSR, *European Roma and Travellers Forum v. France*, 24 January 2012, collective complaint No. 64/2011, §§ 55–66).

120 ECSR, Conclusions (2011), the Netherlands. See also: ECSR, Conclusions XIX-4 (2019), United Kingdom.

121 ECSR, Conclusions (2015), the Netherlands.

122 ECSR, Conclusions V (1977), United Kingdom.

123 ECSR, Conclusions XX-4 (2015), United Kingdom; ECSR, Conclusions (2015), the Netherlands.

Collective expulsions are not in conformity with the Charter; decisions on expulsion may be made only on the basis of a reasonable and objective examination of the particular situation of each individual.[124]

X Article 19 § 9: Right of Transfer of Earnings and Savings

This provision obliges States Parties not to place excessive restrictions on the right of migrants to transfer earnings and savings, either during their stay or when they leave their host country.[125] Migrants must be allowed to transfer money to their own country or any other country. The right to transfer earnings and savings includes the right to transfer movable property.[126] Limits to the amount of the transfer may be permitted,[127] as well as its submission to formal requirements.[128] A migrant worker must not be subject to restrictions that are more severe than those found reasonable by the Committee, irrespective of the treatment given to nationals.[129]

XI Article 19 § 10: Extension to Self-Employed Workers

According to this provision, States Parties must extend the rights provided for in paragraphs 1 to 9, 11 and 12 to self-employed migrant workers and their families.[130]

States Parties must ensure that there is no unjustified treatment, in law or in practice, between wage-earners and self-employed migrants. In addition, equal treatment between self-employed migrants and self-employed nationals

---

124 ECSR, *Centre on Housing Rights and Evictions* (COHRE) *v. Italy*, collective complaint No. 58/2009, decision on the merits of 25 June 2010, §§ 155–158; ECSR, *Centre on Housing Rights and Evictions* (COHRE) *v. France*, collective complaint No. 63/2010, decision on the merits of 28 June 2011, §§ 68–79; ECSR, *European Roma and Travellers Forum* (ERTF) *v. France*, collective complaint No. 64/2011, decision on the merits of 24 January 2012, §§ 51–67; ECSR, *Médecins du Monde – International v. France*, collective complaint No. 67/2011, decision on the merits of 11 September 2012, §§ 112–117. For references to similar case law of the ECtHR, concerning article 8 of the ECSR, see Karin Lucas, *The Revised European Charter, cit.*, p. 255.

125 ECSR, Conclusions I (1969), Norway, Conclusions XIII-1 (2006), Greece.

126 ECSR, Conclusions (2011), Statement of Interpretation of Article 19 § 9.

127 ECSR, Conclusions I (1969), United Kingdom.

128 ECSR, Conclusions XI-2 (1990), France.

129 ECSR, Conclusions IV (1975), Italy, Conclusions V (1977), France.

130 ECSR, Conclusions I (1969), Norway.

must be guaranteed in the areas covered by this provision. A finding of non-conformity under §§ 1 to 9, 11 and/or 12 of Article 19 may lead to a finding of non-conformity under § 10.[131]

XII Article 19 § 11: Right to the Teaching of the National Language(S) of the Receiving State

In Article 19 § 11, the ESC establishes the Parties' obligation to facilitate and promote the teaching of the national language of the host State, or at least one of the national languages, among migrant workers and their family members. Yet this commitment only binds certain States, which decided to prioritize the importance of knowing the language of the host State as an instrument of integration into the labour market and the society.

Introduced by the Revised Charter, such provision demonstrates a willingness to enhance the protection of social rights in the European context. This obligation was not reflected in the ESC of 1961, since it is a result of current international concerns regarding migrant workers and their families. In fact, as social changes determined the need for renovation, they gave the ESC a "fresh impetus"[132] not only with respect to rights already declared but also by enshrining new rights, including the teaching of the host State's language to migrant workers and their families. It represents a step towards a broader protection and a recognition of the importance of language skills in the lives of those who are trying to succeed socially and professionally in a different State.

Migration is an unavoidable element of human life[133] and should not be a rhetorical or isolated concern of States. In this regard, knowing the language of the host State is essential for the integration of both workers and their family members and for a better understanding of the working context, daily life, functioning of national institutions, and rights and mechanisms provided for their protection. Thus, this is a fundamental right with a social nature founded in the principle of human dignity, requiring national consideration and implementation within a framework of social priorities assumed by the State. Yet,

131 ECSR, Conclusions XIV-1 (1998), Germany.

132 See Preamble of the Revised Charter.

133 See Pilar Charro Baena, «Derecho de los Trabajadores Nigrantes y sus Familias a Protección y Asistencia – Artículo 19 de la Carta Social Europea», in Cristina Monereo Atienza and José Luis Monereo Pérez (eds.), *La Garantía Multinivel de los Derechos Fundamentales en el Consejo de Europa: el Convenio Europeo de Derechos Humanos y la Carta Social Europea*, Granada (Spain), Comares, 2017, p. 746.

it should be noted that not all States possess the same level of social development (or State budget) to effectively ensure this commitment.[134]

Understanding the application of the ESCR requires the recognition that the Charter, regardless of its *nomen iuris*, is an international treaty to which States are bound only if they wish to and in a way that matches their will, and to which the Vienna Convention on the Law of Treaties of 1969 is applicable. The interpretation of the ESCR entails the perception of social rights as a States' political commitment.

Regarding to the Parties' commitment, the Committee, in its Conclusions of 2015, affirmed that situations in Armenia, Georgia, the Netherlands and Turkey were not in conformity with the Revised Charter and, in 2017, it maintained its position with respect to Turkey's case and deferred its decision on Georgia pending the receipt of further information. These non-conformity assessments resulted mainly from the absence of adult education programmes or the non-gratuity of such programmes.[135]

On 29 March 2021, Germany deposited an interpretative declaration, simultaneously with its instrument of ratification, in which it clarified its understanding of the obligation to promote and facilitate the teaching of the German language. According to this declaration, Germany believes that the obligation provided for in Article 19 § 11 is only applicable to migrant workers in need of integration into society who lawfully and permanently reside in the country's territory to engage in a gainful occupation. Regarding family members of those migrant workers, such obligation only exists, for the Federal Republic of Germany, to the extent that they lawfully and permanently reside in German territory and that they are in need of social integration. In accordance with the principle of equal treatment laid down in Article 19 § 10 of the ESCR, the scope of the right at issue includes migrant workers either employed or self-employed, regardless of gender,[136] and their family members. The decisive criterion regarding this right is not the nature of the work, but its regularity or the duration of legal residence. It should be noted that the scope of the ESCR,

---

134 Social rights need legislative intervention regarding implementation of their content, which depends on economic fluctuations and available resources at that historic moment. About social rights, see Marie-Françoise Vallette, «Chronique Juridique – Protection et Promotion des Droits Sociaux des Migrants par le Comité Européen des Droits Sociaux», *cit.*, pp. 157 ff.; Catarina Santos Botelho, «40 anos de Direitos Sociais – Uma Reflexão sobre o Papel dos Direitos Fundamentais Sociais no século XXI», *Julgar*, No. 29, 2016, pp. 197–216; Manuel Afonso Vaz *et al.*, *Direito Constitucional o Sistema Constitucional Português*, 2nd ed., Universidade Católica Portuguesa, Porto, 2015, pp. 285 ff.

135 ECSR, Conclusions (2015), Armenia, Georgia, The Netherlands, Turkey.

136 ECSR, Conclusions IV (1972), Statement of Interpretation of Article 19 § 6.

established in the Appendix, refers to «persons» and not to «workers»,[137] which encompasses the protection of job seekers as well. Regarding migrant workers' families, the Appendix clarifies that at least workers' spouses and minor children should be considered family members for the purposes of Article 19 § 6. Thus, if this is the minimum standard for the right to family reunification, allowing a reunion of workers' families in the host State should also guarantee other rights, such as the right to learn the language of the host State.

The monitoring of the application of the Revised Charter – through reports in which States set out the conditions for the application of the provisions they have accepted – allows for the elaboration of Conclusions. The Committee had already indicated the effort States should make to provide additional assistance to migrants' children who had not attended primary school from the beginning and who therefore fell behind their fellow national students.[138] As regards adult migrant workers and their adult family members, the Committee recalled that the ESCR established the obligation to encourage employers, voluntary organizations, and public establishments, such as universities, to organize, free of charge, national language courses.

It can also be inferred that Article 19 is not included in the list of Articles whose protection applies only to nationals of Contracting Parties and who legally reside or regularly work in the territory of one of these States; this would appear to reflect the intention to not exclude the protection of other individuals. Turning attention back to the original Charter, it did not intend to be applicable to all individuals on the Parties' territory[139] as reaffirmed by the Revised Charter's Appendix. Therefore, at first sight, it appears that nationals of third States would be excluded from its scope, except for refugees and stateless persons, entitled to the treatment in accordance with the abovementioned Appendix. However, in the collective complaint *International Federation of Human Rights Leagues (FIDH) v. France*, the Committee conceded the extension of some level of protection to nationals of other States.[140] Motivated by the emergence of the need to protect families and their integration into society, the international legislator seems to have admitted that this right is not

137 On this issue, see Stefan Clauwaert, «The Right of Migrant Workers and their Families to Protection and Assistance», *cit.*

138 ECSR, Conclusions 2006, Portugal.

139 Colm O'cinnéide, «Migrant Rights under the European Social Charter», *cit.*, p. 288.

140 ECSR, *International Federation of Human Rights Leagues (FIDH) v. France*, collective complaint No. 14/2003, decision on the merits of 8 September 2004. In this case, the Committee extended the scope of the right to emergency social and medical assistance to foreigners in an irregular situation. See Colm O'Cinnéide, «Migrant Rights under the European Social Charter», *cit.*, pp. 290–291.

limited by law to nationals of contracting States and that it should at least be granted to members of migrant workers' families, regardless of their nationality and their residence in the receiving State.[141] This option may be grounded on the protection against any form of discrimination under Article E of the ESCR (which already resulted from the Preamble of the Charter of 1961) and on its universal ambitions,[142] even with the limitation regarding the compliance with certain conditions, such as the requirement of legal residence or regular work in the host State.

International recognition of the importance of knowing the language of the host State is transversal to other institutions such as the Council of the European Union, which has long stated that "basic knowledge of the host society's language, history, and institutions is indispensable to integration",[143] and the ILO has stressed that learning the national language is essential to ensuring the transition to the country of employment and avoiding marginalization, and considers language the most important tool for success in the labour market and a prerequisite for social integration.[144]

XIII Article 19 § 12: Children's Right to Learn the Migrant Worker's Mother Tongue

Article 19 § 12 of the ESCR enshrines the commitment to promote and facilitate, as far as practicable, the teaching of the migrant workers' mother tongue to their children, seeking to complement the previous provision and to protect the education of migrant workers' children with unequivocal similarities to the protection under Articles 14 § 2 and 15 of the European Convention on the Legal Status of Migrant Workers.[145] Education is undoubtedly a central concern of the ESCR, also reflected in other provisions, such as Article 7(3), 9, 10 and 17 § 1(a) and § 2. However, the expression 'as far as practicable' gives "a wide margin of discretion in its implementation".[146]

---

141 Colm O'Cinnéide, «Migrant Rights under the European Social Charter», *cit.*, pp. 288–289.

142 *Ibid.*

143 Brussels, 19 November 2004, 14615/04 (Presse 321).

144 See for instance: ILO, Report III (1B), *Migrant Workers*, 87th Session, Geneva, June 1999. OECD, ILO, World Bank IMF, *Towards a Framework for Fair and Effective Integration of Migrants into the Labour Market*, 19–21 December 2016.

145 Klaus Dieter Beiter, *The Protection of the Right to Education by International Law: Including a Systematic Analysis of* Article *13 of the International Covenant on Economic, Social and Cultural Rights*, Brill/Nijhoff, 2006, p. 177 ff.

146 Karin Lucas, *The Revised European Charter, cit.*, p. 257.

The Revised Charter constitutes a broad and complex international instrument for the protection of social rights,[147] whose provisions reflect States' political commitments in this respect.[148] This provision is part of Article 19, which has been excluded from the range of Articles to which the Appendix recognises exclusive application to contracting States' nationals. Accordingly it forms a part of the cornerstone for universality: at least in regards to workers' children, no contracting Party's nationality is required, in order to grant them the right to learning their parents' mother tongue.

In 2006, the Committee's Conclusions on French Report indicated that, in secondary school, those children should have a real opportunity to choose a foreign language so they could effectively study the language of their country of origin.[149] Five years later, the Committee[150] clarified that teaching migrant workers' mother tongue to their children contributed to the preservation of their cultural identity and the promotion of their psychological and mental balance which, consequently, would be beneficial for their active participation in society and their understanding of different cultural identities. Contracting States should, accordingly, teach the most widely represented/spoken languages (and not all languages spoken) to migrants legally resident or regularly employed in their territory, either in schools or in other contexts, such as voluntary associations or non-governmental organizations.

Finally, in the Conclusions presented in 2015, the Committee considered that Turkey was not respecting the application of this provision (as reiterated in its Conclusions of 2017) and requested further information to take a position on compliance with the ESCR in relation to Armenia, Cyprus, Georgia, Latvia and Montenegro as well.

Concluding Remarks

This provision aims to protect migrants through a multidimensional perspective that goes beyond the auspices of other regulations of this kind, given its

147 Giuseppe Palmisano, «Sui Limiti di Applicazione della Carta Sociale Europea in Termini di Persone Protette», in Marilisa D'Amico, Giovanni Guiglia and Benedetta Liberali (eds.), *La Carta Sociale Europea e la Tutela dei Diritti Sociali. Atti del Convegno del 18 gennaio 2013 Università degli Studi di Milano*, Edizioni Scientifichi Italiane, Napoli, 2013, pp. 39–58 and sp. 39–60.

148 Colm O'Cinnéide, «Migrant Rights under the European Social Charter», *cit.*, p. 302.

149 ECSR, Conclusions 2006, France.

150 ECSR, Conclusions 2011, Statement of Interpretation of Article 19 § 12.

wording and the jurisprudence of the ECSR. It enshrines a fuller and richer approach to the issue of migration and migrants' protection (an issue that, due to recent events, has assumed greater pertinence), conveying the social dimension of the (R)ESC.

Still, as noted by Karin Lukas,[151] Article 19 is among the least ratified and most difficult provisions to implement, which is closely related to the sensitive nature of its themes. This is a scenario that, in all probability, will not be soon reversed, given the economic crisis and the so-called "refugee crisis".

---

151 Karin Lukas, *The Revised European Social Charter*, *cit.*, p. 258.

Selected Bibliography

Açimuz B. and Akbulut O., "The Values Underlying the European Social Charter", in Angeleri S. and Nivard C. (eds.), *The European Social Charter: A Commentary,* vol. 1, *Cross-cutting Themes*, Leiden, Brill/Nijhoff Academic Publishers, 2022, pp. 264 ff.

Akandji-Kombé J-F., "La justiciabilité des droits sociaux et de la Charte sociale européenne n'est pas une utopie", *in L'Homme dans la société internationale: Mélanges en hommage au professeur Paul Tavernier*, Brussels, Bruylant, 2013, pp. 475 ff.

Ales E. *et al.* (eds.), *International and European Labour Law: A commentary*, Nomos Verlagsgesellschaft mbH and Co. KG, 2017.

Alston P., "Report of the Special Rapporteur on extreme poverty and human rights. The implementation of the right to social protection through the adoption of social protection floors", A/69/297, 11 August 2014.

Aneja N., "Human Rights of Persons with Disabilities: Contemporary Developments", *International Journal of Law Management & Humanities*, no. 5, 2022, pp. 1004 ff.

Angeleri S. and Nivard C. (eds.), *The European Social Charter: A Commentary*, vol. I: *Cross-cutting Themes,* Leiden, Brill, 2022.

Angeleri S., 'The Impact of the Economic Crisis on the Right to Health of Irregular Migrants, as Reflected in the Jurisprudence of the UN Committee on Economic, Social and Cultural Rights', *European Journal of Migration and Law*, No. 19(2), 2017, pp. 165–190.

Aranguiz A. and Quené M., "Is There a Way Where There's a Will? The Tensions between the Court's Case Law and the Pillar in Delimiting Transnational Solidarity", *European Journal of Migration and Law*, no. 21, 2019, pp. 509 ff.

Association of Research on Constitutional Law (ARCL), "Statement on the Presidential Decision on the Istanbul Convention", available at https://anayasader.org/statement-from-the-association-of-constitutional-research-on-the-presidential-decision-on-the-istanbul-convention.

Awad I., "Les travailleurs migrants", in Thouvenin J-M. et Trebilcock A. (eds.), *Droit international social. Droits économiques, sociaux et culturels*, tome 2, *Règles de droit international social*, Bruxelles, Brulant, 2013.

Bahle T., Pfeifer M. and Wendt C., "Social Assistance", in Castles F. G. *et al.*, in Kotkas T. and Veitch K. (eds.), *Social Rights in the Welfare State: Origins and Transformations*, London, Routledge, 2016, pp. 448 ff.

Beiter K. D., *The Protection of the Right to Education by International Law: Including a Systematic* Analysis of Article 13 of the International Covenant on Economic, Social and Cultural Rights, Brill/Nijhoff, 2006.

Baldwin P., "The Scandinavian Origins of the Social Interpretation of the Welfare State", 31 *Comparative Studies in Society and History*, vol. 31, no. 1, 1989.

Bamu P. H. and Alfres L., "Why an Enforceable Protocol on Social Protection Is Essential in Africa" (*wiego.org,* 2022), available at https://www.wiego.org/blog/why-enforceable-protocol-social-protection-essential-africa#:~:text=The%20protocol%20calls%20for%20states,and%20adaptation%20of%20general%20schemes.

Baruffi M. C., "Surrogacy in the recent 'multilevel' case law", in Corso P. and Wautelet P. (eds.), *L'accès aux droits de la personne et de la famille en Europe*, Bruxelles, Bruylant, 2022, pp. 85 ff.

Bell M., "Article 15 RESC", in Ales E., Bell M., Deinert O. *et al.* (eds.), *International and European Labour Law*, Baden-Baden, Beck/Hart/Nomos, 2018.

Bestagno F., "La tutela della salute tra competenze dell'Unione europea e degli Stati membri", in Pineschi L. (ed.), *La tutela della salute nel diritto internazionale ed europeo tra interessi globali e interessi particolari,* Napoli, Editoriale Scientifica, 2017, pp. 119 ff.

Betaille J., *Les conditions juridiques de l'effectivité de la norme en droit public interne, illustrations en droit de l'urbanisme et en droit de l'environnement*, Thèse, Université de Limoges, 2012.

Beveridge W., "Full Employment in a Free Society" (The New Statesman and Nation and Reynolds News, 1944) available at http://lib-161.lse.ac.uk/archives/beveridge/9A_79_Full_employment_in_a_free_society.pdf.

Beveridge W., "The Beveridge Report: Social Insurance and Allied Services" (Majesty's Stationery Office, 1942), available at http://news.bbc.co.uk/2/shared/bsp/hi/pdfs/19_07_05_beveridge.pdf.

Biondi Dal Monte F., "Lo Stato Sociale di Fronte alle Migrazioni. Diritti Sociali, Appartenenza e Dignità della Persona", *Rivista del Gruppo di Pisa*, no. 3(12), 2012, pp. 1 ff.

Bleckmann A., "Interprétation et application en droit interne de la Charte sociale européenne, notamment du droit de grève", *Cahiers de droit européen*, no. 4, 1967, pp. 388 ff.

Bothe M., "Les concepts fondamentaux du droit à la santé: le point de vue juridique", in Dupuy R. J., *The Right to Health as a Human Right*, Brill-Nijhoff, Leiden Boston, Colloques/Workshop Series, The Hague Academy of International Law, 1979, pp. 14 ff.

Botelho C. S., "40 anos de Direitos Sociais – Uma Reflexão sobre o Papel dos Direitos Fundamentais Sociais no século XXI", *Julgar*, No. 29, 2016, pp. 197 ff.

Boucaud P., *Migrant Workers and their Families Protection within the European Social Charter*, Strasbourg, Council of Europe Publishing, 1996.

Boyd D. R., "Catalyst for Change. Evaluating Forty Years of Experience in Implementing the Right to a Healthy Environment" in Knox J. H. and Pejan R., *The Human Right to a Healthy Environment*, Cambridge University Press, 2018, pp. 17 ff.

Bredimas A., "The 'decisions' of quasi-judicial bodies on human rights and their place in the domestic legal order of states", *Nomiko Vima*, vol. 66, issue 3, 2019, pp. 417 ff (in Greek).

Brems E., "Indirect Protection of Social Rights by the European Court of Human Rights", *Exploring Social Rights Between Theory and Practice*, in Barak-Erez D. and Gross A. M. (eds.), Oxford/Portland, Hart Publishing, 2007, p.135 ff.

Çali B. and Helfer L., "The Gender of Treaty Withdrawal: Lessons from the Istanbul Convention", available at https://www.ejiltalk.org/the-gender-of-treaty-withdrawal-lessons-from-the-istanbul-convention/.

Casla K., *Politics of International Human Rights Law Promotion in Western Europe*, 1st ed, Routledge, 2022.

Castles F. G. *et al.* (eds.), *The Oxford Handbook of the Welfare State*, Oxford, OUP, 2010.

Chapman A. R. and Russel S. (eds.), *Core Obligations: Building a Framework for Economic, Social and Cultural Rights*, Intersentia NV, Mortsel, 2002.

Charro Baena P., "Derecho de los Trabajadores Migrantes y sus Familias a Protección y Asistencia – Artículo 19 de Carta Social Europea", in Cristina Monereo Atienza C. and Monereo Perez J. L. (eds.) *La Garantía Multinivel de los Derechos Fundamentales en el Consejo de Europa: el Convenio Europeo de Derechos Humanos y la Carta Social Europea*, Granada (Spain), Comares, 2017, pp. 745 ff.

Cholewinski R., *Migrant Workers in International Human Rights Law: Their Protection in Countries of Employment*, Oxford, Clarendon Press, 1997.

Cholewinski R., *The Legal Status of Migrants admitted for Employment. Committee of experts on the legal status and rights of immigrants. A comparative study of law and practice in selected European states*, Strasbourg, Council of Europe Publishing, 2004.

Clauwaert S., "Article 19, § 4. The right of migrants workers and their families to protection and assistance", in Bruun N. *et al.* (eds.), *The European Social Charter and the Employment Relation*, Oxford, Hart Publishing, 2017.

Clifford J., "The UN Disability Convention and its Impact on European Equality Law", *The Equal Rights Review*, vol. 6, 2011, pp. 11 ff.

Council of Europe, *Case-law on the European Social Charter, Supplement No.3*, Council of Europe 1993.

Council of Europe, "Digest of the case law of the European Committee of Social Rights"(CoE, 2022), available at https://rm.coe.int/digest-ecsr-prems-106522-web-en/1680a95dbd.

Council of Europe, *Conclusions of the Committee of Independent Experts of the European Social Charter – Conclusions XIII-1*, Council of Europe, 1998.

Cullen H., "The Collective Complaints System of the European Social Charter: Interpretative Methods of the European Committee of Social Rights", *Human Rights Law Review*, no. 9(1), 2009, pp. 61 ff.

Cullen H., "Is the European Social Charter a Charter for children?", *Irish Jurist*, 2005, vol. 40, pp. 60 ff.

Dalli M., "The Content and Potential of the Right to Social Assistance in Light of Article 13 of the European Social Charter", *European Journal of Social Security*, vol. 22, issue 1, 2020.

D'Amico M. and Guiglia G. (eds.), *European Social Charter and the challenges of the XXI century*, Napoli, Edizioni Scientifiche Italiane, 2014.

D'Auchamp Marie, *Rights of migrant workers in Europe*, published by the Regional Office for Europe of the UN High Commissioner for Human Rights, 2011, available at https://ec.europa.eu/migrant-integration/library-document/migrant-workers-rights-europe_en.

De Beco G., Quinlivan S., and Lord J. E. (eds.), *The Right to Inclusive Education in International Human Rights Law*, Cambridge University Press, 2019.

De Guchteneire P. and Pécoud A., "Introduction: The UN Convention on Migrant Workers' Rights", in Cholewinski R., De Guchteneire P. and Pecoud A. (eds.), *Migration and Human Rights: The United Nations Convention on Migrant Workers' Rights*, Cambridge, Cambridge University Press, 2010.

De Schutter O. and Sant'ana M., "The European Committee of Social Rights (the ECSR)", in De Beco G. (ed.), *Human Rights Monitoring Mechanisms of the Council of Europe*, Oxfordshire, Routledge, 2012, pp. 71 ff.

De Schutter O., "The European Pillar of Social Rights and the Role of the European Social Charter in the EU Legal Order", Study for the Secretariat of the European Social Charter and of the CoE-FRA-ENNHRI-Equinet Platform on Economic and Social Rights, 14 November 2018.

De Schutter O., "The European Social Charter as a tool for the protection of the rights of persons with disabilities, with an emphasis on inclusive education", Work Forum on the Implementation of the UN Convention on the Rights of Persons with Disabilities.

De Schutter O., *The European Social Charter in the context of implementation of the EU Charter of Fundamental Rights*, Study for the European Parliament (PE 536.488), 2016, available online at https://www.europarl.europa.eu/RegData/etudes/STUD/2016/536488/IPOL_STU(2016)536488_EN.pdf.

De Schutter O., "The Two Lives of the European Social Charter", in Carlier J-Y., De Schutter O. and Verdussen M. (eds.), *The European Social Charter: A Social Constitution for Europe*, Cheltenham, Edward Elgar Publishing, 2010.

Dewhurst E., "Article 18 RSCE. The right to engage in gainful occupation in the territory of other Parties", in Ales E. *et al.* (eds.) *International and European Labour Law: A commentary*, Nomos Verlagsgesellschaft mbH and Co. KG, 2017.

Donnelly J. and Whelan D. J., *International Human Rights*, 5th ed, Routledge, 2018.

Ducoulombier P., "La liberté des États parties à la Charte sociale européenne dans le choix de leur engagement: une liberté surveillée", *Revue trimestrielle des droits de l'homme*, no. 96, 2013, pp. 829 ff.

Dunaj K. and Ryszka J., "The Protection of Vulnerable People in the Charter System", in Angeleri S. and Nivard C. (eds.), *The European Social Charter: A Commentary*, vol. 1, *Cross-cutting Themes*, Leiden, Brill/Nijhoff Academic Publishers, 2022, pp. 319 ff.

Eardley T. *et. al.*, "Social Assistance in OECD Countries: Synthesis Report", *Research Report – Department of Social Security*, no. 46, London, HMSO.

Egorov A. and Wujczyk M., *The Right to Social Security in the Constitutions of the World: Broadening the Moral and Legal Space for Social Justice*, Geneva, ILO, 2016.

Eleanor K. and Brian C., "Provisions for Health and Health Care in the Constitutions of the Countries Around the World", *Cornell International Law Journal*, 2005, pp. 285 ff.

Evju S., "Application by Domestic Courts of the European Social Charter", *Nordic Journal of Human Rights*, vol. 28, nos. 3–4, 2010, pp. 401 ff.

Evju S., "The European Social Charter and the International Labour Organisation-Interlinks Past and Present", in Däubler W. and Zimmer R. (eds.), *Arbeitsvölkerrecht. Festschrift für Klaus Lörcher*, Baden-Baden, Nomos, 2013.

Gaffney A., *To Heal Humankind: The Right to Health in History*, New York-London, Routledge, 2018, p. 240.

Gomien D., Harris D. and Zwaak L., *Law and Practice of the European Convention on Human Rights and the European Social Charter*, Strasbourg, Council of Europe Publishing, 1996.

Gori G., "Domestic Enforcement of the European Social Charter: The Way Forward", in De Búrca G., De Witte B. (eds.), *Social Rights in Europe*, Oxford, Oxford University Press, 2005, pp. 69 ff.

Guild E., "Who is an Irregular Migrant?", in Bogusz B. *et al.* (eds.), *Irregular Migration and Human Rights: Theoretical, European and International Perspectives* (*Immigration and Asylum Law and Policy in Europe*), Leiden, Martinus Nijhoff Publishers, 2004, pp. 3 ff.

Hachez I., "Article 26. Intégration des personnes handicapées", in Picod F. and Van Drooghenbroeck S., "Charte de droits fondamentaux de l'Union européenne. Commentaire article par article", Bruxelles, Bruylant, 2018.

Harrington J., "The Human Rights Committee, Treaty Interpretation, and the Last Word", EJIL: Talk! 5 August 2015, available at https://www.ejiltalk.org/the-human-rights-committee-treaty-interpretation-and-the-last-word/.

Harris D. *et al.* (eds.), *Law of the European Convention on Human Rights*, 4th ed, Oxford, Oxford University Press, 2018.

Harris D. and Darcy J., *The European Social Charter. 2nd edition.* (*Procedural Aspects of International Law Monograph Series; vol. 25*), New York, Transnational Publishers, 2001.

Harris D. J., O'boyle M., Bates E. P. and Buckley C. M., *Law of the European Convention on Human Rights*, 4th ed., Oxford, Oxford University Press, 2018.

Hervey T. K., "We Don't See a Connection: The 'Right to Health' in the EU Charter and European Social Charter", in De Búrca G., De Witte B. and Ogertschnig L. (eds.), *Social Rights in Europe*, Oxford, OUP, 2005, pp. 305 ff.

Hohmann J., *The Right to Housing, Law, Concepts, Possibilities*, Oxford, Hart Publishing, 2013.

Howard-Jones N., *The Scientific Background of the International Sanitary Conferences 1851–1938*, World Health Organization, Geneva 1975, p. 110.

Ippolito F., "The Convention on the Rights of the Child in Litigation Before the European Social Charter Committee and the European Court of Human Rights: «Why Then, Can One Desire Too Much of a Good Thing?»", *Diritti umani e diritto internazionale*, no. 1, 2020, pp. 93 ff.

Kajtar E., "Changing Perspective on Social Inclusion of People with disabilities: A European-Hungarian Outlook", *Studia iuridica auctoritate Universitatis Pécs Publicata*, no. 141, 2008, pp. 167 ff.

Kanti Ghoshal S., "Concept of Disability – The Dynamic Trend", *International Research Journal of Commerce Arts and Science*, vol. 9, issue 4, 2018, pp. 233 ff.

Karin L., *The Revised European Social Charter: An Article by Article Commentary*, Cheltenham, UK, Edward Elgar Publishing Limited, 2021.

Katrougalos G., "Social Security in the 'Case Law' of the Social Rights Committee", in Pennings F. and Vonk G. (eds.), Research Handbook on European Social Security Law, Cheltenham, Edward Elgar Publishing, 2015, pp. 84 ff.

Katrougalos G., "The (Dim) Perspectives of the European Social Citizenship", *Jean Monnet Working Paper NYU School of Law*, no. 5(7), 2012, pp. 1 ff.

Kilkelly U. and Liefaard T. (eds.), *International Human Rights of Children*, Singapore, Springer Nature, 2019.

Kori K., "Safeguarding the Human Rights of Persons with Disabilities: An Analytical Approach", *International Journal of Law Management & Humanities*, no. 4, 2021, pp. 1248 ff.

Kotkas T., "The Short and Insignificant History of Social Rights Discourse in the Nordic Welfare State", in Kotkas T. and Veitch K. (eds.), *Social Rights in the Welfare State: Origins and Transformations*, London, Routledge, 2016, pp. 15 ff.

Kramer D., "Earning Social Citizenship in the European Union: Free Movement and Access to Social Assistance Benefits Reconstructed", *Cambridge Yearbook of European Legal Studies*, no. 18, 2016, pp. 270 ff.

Ktistakis Y., *Protecting Migrants under the European Convention on Human Rights and the European Social Charter: A Handbook for Legal Practitioners*, 2nd ed., Strasbourg, Council of Europe Publishing, 2016.

Leach P., *Taking a Case to the European Court of Human Rights*, 4th ed., Oxford, Oxford University Press, 2017.

Le Floch G., "Rapport introductif-Santé et droit international: l'ébullition permanente", in Guillaume Le Floch G. and Fleury Graff T. (ed.), *Santé et droit international : colloque de Rennes*, Pedone, 2019, pp. 7 ff.

Leijten I., *Core Socio-Economic Rights and the European Court of Human Rights*, Cambridge, Cambridge University Press, 2018.

Leijten I., "Defining the Scope of Economic and Social Guarantees in the case law of the ECtHR", in Brems E. and Gerards J. (eds.), *Shaping Rights in the ECHR*, Cambridge, Cambridge University Press, 2014, p. 109 ff.

Leijten I., "The Right to Minimum Subsistence and Property Protection under the ECHR: Never the Twain shall Meet?", *European Journal of Social Security*, no. 21(4), 2019, pp. 307 ff.

Liberali B., "L'importanza delle parole e della tecnica decisoria in due recenti pronunce della Corte costituzionale in materia di omogenitorialità", *Studium Iuris*, no. 1, 2021, pp. 1190 ff.

Lougarre C., "What does the Right to Health Mean. The Interpretation of Article 11 of the European Social Charter by the European Committee of Social Rights", *Netherlands Quarterly of Human Rights*, vol. 33, no. 3, 2015, pp. 326 ff.

Lukas K., *The Revised European Social Charter. An Article by Article Commentary*, Cheltenham (UK)/Northampton (USA), Edward Elgar Publishing, 2021.

Mantu S. and Minderhoud P., "Exploring the Links between Residence and Social Rights for Economically Inactive EU Citizens", *European Journal of Migration and Law*, no. 21, 2019, pp. 313 ff.

Mantu S. and Minderhoud P., "Social rights as a case of Europeanization through law – the role of CJEU jurisprudence", *Nijmegen Migration Law Working Papers Series*, no. 1, 2016, pp. 1 ff.

Mcglynn C., *Families and the European Union: Law, Politics and Pluralism*, Cambridge, Cambridge University Press, 2006.

Mikkola M., "Migrants", in Mikkola M. (ed.), *Social Human Rights of Europe*, Porvoo, Karelactio Legisactio, 2010.

Mikkola M., "Social Human Rights of Migrants under the European Social Charter", *European Journal of Social Security*, vol. 10, no. 1, 2008.

Mola L., *La Carta sociale europea e il controllo internazionale sulla sua applicazione*, Torino, Giappichelli, 2022.

Molina Navarette C., "Derecho a los beneficios de los servicios sociales: Articulo 14 de la Carta Social Europea", in Monereo Atienza C. and Monereo Pérez J. L. (eds.), *La garantía multinivel de los derechos fundamentales en el Consejo de Europa: el Convenio Europeo de Derechos Humanos y la Carta Social Europea*, Granada, Editorial Comares, 2017, pp. 669 ff.

Momm W. and Konig A., "Community Integration for Disabled People – A New Approach to Their Vocational Training and Employment", *International Labour Review*, vol.128, no. 4, 1989, pp. 497 ff.

Nivard C., *La justiciabilité des droits sociaux: étude de droit conventionnel européen*, Brussels, Bruylant, 2012.

Nolan A., " 'Aggravated Violations', Roma Housing Rights, and Forced Expulsions in Italy: Recent Developments under the European Social Charter Complaints System", *Human Rights Law Review*, 2011, 11 (2), pp. 343 ff.

Nolan A., *Protecting the Child from Poverty: The Role of Rights in the Council of Europe*, 2019, available at https://rm.coe.int/protecting-the-child-from-poverty-the-role-of-rights-in-the-council-of/168098c54c.

O'Cinneide C., "Migrant Rights under the European Social Charter", in Costello C., and Freedland M. (eds.), *Migrants at Work: Immigration and Vulnerability in Labour Law*, Oxford, Oxford university press, 2014.

O'Leary S., "Solidarity and Citizenship Rights in the Charter of Fundamental Rights of the EU", in De Búrca G. (ed.), *EU Law and the Welfare State: In Search of Solidarity*, Oxford, Oxford University Press, 2005, pp. 39 ff.

O'Sullivan C. E., "Social Assistance for Economically-Inactive Citizens within the EU's 'Market State' Model", *Irish Journal of European Law*, no. 19(1), 2016, pp. 64 ff.

Palmisano G., *L'Europa dei diritti sociali. Significato, valore e prospettive della Carta sociale europea*, Bologna, Il Mulino, 2022.

Palmisano G., "The Right to a Healthy or Decent Environment as a Social Right: Acquis and Future Prospects of the European Social Charter System", *Roma Tre Law Review*, vol. 2, 2020, pp. 7 ff.

Palmisano G., "Overcoming the Limits of the European Social Charter in terms of Persons Protected: the Case of Third State Nationals and Irregular Migrants", in D'amico M. and Guiglia G. (eds.), *European Social Charter and the challenges of the XXI century/La Charte Sociale Européenne et les défis du XXIe siècle, Napoli*, Edizione Scientifiche Italiane, 2014, pp. 171 ff.

Palmisano G., "Sui Limiti di Applicazione della Carta Sociale Europea in Termini di Persone Protette", in D'amico M., Guiglia G. and Liberali B. (eds.), *La Carta Sociale Europea e la Tutela dei Diritti Sociali Atti del Convegno del 18 gennaio 2013 Università degli Studi di Milano*, Napoli, Edizioni Scientifichi Italiane, 2013, pp. 39 ff.

Panzera C., "The Personal Scope of the European Social Charter: Questioning Equality", *Revista Europea de Derechos Fundamentales*, vol. 24, 2014, pp. 51 ff.

Papadopoulos N. A., "Revisiting the Preamble of the European Social Charter: Paper Tiger or Blessing in Disguise?", *Human Rights Law Review*, vol. 22, issue 1, 2022, pp. 1 ff.

Peroni L. and Timmer A., "Vulnerable Groups: The Promise of an Emerging Concept in European Human Rights Convention Law", *International Journal of Constitutional Law*, no. 11(4), 2013, pp. 1056 ff.

Rainey B., Wicks E. and Ovey C., *Jacobs, White & Ovey: The European Convention on Human Rights*, 6th ed., Oxford, Oxford University Press, 2014.

Reich M. R., "Public-Private Partnerships for Public Health", in Reich M. R., (ed.), *Public-Private Partnerships for Public Health*, Cambridge, Harvard University Press, 2002, pp. 1 ff.

Reyes Fernandez M., "El Pacto Mundial para Una Migración Segura, Ordenada e Regular desde La Perspectiva del Ministerio de Trabajo, Migraciones y Seguridad Social", *Revista del Ministerio de Trabajo, Migraciones y Seguridad Social*, 2019, no. 140, pp. 67 ff.

Roscam Abbing H., "The Right to Care for Health: The Contribution of the European Social Charter", *European Journal of Health Law*, vol. 12, no. 3, 2005, pp. 183 ff.

Rothmar Herrmann J. and Toebes B., "The European Union and Health and Human Rights", in Toebes B. *et al., Health and Human Rights in Europe*, Cambridge, Intersentia, 2012, pp. 51 ff.

Sainsbury D., *Welfare States and Immigrant Rights. The Politics of Inclusion and Exclusion*, Oxford, Oxford University Press, 2012.

Samuel L., *Fundamental Social Rights – Case-law of the European Social Charter*, 2nd ed, Strasbourg, Council of Europe Publishing, 2002.

Sanz Caballero S., "The European Social Charter as an instrument to eradicate poverty: failure or success." *Cuadernos Constitucionales de la Cátedra Fadrique Furió Ceriol*. Valencia: Universitat de València, Departamento de Derecho Constitucional y Ciencia Política. N. 64/65, 2008.

Saul B., Kinley D. and Mowbray J., *The International Covenant on Economic, Social and Cultural Rights: Commentary, Cases, and Materials*, Oxford, OUP, 2014, p. 1358.

Sepúlveda Carmona M. and Nyst C., *The Human Rights Approach to Social Protection*, Helsinki, Ministry of Foreign Affairs of Finland, 2012.

Slingenberg L., "Social security in the case law of the European Court of Human Rights" in Pennings F. in Vonk G. (eds.), *Research Handbook in European Social Security Law*, Cheltenham, Edward Elgar Publishing, 2015.

Slingenberg L., *The Reception of Asylum Seekers under International Law. Between Sovereignty and Equality*, Oxford, Hart Publishing, 2014.

Scheinin M., "Economic, Social and Cultural Rights as Legal Rights", in Eide A., Krause C. and Rosas A. (eds.), *Economic, Social, and Cultural Rights: A Textbook*, 2nd rev. ed., Leiden, Martinus Nijhoff Publishers, 2001.

Schmid E., "Part V, Art I – Implementation of the undertakings given", in Academic Network on the European Social Charter and Social Rights *et al* (ed.) *The European Social Charter: A Commentary* (forthcoming), Leiden, Brill/Nijhoff Academic Publishers, 2024, available at https://serval.unil.ch/resource/serval:BIB_A6B49C5487E2.P001/REF.

Smusz-Kulesza M., Manasyan A. and Fedorova A., *Training programme for judges. European Social Charter and case law of the European Committee of Social Rights*, 2021, available online at https://rm.coe.int/15-judges-training-eng-soft/1680a39c11.

De Sousa C.U., "A Securitização da Imigração e o Imperativo de Uma Gestão da Migração Baseada no Respeito pelos Direitos Humanos", *Revista del Ministerio de Trabajo, Migraciones y Seguridad Social*, 2019, no. 140, pp. 35 ff.

Stangos P., "Challenges and reasons for reforming the collective complaints procedure of the European Committee of Social Rights – Towards a 'third life' of the European Social Charter?", *Epitheoressis Ergatikou Dikeou*, vol. 79, issue 10, 2020, pp. 1193 ff (in Greek).

Swiatkowski A. M., *Labour Law: Council of Europe*, 2nd ed, Kluwer, 2016.

Tobin J., *The Right to Health in International Law*, Oxford, OUP, 2012, p. 416.

Tooze J., "The Rights to Social Security and Social Assistance: Towards an Analytical Framework", in Baderin M. A. and Mccorquodale R. (eds.), *Economic, Social and Cultural Rights in Action*, Oxford / New York, Oxford University Press, 2007, pp. 331 ff.

Torchia M., Calabrò A. and Morner M., "Public-Private Partnerships in the Health Care Sector: A Systematic Review of the Literature", *Public Management Review*, vol. 17, no. 2, 2015, pp. 236 ff.

Trilsch M., "European Committee of Social Rights: The Right to a Healthy Environment", *International Journal of Constitutional Law*, vol. 7, no. 3, July 2009, pp. 529 ff.

Válková L., "The Commission Proposal for a Regulation on the Recognition of Parenthood and Other Legislative Trends Affecting Legal Parenthood", *Rivista di diritto internazionale privato e processuale*, 2022, no. 4, pp. 854 ff.

Valette M.-F., "Protection et Promotion des Droits Sociaux des Migrants par le Comité Européen des Droits Sociaux", *Revue Européenne des Migrations Internationales*, 2016, 32 (3 & 4), p. 337 ff.

Vandamme F., "Les droits protégés par la Charte sociale. Contenu et portée", in Leclerc S. et Akandji-Kombé J-F. (eds.), *La Charte sociale européenne*, Bruxelles, Bruylant, 2001.

Vaz M. A., Carvalho R., Botelho C. S., Folhadela I. and Ribeiro A. T., *Direito Constitucional – o Sistema Constitucional Português*, 2nd ed., Porto, Universidade Católica Portuguesa, 2015.

Vonk G. and Olivier M., "The Fundamental Right of Social Assistance: A Global, a Regional (Europe and Africa) and a National Perspective (Germany, the Netherlands and South Africa)", *European Journal of Social Security*, no. 21(3), 2019, pp. 219 ff.

Wachsmann P., *Les droits de l'homme*, 5th ed., Paris, Dalloz, 2008.